TO THE BELOVED MEMORY

OF

HELEN ROSSETTI ANGELI

FOREWORD

WHILE burrowing amongst the treasures hoarded up over the years in the house inhabited by William Michael Rossetti during the last twenty-nine years of his life,[1] and while working in his own library, I came across a thick bundle of papers which he had prepared for publication in 1903 and to which he had given the title *Rossetti Papers, 2nd Series, 1870–1876*.

These were not the first 'Rossetti Papers' edited by William Michael Rossetti. In 1899 he had published *Ruskin: Rossetti: Preraphaelitism* with the sub-title *Papers 1854 to 1862* (George Allen); in 1900 *Præraphaelite Diaries and Letters* (Hurst and Blackett); in 1903 *Rossetti Papers, 1862 to 1870* (Sands & Co.).

The unpublished *Rossetti Papers, 2nd Series* included:

1. Letters from Dante Gabriel Rossetti to various correspondents;[2]

2. Letters to D. G. Rossetti from some of his friends and patrons;

3. Letters to William Michael Rossetti from various contemporaries;

4. W. M. Rossetti's Diary covering the period 1870–3.

It is the latter item which is here presented for the first time.

Among the more important topics to which this diary refers, I will merely mention the following:

1. The publication of D. G. Rossetti's *Poems* in 1870 and the reception with which they met from fellow poets and writers, Tennyson, Browning, Meredith being among them.

2. The growing dismay succeeded by anger caused in Preraphaelite circles by the publication of Robert Buchanan's scandalous article and pamphlet, *The Fleshly School of Poetry* (1871).

3. The collapse of D. G. Rossetti's health in 1872. Although some details had already been given by W. M. Rossetti in his

---

[1] At 3 St. Edmund's Terrace, London N.W.3. In 1890, Mrs. Lucy Madox Brown Rossetti had bought the leasehold from Richard Garnett. The house was destroyed by a V2 in June 1944.

[2] These have since been incorporated into the correspondence of D. G. R. edited by Oswald Doughty and J. R. Wahl, and published under the title: *Letters of Dante Gabriel Rossetti* (4 vols., O.U.P., 1965–7).

Memoir of his brother published in 1895, the Diary throws interesting sidelights on the poet's illness during those crucial months.

4. Numerous references to D. G. R.'s activities as a painter during the period.

5. The very serious illness of Christina G. Rossetti between 1870 and 1873.

6. The contribution made by W. M. Rossetti and his friends, Trelawny, D. MacCarthy, R. Garnett, and E. Dowden to the study of Shelley's life and writings, and a few revelations about Byron.

7. The part played by W. M. Rossetti as literary critic in promoting the recognition of James Thomson and of the American poets Walt Whitman and in a lesser degree of Joaquin Cincinnatus Miller who were still almost completely unknown in England at that time.

The diary which is here presented forms part of the Angeli Collection, and constitutes an invaluable source for the history of English literature and art between 1870 and 1873; indeed so wide was the circle with which the Rossettis were acquainted that few of the great names of the period are left unmentioned.

The present edition would never have appeared if it had not been for the extraordinary chance that led me to meet W. M. Rossetti's daughters, Helen Rossetti Angeli and Mary Rossetti, just before the Second World War. They allowed me to consult the bulk of family documents which were in their possession; their generosity was, from the first, boundless. But everything came to an end when the war broke out. When the tragedy was over, the St. Edmund's Terrace house so full of precious memories had been destroyed; the two ladies had taken refuge in furnished rooms in London. Miss Mary Rossetti soon died of the shock; Mrs. Angeli fled to Rome, where she still owned a house. All the priceless papers had been scattered, some of them lost, and it was only after a long time that I could resume my friendly and fruitful visits to Helen Rossetti Angeli. I was no longer in a position to publish the whole of *Rossetti Papers II* and my ambition was henceforward to edit W. M. R.'s diary.

Up to 12 May 1871 the text has been checked against the typed version which W. M. R. prepared for the press, as the original manuscript for that period has disappeared; from 14 May 1871,

I have been able to consult both versions, and the diary is there-fóre printed here in its complete and original form. Yet, the spelling is not always consistent; W. M. R. prepared his typescript some thirty-five years after the actual composition of the diary. The spelling often reflects the earlier period, but sometimes he did modernize it, although not consistently. On 5 June 1872, W .M. R. decided to cease keeping a diary as his brother's con-dition had become so serious that recording 'unimportant matters' seemed futile and the important ones too painful to be mentioned. He did not resume writing it until nearly four months later.

W. M. R.'s policy when preparing the typescript was to expand all the names when initials appeared originally except for F. (Fanny). I followed the course he regarded as an improvement.

The few notes which W. M. R. added to the typed version have been retained throughout and appear followed by his initials in round brackets.

Dante Gabriel Rossetti is constantly referred to as 'Gabriel' by his brother; in my notes, he is referred to by his initials and so is William Michael Rossetti; their father is referred to by his Christian name 'Gabriele'.

CONTENTS

ABBREVIATIONS AND SHORT TITLES

D. G. R., *Letters*	*Letters of Dante Gabriel Rossetti*, ed. O. Doughty and J. R. Wahl, 4 vols., Oxford, 1965–7
Family Letters	*Dante Gabriel Rossetti: His Family Letters, with a Memoir*, ed. W. M. Rossetti, 2 vols., London, 1895, vol. ii (*Family Letters*)
Letters about Shelley	*Letters about Shelley Interchanged by Three Friends. Edward Dowden, Richard Garnett and Wm. Michael Rossetti*, ed. with an Introduction by R. S. Garnett, London, 1917
Memoir	*Dante Gabriel Rossetti: His Family Letters, with a Memoir*, ed. W. M. Rossetti, 2 vols., London, 1895, vol. i (*Memoir*)
Reminiscences	W. M. Rossetti, *Some Reminiscences*, 2 vols., New York, 1906
R.P.	*Rossetti Papers (1862–70)*, ed. W. M. Rossetti, London, 1903
Shelley, *Letters*	*The Letters of Percy Bysshe Shelley*, ed. F. L. Jones, 2 vols., Oxford, 1964
Surtees	*The Paintings and Drawings of Dante Gabriel Rossetti (1828–1882). A Catalogue Raisonné*. By V. Surtees, 2 vols., Oxford, 1971
Swinburne, *Letters*	Algernon C. Swinburne, *Letters*, ed. C. Y. Lang, 6 vols., New Haven, Conn., 1959–62
Trelawny *Recollections*	E. J. Trelawny, *Recollections of the Last Days of Shelley and Byron*, ed. E. Dowden, London, 1906
Works	D. G. Rossetti, *Works*, ed. W. M. Rossetti, London, 1911

INTRODUCTION

W. M. ROSSETTI's work as a man of letters cannot be overlooked when studying the period extending from 1850 to the end of the century without ignoring a very abundant and accurate source of information.

No man, perhaps, has ever been in a better position to be both a critic and a memorialist: he was the brother of two of England's outstanding poets; he was personally acquainted with most of the writers and artists of his time, while his extraordinary capacity for work and his long life enabled him to read almost every book of value published between 1848 and 1919.

W. M. Rossetti was not a critic in the narrow sense of the word, that is to say a theorist of the canons of literature, who would apply rigorous principles to every work and judge of their value according to a well-defined standard. He was a critic who endeavoured to discover among the enormous production of literary matter what is destined to live and what is doomed to disappear, who noticed the inspiration which raises a work above the common level, who approached the author's inner meaning more closely than most men do. He endeavoured to perform this task throughout his career—in the reviews he wrote for the several papers and magazines to which he regularly contributed. But he was first of all a historian of literature; his natural tendency was to record facts as illustrative of men's character and genius, and as liable to illuminate their works. To those who wish to rediscover the atmosphere of those days, his books are invaluable. His brother Dante Gabriel, his sister Christina, and, to a lesser degree, his father, will never have a better biographer and bibliographer. He had a passion for statistics and compilation—perhaps we may detect here 'the mark of the beast' in a clerk of the Inland Revenue Office; this is even more evident in the many manuscripts he left, which he intended to be the starting-points of several studies, than in his printed books.

He was also, to a certain extent, a technician of form who enjoyed discussing the appropriateness or value of a word in a particular context; his brother, Dante Gabriel, and his friend Swinburne continually asked his opinion about the choice of words and often took his advice. He had something of the exegetist in him and loved to interpret a text—his edition of Shelley warrants this statement; philology and phonetics had their charms for him; I have seen a short essay in which he recorded the changes that had occurred in the English language (vocabulary, syntax, and pronunciation), during the time which had elapsed since his mother's youth and the date at which he wrote. Most of his remarks show a keen ear and a subtle sense of linguistic observation.

A loving son,[1] a devoted brother,[2] a fond husband and father, a loyal friend, such was W. M. R. throughout his life from the evidence of those who were most closely related to him. Kindness, generosity, courtesy, honesty seem to have been his distinctive qualities.[3]

A peace-lover at home, he was a revolutionary in theory if we are to believe his declarations in his *Democratic Sonnets* (1881); later in life, he declared himself to be a 'theoretic republican';[4] even in old age his spirit of independence had never subsided. His philosophy of life was pessimistic, but his soul was serene and he took a great interest in all the events of his time, both domestic and public.

So far as his religious points of view were concerned, he repeatedly, at different periods of his life, declared himself to be an agnostic,[5] but when Swinburne, having prepared a motion for the Atheistic Congress convened by Ricciardi in Rome (1869) as an 'Anticoncilio' to the Vatican Council I, asked W. M. Rossetti to sign it, the latter refused giving the following reasons: 'Having now fully considered the matter, I find myself quite ready to adopt your eloquent manifesto in a modified form, but not *without* some modification. I never have professed myself, and never have been nor am, an atheist. The utmost I can truthfully say about that is that theism appears to me an unfathomable mystery, and atheism another quite as unfathomable: I can therefore, in many moods

---

[1] When in July 1873 William announced his engagement to Lucy Madox Brown to his mother, she answered: 'Few mothers have enjoyed so long an experience of the unvaried domestic affection of a son, and still fewer fathers have one like you. From what you have proved as a son and a brother, it is easy to deduce what a good husband you will be.' (Unpublished letter in the Angeli Collection.)

[2] Christina declared that he was 'the brother of brothers'.

[3] Cf. Sir William Rothenstein, *Men and Memories*, 1931, *passim*, and Richard Curle, *Caravansary and Conversation*, 1937, pp. 76 ff.

[4] *Reminiscences*, p. 450.　　　　　　　　　　　　[5] Ibid., p. 122.

and for many purposes of discussion or speculation, stop short of theism as an alien hypothesis, but cannot affirm atheism.'[1] Furthermore, he always professed the greatest respect for his mother's and sisters' religious feelings; in answer to Swinburne, who although a great admirer of Christina's poetry had shown a deplorable want of understanding of her Christian beliefs, W. M. Rossetti wrote 'those ideas (religious), however irrational I may consider them, do produce a beautiful type of character. I knew it in my mother and both my sisters—and have no doubt you have known and reverenced it too'.[2]

W. M. R.'s love for intellectual concerns was derived from the very atmosphere he breathed from his tenderest youth. His father, Gabriele Rossetti, the Italian patriot, was an idealist. He had gone through many painful ordeals that had endangered his life and personal liberty, and as they had driven him away from his mother-country, so they had estranged him, as it were, from the commonplace realities of this life. Idealism appears indeed as one of the characteristics of the family.

In Italy, Gabriele Rossetti had become well known as a lyric poet and showed extraordinary facility in the art of extemporization, especially when under the influence of political passion.

It was on his voyage from Malta to England in 1824 that the young exile perceived, standing against a dark cloud, the 'shadow' of Dante which beckoned to him and spoke to him. Henceforth, the poet's life, and in a minor degree that of his family, was to be dominated by the 'Shadow of Dante'.[3]

Even the political activities of Gabriele Rossetti were not devoid of a sense of mystery: he had become a Freemason in 1809, and later joined the Carbonari. In his English home, he received the visits of fellow members or other compatriots, and his children, lying on the floor,[4] could listen to the sonorous voices, to the fiery declaration of these Southern men, endlessly discussing the excellences of freedom and the abomination of tyranny.

The four children, Maria, Gabriel, William, and Christina, were

---

[1] W. M. Rossetti to Swinburne, 24 October 1869 (unpublished letter in the Angeli Collection).
[2] W. M. Rossetti to Swinburne, 11 February 1904 (id.).
[3] The title of the book written by Maria F. Rossetti and published in 1871.
[4] See the wonderful reconstitution of the scene by Max Beerbohm in *Rossetti and His Circle*, London, 1922 (facing the title-page).

extraordinarily precocious and all of them showed a keen taste for art and literature. William was Gabriel's junior by little more than a year, and shared all his brother's attempts at writing or sketching. Commenting upon Gabriel's first letter to Ford Madox Brown (March 1848), William wrote: 'How many hours, which in retrospect seem glorious hours, have I not passed with my brother! how many books have we not read to one another, how many *bouts-rimés* sonnets have we not written, over the scanty fire-place!'[1] and further, he added: 'Most things, whether books or ideas were in common, at this time and for years afterwards, between my brother and myself, and whatever one of us lighted upon was rapidly imparted to the other.'[2]

In those days, all the Rossetti children sketched and drew, and William, who, as early as 1845, had entered the Excise Office as a clerk in spite of his desire to become a doctor, devoted some of his free time to sketching and portrait-drawing; he even joined his brother in the Life School which he attended at night, after his work at the Inland Revenue Office, and Holman Hunt[3] tells us that Gabriel hoped that William would soon be able to throw up his appointment at Somerset House and take to painting. In 1857 William had not lost his interest in drawing as he attended Ruskin's class at the Working Men's College for two or three months.[4]

In 1848 the Pre-Raphaelite Brotherhood was founded. Its aims and doctrines have been set forth at length by various and not always concordant hands. The most interesting studies on the subject are the excellent preface of thirty pages written by W. M. Rossetti in 1899 for the facsimile reproduction of the four numbers of *The Germ*, and the somewhat ponderous but well-informed book of Holman Hunt: *Pre-Raphaelitism and the Pre-Raphaelite Brotherhood* (1905). These are first-hand documents written by men who were actually members of the Brotherhood. Holman Hunt, Millais, Woolner, and Dante Gabriel Rossetti were the founders of the association; they were soon joined by J. Collinson, F. G. Stephens, and William Michael Rossetti, who, though not looked upon by his fellow members as an artist, became the secretary of the Brotherhood; from 1849 to 1855, he kept the

---

[1] *Memoir*, i. 117.   [2] Ibid., i. 125–6.
[3] Holman Hunt, *Pre-Raphaelitism*, p. 128.
[4] W. M. R., *Ruskin: Rossetti: Preraphaelitism*, p. 186.

P.R.B. Journal[1] in which he recorded the proceedings of all the members and also their struggles, their successes—if any—their hopes, and their disappointments.

The Brotherhood, being full of energy and enthusiasm, felt the need of a periodical organ which would enable them to propagate their doctrines; Dante Gabriel Rossetti, more especially, was anxious for their principles to be presented to the public. There was a lengthy discussion as to what the title of the new magazine should be. Sixty-five titles were suggested.[2] *The Germ* was chosen as revealing the hopes and prospects that were embodied in this humble seed. W. M. Rossetti was appointed the responsible editor, and, as such, was expected 'to do the sort of work for which other proprietors had little inclination',[3] and to fill the gaps with whatever he could think of or had ready in some drawer: *bouts-rimés*, poems, or others. He contributed the sonnet which appeared on the wrapper; it was intended 'to express the spirit in which the publication was undertaken'.[4] Four numbers of *The Germ* came out[5] in spite of the difficulties which thickened after each number, thanks to the never-failing perseverance of William and to the generosity of Messrs. Tupper, the printers. W. M. Rossetti's sonnet was pronounced unintelligible by William Bell Scott, who never liked the Rossettis, though he declared himself to be their close friend.[6] The painter Arthur Hughes, however, plainly admitted the influence this sonnet had on him at the dawn of his artistic career: in a speech delivered at the opening of the 'Loan Exhibition of Works by Ford Madox Brown and the Pre-Raphaelites' at the Manchester Art Gallery on 13 September 1911 and published *in extenso* in the *Guardian* (14 Sept.), Hughes, recalling his early reminiscences, said: 'I was drawing in the Academy School one evening when a young sculptor Alexander Munro, standing behind me had brought with him a slender pamphlet.[7] It passed around from hand to hand eliciting shouts of laughter! In the end it came to me and I saw the strangely interesting and pathetic etching by Holman Hunt[8] inside, and that quaint but

---

[1] See *The P.R.B. Journal* edited by Professor William E. Fredeman, Oxford, 1975.

[2] See the full list in *Letters of Dante Gabriel Rossetti to William Allingham*, 1897, pp. 65–7.   [3] Preface to *The Germ*, p. 20.   [4] Ibid., p. 15.

[5] In Jan., Feb., Mar., and May 1850.

[6] W. B. Scott, *Autobiographical Notes*, i. 324.   [7] The first number of *The Germ*.

[8] *The Germ*, No. 1. Holman Hunt's etching illustrates a poem by Thomas Woolner, entitled 'My Beautiful Lady'.

inspiring sonnet on the cover, and I could only wonder where the joke came in.' Arthur Hughes then quoted W. M. Rossetti's sonnet and added, 'whatever else William Rossetti may have to answer for, he will certainly have to answer for that, I know of one who thanked him for it'.[1]

Arthur Hughes is not the only artist and poet who had to thank William M. Rossetti for encouragement or help. Some passages of the diary reveal how much James Thomson, Joaquin Miller, and Walt Whitman owe him and show that his friendship for Swinburne helped the unfortunate poet along many a difficult path. Beside those he helped, he was in frequent touch with the greatest men of the period; we have only to cast a glance at the names that appear in the index of his *Reminiscences*.

Gabriele Rossetti had won fame in Italy as a patriotic poet calling for the liberation of his country; once in England, his name attracted attention with the publication of two volumes of commentaries on Dante's *Divine Comedy*,[2] in which he alleged that Dante belonged to an occult society which resembled that of the Freemasons, and that the narrative of the epic concealed a political and religious message. This theory met with widespread opposition, but was reasserted from time to time by a number of distinguished Dantean scholars. In 1901 W.M.R. decided to offer 'to the British public a record of his patriotic, highly gifted, laborious and loving father' by translating into English Gabriele Rossetti's versified autobiography.[3]

As for Dante Gabriel Rossetti, the labour of love performed on his behalf by W. M. R. is summed up by the title of the book he wrote in 1889, *Dante Gabriel Rossetti as Designer and Writer*. He not only wrote a biography of his brother, and in the various 'Rossetti Papers' related all the facts and 'events' that accounted for the extraordinary influence D. G. R. exercised over his friends and companions in the first period of his artistic career, he also collected his *Family Letters*, throwing a veil over what might be con-

---

[1] The typescript of this lecture was kindly communicated to me by the late Miss Hale-White, Arthur Hughes's granddaughter.

[2] *La Divina Commedia di Dante Alighieri con comento analitico di Gabriele Rossetti. In sei volumi.* Vol. i, London, 1826; vol. ii, London, 1827. The other four volumes never appeared.

[3] Gabriele Rossetti, *A Versified Autobiography*. Translated and supplemented by W. M. Rossetti, London, 1901. The elements of this version were taken from *Il Veggente in Solitudine*, Paris, 1846, and the MS. of *La Vita Mia* which was to be published by Prof. Ciampoli in 1910.

sidered as unfortunate, and at the same time showing him as a devoted son and an appreciative brother. He prepared no less than nine editions of his brother's works with lengthy prefaces and explanatory notes. On a lesser scale he did the same for his sister Christina and it is thanks to the various editions of her poems and especially to the complete edition of her poetical works 'with Memoir and Notes by W. M. R.' (1903) that her poetry, both love poems and religious poems, reveals her mastery of poetic technique.

He wrote introductions and prefaces for various works all concerned with literature. He edited the poems of various authors, most of them being published in the *Moxon's Popular Poets* series. He translated the *Comedy of Dante Alighieri—The Hell* and several other Italian works into English.

Ever since his youth, W. M. R. had been a devotee of Shelley and when in 1868 he was commissioned by Moxons to prepare a new edition of Shelley's works, he thought that 'nothing could have been more conformable to [his] liking'.[1] The book was published in 1869. In June 1870 W. M. R. heard that there were papers concerning a young man called Shelley in the State Paper Office. By October, W. M. R. had investigated the question and come to the conclusion that the so-called Shelley Papers included *The Devil's Disciple* and the *Declaration of Rights*, both of which he made known to the public in an article in the *Fortnightly Review* for January 1871. W. M. R.'s acquaintance with Trelawny enabled him to collect interesting and at that time unknown facts about Byron and Shelley. Mrs. Beecher Stowe's infamous assertions about Byron and his half-sister are rejected by a witness of Byron's last days.

W. M. R. never ceased to be fascinated by the personality and poetry of Shelley. Seventy years ahead of his time he studied the symbolism of the themes of Shelley's poetry, on the same line as that of modern critics, one of the most noteworthy being Gaston Bachelard, the French philosopher and physicist who quoted Shelley and W. M. R. in his study of the symbolism of the elements.[2] W. M. R. left an unpublished manuscript entitled *Shelley and the Element of Water*, which was the subject of a lecture delivered to the Shelley Society in 1888. The MS. bears a wistful

[1] See *Reminiscences*, p. 359.
[2] See Gaston Bachelard, *L'Eau et les rêves*, Paris, 1942, p. 221.

remark: 'There was to have been a further lecture (or lectures); but, as people didn't care for this one, I dropped the project.' This remark shows to what extent W. M. R. was in advance of his time. He wrote several articles in various literary reviews to elucidate a newly discovered biographical fact, to correct the reading of a particular line. For W. M. R. the subject of Shelley was inexhaustible; it is a fact that no modern Shelleyan scholar can put forward an opinion or give a new interpretation without mentioning or quoting W. M. R. He was one of the founders of the Shelley Society with Dowden and Garnett in 1886. It is evident from the diary that Shelley was constantly present in his mind, without, however, absorbing all his other literary activities.

It was during the same period that W. M. R. revealed Whitman to the English public: he had edited Whitman's poetical works in 1868; henceforward, there was a constant exchange of letters between the two men. It was to him that Whitman wrote complaining that he had not found a publisher in America. The diary enables us to appreciate their friendly relations; we cannot but admire the insight of the critic who discovered the poetical value of America's great lyrical poet.

Always ready to help and to discover new talent or genius, W. M. R. gave his support to another American poet, Joaquin Miller, who has now become an extinguished star, but who, in his day, knew some recognition, thanks to W. M. R.'s efforts: it is probably in W. M. R.'s diary that we find the most accurate details about the strange personality and the poetry of Joaquin Cincinnatus Miller.

A common admiration for Shelley drew his attention to another poet who was then so little appreciated that he did not write under his own name, James Thomson. W. M. R. encouraged him, supporting him by praising the style and inspiration of the poems of 'B. V.' That profoundly pessimistic mind was fortified by the optimistic, courageous mind of W. M. R. and but for the latter, Thomson would probably never have published his *City of Dreadful Night*.

This diary gives us a vivid picture of the literary circles of the day—but it also brings to life political struggles which have only lately calmed down. These were the great days when the most intelligent and forward women of the time wished to show some independence from their lords and masters. They wished to be financially independent, they wished to have the right to vote. W. M. R. describes their attempts with sympathy and understanding, he himself being a champion of liberty.

A whole portion of the diary includes the narrative of his journey through Germany and Italy. Landscapes, churches, monuments, art galleries, works of art are described with accuracy and a thrilling sense of the picturesque. W. M. R. delights in describing Italy, which is for him a second mother-country. This feeling pervades the whole narrative. Some of his remarks show an eye highly sensitive to beauty and to follow so well informed and so sensitive a guide is immensely gratifying.

He displayed equal activity as an art critic. He published *Fine Art: Chiefly Contemporary* in 1869, which consists of the reprint of articles he had written for various reviews and magazines; in his dedication to his mother, he expressed his intentions and aim when he wrote criticism: 'To my Mother, whose dear example ought to have taught me the critical virtue of sound judgment, perfect modesty, and infallible truth-feeling.' As we look back on his career, we may say that, within human limits, he kept to that ideal. We can see from the diary that no exhibition of importance was held in London at the R.A. or in other important galleries without being visited by W. M. R., who regularly published his 'notes' on the paintings exhibited in the *Athenaeum*, *Fraser's Magazine*, *The Magazine of Art*, etc. By so doing he helped to form the taste of the public who tend to remain behind the time when works of art are concerned.

If we were to characterize W. M. R.'s personality through the reading of the portion of the diary presented here, we are struck by the extensive range of his interests, and by the sincerity, the objectivity, the generosity, and the subtle intuition with which he relates the facts, circumstances, and tragedies in which he had, in spite of himself, to play his own part.

When in 1917 Richard Garnett observed that 'perhaps no man of his day has been more constantly before the public as a man of letters',[1] it was not merely W. M. R.'s career as a literary critic or as a literary editor that he was describing. He was referring to W. M. R.'s remarkable talent for minute and dispassionate scrutiny which enabled him to convey to his readers his calm enthusiasm.

[1] Richard Garnett, *Letters about Shelley*, 1917, p. 4.

William Michael Rossetti's
DIARY
1870—1873

1870

Monday 25 April   Stillman[1] says that Mrs Bodichon,[2] himself, and others, are thinking of entering into a pact—to include as many people as they can prevail upon—to keep up a simple economical style of living—as, for instance, to limit dinner to three courses. The plan is not to affect expenditure upon works of art. Gabriel (Stillman says) likes the idea, and inclines to join; and Stillman has advised him to sell off all his china[3] etc. (which I dissent from), and leave the Chelsea house,[4] clear off debts, and economise. I told Stillman it would be a waste of faith to suppose Gabriel will ever deny himself any expenditure he feels disposed for.

Thursday 28 April   Gabriel's volume of *Poems*[5] reaches us today. Replied to a letter from Moxon's about the Longfellow notice (in

[1] William J. Stillman (1828–1901), American landscape-painter and journalist. He came to England in 1849, met Turner and Ruskin; then returned to America and founded an art-review, *The Crayon*, to which W. M. R. was attached as English correspondent through the recommendation of Ruskin. In 1860 he came back to Europe and was successively American consul in Rome and in Crete. In 1869, his wife, Laura Mack, exhausted by the terrible conditions of their life during the Cretan insurrection, committed suicide, leaving him with three young children. He then went to England and settled in London. He met the Rossettis; of W. M. R. he wrote: 'He was for many years my most valued English friend.' In America he had met Madame Bodichon who offered him her house at Scalands in Sussex. He asked D. G. Rossetti to share it and, while staying there, recommended him chloral for sleeplessness, but soon realized the disastrous effect of the drug on D. G. R.'s health and mental balance. See W. J. Stillman, *The Autobiography of a Journalist*, London, 1900, i. 252; ii. 68, 79.

[2] Madame Bodichon, *née* Barbara Leigh-Smith (1827–91), one of the founders of Girton College, Cambridge. She was a promoter of women's rights and advocated 'the responsible and practical work of women in the various duties of life'. With two friends, she founded a literary and artistic club called the Portfolio Club which Christina Rossetti joined. See H. Burton, *Barbara Bodichon*, London, 1949, p. 41.

[3] D. G. R. had been for years an enthusiastic collector of blue and white Nankin. When, in 1872, D. G. R.'s illness made money matters difficult, W. M. R. sold the collection of blue china to the dealer Murray Marks for £650. See *Memoir*, p. 320, and D. G. R., *Letters*, iii. 1051.

[4] D. G. R. had moved into Tudor House, 16 Cheyne Walk, Chelsea, on 24 October 1862, eight months after his wife's death.

[5] This volume contained the poems that had been buried with D. G. R.'s wife,

Moxon's Popular Poets).[1] In consideration of its shortness,[2] I volunteered to reduce the price from £21 to £12 rather than spin it out, which I am by no means inclined to do. Declined to omit the concluding reference to Whitman;[3] and explained that I shall decidedly include Whitman in the volume of American selection,[4] or if Moxons demur to this, shall have nothing to do with that volume. Wrote also to Mr. Roberts who is in Moxon's firm (whether as partner or assistant) and who turns out to be the editor of Nimmo's *Burns*.[5] I expressed my opinion that that edition should be adhered to for Moxon's as far as practicable and convenient; that his name as editor of the forthcoming Moxon *Burns* should appear along with mine; and that he ought also to share in the remuneration.

Friday 29 April   Christina received the last proof of her volume of *Commonplace*.[6]

Saturday 30 April   Swinburne's tremendous laudation of Gabriel's poems appears in today's *Fortnightly Review*. Ellis[7] sent Christina

Elizabeth Siddal, in 1862 and recovered from the grave with the help of Charles Augustus Howell in 1869, and also other poems written between 1862 and 1870. They were published by F. S. Ellis in April 1870. See 'C. A. Howell and the Exhumation' in *Three Rossettis: Unpublished Letters to and from Dante Gabriel, Christina, William*; ed. J. C. Troxell, Cambridge, Mass., 1937, pp. 109–23.

[1] From 1870 to 1880 W. M. R. edited selections of the works of well-known poets, with a critical memoir. Most of them were published by Moxon, and later by Ward, Lock and Co., in the series *Moxon's Popular Poets*. The P.R.B. connection with Moxon dates from their enthusiasm about Tennyson's *Morte d'Arthur* in 1855. See *Ruskin: Rossetti: Pre-Raphaelitism*, p. 34. E. Moxon and Co. had published Tennyson's *Poems* (2 vols.) in 1842 and the *Idylls of the King* in 1859.

[2] *The Poetical Works of Henry W. Longfellow*. Edited, with a Critical Memoir, by William Michael Rossetti, London, Moxon, 1870. The notice on Longfellow consisted of sixteen pages.

[3] The 'concluding reference to Whitman' reads as follows: 'The real American poet is a man enormously greater than Longfellow or any other of his poet compatriots—Walt Whitman.'

[4] Whitman is represented by thirty-two poems in W. M. R.'s volume, *American Poems* published in 1872 and 'dedicated with homage and love to Walt Whitman'.

[5] *The Complete Poetical Works of Robert Burns*, ed. John S. Roberts, with an Original Memoir by William Gunnyon, William P. Nimmo, Edinburgh, 1865.

[6] (*Commonplace and Other Short Stories*, Ellis, 1870, W. M. R.)

[7] Frederick Startbridge Ellis (1830–1901), bookseller, then publisher. After 1869 he became intimate with the Pre-Raphaelites. He had already published W. B. Scott's *Dürer* when D. G. R. thought it desirable that their 'little knot of congenial writers' should be published by the same firm. Thus, Ellis published D. G. R.'s *Poems* just recovered from his wife's grave, and works by William Morris, Swinburne, Ruskin, Christina Rossetti. See *The Letters of D. G. Rossetti to F. S. Ellis*, ed. O. Doughty, 1928.

£46. 17. 6 as the quarter due to her upon the published price of
the first issue (500 copies) of her prose book.

Tuesday 3 May   The Scotts[1] and others at Euston Square.[2] Miss
Boyd[3] asked me down to Penkill[4] when Scott is to be there, and
I fancy someone else. I replied that I would gladly come, but that
at present the question of going to Florence with Gabriel is still
pending, and at any rate I should take out the bulk of my leave
somewhere on the continent. Answering another letter from
Hotten[5] about Swinburne's affairs: saying that were I to inform
him of everything Swinburne has told me, I might possibly
(though I do not admit that I should) be laying Swinburne open
to an action for libel. I have, therefore, only told Hotten in a
general way that I wished to be satisfied as to accounts, and that
I do not know—as indeed I do not—whether Swinburne, now
that he has seen the accounts, considers them complete or satisfactory; also that I adhere to my former statement as to the amount

[1] William Bell Scott (1811–90), poet, painter, literary and art critic. His connection
with the Rossettis began as early as 1847. He was then an enthusiastic admirer of
them all, but as time passed his outlook changed and a certain amount of spite
appears in his *Autobiographical Notes* (1892). Some of his statements about D. G. R.
were refuted by W. M. R. in *Memoir*. Just before Scott had married Letitia Margery
Norquoy in 1852, they had consulted Varley the astrologer who had foretold 'a
highly favourable scheme of fortune for her'. W. B. S. adds 'after forty years, I fear
either the planets or the expositor have made a mistake!' W. B. Scott, *Autobiographical Notes*, i. 118. Mrs. Scott died in 1898 in London; her remains were cremated.
[2] 56 Euston Square (afterwards 5 Endsleigh Gardens) was the family residence
in which W. M. R. lived with his mother and sisters, while the second floor of the
house was assigned to his aunts, Eliza and Charlotte Polidori. In 1871 Charlotte
bought the lease and later bequeathed it to W. M. R. See the entry for 29 June 1871.
[3] Miss Alice Boyd (1823–97), the owner of Penkill Castle, Ayrshire. In 1859 she
met W. B. Scott and then began a 'perfect intercourse' of thirty-one years. Scott and
his wife used to spend the summers at Penkill and Alice Boyd visited them in London
every winter. Her admiration and affection for Scott were passionate, as can be seen
in her diaries, discovered at Penkill in 1963. Scott and Miss Boyd are buried in the
same grave in Girvan Cemetery. (I am grateful to Mr. Leslie Cowan of the Oxford
College of Technology for information concerning the burial.) Miss Boyd's diaries
and letters are now in the special collections of the Library of the University of
British Columbia. See W. E. Fredeman, 'A Pre-Raphaelite Gazette', *Bulletin of the
John Rylands Library*, xlix, 1967, 323 and l, 1967, 34.
[4] D. G. R. visited Penkill in 1868 and 1869, and thought of going back there in
1871. See D. G. R., *Letters*, iii. 938. At Penkill he wrote several poems, 'The Orchard
Pit', 'Troy Town', 'Eden Bower', and some of the sonnets which were to form part
of the 'House of Life'; he also began 'The Stream's Secret'.
[5] John Camden Hotten (1832–97), the publisher who had undertaken the publication of Swinburne's *Poems and Ballads*, withdrawn by Moxon and Co., in 1866,
'through fear of consequence'.

of engagement entered into originally by Swinburne for continuing to publish with Hotten.

Wednesday 4 May   Stillman says that he was told the other day
that Gabriel's book (edition of 1000) had already been sold off
up to 250 copies or so remaining on hand; and that a second, and
then probably a third edition would be pressed forward. This is
rapid indeed. Gabriel gets £150 for the first edition and is to have
the same sum for each succeeding 1000.[1]

Thursday 5 May   Went to Royal Academy, looking deliberately
through the first two rooms and casually through the others.
Maclise's[2] *Desmond* and Millais's *Flood*[3] appear to me about the
finest things; the former beats almost everything Maclise has
done.

Friday 6 May   Gabriel, writing to Mamma, says his health has
been 'wonderfully better' within the last month—his eyes sharing
in the improvement. Stillman is going to bring his album of
Grecian photographs published by Ellis.

Sunday 8 May   Whistler,[4] whom I had not seen for long was here;
and, in walking home, told me all about the clever way he had
managed to stave off a threatened expulsion of Swinburne from
the Arts Club[5] (some little while back) consequent upon his getting

---

[1] Up to 1872 there were six editions of the volume of *Poems*, four in 1870, one
in 1871, and one in 1872, published by Ellis's firm.

[2] Daniel Maclise (1806–70), Irish painter who owed his first success to a sketch
of Walter Scott he made while the latter was travelling in Ireland. There are two
versions of the drawing: one in the Victoria and Albert Museum, the other in the
British Museum. He came to London and became an R.A. in 1840. He decorated
the House of Lords with historical pictures, *Waterloo* and *Trafalgar*. D. G. R.
wrote an article on 'Maclise's Character-portraits' in the *Academy* for 15 April 1871
in which he considered Maclise as 'a great master of tragic satire'. His portrait
drawings are in the Victoria and Albert Museum. See W. Bates, *The Maclise Portrait
Gallery*, London, 1883.

[3] An oil painting executed in 1870. It depicts the flood that followed the bursting
of the Greenfield reservoir. D. G. R. had seen the design of this picture as early as
December 1850 and 'pronounced it to be immeasurably the best thing he (Millais)
has done'. See W. M. R., *Præraphaelite Diaries and Letters*, 1900, p. 292. It is now in
Manchester City Art Gallery.

[4] James McNeill Whistler (1834–1903) was at that time intimate with the Rossettis.
In 1867 D. G. R. and W. M. R. resigned when Whistler was expelled from the
Burlington Club after a row with his brother-in-law. Sir Seymour Haden. See *R.P.*,
pp. 234 ff.   [5] See p. 16, the entry for 29 June.

drunk there with Consul Cameron,[1] and indulging in any amount
of offensive talk. Whistler settled the matter in masterly style, but
he fears something of the sort is again likely to be coming up.

Tuesday 10 May   Finished the notice of Cowper, and have now no
more of such notices to write; the major part of the work on the
volumes of Poetic Selections[2] remains to be attended to. Gabriel
now back from Scalands,[3] and called in Euston Square. He is
considerably thinner than he has been for years, but looking and
feeling greatly better—although today on re-entering London, he
again felt some return of pain in the eyes. Only 30 copies of his
book remained unsold this afternoon. Christina left today for a
month in Gloucester.[4]

Wednesday 11 May   Today Christina's book (*Commonplace* etc.)
reaches us. Swinburne called. Gabriel had told me yesterday that
two poems of Swinburne's for the forthcoming *Songs before Sunrise*—one raising a comparison between the birth of L. Napoleon
and that of Christ,[5] and the other blaspheming the three Persons of
the Trinity[6]—are so alarming to the publisher Ellis that, when it
comes to the scratch, he will absolutely decline to publish them,
or the book with them included. I named this matter to Swinburne
and find that he is a little put out by Gabriel's course of action in
more than once (as he believes) pressing upon Ellis the objections to
the publishing of these poems. Swinburne exhibited considerable

[1] Charles Duncan Cameron (d. 1870), army officer and British Consul, was an
acquaintance of Swinburne, for whom he had conceived 'an excessive affection'.
See *R.P.*, p. 394.
[2] (Only two such volumes came out eventually—*American Poems* and *Humorous
Poems*. W. M. R.)
[3] D. G. R. had been invited to stay at Mme Bodichon's country house at Scalands,
Sussex, which she had built in 1860 on the family estate. The Scalands Farm, where,
as Barbara Leigh-Smith, she had entertained D. G. R. and Lizzie in 1854 when they
were staying at Hastings, was at some distance from the house now called Scalands
Gate. See D. G. R., *Letters*, ii. 814. D. G. R. remained at Scalands from 11 March to
9 May 1870 with Stillman for part of the time; he also invited other friends, among
them the Morrises; he made a crayon portrait of Stillman (Surtees, no. 518) and a
crayon portrait of Mrs. Morris (Surtees, no. 376).
[4] (To stay with her uncle Henry Polydore. W. M. R.)
[5] *The Saviour of Society*, Bonchurch edition, ii. 360. Ellis did refuse to publish
Songs before Sunrise should they include *The Saviour of Society*. The latter was published
in *The Examiner*, May 1873, and immediately attacked in the press. See D. G. R.,
Letters, ii. 859, and Swinburne, *Letters*, ii. 243–50.
[6] *Celaeno*, Bonchurch ed., ii. 353. It was printed in *The Examiner*, April 1873.

excitability on this subject, but still all sorts of cordial goodwill
to Gabriel. I heard the poems (among others, mostly sonnets,
all very masterly). Swinburne spoke a good deal about the very
strong religious Christian feelings he used to have from the age
of fifteen to eighteen or so; and attributes partly to this fact the
continual use which he makes of Christian or biblical framework
in his poems, even when the gist of them is of the most extraneous
or conflicting kind. He repudiates the idea that Ellis will—or, in
accordance with his engagements, now can—decline to publish
the book.

Saturday 14 May   Gabriel expresses himself unlikely to settle for
the present for going to Florence; as he wishes to begin at once
on his large picture of the *Death of Beatrice*.[1] He has bought a new
wombat, and his kangaroo has a young one borne in her pouch.

Monday 16 May   Met Allingham[2] again at Chelsea after a long
while; he is acting as sub-editor of *Fraser*.[3] Gabriel has resumed
his old picture of *Found*[4] and has painted the man's head with great
intensity of expression. Allingham tells me that (as I had always
anticipated) some passages in my Memoir of Shelley[5] do not please

---

[1] Generally known as *Dante's Dream*. An earlier version of the subject in water-
colour had been done by D. G. Rossetti in 1856. The picture mentioned here is an
oil-painting 7 ft. 1 in. by 10 ft. 6½ in. The subject was taken from Dante's *Vita
Nuova* and represents the vision Dante had of the imminent death of Beatrice. It is
now in the Walker Art Gallery, Liverpool. The water-colour is in the Tate Gallery.
See Surtees, No. 81, pp. 42–8.

[2] William Allingham (1824–89), Irish poet, was introduced into the Pre-Raphaelite
circle by Coventry Patmore as early as 1849; for a while he became a close friend
of the Rossettis. In 1850 W. M. R. had written a review of Allingham's first poems
in *The Critic*, and in 1855, on the eve of the publication of his *Day and Night Songs*,
Allingham wrote to W. M. R.: 'You were the reviewer "par excellence" of my
volume of 1850. Could you possibly be persuaded to review that of 1855 in *The
Critic*?' See W. M. R., *Ruskin, Rossetti, Pre-Raphaelitism*, 1899, p. 88. Allingham's
volume (1855) was illustrated by D. G. Rossetti, J. E. Millais, Arthur Hughes, and
Lizzie Siddal, whose designs for 'Clerk Saunders' are among the best. See Allingham
& Radford, *Allingham's Diary*, 1907, p. 186, and *Letters of D. G. Rossetti to W.
Allingham* (1864–70), ed. G. B. Hill, London, 1897.   [3] *Fraser's Magazine*.

[4] According to W. M. R., *Found* was begun in 1853. D. G. R. was still working
on it in 1881. He had made numerous studies for it in pen-and-ink or pencil, and at
intervals returned to a subject which had appealed to him when a young man—
the redemption of a prostitute by her lover. He explained the meaning of the picture
in a sonnet entitled 'Found' dated 1881 (*Works*, p. 233.) The picture is now in the
Bancroft Collection, Wilmington, Delaware. See Surtees, no. 64, p. 26.

[5] The Memoir which W. M. R. had written for his recent edition of *The Poetical
Works of Percy Bysshe Shelley*, London, Moxon, 1870.

the Shelley family, but he has not broached the subject in its minutiae to them. Lastly Lady Shelley[1] destroyed a packet of Shelley letters and papers, and Allingham rather fears the correspondence bearing on the separation from Harriet may have been included in the destruction. This would be bad news.

Saturday 21 May   Went on with the arrangement of Keats's poems[2] for the cheap edition—which will not be a satisfactory affair, as Moxon wants, with a view to his publishing interests, only about two thirds of the total bulk of the Library Edition to appear in the cheap edition.

Tuesday 24 May   Gabriel says he has now taken for a month—with probable continuance—half a farmhouse at Scalands,[3] which he was thinking about when lately down at Mrs. Bodichon's house there. The new wombat seems ill, and causes anxiety.

Thursday 26 May   The poor wombat is defunct. Dr. Hake[4] and Allingham dined at Chelsea. The former is looking up *Valdarno*,[5] etc. and revising that set of tales with a view to republication.

[1] Lady Shelley (1819–89), the wife of Sir Percy Florence Shelley, son of the poet. On several occasions she suppressed the papers that appeared to her detrimental to the 'image' of Shelley. The letters mentioned here were not Shelley's last letters to Harriet. After her death they were presented to the Court by the Westbrook family as evidence against Shelley, but the originals have not been traced, though T. L. Peacock and Kegan Paul searched for them. In 1930 the copies of the letters were discovered by Leslie Hotson in the Public Record Office (Chancery Masters' Papers); he published them immediately: *Shelley's Lost Letters to Harriet*, ed. Leslie Hotson, London, 1930. They are reproduced in Shelley, *Letters*, i, nos. 258 to 270. The letter dated 13 August 1814 (Jones, no. 259) is a copy by Lady Shelley and is in the Bodleian Library.

[2] *The Poetical Works of Keats*, ed. W. M. Rossetti. Moxon and Co., 1872.

[3] (He never lived there. W. M. R.)

[4] Thomas Gordon Hake (1809–95), physician, romanticist, minor poet, had published *Vates or the Philosophy of Madness* in 1840, first anonymously as a serial, then as a book which D. G. R. read in 1844 with great interest; and having discovered the name of the author in 1860, wrote to him enthusiastically and they met in 1869. When in 1871 D. G. R.'s hypochondria came to an alarming crisis, he was taken to Dr. Hake's house at Roehampton, after which they spent six weeks in Scotland: 'I walked with him by day, I sat with him by night,' Dr. Hake wrote in his *Memoirs*. W. M. R. considered him as 'the earthly Providence of the Rossetti family in those dark days'. Dr. Hake published several books of poems, among them *Madeline with Other Poems and Parables* (1871), reviewed by D. G. R. in the *Academy*, 1 Feb. 1871; *Parables and Tales*, illustrated by Arthur Hughes, also reviewed by D. G. R. in the *Fortnightly Review*, Apr. 1873. See *Memoir*, 310; also T. G. Hake, *Memoirs of Eighty Years*, London, 1892.

[5] (*Valdarno or the Ordeal of Art-Worship*—originally called *Vates*—was a romance of old date by Dr. Hake. W. M. R.)

Gabriel offers to propose it to Ellis. Allingham has abandoned the Customs once more, and seems to rely upon his sub-editorship of *Fraser* as a main part of his future income.[1] While we were at dinner in the tent, Swinburne came to the house; but as Emma's[2] account of his intoxicated state menaced serious inconvenience had he been admitted, an excuse was made for getting him to go away.

Monday 30 May O'Connor[3] informs me that the article written by Mrs Gilchrist[4] on Whitman some while ago is appearing in the May number of *The Radical*, a paper of high character, circulating chiefly among Unitarians.

Tuesday 31 May Stillman called: he expects to start for Liverpool on Sunday, en route for America. He says that Kossuth[5] once told him that, when Kossuth held a ministerial appointment in the Austrian dominions, he found among the archives documents wherein Marie-Louise betrayed to the Austrians all the movements of her husband Napoleon prior to his downfall . . .

Wednesday 1 June Lucy Brown[6] called with a letter addressed by

[1] Allingham gave up the Customs in April 1870 when the post of sub-editor of *Fraser's Magazine* with Froude as editor, was offered to him. He became editor in 1874 and remained in that position till the publication of the *Magazine* ceased in 1879.   [2] Rossetti's servant.

[3] William Douglas O'Connor (1832–89), American journalist and civil servant. He was a friend and supporter of Walt Whitman. He wrote *The Good Gray Poet* (1866) as a vindication of the poet who had been dismissed from his clerkship by James Harlan, the American Secretary of the Interior, on the grounds of immorality. W. M. R. exchanged several letters with him about the publication of *Poems by Walt Whitman*, selected and ed. by W. M. R., Hotten, London, 1868. Some of these letters appear in *R.P.*; others are still unpublished.

[4] Anne Gilchrist (1828–85), widow of Alexander Gilchrist (1828–61), author of the *Life of Blake* which she completed after his death with the help of the Rossettis and published in 1863. The article mentioned here was composed of enthusiastic letters she had written to W. M. R. about Whitman, and was published under the title of 'A Woman's Estimate of Walt Whitman' (from late letters by an English Lady to W. M. R.) in the *Radical* of May 1870. A few months later, Mrs. Gilchrist proposed marriage to Whitman; he declined. See H. H. Gilchrist, *Anne Gilchrist*, London, 1887, and also Elizabeth Porter Gould, *Anne Gilchrist and Walt Whitman*, Philadelphia, 1900.

[5] Lajos Kossuth (1802–94), the Hungarian patriot. In 1853 he went to America to raise funds to arm his country and enrolled young Stillman, whom he sent to Hungary. During his stay in England, he was connected with Mazzini and joined the Revolutionary Committee. See W. J. Stillman, *Autobiography*, p. 466 and a small pamphlet, *Kossuth and The Times*, London, 1851.

[6] Lucy Madox Brown (1843–94) was Ford Madox Brown's daughter by his first

Gabriel to Brown[1] concerning the pressing necessity which Inchbold[2] is under for getting something sold. Lucy says that Spartali[3] has expressed some sort of intention to buy some view painted by Inchbold in the Isle of Wight.

Friday 3 June   Ellis writes to Christina that, in consequence of an objection raised (originally by Gabriel) to the larger figure-subjects among the illustrations which Miss Boyd is producing for Christina's *Nursery Songs*,[4] he feels a little uncertain how to act. The object would be to eliminate these subjects without offending Miss Boyd or leading to an offer from Scott to supply her place with similar subjects. My advice to Christina is to tell Ellis that she, although not exactly an admirer of these examples by Miss Boyd, is quite content to let them pass—thus leaving Ellis to do

wife Elizabeth Bromley. Like her half-sister and half-brother, she had artistic gifts and left several paintings. Lucy Brown married William Michael Rossetti in 1874. See William M. Hardinge, 'A Reminiscence of Mrs. W. M. Rossetti', *Magazine of Art*, 1895, pp. 541–6; also 'The Younger Madox Browns: Lucy, Catherine, Oliver', *Artist*, xix, February 1897, pp. 49–56.

[1] Ford Madox Brown (1821–93), painter, studied art in Belgium and in Paris. In 1848 D. G. R. became his pupil and introduced Holman Hunt and Millais to him. Though Madox Brown was never an actual member of the Pre-Raphaelite Brother-hood, he remained in constant association with the P.R.B. painters and writers, especially with the Rossettis. See Ford Madox Hueffer, *Ford Madox Brown, A Record of his Life and Work*, London, 1896, and Helen Rossetti Angeli, *Ford Madox Brown*, London, 1901.

[2] J. W. Inchbold (1830–88), one of the minor painters associated with Pre-Raphaelitism through Ruskin. His career was described as 'unsuccessful' by W. M. R. In 1872 he was homeless, and for many months lived in Madox Brown's house. Swinburne, whose affection for him never wavered, thought that his landscapes could be compared to Turner's. When he died, Swinburne sent to the *Athenaeum* (29 December 1888), a poem, 'In Memory of John William Inchbold'. See *Swinburne's Works*, ed. Bonchurch, iii. 235.

[3] Michael M. Spartali (1818–1914), a Greek merchant established in London, Greek Consul-General from 1866 to 1882. His daughter Marie married W. J. Stillman in 1871.

[4] In a letter to Ellis, dated 7 March 1870, Christina quoted what D. G. R. wrote to her about the illustrations for *Sing-Song*: 'Scott was mentioning to me an idea that Miss Boyd would have been very glad to put those things on the blocks for your Nursery Rhymes. I fancy she would probably do them with more fun and zest than Murray [see p. 224, n. 3] though perhaps not so artistically.' But on 1 June 1870 Christina wrote again to Ellis: 'I ventured to mention my brother Gabriel's remarks to you: but certainly I do not venture to urge them, sharing, as I do, neither risk nor responsibility. It strikes me that if anything could be done to lessen the evil we both perceive, it might be to suggest to Miss Boyd to make no more *large* figure designs; thus the bulk of the illustrations might be rescued from the misfortune which has already befallen some.' See *The Rossetti–Macmillan Letters*, ed. Lona Mosk Packer, Berkeley, Calif., 1963, pp. 78 and 88.

on his own hook what else he considers desirable for his own interests as publisher . . .

Thursday 9 June   Saw reviews of Christina's book in the *Pall Mall Gazette*[1] and *Victoria Magazine*.[2]

Friday 10 June   Swinburne called, saying that Hotten threatened to take an injunction to impede publication of Swinburne's books by any person other than Hotten. The lawyers advise Swinburne that the action would probably not lie, but would cause a good deal of expense. Ellis is unwilling to undertake this; and the device suggested to Swinburne to escape from the difficulty, is to make over to someone else the property in his forthcoming book—so that this someone else being wholly uncommitted to Hotten, may publish the book where he chooses, of course holding the receipts in trust for Swinburne. Swinburne asks whether I will act in this matter. I would much rather keep out of this additional bother and responsibility, but would not like to say no without full consideration: I therefore agreed with Swinburne to accompany him tomorrow to his lawyers, and hear more precisely how the facts or contingencies of the case stand. Wrote Pollen[3] (at his request) a letter by way of testimonial in his forthcoming candidateship for the Slade Professorship in London.

Monday 13 June   Several men dining at Chelsea. Ellis brought a

---

[1] *Commonplace, a Tale of To-day and other Stories* was advertised in the *Pall Mall Gazette* for 2 June 1870 and an unsigned laudatory review, in which 'Miss Rossetti' is compared with Mrs. Gaskell and the 'subdued intensity of her manner' is praised, appeared in the *Pall Mall Gazette* for 7 June 1870.

[2] *Victoria Magazine*, xv (May–October 1870). In the issue for June 1870, p. 191, the anonymous review of *Common Place* [*sic*] is by no means so laudatory as that of the *Pall Mall Gazette*, but admits that when 'Miss Rossetti wings her way to fairyland, she writes charmingly'.

[3] John Hungerford Pollen (1820–1902), one of the artists who, under the leadership of D. G. R., undertook to decorate the walls of the Oxford Union Debating Hall with tempera paintings from the Arthurian legend in 1857. His subject was *King Arthur obtaining the Sword Excalibur from the Damsel of the Lake*. Originally a clergyman in the Church of England, he became a convert to Roman Catholicism in 1852. He was a friend of Newman, who was then the Rector of the Catholic University of Dublin, and appointed him Professor of Fine Art and asked him to undertake the decoration of the University church. In 1857 Pollen left Dublin and settled at Hampstead. See W. M. R., *Reminiscences*, p. 223; Anne Pollen, *John Hungerford Pollen*, London, 1912; and C. P. Curran, *John Hungerford Pollen and University Church*, Dublin, 1945.

couple of American reviews of Gabriel's poems, both laudatory.
Dr. Hüffer[1] says that he used to know a very old man at Arras
who had known (or I rather think had himself been) a lawyer
there along with Robespierre. This lawyer, when both were young
men, got into a serious altercation with Robespierre, and went
so far as to say 'Je vous cracherai au visage' or something equally
strong. In the reign of Terror he got into prison. His gaoler, an
Arras man, recommended him to apply to Robespierre, as sole
chance. This the lawyer naturally thought a poor prospect, but at
last acquiesced. Robespierre came to see him and looked at him
with a terrible expression, but said: 'L'homme doit le céder au
citoyen', and took steps for his release. Swinburne tells me Lord
Houghton[2] used to know a sister of Marat:[3] she had a great
regard for her brother. Henry Kingsley[4] declares him to be *the*
great man of the Revolution.

Friday 17 June   Called by invitation to see Tennyson, staying just
at present with his architect Knowles[5] at 16, Albert Buildings,
Westminster. He looks well and brisk, and hardly older than
when I saw him last—I daresay four or five years ago. His younger
son has a *slight* tendency to verse-writing. He expressed to me
admiration of some of Gabriel's poems, to others he objects, also
to a rhyme here and there, as 'water' and 'clear'. Saw here Lecky,[6]

---

[1] Franz Hüffer (1845–89), afterwards Francis Hueffer, a German music critic
who came to England in 1868, settled there, became a British subject, and married
Ford Madox Brown's second daughter, Catherine, in 1872. *Reminiscences*, p. 332.

[2] Richard Monckton Milnes, first Lord Houghton (1809–85) published the *Life
and Letters of Keats* in 1848. He was one of the earliest champions of Swinburne to
whom he revealed the works of the Marquis de Sade. In a letter to George Powell
(see p. 33, n. 5) dated 29 July 1869, Swinburne wrote about Lord Houghton's
library of erotica at Fryston. 'There is every edition and every work of our dear
and honoured Marquis.' Swinburne, *Letters*, ii. 20. Florence Nightingale (1820–
1910) spoke of Monckton as 'the man I adored'. He proposed to her, and waited
nine years for an answer before she refused him for the sake of a higher destiny.
See C. Woodham Smith, *Florence Nightingale*, London, 1949.

[3] Jean-Paul Marat (1743–93), the French revolutionary murdered in his bath by
Charlotte Corday.

[4] Henry Kingsley (1830–76), the younger brother of the Revd. Charles Kingsley.
He wrote novels about Australia where he had travelled.

[5] James Thomas Knowles (1831–1908), architect. He built Tennyson's house,
Aldworth, near Haslemere, Surrey. Founded and edited the *Nineteenth Century*;
also editor of the *Contemporary Review* from 1870 to 1877.

[6] William E. H. Lecky (1838–1903), historian and essayist. He had recently
published his *History of European Morals from Augustus to Charlemagne*, 1869.

Leyland,[1] and Mrs. Procter,[2] whom I never met before. A friend of the architect Hewlett[3] tells me that he lately found in the State-paper Office some reports from the authorities that a young man named Shelley, living at Lynmouth, made himself obnoxious, distributing Coleridge's *Devil's Walk*[4] and other exciting writings from a boat. He promised to send me particulars whereby I may trace out the documents.[5]

Monday 20 June A Signor Damiani,[6] who used to know my Father years ago, called on the part of Ricciardi,[7] to see what could be done through me towards the publication of an English version of the book on the *Anticoncilio*,[8] I promised to see what can be done with Trübner,[9] but am far from confident of getting any publisher for the book. Damiani is an ardent spiritualist, and

[1] F. R. Leyland, ship-owner, became one of the main purchasers of D. G. R.'s paintings after 1868. By 1882, at the time of the painter's death, Leyland possessed an important collection of his pictures. When he himself died in 1892, it was sold at Christie's. For details of the sale and prices, see Christie's Sale Catalogue, 8 May 1892, and *Daily News*, 30 May 1892.

[2] Adelaide Anne Proctor (1825–64), author of *Legends and Lyrics*, 1858–62. When J. H. Ingram was projecting his *Eminent Women Series* in 1882, he asked Christina if she would write a biography of A. A. Proctor, but she declined. See Mackenzie Bell, *Christina Rossetti, A Biographical and Critical Study*, London, 1898, pp. 89–90.

[3] On 21 June 1870, W. M. R. wrote to R. Garnett: 'A Mr. Hewlett whom I met the other day told me that a friend of his had come on a trace of Shelley at the State-paper Office, and he has now sent me the enclosed note of the facts.' See *Letters about Shelley*, p. 35.

[4] In 1799 Coleridge composed a ballad entitled *The Devil's Thoughts* which first appeared in the *Morning Post* of 6 September 1799; according to the Editor of that Journal, 'it made so great a sensation that several sheets extra were sold by them, as the paper was in request for days and weeks afterwards'. In the Moxon edition of the *Poems of S. T. Coleridge* (1859), Sarah Coleridge declares in a note on p. 193 that 'the 1st, 2nd, 3rd, 9th and 10th stanzas were dictated by Mr. Southey'. It was probably his own *Devil's Walk*, a ballad composed in 1812 and published as a broadside that Shelley was distributing. See the Oxford edition (Hutchinson) of Shelley's *Poetical Works*, p. 867, and Shelley, *Letters*, p. 235.

[5] Some six months later W. M. R. wrote to Mrs. Gilchrist that he had found these documents at the Record Office. See *Letters of W. M. R. to Anne Gilchrist and her Son*, ed. C. Gohdes and P. F. Baum, Durham, N. Carolina, 1934, p. 69.

[6] Signor Damiani was an earnest spiritualist; he 'sat' with Mrs. Marshall and Mrs. Guppy (see p. 15, nn. 4 and 5) and was well known by the spiritualists of the time.

[7] Giuseppe Napoleone Ricciardi (1808–82) was an old friend of Gabriele Rossetti, like him a revolutionary patriot who had taken refuge in London. He published *The Autobiography of an Italian Rebel*, London, 1860. When W.M.R. met him in Florence in 1869, he had become a member of the Italian Parliament. See *Reminiscences*, p. 351. [8] (Compiled by Ricciardi, Conte Giuseppe. W.M.R.)

[9] Nicholas Trübner (1817–84), publisher of German origin, began his career as clerk at Longman's.

told me all sorts of things about his own and other people's experiences; he seems to be genuinely happy in this sphere of life and thought. It was he who offered to deposit £500 to test the truth of spiritualism: he says Lewes[1] and Tyndall,[2] to whom the challenge was addressed, made no response. He fully believes in the Davenports,[3] Mr and Mrs Guppy[4] and Mrs Marshall. The latter, he says, (the younger Mrs Marshall) has been lately claimed by a man of fortune as his natural daughter, and now lives in style, acting no longer as a professional medium. Damiani is nothing of a medium himself. The elder Mrs Marshall[5] is regarded by Damiani as having, through age etc., lost her powers as a medium. Damiani says that the real secret about John Brown[6] and the Queen is that Brown is a powerful medium, through whom Prince Albert's spirit communicates with the Queen: hence Brown remains closeted with her alone sometimes for hours together. Victor Emmanuel is also a spiritualist.[7]

Tuesday 21 June   Sent Garnett,[8] for any use he may like to make of

[1] George Henry Lewes (1817–78), the life-long companion of George Eliot and a versatile writer; edited the *Fortnightly Review*, in 1865–6. On several occasions he was invited to give an opinion about spiritualism. He attended several seances, but his conclusion was: 'The instructive, though deplorable hypothesis of spirit-rapping is an indelible disgrace to the education of our age.' See Horace Wyndham, *Mr. Sludge, the Medium*, Edinburgh, 1937, p. 27.

[2] John Tyndall (1820–93), physicist, Professor at the Royal Institution of London. He greatly advanced the study of radiant heat and molecular physics. He tried to popularize science by his lectures and publications. He was also an enthusiastic mountaineer and studied the motion of glaciers in *The Glaciers of the Alps*, (1860).

[3] The Davenport Brothers, Ira and William, were the sons of a New York policeman. They arrived from America when Home (see p. 184, n. 3) crossed the Atlantic; in 1864 'they electrified London by performing various surprising feats'; but their conjurers' tricks were denounced, and in spite of Adah Menken's protection they had to leave England in 1865. See *R.P.*, p. 68 and for Adah Menken, p. 77, n. 3 of this diary.

[4] Mrs. Guppy, *née* Elizabeth Nicol, had begun her career as a photographer. While acting as companion to Professor Wallace's sister she became a medium; hence Professor Wallace's interest in spiritualism.

[5] The elder Mrs. Marshall, a laundress, became a medium of some vogue and held many seances.

[6] John Brown (d. 1883) was originally a gillie to the Prince Consort at Balmoral. He came into prominence after the latter's death in 1861 when he became Queen Victoria's favourite servant accompanying her on all her travels.

[7] Victor Emmanuel II (1820–78), King of Italy.

[8] Richard Garnett (1835–1906), man of letters, poet, essayist, Keeper of Printed Books in the British Museum from 1890 to 1899. He was a friend of Madox Brown and of W. M. R. Like the latter, he was an enthusiastic Shelleyite and kept an active

it the memorandum which Mr Hewlett forwarded to me the other day about Shelley at Lynmouth, consequent on what he had said on Saturday last.

Thursday 23 June   Swinburne writes me that Hotten wishes to refer to Howell[1] and me the matters in dispute between Swinburne and himself.[2] I reply that I consent if Swinburne wishes it, but that my opinion will be contingent upon the evidence to be adduced.

Monday 27 June   Garnett tells me he has made some interesting discoveries as to the true MS readings in *The Triumph of Life*[3] which is perhaps still more in need of such aid than any other of Shelley's long poems.

Wednesday 29 June   Gabriel says that Swinburne, who has lately been staying with Gabriel a few days, came in last Sunday much muddled, and Gabriel remonstrated very sharply with him and seemed to make some faint sort of impression. Gabriel tried (what he has long thought of) to get Swinburne to sign a written pledge for a year to come, but could not prevail on him to do so. Swinburne had recently quitted his lodgings in Dorset Street, but has now returned to them. After innumerable rows and manoeuvrings, he has at last ceased to be a member of the Arts Club.[4] The Secretary told him the other day that the question of his compulsory resignation was again about to be mooted, on account of some recent hullabaloo (of which however Swinburne professed

correspondence with him concerning Shelley's life and works. See *Letters about Shelley*.

[1] Charles Augustus Howell (1840–90). His career and dealings were those of an adventurer. He became known to D. G. R. in 1857. The latter introduced him to Ruskin who engaged him as his secretary, but their relationship came to an end in 1870 through the influence of Burne-Jones. In 1869 Howell played an important part in the recovery of the poems from Lizzie Rossetti's grave. See the documents concerned in Troxell, *Three Rossettis*, pp. 114–25. See also Helen Rossetti Angeli, *Pre-Raphaelite Twilight, The Story of Charles Augustus Howell*, London, 1954.

[2] In a letter dated 23 June 1870, Swinburne explained to W. M. R. that he was leaving Hotten as the latter's method of business was 'wholly unsatisfactory' to him. See Swinburne, *Letters*, ii. 114.

[3] *The Triumph of Life* was Shelley's last composition (1822). Interrupted by his death at line 544, first published by Mary Shelley in the *Posthumous Poems*, 1824. Roger Ingpen in the *Complete Works of P. B. Shelley*, iv. 417, writes: 'Dr. Garnett who examined the MS then at Boscombe Manor (1870) kindly allowed us to use the text of a leaf of Shelley's MS in his possession.'

[4] To which Swinburne had been elected in 1864.

entire oblivion), and at once withdrew his name from the books of the Club. It was probably the only thing to be done; but I fear this cessation of Club membership will be a daily and serious inconvenience to him. His getting elected elsewhere seems to be most dubious.

Thursday 30 June   Received the first lot of proofs that has reached me of the text of the Poets for the cheap series—Scott[1] and Wordsworth.[2] Began reading through Scott. I go on the principle of making as few alterations as possible, and am indeed not responsible for the correctness of the text, according to the stipulations made at starting. . . .

Monday 4 July   Went to Brown's soirée—the last for the present year.

Tuesday 5 July   About 10.15 tonight Nolly Brown[3] called on me, saying that someone from Swinburne's had just been round to Brown's to say that Swinburne is raving with 'delirium tremens', and has cut himself in smashing windows, and they do not know what to do with him. I therefore went round to Brown, and thence to Swinburne's. By that time Swinburne was quiet and had been got to bed; and Dr Bird[4] had done what I thought from the first the only feasible thing—sent a male nurse or attendant to see to Swinburne. Fearing that my appearance might do more harm than good, by re-exciting him now that he is quiescent, I left and returned to Brown's. We debated whether to write at once to Swinburne's father—as it seems the attack is an uncommonly bad one, and his proceedings of late more reckless than ordinary:

[1] *The Poetical Works of Sir Walter Scott.* Edited, with a Critical Memoir, by W. M. R., London, Moxon, 1870.

[2] *The Poetical Works of William Wordsworth.* Edited, with a Critical Memoir, by W. M. R., London, Moxon, 1870.

[3] Oliver Madox Brown (1855–74), only son of Ford Madox Brown. 'Nolly' was a youth of talent. He had been a painter from the age of 13; one of his paintings, *Exercise*, is in the Manchester Art Gallery. He wrote a short romance, *Gabriel Denver* in 1873, and a tale, *The Dwale Bluth*, both mentioned later in this Diary. His premature death was a great blow to his father and his family. See *Reminiscences*, p. 425; John H. Ingram, *Oliver Madox Brown*, London, 1883; W. E. Fredeman, 'Pre-Raphaelite manqué: Oliver Madox Brown', *Bulletin of The John Rylands Library*, vol. li, no. 1, autumn 1968.

[4] Dr. George Bird (1817–99), Swinburne's physician and friend; he helped him through many difficulties, especially when the poet's intemperance brought him into conflict with his father.

finally we agreed to wait till after I shall have again called at Swinburne's tomorrow.

Wednesday 6 July   Called again to see Swinburne. He was again somewhat violent in the course of the day, but was sleeping when I arrived. The attendant says that Dr Bird proposed to write to his father.

Wednesday 13 July   Paid at last a second visit to the Royal Academy. Millais's *Widow's Mite*[1] is a very fine piece of painting. Generally a poor and uninteresting exhibition.

Friday 15 July   This is the day that the hellish ruffian Napoleon declares war against Prussia. The best (but hardly the most likely) issue might be an early reverse of the French so disastrous as to tumble the beast from his burglarious throne . . .

Monday 18 July   Cayley[2] showed us an Italian review (*Europea*) containing a laudatory notice of Gabriel's poems, and something about Christina's prose stories[3] . . .

Friday 22 July   Went to a party at Conway's[4] where I saw (but was not introduced to) the Indian theistic reformer Chunder Sen.[5] Also made the acquaintance of Karl Blind,[6] whom I am pleased to know. He thinks there is a danger that, if Prussia should obtain conspicuous advantages over France, such as to lead to the dethronement of Napoleon, the influence of Prussia may avail to

[1] *The Widow's Mite*, begun in 1846 was finished in 1870 and exhibited at the R.A. in the same year. It is now in Birmingham Art Gallery.

[2] Charles Bagot Cayley (1823–83), translated the *Divina Commedia* into English. He was very devoted to Christina Rossetti to whom he proposed marriage several times, but she never accepted although she always looked upon him as a friend.

[3] *Commonplace and Other Stories.*

[4] Moncure Daniel Conway (1832–1907), an American Unitarian Minister who advocated abolitionism and had come to England for conscience' sake, on the outbreak of the War of Secession. He returned to the United States in 1884. W. M. R. had met him at W. B. Scott's house in 1863; he and his wife became friends of the Rossetti family. He made a funeral speech at the graveside of Oliver Madox Brown in 1874, and of Ford Madox Brown in 1893. See his *Autobiography, Memoirs and Experiences*, 2 vols., London, Paris, New York, 1904, and *Reminiscences*, p. 492.

[5] Keshub Chunder Sen (1838–84) led a reform movement of Hinduism, developing a tendency towards mysticism. In 1870 he came to England where he was warmly welcomed. *Encyclopaedia Britannica* (1961), xiii. 353.

[6] Karl Blind (1826–1907), a German political refugee named Cohen; he took the name of Blind when he settled in England in 1852. He introduced Mazzini to Swinburne. 'Scott says that Swinburne, being at Karl Blind's the other evening, met Mazzini personally for the first time. Mazzini walked straight up to Swinburne, who fell on his knee before him and kissed his hand.' See *R.P.*, p. 230.

restoring the Orléans family rather than to the alternative of a Republic. I fear there is considerable reason in this; however, the contingency which could alone lead to such a solution is itself a very questionable probability. Blind agrees with me that there is danger of a long continuance of the war—both parties being so strong and neither capable of accepting as final anything short of successive or overwhelming defeats.

Sunday 24 July   Went in the evening to Karl Blind's. Mrs. and Miss Blind[1] inform me that Ledru-Rollin[2] lived an exceedingly retired life in England, was hardly ever to be seen anywhere—the exact reverse of Louis Blanc,[3] whom they evidently like less well. Ledru-Rollin has a bitter dislike of Victor Hugo, whom he considers to have been an opponent of himself and of republicanism in 1848–9. Mrs and Miss Blind think that Hugo was an avowed anti-republican up to about 1850; for myself, I think the contrary was the fact, and that he was a known republican as soon as the Republic was established in 1848, or even a year or two earlier.

Tuesday 25 July   Called to see Vedder's[4] pictures and sketches. He is certainly one of the most talented American painters of whom I have any knowledge.

Wednesday 27 July   Dined at Gabriel's, where a curious man Bergheim (German Jew or German Arab by parentage) held a

---

[1] Mathilde Blind (1841–96), stepdaughter of Karl Blind. She became an intimate friend of the Madox Brown family, took a great interest in English literature; when the Shelley Society was founded she was one of its most active members. She wrote several volumes of verse, edited by Arthur Symonds, with a Memoir by Richard Garnett, London, 1900. She published a study of George Eliot in the *Eminent Women Series* (1883) and a translation of the *Journal of Marie Bashkirtseff* (1890). Ford Madox Hueffer, who knew her personally, wrote in *Ancient Lights*, p. 50: 'She was a favourite pupil of Mazzini, and a person of extreme beauty and fire.'

[2] Alexandre Ledru-Rollin (1807–74), a member of the Provisional Government after the fall of Louis-Philippe in 1848. He was an exile in London from 1849 to 1870, returning to Paris on 27 March 1870 as a result of Napoleon III's last amnesty. See Karl Blind, 'Personal Reminiscences of Ledru-Rollin', in *Fraser's Magazine*, 1891, pp. 243–63.

[3] Louis Blanc (1811–82), French politician. His pamphlets *L'Organisation du Travail* (1840) and *Histoire de Dix Ans* (1841), contributed to the fall of King Louis-Philippe early in 1848. As a member of the Provisional Government, he was responsible for the organization of National Workshops in Paris, but after the outbreak of working class risings against the Government, he had to leave France and took refuge in London where he stayed until 1870.

[4] Elihu Vedder (1836–1923), American painter of abstract ideas rather than of visible realities, came to Europe at the age of 20. He illustrated the *Rubaiyat of Omar Khayyam* in 1888.

mesmeric séance a short while back,[1] but I was not present. On the present occasion some very surprising things were certainly done, in the way of making the somnambule do and think whatever Bergheim chose. Three men (Leyland, I, and Whistler) also submitted to Bergheim's manipulations, but not one of us was in the slightest degree affected.

Thursday 4 August   Gabriel tells me that *Blackwood*[2] for this month contains a review of his poems, about the severest that has yet appeared. To his surprise and also to mine, Woolner[3] called at his house some three weeks ago; Gabriel however had given orders that he was 'not at home' to any one, and so did not, until after Woolner had left, so much as know that he had come. He is going on steadily with his large picture of *Dante's Vision of the Death of Beatrice*; paints heads and hands from nature—draperies first by way of study from nature, and then from the study on to the canvas; can do a head at a sitting (but I think this must practically be overstated). Intends when this picture is done, to do the *Magdalene*[4] and *Cassandra*[5] subjects; there are also in progress the *Medusa*,[6] *Found*, and *La Pia*.[7] Watts[8] lately painted a portrait of

[1] Details are given in Treffry Dunn's *Recollections of Dante Gabriel Rossetti*, London, 1904, p. 55.

[2] The review appeared in *Blackwood's Magazine* for August 1870, p. 178. One of the most positive statements found there reads thus: 'In none of these poems is there the least indication of a new poet arisen to bless us. They are all sufficiently interesting, pleasantly readable, some of them suggestive, but they lay no hold upon the imagination, or even on the ear and memory.' 'The Blessed Damozel' is described as 'fleshly', the refrains as 'unbearable'.

[3] Thomas Woolner (1828–92), the sculptor, and one of the seven members of the Pre-Raphaelite Brotherhood. In an article written for *The Portfolio*, 1871, p. 97, J. L. Tupper declares that Woolner's name 'is to shed splendour upon the R.A. as well as upon his country'. He contributed several poems to the *Germ* in 1850. See Amy Woolner, *Thomas Woolner, Sculptor and Poet*, London, 1917.

[4] The *Magdalene at the door of Simon the Pharisee* was begun in 1853 by D. G. R., and completed in 1858 as a pen-and-ink drawing. For further versions, see Surtees, no. 109, p. 62. D. G. R. wrote a sonnet on the subject, *Works*, p. 214.

[5] The *Cassandra* is a pen-and-ink drawing now in the British Museum. See Surtees, no. 127, p. 80. In 1869 D. G. R. wrote two sonnets for the drawing. See *Works*, p. 213.

[6] The *Aspecta Medusa*, a pencil-and-crayon design begun in 1861, practically completed in 1866, and improved in 1867. It is now in the Birmingham Art Gallery. In 1865 D. G. R. wrote nine lines of verse to accompany the drawing. *Works*, p. 209. See Surtees, no. 183, p. 106.

[7] *La Pia de' Tolomei*. The subject was taken from Dante's *Purgatorio*, Canto V. It was D. G. R.'s last major work. It is now in the University of Kansas Museum of Art, Lawrence, Kansas. See Surtees, no. 207, p. 118.

[8] George Frederic Watts (1817–1904), met D. G. R. who was ten years his junior,

Gabriel;[1] the latter does not much like it, but Mrs Stephens[2] admires it hugely.

Friday 5 August   Swinburne having again consulted me about Hotten's affair, I wrote recommending him to do what he chooses as to selection of publisher, but to offer Hotten £50 as indemnity for any detriment he may have suffered.

Sunday 7 August   Battle of Haguenau—an important Prussian victory—along with other Prussian successes. I strongly suspect a republic will be proclaimed in Paris within two or three days— and proclaimed with a pretty fair start and chance of success. Assuming this to be done, and Napoleon and his son kept at arm's length, the difficulty is to guess what will be done with the Prussian war. Will it be a *levée en masse*, against which the Prussians will be powerless, or an immediate cessation of hostilities? I incline to the former surmise, but should hope that the French, after satisfying the national honour, would be disposed to close the war as soon as possible. The first thing however is to get rid of Napoleon; I hope I am not wrong in thinking that there is a considerable chance of that—unless indeed he could succeed *very* soon in turning the tables on the Prussians. We are close to the '*dix Août*';[3] 'le jour de gloire est arrivé'. What a tremendous *rapprochement* and maddening suggestion to the Parisians!

in the heyday of the Pre-Raphaelite Brotherhood. Watts had gathered round him at Little Holland House, under the dominating patronage of Mrs. Prinsep, a group of admirers. In 1864 he married Ellen Terry, but they separated after eighteen months, and were divorced in 1877; in 1886 he married Mary Fraser Tytler. See M. S. Watts, *George Frederic Watts, the Annals of an Artist's Life*, London, 1912, 3 vols., and Ronald Chapman, *The Laurel and the Thorn*, London, 1945.

[1] At first D. G. R. thoroughly disliked the portrait and sent a chalk drawing to Watts in exchange for the portrait. D. G. R. did not keep it and loaned it to Mrs. Hughes who after D.G.R.'s death sold it to Leyland. See *Memoir*, pp. 348–9. The portrait is now in the National Portrait Gallery, London. See R. Chapman, op. cit., p. 78.

[2] In 1865 F. G. Stephens, one of the first Pre-Raphaelite Brethren, had secretly married a widow, Mrs. Clara Charles. In 1868 a son was born to them and was named Holman after his godfather, Holman Hunt. For F. G. Stephens, see p. 122, n. 3.

[3] It was on 10 August 1792 that the Paris mob stormed the Tuileries where Louis XVI and his family were residing, thus securing his deposition from the throne.

Wednesday 10 August   Overturn of the Ollivier Ministry.[1] The agitation in Paris looks black for Napoleon; but perhaps hardly likely to amount to a revolution, unless further disasters ensue to the French arms. But at any rate, unless some decided success is soon achieved by Napoleon, I greatly doubt whether he will ever be Emperor again in Paris; for his son I see still less chance.

Saturday 13 August   My article on Miss Spartali[2] etc. is now published in the *Portfolio*.[3]

Tuesday 16 August   Gabriel says he has now got on considerably with his large Dante picture. His racoon has disappeared, which he does not regret as it used to lie *perdu*, and was dangerous to other animals. The second of his Virginian owls died some little while ago, being found with its head thrust forward into the ground. The raven also is dead. He has lately got a mole for Nolly Brown.

Thursday 29 September . . . Started at 8.30 p.m. for Ostend and Brussels—intending to go up the Rhine, and probably into Italy, but not very clear as to what the trip will really come to.

Friday 30 September   Landed at Ostend. Started for Brussels towards 7. Here I found considerable difficulty in getting a hotel, having called altogether at seven places. Had to content myself with a small room at Hôtel de Dunquerque [*sic*] without a fireplace or a table. But it does well enough. The great influx of French people taking refuge in Belgium and prolonging their stay as the

---

[1] Jules Ollivier (1825–1913) had been the French Prime Minister since 2 January 1870. He advocated a liberal Empire and declared that he was ready to accept the responsibility for the war. The defeats suffered by the French army brought about his downfall and henceforth his activities were only literary. He became a member of the French Academy in 1870.

[2] Marie Spartali (1844–1927) was the beautiful daughter of the Greek Consul-General in London. She studied painting under Madox Brown, and in 1871 exhibited for the first time in the Dudley Gallery. In the same year she married a widower, W. J. Stillman, to the great displeasure of her father. See the obituary notice in *The Times*, 8 March 1927, by J. W. Mackail, and an article on Marie Spartali by R. L. Ormond in *Country Life*, 30 December 1965.

[3] W. M. R.'s article in the *Portfolio*, no. 8, was entitled 'English Painters of the Present Day'. It concerned Arthur Hughes, Windus, Miss Spartali, Lucy and Oliver Madox Brown. Facing p. 113 is a reproduction of a drawing in chalk by Marie Spartali, called 'Fear'.

war continues, is the cause of the glut; got three French 100-franc notes changed at a discount of 2·50%. To the Wiertz Museum. It ought not, I think, to be denied that Wiertz[1] was a man of genius, and a painter of considerable attainment. The immense scale of several of his works is beyond what I had surmised. In execution Rubens seems to have been his ideal; and something between Rubens and David Scott[2] might give the nearest idea of his most marked style.

Sunday 2 October   Took a carriage and went to Waterloo. At the Hôtel des Colonnes, where I made an early dinner, there is framed an autograph note from Victor Hugo testifying his great satisfaction at the treatment he experienced there in 1861. The landlady tells me he stopped about a fortnight, collecting the facts concerning Waterloo for the *Misérables*,[3] and writing some of the work. In Brussels dog-carts (literal) are very prevalent, especially for milk-carts, the dogs don't seem to consider themselves aggrieved.

Monday 3 October   Left Brussels at 9.45 and went on to Louvain.

Thursday 6 October   Cologne ... To the Walraff Richarts Museum, which I find so rich in old paintings and other objects that I resolve to stay here to-morrow also, to continue exploring it. Spent three or four hours looking mostly at the old German paintings, a collection which includes many highly wrought and characteristic specimens; also at the painted glass, the Roman antiquities, and glancing also at the less ancient paintings. There is a most beautiful Bordone,[4] bought for the Museum out of the endowment, and not described in the catalogue; represents a woman bathing in a palace court, with two other figures, perhaps

---

[1] Antoine-Joseph Wiertz (1806–65), Belgian painter who executed gigantic pictures. He invented 'la peinture mate' which combines the effects of oil painting with the fresco technique.

[2] David Scott (1806–49), designer and painter, elder brother of William Bell Scott who wrote a *Memoir of David Scott*, containing his journals in Italy, notes on art, and other papers, Edinburgh, 1850.

[3] Published in 1862.

[4] Paris Bordone (1500–71), Venetian painter, pupil of Titian. He also worked in Germany and France. The picture mentioned by W. M. R. represents Bathsheba at the bath attended by two servants, and King David watching the scene from a window; it was painted between 1540 and 1557.

an allegorical subject, for beauty I know few pictures to surpass it. A very fine Rubens, *Francis receiving the stigmata*: Tintoretto[1] of *Ovid and Corinna*, admirable, and very novel composition. Piloty's *Galileo in Prison*[2] is a most excellent work of the intellectual-art class, interesting the mind in a very high degree.

Friday 7 October   Came on to Coblentz by rail.

Saturday 8 October   I purposely miss out in this diary everything I see bearing upon the war—thinking this the more prudential course in case any extraneous person should demand or come across my diary. In point of fact however, though I could note down a variety of details here and there, things in general seem to be going on very much in their normal condition, the German people calm and undemonstrative, and since Brussels no difficulty whatever in obtaining Hotel accommodation. Before going to bed I considered (for the first time with any degree of precision) what my ultimate destination shall be; and came to the conclusion that I am not very likely to cross the Alps or reach Italy. The short days are against long continued railway, etc. journeys, and the alternative road home through France is closed by the war. I propose to go on to Munich, thence, if convenient, to Inspruch,[3] Trient,[4] and conceivably but not probably Verona; and home by Nuremberg, Frankfort, Antwerp, etc. Anything beyond Munich I should make contingent on the time etc. remaining after I shall have seen what I want in that city.

Wednesday 12 October   Left Mainz in the morning, and came on to Würzburg as the only available midway station towards Munich, which one can only reach after 9 p.m. I may congratulate myself upon having stopped at Würzburg, which is one of the most old-charactered picturesque places I ever was in. Walked through the streets, in which churches are numerous.

[1] The 'Tintoretto' mentioned by W. M. R. was a copy of the picture *Tarquin and Lucrezia* in the Prado. This copy disappeared from the Wallraf Museum forty years ago; its present whereabouts is unknown.
[2] Charles-Théodore de Piloty (1826–86), German painter; the 'Galileo' picture was painted in 1864.   [3] Innsbruck.
[4] Trient became Italian in 1919 by the treaty of Versailles and the name changed to Trento.

Thursday 13 October   Looked into the Neumunster,[1] the interior of which has been considerably renovated within these few years, there are various old monuments of a memorable kind. This is more especially the case with the Cathedral,[2] which is truly rich in episcopal and other brasses, effigies, etc., many of them uncommonly fine. Also an ample series of paintings which, without being particularly fine, are of a creditable class. Left Würzburg for Munich about 3, and arrived there about 10. Hôtel de Bavière.

Friday 14 October   Took a guide, and (with the interval of dinner) went about with him all day.

Saturday 15 October   Went to the Ludwigskirche,[3] to see the vast fresco of *The Last Judgement* by Cornelius.[4] It is a very complete piece of work, and must I think be numbered among fine things. Other frescoes in this church by Hess[5] and Schraudolph[6] are considerably less good. Then to the Royal Palace, and saw the old and the new apartments—the frescoes, I believe by Schnorr,[7] of *Charlemagne*, *Barbarossa* and *Rudolph of Hapsburg*, do not interest me much, though their merit from a certain point of view is no doubt considerable. Those from the *Niebelungen*, also by Schnorr, are much finer. Some of the great pieces of action, such as *Murder of Siegfried, Fight of Hagen and others in Etzel's Palace*,[8] are very

[1] The Neumunster is a thirteenth-century Romano–Gothic church, the interior of which was completely renovated in the eighteenth century when a baroque facade was added.

[2] The Cathedral is a Romanesque edifice begun in the twelfth century and enlarged in 1240, but its style was altered by eighteenth-century modifications. It was damaged in 1945 by a great fire and many of its artistic treasures mentioned by W. M. R. were destroyed.

[3] The Ludwigskirche was built by Gärtner between 1830 and 1844. The interior is decorated with frescoes executed on designs by Cornelius. The main piece is the *Last Judgement*, a colossal composition painted by Cornelius himself.

[4] Peter von Cornelius (1783–1867), German painter, Director of the Academy of Munich was, with Overbeck, one of the leaders of the Nazarene painters. See p. 27 n. 3.

[5] Heinrich von Hess (1798–1863), German painter, Art Professor at the Academy of Music; decorated several churches in Germany.

[6] Johann von Schraudolph (1808–79), German painter, a pupil of von Hess and, like his master, he executed decorative frescoes.

[7] Julius Schnorr von Karolsfeld (1794–1872), was commissioned by King Ludwig I of Bavaria to decorate the new apartments of the Royal Palace at Munich.

[8] In the Nibelungenlied, the hero Siegfried is murdered by Hagen, a retainer of the Burgundian King. Siegfried's widow marries Etzel, King of the Huns. After the arrival at Etzel's palace of the Queen's brothers, they are attacked. Hagen is

powerful and striking. I knew these works already as com-
positions, many of the subjects, even of leading importance,
are merely on a comparatively small scale, such as lunettes in
monochrome, etc. Bought various caricatures, etc. of the present
war.

Monday 17 October Returned to the old pictures, and found
among the smaller works many masterpieces; an *Adoration of
Shepherds* and *Entombment* by Rembrandt, finished sketches, are
among the very finest works I know of the master. Had to leave
at 11.45 to keep an appointment which had been made in the
morning to see Kaulbach's[1] studio. He received me kindly and,
on my naming Miss Howitt,[2] almost affectionately. He is a
younger-looking man than I had expected, hair still dark.[3] I find
however his age must be 65. Speaks neither French, English, nor
Italian. Is engaged on a subject of *Nero carousing in his Golden
House*, while Peter, Paul, and other Christians are martyred.
Also an impressive subject of *The Inquisition*: an old blind Inquisi-
tor touching with his staff a girl of thirteen or so as next victim.
He has done two very excellent designs *de circonstance*, to be engraved on wood: *The Dance of Death with Pius IX and Napoleon I.*
1st, Death, as Protestantism, knocks at the door of Vatican; Pius
thinks he is safe, having locked door with Peter's keys, but
meanwhile another Death, as Red Revolution, is lying in wait at
his feet. 2, Napoleon measures a globe with compasses, and
thinks it too small for his ambition. Death comes, and shows him
a skull, as if that too were a sort of globe. He gave me a photograph of one of his designs for Anna Mary.[4] Talked a good deal

slain by the Queen with Siegfried's magic sword. This legend has a historical nucleus
provided by the overthrow of Gundahar, King of the Burgundians, by Attila (Etzel)
in 436. See J. B. Bury, *History of the Later Roman Empire* (1923), I, 249.

    [1] Wilhelm von Kaulbach (1805–74), prolific German painter.
    [2] Anna Mary Howitt (d. 1884) who became Mrs. Alaric Alfred Watts, a colleague
of W. M. R. in the Inland Revenue Office, had been a pupil of Kaulbach towards
1850 and published a book about her artistic experiences in Munich, *An Art-
student in Munich*, 2 vols., London, 1853. She was a great friend of Mme Bodichon
as was her mother Mary Howitt, the author of books for children. It was through
the Howitts that the Rossettis became acquainted with Barbara Leigh-Smith. See
Reminiscences, pp. 170–1, and H. Burton, *Barbara Bodichon*, London, 1949, *passim*.
    [3] W. M. R. adds an amusing note to this remark: 'Yes, but it was a wig which
I did not then observe.'
    [4] Anna Mary Howitt.

of the war; deplores it, but says the French must be smashed. A relative of his was wounded in the arm at Sedan, and was being transported thence with other wounded: all were killed by peasants. Then the Germans burned down the peasants' village, and destroyed many of the inhabitants. Kaulbach is a Republican, but seems to have no belief in the present French Republic. Honours Jules Favre[1] but thinks him no statesman. Has no admiration for Victor Hugo. Kaulbach called me '*mein lieber Freund*'; told me to call if I am again in Munich, saw me home to my Hotel, and gave me a cigar to smoke in his studio. I smoked a little of it, and ought perhaps to preserve the rest as a souvenir. I liked him much.

Tuesday 18 October To the Exhibition of New Paintings, which is a miserable show. Kaulbach's *Jerusalem*[2] is about the most valuable work, and of course fine from its point of view. One or two Overbecks,[3] a highly respectable Piloty, etc. are to be observed, but, with a few exceptions, the Gallery lowers even a low estimate of modern German art. Wilkie's *Reading the Will*[4] is quite a masterpiece amid its surroundings.

Wednesday 19 October Left Munich about 1. Reached Nuremberg about 8.15 p.m, and put up at Hôtel de Bavière.

Thursday 20 October Nuremberg is certainly an astonishingly picturesque place. I think it beats everything I had seen in this way; and this although I see it to-day under much disadvantage, there being no single gleam of sunshine to give colour and throw shadows. Looked through the Rathhaus, with Dürer's *Triumph of*

---

[1] Jules Favre (1809–80), French politician who was a staunch Republican and opposed to Napoleon III; he became Vice-President of the French Government and Foreign Minister in 1870.

[2] Kaulbach's *Jerusalem* is now in the New Pinacothek of Munich.

[3] Johann Friedrich Overbeck (1789–1869), German painter who with Cornelius had founded in 1810 a group called the Nazarenes, which has been likened to the Pre-Raphaelites. They rebelled against their national schools of art and attempted to return to the Italian early masters' principles and adopted monastic customs, wearing long robes with girdles of rope. Madox Brown visited the studios of Overbeck and Cornelius on a visit to Rome in 1845. See the descriptions of this visit in F. M. Hueffer, *Ford Madox Brown*, pp. 43–5.

[4] David Wilkie (1785–1841), appointed Painter in Ordinary to King William IV in 1830 after Lawrence's death. R.A. in 1811. A study for a portion of the picture mentioned here is in the Tate Gallery. The picture itself is in Munich Pinacothek.

Maximilian,[1] but it was dark and rather late, and I had but an imperfect view of this work. Fine old hall.

Saturday 22 October   Went over the Castle; containing some pictures, excellent old stoves, fine views of Nuremberg, room of instruments of torture, etc. Also to the other torture place, Heimliches Gericht,[2] with the Eiserne Jungfrau.[3] I sat down in a spiked chair, just to find what it was like. The spikes are not such as would pierce the flesh even if bare, and for a minute or so (all I tried) the feeling does not extend beyond a moderate degree of discomfort. Looked again at Dürer's *Maximilian's Triumph* in Rathhaus, so as to see it with a reasonable amount of light. Was pleased at the uncommon incident of refusal of gratuity by the old lady who shows this place. Even after I had actually put a half florin in her hand, she declined it; seeming to think that, as I had had to return to make up for the darkness of the preceding visit, it ought to go into the original payment.

Sunday 23 October   Left Nuremberg at noon, and travelled all day, reaching Frankfurt at 8.30.

Monday 24 October   To the house where Goethe was born in the Hirschgraben,[4] it is now public property, though some of the purchase money remains to be cleared off. Looked all over the house, which contains many items of interest, among others a pen-and-ink sketch by Goethe of a *Witches' Sabbath*,[5] done at some late period of his life; it has no artistic merit or executive skill, but expresses its meaning. The house generally had a very comfortable family air, not unlike that given in Dutch pictures of the better class of houses of the late seventeenth century.

Wednesday 26 October   Started about noon, and reached Antwerp about 6.30. To the Hôtel de Ville, to see Leys's[6] frescoes. Most of

[1] Albert Dürer (1471–1528), the greatest German painter who was also an engraver and a sculptor. The *Triumph of Maximilian* is a series of large wood engravings executed between 1512 and 1515 by Dürer and other artists.

[2] Secret court of justice.   [3] An instrument of torture: 'the iron maiden'.

[4] Goethe was born in 1749; the house was badly damaged during the Second World War, but has since been entirely restored.

[5] There are two pen-and-ink designs by Goethe representing *The Witches' Sabbath* in the Frankfurt Goethe Museum. They were probably executed after 1820.

[6] Jean Auguste Leys (1815–69), Belgian historical painter.

them were already known to me by the oil-pictures, the tone of colour is very fine and solid for fresco. I observe that one of the secrets of Leys's positivism in art is never to paint a mouth open. I thought the scenes of old Burgher-life were also at the Hôtel de Ville; but the gardienne says there is nothing beyond what I saw, viz. the *Charles the Fifth, Pallavicini*, etc. She says Leys was very agreeable and pleasant to deal with; his wife (who survives) somewhat grasping, and made him sell as fast as he painted, to the ultimate detriment of his fortune. He was a large eater—caught a cold in a storm after a hearty meal, and died in a day or two— was besides a sufferer from asthma. Had come back from London with some digestive pills which he valued highly. His wife and two daughters are painted seated in the *Pallavicini* picture; his son, as a drummerboy in the *Rubens* picture in the Musée.

Friday 28 October   Started about 5 for London. Reached London early on Saturday 29th October.

Saturday 5 November   Returned to Somerset House. Received from Froment the concluding transcript of the Shelley papers at the Record Office. *The Devil's Walk*[1] is evidently Shelley's own composition—not, as I had supposed, a mere appropriation of Coleridge's poem. Both this and *The Declaration of Rights*[2] are valuable finds for Shelleyites, and I shall see at my convenience about getting them published.

Sunday 6 November   Allingham called. I offered him the above Shelley papers for *Fraser*. For himself, he would be glad to secure them; but says that specially literary matter is not particularly welcomed by Froude,[3] who submits his judgment greatly to

---

[1] In 1812, Shelley, writing to Elizabeth Hitchener, sends her nine stanzas on the Devil, 'I was once rather fond of the Devil'. Then he considerably enlarged the poem, remotely imitated from Coleridge's ballad, entitled it *The Devil's Walk* and published it as a broadside in 1812. See *The Complete Works of P. B. Shelley*, ed. Hutchinson, 1912, p. 867.

[2] A paper in which Shelley proclaimed the rights of governments and individuals. Shelley made his servant, Daniel Hill, paste it upon the walls of houses in Barnstaple. The correspondence between the Barnstaple Town Clerk and the Home Secretary about the affair was traced at the Record Office by a friend of W. M. R.

[3] James Anthony Froude (1818–94), historian and man of letters, the editor of *Fraser's Magazine* from 1860 to 1874; he had met Carlyle in 1849 and was greatly influenced by him. Later he became Carlyle's literary executor.

Carlyle's. Carlyle lately condemned the admission into *Fraser* of an article by Horne[1] concerning the burning of Shelley's body, saying that the whole subject was totally insignificant. On the whole, therefore, Allingham does not think it would be desirable for me to offer the paper to *Fraser*.

Wednesday 9 November   Gabriel called. Webb[2] thinks a moderate outlay will suffice to make his present studio adequate. The sale of Gabriel's *Poems* has lately been almost nullified by the war, but it begins to revive now, and a 5th edition is to come out. £450 has already been paid to him through the publisher. Gabriel told me a good deal about Howell, whose connexion with Ruskin, it seems, is about finally to close.[3]

Saturday 12 November   Gabriel tells me that his servant Emma, a person of self-possessed decided character, and not at all superstitious I should say, was about to go to bed on Sunday last, but came out of her room a moment to say good night to some one. On doing so, she saw, standing at the entrance of my bed-room (just opposite to hers) a ghost—i.e. a female-looking figure in white drapery. This so startled Emma that she rushed back into her room, and had a hysterical fit. The other servant Susan, who sleeps in a room between these other two, came out and assisted her. A day or two afterwards, Emma told Gabriel that, on coming down that morning, she found papers strewn about the passage (which, Gabriel knows, were not there the last thing on the previous night); drawings etc. in an adjacent room transposed, a candlestick in another room placed on the ground; and articles of china in that room fantastically displaced. This is strange, and I know no physical explanation of it that can be offered, unless

---

[1] Richard Hengist Horne (1803–84), the author of *Orion*, had just returned from Australia and was still showing an interest in the literary matters which had induced him to write *A New Spirit of the Age* (1844) in collaboration with Elizabeth Barrett.

[2] Philip Webb (1831–1915), the architect who built 'Red House' at Upton for William Morris; he was one of the seven members of the Firm of Decorators founded in 1860, under the name of 'Morris, Marshall, Faulkner and Co.', of which D. G. Rossetti and F. Madox Brown were also members. See *Memoir*, p. 217, and W. R. Lethaby, *Philip Webb and his Work*, London, 1935.

[3] The real reasons for which Ruskin dismissed Howell have never been made quite clear. Howell was accused of dishonesty; in fact, he managed to be involved in 'complicated activities' which led him into endless difficulties. See H. Rossetti Angeli, *Pre-Raphaelite Twilight*, p. 164.

possibly Susan is purposely playing tricks. Gabriel had had no reason hitherto to suspect her of any such tendencies; for myself, I barely know her by sight. The house has had the reputation of being haunted ever since we knew anything about it; and some peculiar things have occurred before, but nothing so marked as this.

Sunday 13 November Finished and sent to Scott the notes I have been making for the revision of his Dürer book.[1]

Thursday 17 November Dined with Scott, apparently the last time I shall see him in his present house, 33 Elgin Road, as he expects to have moved by Wednesday next into the house of which he has bought the lease: Bellevue House, Battersea Bridge.

Saturday 19 November Met Allingham by appointment at the South Kensington Museum. Allingham, some while ago, in reading Chaucer noted down certain words, phrases, etc., which are now out of use in ordinary English, but still current in Ireland; he showed me two or three instances, which appear to me to be in point. He had thought of writing a paper on this subject, but had not yet done so. He tells me that Froude, though still very heterodox in religious matters, makes a practice now of going to church which he justifies to himself by some sideway argument. Allingham is distinctly a theist, and believes in immortality, but not as being proveable.

Monday 21 November Today brings me two letters about Shelley. One from D. F. MacCarthy,[2] who is treating the subject of Shelley

---

[1] W. B. Scott, *Albert Dürer: His Life and Works, including autobiographical papers and a complete catalogue with illustrations*, London, 1869. It was reviewed in The *Academy*, 12 Feb. 1870, by J. A. Symonds who wrote that the 'true life of Dürer remains yet to be written', but that Mr. Scott's book 'leaves the impression of greater gravity and more reliability' than that of Mrs. Heaton, who had also written a life of Dürer which Symonds reviewed in the same article. Some twenty years later, W. B. Scott considered his book as 'good enough for the English public at the time, but now antiquated by the rapidly-developed Dürer literature in Germany'. See W. B. Scott, *Autobiographical Notes*, 1892, ii. 193.

[2] Denis Florence MacCarthy (1817–82) had written an account of Shelley's stay in Ireland in *The Nation*, Dublin, in 1846. In a letter to W. M. R., dated 21 November —the one mentioned here—he complained that when C. S. Middleton wrote his

in Ireland, and wishes to know what is the unpublished correspondence mentioned by me. I replied, naming Mr. Slack[1] as the
owner, but saying that, as Mr Slack keeps the correspondence to
himself, I would thank Mr MacCarthy if he addressed Mr Slack
to explain that I gave the name in confidence, and have not
implied that the letters could be shown. I also mentioned (without
precise details) the papers I have lately traced in the Record Office;
as it seems to me possible that MacCarthy may also have traced
them, and I should wish to avoid any chance of future collision
as to the right of using the papers. If he should really be in possession of them, and be in the way of publishing them earlier than
myself, I should ungrudgingly acquiesce.

Tuesday 22 November   Today, in a reading at the Hanover Square
Rooms,[2] Christina's *Goblin Market* was included. Mamma who
attended (I was prevented from doing so) tells me that it was well

book entitled *Shelley and his Writings*, 1858, he made use of his article without
acknowledgement. In the same letter, he adds:
   'I am engaged on a detailed narrative of Shelley's visits to Dublin in 1812 and
1813 . . . I am sure you would be glad that the truth were told about the whole of
this affair, or at least as much of it as can now be related with absolute certainty.
I believe that I am in a position to make this contribution to a true knowledge of
Shelley's life at the period I refer to.'
In a subsequent letter, dated 22 Nov. 1870, MacCarthy declares:
   'I have in my possession most of the materials:
   1. *The Address to the People of Ireland*
   2. *The Proposals for an Association*
   3. *The Declaration of Rights*, which as promised me by a distinguished gentleman,
      I may rely on.
   4. The *Letters* referring to the seizure of Holyhead, promised me in the same way.
   5. *A Dublin Newspaper* authenticated by Shelley himself . . .
   6. Different versions of Shelley's *Speech*, which in one form I was the first to
      extract. (Unpublished letters in the Angeli Collection.)
The speech mentioned here was made by Shelley on 28 Feb. 1812 at a Roman
Catholic political meeting. It appeared in *The Dublin Evening Post*, of 29 February
1812. D. F. MacCarthy used this material in a volume, *Shelley's Early Life, from
Original Sources*, issued in 1872.
   [1] Henry James Slack (1818–96), author and journalist, was the custodian of a
number of letters addressed by Shelley to Miss Hitchener. In 1869 he allowed
W. M. R. to read them in order to obtain information for his memoir on Shelley,
but not to quote any passages from them. The real owner of the letters was, at that
time, a lady living in Germany. See also entry for 4 May 1873, and *Reminiscences*,
p. 365.
   [2] These 'Poetic Readings' were organized by Frank A. Marshall (1840–89),
journalist and playwright, also editor of Shakespeare.

received, but the audience did not seem to enter much into the
the more sprightly and characteristic details.[1]

Wednesday 23 November   Mr MacCarthy having solicited me to
allow him to see my copy of Shelley's *Declaration of Rights*, I posted
him the whole of the transcripts made at the Record Office,
intimating that, if he is in the way of using them before myself,
he is welcome to do so.[2] Gabriel says that, with a view to pre-
venting any posthumous publication of poems of his which he
considers not good enough to be published, he has lately looked
up all those which he considers *just* good enough, and has put
them into such a state as would render their publication practically unobjectionable; any other poems not thus revised, are such
as he considers positively below the mark.

Thursday 24 November   Finished the biographical notice of Hood.[3]
Brown tells me that Swinburne is recently back from Holmwood,
and has been seeing to the settlement of his affairs with Hotten.
An appointment was made the other day for a meeting at Swinburne's lawyers—with Swinburne himself, Hotten and Howell
and Moy Thomas[4] as the respective referees. Swinburne having
breakfasted with Powell,[5] arrived in such a muddled state that it
was found impossible to proceed with the business, and the affair
still hangs over. It seems, however, that the referees agree that

---

[1] *Goblin Market and Other Poems* was published in 1862. It was intended to be a
tale for children; in fact, the symbolism of the poem has not yet been altogether
explained.

[2] (I am now in possession of this transcript—probably the whole of it. W. M. R.)
It appeared as a folio leaf printed on one side only. According to T. J. Wise,
only three copies of this broadside are known. One was sold at Sotheby's in May
1913 for £530 and is now in California. The other two are preserved in the Public
Record Office, London. See T. J. Wise, *A Shelley Library*. One volume from the
Catalogue of the Ashley Library (printed for private circulation), 1924.

[3] For the Moxon Series of English Poets: it was published in 1871 and illustrated
by Gustave Doré.

[4] William Moy Thomas (1828–1910), journalist; in 1866–7 was the London
correspondent of *The New York Round Table*; in 1868 he joined the staff of the
Daily News. He translated Victor Hugo's *Les Travailleurs de la mer* in 1866.

[5] G. E. J. Powell (1842–82), a young Welsh squire who was so struck by the
beauty of *Atalanta in Calydon* that he wrote to Swinburne to express his admiration.
They became close friends. He shared Swinburne's appreciation of the Marquis
de Sade and admiration of Simeon Solomon (see p. 120, n. 1); but in 1873 Swinburne
strongly advised Powell to keep aloof from Solomon. See Swinburne, *Letters*, ii.
261 and *passim*.

Swinburne ought to give Hotten the publishing of his next two books—including (as Brown understands) the *Songs before Sunrise*, now on the eve of publication by Ellis. The latter is said to be quite tired of Swinburne and his affairs and more than willing to resign him.

Friday 25 November   Mr MacCarthy informs me that he has traced out something definite about the second of the volumes of poetry (both now lost) published by Shelley:[1] this is exciting. Garnett agrees in the probability that Daniel Hill, Shelley's servant at Lynmouth, was the 'Dan' suspected by Hogg of having got up the assassination affair at Tanyrallt,[2] and that Hogg's suspicion was correct.[3]

Thursday 1 December   Maria has about finished her book[4] giving an exposition of Dante's *Commedia*, the next question will be as to the chance of finding a publisher.

[1] In his 'Memoir of Shelley' W. M. R. mentioned two early poetic works. In a letter dated 23 November 1870 MacCarthy wrote to W. M. R.: 'I have discovered the other (published) book of verse, beside *Victor and Cazire* to which you refer in a note to your memoir. I do not mean to say that I have discovered the poem itself, but its title, and all the circumstances connected with it.' (Unpublished letter from the Angeli collection.) In the note mentioned W. M. R. gave the following information: 'The poem was advertised for publication as follows, in the *Oxford University and City Herald* for 9 March 1811: "Just published, price two shillings, *A Poetical Essay on the Existing State of Things*, by a Gentleman of the University of Oxford. For assisting to maintain in prison Mr. Peter Finnerty, imprisoned for a libel."' *Original Poetry by Victor and Cazire* was the second early volume. It was composed by Shelley and his sister Elizabeth and published in 1810, but withdrawn when the printer, Stockdale, found out that some of the contributions had been taken from 'Alonzo the Brave and Fair Imogene' in *The Tales of Wonder* (1801) by Matthew Gregory Lewis ('Monk' Lewis). The whole impression (1,480 copies) was destroyed except for 100 copies which were already in circulation. R. Garnett found a copy of it and republished it in 1899. See *Letters about Shelley*, p. 16.

[2] After their return from Ireland in 1812, the Shelleys (Percy and Harriet) settled at Tanyrallt, in North Wales. One night, on 26 February 1813, Shelley was twice attacked in his home by a man who attempted to murder him. No trace of the assassin could be found. A more recent interpretation of the fact has been given by H. M. Dowling in *The Keats–Shelley Memorial Association Bulletin*, xii, 1961, 28: 'Shelley being considered as wholly undesirable, because of his "radical" ideas was attacked by some hardy citizen to drive him away from their town; the "trick" succeeded, since the Shelleys fled from Tanyrallt the next morning to Gwynfryn, seven miles away.'

[3] See T. J. Hogg, *The Life of Percy Bysshe Shelley*, with an introduction by Professor Edward Dowden, London, 1906, pp. 392–3.

[4] *A Shadow of Dante*, published in 1871, by Rivingtons.

Saturday 3 December   Swinburne called, asking whether I would accompany him to hear a lecture at St George's Hall by Wilfred[1] (brother of Ulric de Fonvielle,[2] who has come over from Paris by balloon). We went; attendance rather scanty, and to a great extent foreigners: lecture partly English and partly French, and moderately interesting, as to state of Paris etc. The gist of it was denunciation of Prussian barbarism, French resistance to the death etc. Nothing very much like grappling with the precise facts. Brown asked me to write (which I did) to Appleton,[3] Editor of the *Academy*, recommending Hüffer as musical critic. Hüffer would like to get the post—for which it seems a son of Hullah[4] is also looking out.

Sunday 4 December   Began the article, to be offered to the *Fortnightly*[5] embodying the Shelley papers from the Record Office.

Monday 5 December   Went on with this—Hüffer, as Appleton informs me, *will* be selected as musical critic for the *Academy*, and is also invited to act as sub-editor.

Friday 9 December   Bought a Southey, so as to settle the question about the relation of his *Devil's Walk*[6] to Shelley's. I see there is no direct borrowing (apart from the portion ascribed to Coleridge), and so finally settled the Shelley article for the *Fortnightly*.

Sunday 11 December   Brown called with Hüffer, also invited as subeditor of the *Academy* at £100 per annum . . .

Monday 12 December Dined with Watts and his wife. She does not now pursue art, except under the form of 'Spirit Drawings'. Morley[7] accepts my Shelley article for the *Fortnightly*.

---

[1] Wilfred de Fonvielle (1824–1914), French journalist and writer, played a part in the Revolution of 1848; he founded the French Aero Club.

[2] Ulric de Fonvielle (1833–1911), French journalist, fought under Garibaldi in the campaign for Sicily in 1860, challenged Prince Pierre Bonaparte to a duel in 1870, commanded a battalion during the siege of Paris in the Franco-Prussian War.

[3] Charles E. Appleton (1841–79) founded the *Academy* in 1869, and invited W. M. R. to write some literary critiques for it. See *Reminiscences*, p. 468.

[4] John Pyke Hullah (1812–84), composer and teacher.

[5] The article was published in the *Fortnightly Review* for January 1871, under the title 'Shelley in 1812–13, an Unpublished Poem, and other Particulars'.

[6] See p. 14 n. 4.

[7] Editor of the *Fortnightly Review*. See p. 141 n. 2.

Thursday 15 December   Dined at Brown's—partly in order to hear Hüffer's music, which I like much, to Christina's song, 'When I am dead, my dearest'.[1] Brown has done a goodish-sized water-colour of young Foscari in prison, the same design as in the Byron volume;[2] very fine, though with some peculiarity of designing arrangement. Gabriel read the plan he has laid out for his pro-posed lyrical drama of *The Sirens*.[3] He wishes to have music com-posed for it, and seems to think of Hüffer. I confess to some doubts whether the idea is a well-conceived one, and feel some demur even at points in the story itself, as planned out. Brown, Hüffer, and Swinburne, who was also present, all raised some questions as to details, though generally approving. Swinburne came more especially to consult me, as proposed by Ellis the publisher, on the contract Ellis offers regarding the publication of the *Songs before Sunrise*. I saw nothing that occurs to me as unfair or objectionable: as regards one point, probable purchase by Swinburne of the stereotype plates, Gabriel and Brown thought that some modification to Swinburne's advantage should be introduced, and I made a pencil note accordingly, though without thinking the point of any great importance.

Thursday 22 December   Called on the bookseller Pearson, to see after some Shelley and other items. He showed me an entry in a catalogue (some years old) of the sale of the library of a Mr Edward Higgs, wherein the *Epipsychidion* of 1821 is shown as one of the books for sale; this is the only time I have ever seen or heard of any actually existing copy of that edition.[4] Pearson expects to get

[1] *The Poetical Works of Christina G. Rossetti*, 1904, p. 290. After Hüffer, other composers wrote music for this song; Ralph Vaughan Williams in 1903; John Ireland in 1928.

[2] The subject was taken from Byron's historical tragedy *The Two Foscari* written in 1821. Ford Madox Brown contributed some illustrations to *The Poetical Works of Lord Byron*, ed. W. M. R., and published by Moxon in 1872.

[3] The full title was *The Doom of the Sirens*, 'a lyrical tragedy'. It was never written, but the prose outline, composed at Penkill in 1869 and mentioned here, was pub-lished first in the 1886 edition of *The Collected Works of D. G. R.*, vol. i.

[4] *Epipsychidion* was published by the Olliers in 1821. In sending the poem with the *Ode to Naples* to Ollier, Shelley wrote: 'The longer poem I desire should not be considered as my own; indeed, in a certain sense, it is a production of a part of me already dead.' The Ollier edition of 100 copies was reprinted for private circulation with notes by H. Buxton Forman in 1876. A facsimile reprint was published by the Shelley Society in 1887 with an introduction by Stopford Brooke and a note by Swinburne. See F. L. Jones, *The Letters of Shelley*, ii. 262, and R. S. Granniss, *A Descriptive Catalogue of the First Editions of the Writings of Shelley*, New York, 1923, p. 65.

soon some of the letters by Shelley belonging to the Stockdale[1] correspondence which Garnett brought to light.

Monday 26 December   Gabriel sent lately to Macmillan's to get copies of Christina's poems and was informed they could not possibly be had at present, but are in course of printing. This looks somewhat suspicious. When Christina proposed to transfer the books from Macmillan to Ellis,[2] a certain stock of one of them was said to be on hand, beyond what one could well expect to be now exhausted. I can't suppose he has any right to reprint it without consulting Christina. Gabriel proposes to write to Macmillan, enquiring, and not to allow the matter to drop unless properly explained. He tells me (what I did not know before) that Mrs. Zambaco[3] is a woman of great talent in a variety of ways, and with remarkable capacities for painting, which she is now cultivating to good effect. Scott's new house at Battersea is so cold as to distress the inmates; and Gabriel says he cannot go there again unless the objection is remedied. I took up the affair of my will, which I planned in March '69 and copied it out for execution: some questions however present themselves as to which I

[1] John Joseph Stockdale (1770–1847) was Shelley's first publisher and one of the poet's earlier correspondents. In 1826, four years after Shelley's death, Stockdale printed the eleven letters he had received from him in *Stockdale's Budget* (1826–7). They remained largely unknown until Richard Garnett secured a copy for the British Museum and reprinted Shelley's letters in *Macmillan's Magazine*, June 1860, pp. 100–10.

[2] *Goblin Market and Other Poems* had been published in 1862 by Macmillan and a second edition had come out in 1866. In Feb. 1870, F. S. Ellis—through the influence of D. G. R.—took an interest in Christina's poems and contemplated publishing the whole of her production, as appears in a letter, dated 23 February 1870, from Christina to F. S. Ellis: 'Sir, I understand from my brother Mr. Rossetti that you are desirous of seeing some Nursery Rhymes I have just completed, and which I send you by book-post. I shall be very glad if we can come to terms for their publication. I fear you may have misconceived what the illustrations amount to, as they are merely my own scratches and I cannot draw, but I send you the MS. just as it stands. As regards the complete edition of my former vols. this cannot be done until the matter has been discussed with Mr. Macmillan . . .' See Packer, *The Rossetti–Macmillan Letters*, p. 74.

[3] Mary Zambaco, *née* Cassavetti, was a cousin of the Ionides, well-known members of the Greek community in London. She was a beautiful woman who sat for D. G. R. Her own cousin wrote that she had 'a large heart' and several 'affaires de cœur'. The most notorious was that with Burne-Jones who tried to escape by going to Rome, 'leaving the Greek damsel beating up all the quarters of all his friends for him and howling like Cassandra'. See D. G. R., *Letters*, ii. 685, and A. C. Ionides Jr., *Ion, a Grandfather's Tale*, London, 1927 (privately printed).

shall consult Uncle Henry[1] before completing the document. Meanwhile, to provide against casualties, I had, just before going abroad in September last executed a short will, leaving everything to Mamma.

Friday 30 December   Resumed, after a considerable interval, the reading of poems with a view to the volumes of Selections. Also looked through the proofs of the two-volume Shelley.[2] Made three other alterations—i.e. restoration of the original punctuation, which I had altered in the two-volume edition, for after all I think the original the better of the two. Certainly one cannot be too chary of conjectural emendations, which, even if unsatisfactory to no one else, are more than likely to pall upon oneself in the long run.[3]

[1] Henry Francis Polidori (d. 1885), one of Mrs. Rossetti's brothers. He was a lawyer and had anglicized his name into Polydore.

[2] W. M. R. was preparing a second edition of *The Poetical Works of P. B. Shelley* which was to be unannotated and with the memoir made shorter.

[3] The first two-volume edition had been reviewed in the *Academy* for April 1870 by J. A. Symonds, who reproached W. M. R. for having 'emended the text without sufficient MS. authority'. See also p. 240 n. 1.

Monday 2 January   Swinburne's *Songs before Sunrise* are at last published by Ellis. A copy reached us today.

Wednesday 4 January   . . . Began reading through, and making a few notes on, Maria's book on Dante. I consider it amply good enough to be published, and think that it offers *some* chance of commanding a sale. It would certainly be a very suitable book for people to read, as an incentive and introduction to the study of Dante in Italian. . . .

Monday 9 January   I am sorry to see in today's paper the death of Alex Munro,[1] though the wonder has for years been how he could possibly survive: Gabriel never had a more admiring or attached friend than Munro.

Sunday 15 January   Answered a letter from Moxon, who sent me a letter from a son of Wordsworth, correcting two details in my Memoir, and also objecting to an expression that Wordsworth was not self-sacrificing or generous.[2] I explained to Moxon that this was taken (and softened) from De Quincey: but, as Wordsworth affirms it to be untrue, I modified it. Gabriel tells me that Stillman is now on his voyage back to England. Gabriel has undertaken to review Hake's poems in the *Academy*.[3]

[1] Alexander Munro (1825–71), the sculptor who had been associated with the Pre-Raphaelites since the earlier days of the Brotherhood; he was blamed for having revealed the meaning of the mysterious letters P. R. B. He went to the South of France for his health and died in Cannes where he was buried.

[2] The opinion of William Wordsworth the Younger on the question is given in a letter to Moxon dated 24 January 1871: 'Had Mr. Rossetti known anything of Mr. De Quincey's private character, he could not, notwithstanding Mr. De Quincey's brilliant talents, have relied upon him as an authority for the numerous false statements he published in reference to my Father and members of his family; which, in charity, could only be accounted for by their having been written when he was under the influence of opium, or irritation at my Father's frequent refusal to lend him money.' (Unpublished letter in the Angeli Collection.)

[3] This review appeared in the *Academy*, 1 February 1871, and was reprinted in *Works*, p. 621.

Sunday 22 January   Began another section of the Chaucer work,[1] viz: the summarizing of those portions of the *Filostrato* which have not been adapted by Chaucer.

Thursday 26 January   Gabriel says Miss Wilding[2] (who sat for him for *Sibylla Palmifera*, etc.) knows something of a George Ernest Shelley, who has been in the army, and calls himself a nephew of the poet[3]—for whom he professes no great reverence. This must, I suppose, be a son of Shelley's younger brother John who died in 1866.

Friday 27 January   Several friends dined at Chelsea: among them Westland Marston,[4] of whom practically I have seen nothing since about 1851. He tells me that Dobell's[5] *Balder* was planned to be in four parts, and its main idea was to exhibit the necessity of a literal millennial reign of Christ on the earth: I should almost doubt whether this is quite accurately stated. I saw some of Gabriel's recent works:—Red-chalk design, *Wedding of Michael Scott*;[6] red-chalk heads of Stillman,[7] full face; Mrs. Morris[8] with

[1] (This was a work which I had begun in September 1868 for the Chaucer Society: a collation of the *Troylus and Cryseyde* with the *Filostrato* of Boccaccio. W. M. R.)

[2] Miss Alexa Wilding, 'a damsel of respectable parentage whom he [Dante Gabriel] saw casually in the street, in April 1865, and whom he at once determined to paint from'. He paid her a regular annual salary as a model. She sat for *Sibylla Palmifera*, *Monna Vanna*, *Veronica Veronese*, and *The Blessed Damozel*, among others. See *Family Letters*, vol. i, p. 242.

[3] George Ernest Shelley (1840–1910), Captain in the Grenadier Guards, was the third son of John Shelley (1806–66), younger brother of the poet.

[4] Dr. J. W. Marston (1819–90), the dramatist and father of P. B. Marston; he wrote a review of Swinburne's *Atalanta in Calydon* in the *Athenaeum* of 1 April 1865.

[5] Sydney Dobell (1824–74), poet and critic. His *Balder* was published in 1853.

[6] *The Wedding of Michael Scott* was sold to Leyland. It is now in the William Morris Gallery, Walthamstow. It appears in Surtees, no. 222, p. 124, with the title *Michael Scott's Wooing* which is the title given by D. G. R. to the 'illustrative verse', *Works*, p. 214, and to the prose narrative, *Works*, p. 616. In the Notes, W. M. R. wrote: 'My brother made two or three drawings of this subject of invention. He contemplated carrying (it) out in a large picture which was never executed.' *Works*, p. 668.

[7] The red chalk portraits of Stillman mentioned here were studies for the finished portrait which is now in the Boston Museum of Fine Arts and reproduced in the *Autobiography of a Journalist*. It appears more as a 'red chalk' than as a 'pastel' as recorded in the Museum catalogue, though the eyes are slightly tinted. Surtees, no. 518, p. 197.

[8] William Morris (1834–96), poet and artist, married Jane Burden in April 1859;

a pomegranate, the same as *Silence*;[1] oil-picture of Mrs. Morris listening to a song sung by a girl (this was begun as a portrait, but now rather to count as a subject).[2] The picture of *Beatrice in Trance*[3] symbolizing her death, begun perhaps fifteen years ago, seems about finished; the *Pandora*[4] picture, ditto; but Gabriel is inclined to make another picture of this, giving the figure at full length. E. B. Jones[5] expresses himself rather disposed to leave off exhibiting altogether—or at least to miss the current year. Morris[6] has some idea, now *The Earthly Paradise*[7] is done, of writing a drama, or a prose romance—not another narrative poem; he cannot however settle upon any subject.

she had been associated with the young decorators of the Oxford Union Debating Hall since 1857; they all thought that her enigmatic beauty was peerless and she regularly sat for them. Between 1857 and 1875, D. G. R. painted or drew no less than thirty-nine portraits of Mrs. William Morris. She also sat for him when he executed some of his most characteristic pictures. In Henry James's words, she represented 'a grand synthesis of all the Preraphaelite pictures'.

[1] *Silence*. There are at least two versions of this drawing. See Surtees, nos. 214, and 214 A, p. 122. According to D. G. R.'s letter quoted by Mrs. Surtees, the fruit is not a pomegranate, but a peach.

[2] This subject was *Mariana*. The song is sung not by a girl, but by a page-boy See Surtees, no. 213, p. 121.

[3] A name often given by D. G. R. to the picture known as *Beata Beatrix*. The original oil-painting was begun in 1863; Rossetti had conceived it as a memorial to his wife, Lizzie Siddall. He made several replicas of it, three in oil, several in crayon, and a small one in water-colour. The original, completed in 1871, was bought by Lord Mount-Temple and is now in the Tate Gallery, London. See Surtees, no. 168, p. 93.

[4] Several crayon studies for *Pandora* had been made in 1869. The head was done from Jane Morris. D. G. R. was then beginning an oil picture of this same subject which he completed during the following year. The full-length figure mentioned here was never executed. See Surtees, no. 224, p. 125. D. G. R. had written a sonnet to accompany the picture. See *Works*, p. 211.

[5] Sir Edward Coley Burne-Jones (1833–98), the famous painter who remained a loyal friend and admirer of D. G. R. to the end. See G. Burne-Jones, *Memorials of E. Burne-Jones*, 2 vols., London, 1904.

[6] William Morris founded in 1861 the manufacturing and decorating firm of Morris, Marshall, Faulkner and Co. in which D. G. R., Burne-Jones, Madox Brown, and Philip Webb were partners. It was in 1856 that Burne-Jones and William Morris, aged 22, were introduced to D. G. R. who immediately exercised an overpowering influence on them which was gradually to decline. In later years, Morris's interest in socialism grew deeper and he became one of the leaders of the movement. He started the Kelmscott Press in 1890. See Philip Henderson, *William Morris, His Life, Work and Friends*, London, 1967.

[7] *The Earthly Paradise*, a narrative poem published in 1868–70 consisting of a prologue and twenty-four tales in Chaucerian metres in which the heroes alternately tell Greek and Norse legends. Yet, Morris's biographers and his daughter May Morris have suggested the personal significance of the poem.

Sunday 29 January   Called by appointment on Woolner—who, as I see, has just been elected A.R.A. He seems to care little about this, but to think acceptance the only rational course, in which I agree with him. Looked a great deal at his pictures—including undoubtedly some very fine and important Turners and other works: there are however some that I think disputable, and some others more probably not genuine. His delight in the ordinary sort of English landscape seems to me disproportionate. The number of his pictures is now very large—including some at high prices—£1,400 for Turner's *Newark* etc. Saw his four children for the first time.

Tuesday 31 January   Brown called—indignant at the bad hanging of Marie Spartali's picture at Dudley Gallery, and not particularly pleased at the rejection of works by Cathie[1] and Nolly: he attributes these proceedings mainly to Marks,[2] and thinks of not countenancing any further offer of pictures by his family in future years. He is also indignant with Karl Blind for going against the Republican French in the present horrible war (now presumably nearing its close) and even speaks of dropping his acquaintance altogether. He tells me that Morris has been translating the *Frithiof* and some other sagas. As the prospect of sale is indifferent, he does not propose to publish these;[3] but has written them out in elaborate black-letter calligraphy with initial letters etc.

Friday 3 February   Gabriel is proposing to write for the *Academy*[4] a notice of the series of portraits done by Maclise in *Fraser*.

Monday 6 February   Appleton sends a circular, asking whether

[1] Catherine Madox Brown, second daughter of Ford Madox Brown by his second wife, Emma Hill. She married Francis Hüffer in 1872. She was a portrait and subject painter and exhibited several pictures at the Dudley Gallery.

[2] Murray Marks (1840–1918), the famous art dealer of 395 Oxford Street. His trade card, adorned with a Chinese ginger jar and peacock feathers is supposed to have been the joint work of D. G. R., Whistler, and William Morris. D. G. R. made two chalk portrait heads of Mrs. Murray Marks. See Surtees, nos. 350 and 351. See G. C. Williamson, *Murray Marks and his Friends*, London, 1919.

[3] In 1868 William Morris had plunged into the study of Icelandic language and literature under the guidance of Magnus Magnússon. In January 1869 Morris and Magnússon's translation of the *Saga of Gunnlaug Worm-Tongue* came out in the *Fortnightly Review. The Frithiof Saga* was published in March 1871 in the *Dark Blue*. See J. W. MacKail, *The Life of W. Morris*, 2 vols., London, 1899, i. 201, 240.

[4] D. G. R. wrote an article: 'Maclise's Character-Portraits' in the *Academy*, 15 Apr. 1871; it was reprinted in *Works*, p. 627.

contributors to the *Academy* will forego their remunerations for 1871, to form a fund for relief of members of the French Academy and Institute, suffering from the war; I replied consenting.

Tuesday 7 February   Dined with Scott . . .

Thursday 9 February   Ellis writes to Christina that he gives up the idea of publishing her *Nursery Rhymes*, because he can't see his way to getting illustrations suitable to his position as connected with the best artists: he sends her £35 by way of compensation for the delay etc. Christina is not inclined—nor should I be—to keep the money. It has been a tiresome affair and I think not well managed on Ellis's part.

Friday 10 February   Gabriel, calling in Euston Square, wrote a sonnet on the French subjugation by Germany—as a sequel to an old sonnet of his on the Italian war of Napoleon III.[1] He suggests to me to write a set of political sonnets—which I am not averse from doing.[2]

Saturday 11 February   Locker[3] called at Somerset House, and showed me a bombastical letter he has lately purchased, addressed by Shelley to Graham,[4] signed 'Philobasileus',[5] and containing a

[1] The 'old sonnet' is 'After the French Liberation of Italy' (1859) and the new 'After the German Subjugation of France' (1871). They were both first published in 1904. See *Works*, pp. 205, 217.

[2] Ten years later W. M. R. took the cue and composed 43 sonnets (one on Hungary dated from 1849) which appeared so incendiary to D. G. R. that he begged his brother not to publish them as they might endanger his position as 'an official of a monarchical government'. W. M. R. acquiesced and had them published only in 1907. See W. M. R., *Democratic Sonnets*, London, 1907, and D. G. R., *Letters*, nos. 2451, 52, 57.

[3] Frederick Locker (1821–95), known as Locker-Lampson after 1885, poet, sometime clerk in Somerset House, where he became acquainted with W. M. R. He was the owner of important Shelleyan documents and he and W. M. R. pursued joint researches about Shelley. He was also a friend and correspondent of Swinburne. See F. Locker-Lampson, *My Confidences*, ed. A. Birrell, London, 1896.

[4] Edward Fergus Graham (1787?–1852), was the son of Shelley's father's 'factotum'. Sir Timothy's notice was attracted by the musical talent of the boy, he took him into his house and provided for his education. Later, Graham became a teacher of music. In 1845 he called on Gabriele Rossetti and became an occasional visitor at the Rossettis' house. W. M. R., who was then a boy, remembered him quite well. See R. Ingpen, *Shelley in England*, London and Edinburgh, 1917, i. 223, and K. N. Cameron, *Shelley and his Circle, 1773–1822*, Cambridge, Mass., 1961.

[5] The letter is published in Shelley, *Letters*, i, 105.

few verses beginning 'Tremble, ye Kings despised by man'.[1]
I know I have seen this somewhere before. Don't however believe
that it is in print, but that it must have been one cut out of the
two or three Shelley letters shown me some twenty years ago by
Graham the Musician, who was son of Shelley's Graham.

Sunday 12 February   Finished the Chaucer work.[2] Nothing, I
think, remains save to give it one final perusal and then hand it in
to Furnivall.

Monday 13 February   Christina wrote offering her *Nursery-Songs* to
Roberts and Co., for American publication,[3] in case that firm will
take steps with some publisher in England so as to save Christina's
rights of copyright in this country. This was in accordance with a suggestion I had made, considering the present position of the matter.

Tuesday 14 February   Maria's turn comes today. She writes offering
her *Shadow of Dante* to Williams and Norgate, saying nothing of
terms. Her idea is to be content if the publishers will simply
undertake the expense.

Wednesday 15 February   Williams and Norgate reply that the book
would not do well in their hands, as they have no adequate country
connexion. Maria therefore wrote offering it to Bell and Daldy.[4]

Friday 17 February   Sandys[5] having asked me the other day

    [1] This was the fourth stanza of a translation of the *Marseillaise Hymn*. It was the
only one published (by Buxton Forman in the 1870 edition of the works of Shelley)
till André Koszul published the whole of the translation in *La Jeunesse de Shelley*,
Paris, 1910, p. 402. He obtained it from Charles Esdaile, the poet's grandson, who
gave permission for the other five stanzas to be published for the first time.
    [2] This was published in 1875 by the Chaucer Society under the title *Chaucer's
Troylus and Cryseyde (from the Harleian M.S. 3943) compared with Boccaccio's Filostrato
translated by Wm. Michael Rossetti*, part i, with the following commentary: 'Those
lines of the Filostrato that Chaucer translated or adapted, are Englisht [*sic*] here:
those which Chaucer did not use—more than half—are only summarized.' The
second part of the work was published in 1883.
    [3] Roberts Brothers, a Boston publishing firm, absorbed late in the nineties by
Little, Brown & Co. Christina Rossetti was put in touch with them by Jean
Ingelow in 1866. See Troxell, *Three Rossettis*, p. 53.
    [4] George Bell (d. 1890), publisher, was joined by F. R. Daldy in 1855, but their
partnership was dissolved in 1872.
    [5] Anthony Frederic Augustus Sandys (1829–1900), the painter, known to Rossetti
since 1857. He stayed more than a year (1866–7) in the Cheyne Walk house, then a

(rather to my surprise, considering his having broken off with Gabriel) to look at his portrait of Clabburn,[1] now on view at Graves's[2] which I did yesterday—I wrote expressing my high opinion of the work. It is indeed very fine, though perhaps a little over-peculiar in style.

Saturday 18 February   Locker and Cincinnatus Miller,[3] a Californian whom Locker made known to me, also Stillman, came to Euston Sq., the former two were introduced to Christina, whom they more especially wished to know.

Sunday 19 February   Gabriel now engaged on a picture of *The Blessed Damozel*[4] for Graham M.P.[5]—the latter commissioned him at the large price of £945 for a duplicate of his *Beatrice in Trance*.[6] He tells me Swinburne's *Songs before Sunrise* are a success in point of sale.

Monday 20 February   Alma Tadema[7] and others dined at Chelsea.

difference arose between them in 1869 and relations were broken off, but were resumed in 1873. For D. G. R.'s conciliatory letter to Sandys, see Troxell, *Three Rossettis*, p. 57.

[1] Clabburn, a Norwich manufacturer interested in Pre-Raphaelite painting; he visited D. G. R.'s studio in 1864. *R.P.*, p. 66.

[2] An art gallery.

[3] Cincinnatus Miller (1839 or 1841–1913), known afterwards as Joaquin Miller: gold-digger, cowboy, teacher, barrister, judge, poet, and dramatist; born in Indiana. Went to England in 1870, met W. M. R., who introduced him to literary circles, and wrote eulogistic reviews of his poems in the *Academy* (15 June 1871) and the *Eclectic Magazine*. Miller published *The Songs of the Sierras* in 1871 (reviewed in the *Athenaeum*, 3 June 1871), and *The Songs of the Sunlands* (dedicated to the Rossettis) in 1873. See M. S. Peterson, *Joaquin Miller*, Stanford, 1937, *passim*.

[4] There are two oil versions of this picture illustrating D. G. R.'s poem, *Works*, p. 3, and also several pencil or ink studies. The one mentioned here was commissioned by William Graham in 1871 and completed in 1877 when Graham asked for a predella to be added. It is now in the Fogg Museum of Art, Harvard University. The other was bought by Leyland in 1881; it is in the Lady Lever Art Gallery, Port Sunlight, Cheshire. See Surtees, no. 244, p. 141 and no. 244 M, R. 1, p. 144.

[5] William Graham (1816–85), M.P. for Glasgow, one of the most liberal purchasers of D. G. R.'s paintings. On his relations with Rossetti, see his daughter's reminiscences: Frances Horner, *Time Remembered*, London, 1933, *passim*.

[6] Graham wished a predella to be added to distinguish the picture from the original. This replica was completed in 1872. It is in the Art Institute of Chicago. See Surtees, no. 168 E, R. 3, p. 95.

[7] Lawrence Alma-Tadema (1836–1912), a painter of Dutch origin. He studied art with Leys and, when visiting Paris in 1864, he met Gérôme and Rosa Bonheur who spoke of him to Gambart, the picture dealer. He came to London in 1870 and

Tadema, whom I now meet for the second time—but the first so as to see anything of his ways—seems to have a remarkable energy of character, and a frank hearty manner and tone of opinion on any subject that is started. He is a devoted admirer of Japanese art—going, I think, as far as anyone I know. He decidedly prepossesses me. Allingham says that Mrs. Esdaile (Shelley's daughter Ianthe) has been brought up in total ignorance of and alienation from her father and his memory; but some little while ago thawed somewhat in this respect under the influence of Lady Shelley. She says she had in her possession some poems by Shelley wholly unknown: not even Lady Shelley has been allowed to see them. I suppose they are of minor or minimum value.

Tuesday 21 February   Bell and Daldy decline Maria's book on Dante on the ground that its prospect of sale is uncertain.

Friday 24 February   Maclennan[1] (author of the book *Primitive Marriage*) called on me at Somerset House. He is now Parliamentary Counsel for Scotland, and has to live in London a good portion of the year; is also employed on the Statute Revision, and apparently to much more satisfactory effect than others who are so employed. He seems thus to be assuming a very good legal position. Took round to Furnivall[2] my work on Chaucer's *Troylus*: he asks me to say something more detailed about the poetic beauties of the work—the other persons concerned with it being, as he says, merely scholars without poetic perception: this I will see to when the occasion comes. He has ceased since the

settled there. He became acquainted with the Rossettis and their circle and achieved a successful career in England. He was elected R.A. in 1879. See Edmund Gosse, 'Alma-Tadema R.A.' in *Modern Artists, A series of Illustrated Biographies*, ed. F. G. Dumas, London (n.d., presumably 1882).

[1] John Ferguson McLennan (1827–81), Scottish sociologist. The full title of the book is *Primitive Marriage: an Enquiry into the Origin of the form of capture in Marriage Ceremonies*, Edinburgh, 1865.

[2] Frederick James Furnivall (1825–1910), scholar and editor. In 1854 he helped to found the Working Men's College, where D. G. R. was a drawing instructor. Then began a life-long friendship between Furnivall and W. M. R. Furnivall was the founder or president of the New Shakespeare Society, the Chaucer Society, the Early English Text Society, the Browning Society, and in 1886 he founded the Shelley Society, together with R. Garnett, E. Dowden, and W. M. Rossetti. See *Reminiscences*, pp. 389–90.

beginning of this year to be a strict vegetarian, finding his digestion bad under that system: seems to think himself improved in health now that he eats a little meat, but doesn't care about it in point of taste: still abstains from all wines etc. Had been a vegetarian about twenty-five years. Two young Japanese are now inmates of his house: Sanjo (son I believe of the Prime Minister) who can speak English now very fairly; and Oshikoji, just arrived —a quaint laughing little chap who can only repeat a word or two now and again. I took round four of my Japanese books, for Sanjo to give some information about. One of them is the book I described in the *Reader*:[1] I find my conjectural suggestions were generally wrong, and the book not offering anything like a consecutive story. Sanjo treated this book slightingly—saying it is merely for children, and not noticeable in point of art: but I know better[2] as far as the last point is concerned. Shall note down, in this and the other books, a few details ascertained from Sanjo. He says he is nominally a Buddhist; but, like the majority of Japanese learned men has no real belief in the religion. He is seventeen years old. Oshikoji sixteen; both short—and the latter almost dwarfish and childish in aspect. Sanjo showed me a letter he had received from his mother. It is a light long piece of paper, painted with flowers in a broad style: across this design the letter-writer indites her epistle—rather confusedly to an English eye. He regards ear-rings as barbarisms—there is no such custom in Japan: the men there are now departing from the habit of shaving the head. He knows Nagai, whom I met years ago at Boyce's, and something of Soogiwoora: they are now back in Japan. He showed me a series of small landscape photographs by Japanese, most skilfully and nicely taken—the focussing in some rather difficult subjects being, I think, almost superior to a good European standard. Says that some Japanese are now studying art on the European system. I told him it would spoil them, but he did not seem to agree. He cited the splendid tiger painted on silk at South Kensington Museum by Ganku (see 19 April 1870)[3] as a

[1] Article published in the *Reader* in 1863.

[2] (I did know better: the designs are by that consummate master Hokusai. W. M. R.)

[3] This refers to jottings in W. M. R.'s diary dated 3 March 1870 and 19 April: 'Went to see at South Kensington an astonishing Japanese silk painting of a tiger— done by a distinguished artist, Ganku, about 1700', *R.P.*, p. 505. W. M. R. was mistaken about the date. Ganku (1749–1838), Japanese painter, specialized in

really good sample of Japanese art. I appointed for him and Oshikoji to pay me a visit on Sunday week. His state-sword (which I saw) cost about £100: he is extremely punctilious about its blade—even the touch of a finger is wrong, as rust may ensue from the moisture. He seems to think the abolition of the Tycoon[1] a national benefit.

Saturday 25 February   Visited the exhibition at 168, Bond Street in aid of the distressed French, and met Legros[2] there—first time this long while. Regnault's[3] *Headsman*[4] and *Prim*[5] are very fine; but the former perhaps rather below than above my expectation. David's[6] *Marat dead in his bath*, most interesting and very good. A fine mournful snow-scene by Legros. The latter tells me that a picture-sketch here by Delacroix,[7] of *Mirabeau and de Brézé*,[8] was

painting tigers, mainly on kakemonos, the silk or paper scrolls which decorate Japanese houses.

[1] A title applied by foreigners to the Shogun of Japan. The Shogun was a Japanese hereditary ruler and commander-in-chief whose office was abolished in 1867 or 1868.

[2] Alphonse Legros (1837–1911), French painter, engraver, and medallist. When an art student in Paris, formed a friendship with Fantin-Latour and Whistler. In 1863, as he was in difficult circumstances after his father's death, Whistler advised him to go to London where he settled and became a British subject. He became a teacher of etching at the South Kensington Museum and in 1875 Slade Professor of Fine Art, University College, London. He was a prolific painter, exhibited at the R.A., and many of his pictures are in English and French galleries. See E. R. and J. Pennell, *The Whistler Journal* (1921), p. 83, and M. Geiger, *Alphonse Legros*, MS. thesis (1954), Bibliothèque de l'École du Louvre, Paris; also the Catalogue of paintings, drawings, and lithographs by A. Legros from the collection of Frank E. Bliss in Boston, Mass., Public Library.

[3] Henri Regnault (1843–71), French painter: he was killed at the siege of Paris, during the Franco-Prussian war.

[4] The full title of the picture is *Exécution sans jugement sous les rois maures de Grenade* 1870).

[5] *Portrait équestre de Juan Prim* (1869). These two pictures by Regnault were purchased for the Luxembourg in 1872, but have now been removed to the Louvre.

[6] Louis David (1748–1825), French painter, famous for his historical pictures of the Revolution and the reign of Napoleon. His picture *Marat assassiné dans sa baignoire* is in the Musée des Beaux-Arts in Brussels. See Jacques Louis David, *Le Peintre Louis David, souvenirs et documents inédits*, Paris, 1880.

[7] Eugène Delacroix (1799–1865), the great French painter, leader of the French Romantic School of painting. Delacroix had been to London where he had met Wilkie. He appreciated contemporary English painting and when he saw Millais's *Order of Release*, exhibited in Paris in 1855, he admired 'the sincerity, keenness of observation and sentiment which pervaded the picture'. See E. Delacroix, *Journal*, ii. 339.

[8] The real title of this picture is *Mirabeau et Dreux-Brézé* which is now in the Glyptothèque Ny-Carlsberg, Copenhagen. A sketch of it is in the Louvre.

sent into a competition, and was rated by the judges at almost the bottom of the list,—towards 1840, I think. At first sight it appeared to myself a very ordinary work; but more careful consideration altered my impression almost entirely, and I think it contains the true essence of the scene in a very satisfactory though rather lax form.

Monday 27 February   No. 1 of *The Dark Blue*[1] out today. The only decidedly good thing is Morris's translation of *The Frithiof Saga*; generally the magazine has an amateurish and vacuous character that threatens no long life, and certainly no distinguished one.

Thursday 2 March   Brown tells me that Hüffer, not being satisfied with his position in relation to the *Academy*, has given notice to resign . . .

Saturday 4 March   Went to the Dudley Gallery: the excellence and completeness of Lucy Brown's picture of *Romeo and Juliet in the Tomb*[2] surprise me, highly promising as her previous works had been.

Sunday 5 March   A visit of the two Japanese Sanjo and Oshikoji with Furnivall and his wife. Sanjo speaks about the Japanese objects we possess.

Monday 6 March   Ricciardi having asked me to see whether anything in the way of publishing a translation of his book on the *Anticoncilio*, can be done through Bradlaugh,[3] as to which I wrote yesterday to Bradlaugh. He replies today accepting the offer for the *National Reformer*.

[1] *The Dark Blue* was a magazine edited by John C. Freund; the first number appeared in March 1871 and the last in March 1873. During these two years of existence the most noteworthy contributors were Karl Blind, Professor Dowden, Franz Hüffer, Andrew Lang, Joaquin Miller, Arthur O'Shaughnessy, D. G. Rossetti, and Swinburne.

[2] On loan to the National Trust (Wightwick Manor, Wolverhampton) from Mrs. Imogen Dennis.

[3] Charles Bradlaugh (1833–91), free-thinker and radical politician; proprietor of the *National Reformer* from 1862. See Hypatia Bradlaugh, *The Life of Charles Bradlaugh*, London, 1895.

Tuesday 7 March   Took tea with Boyce,[1] Wallis,[2] Scott, and Miss Boyd there also . . . Wallis tells me that Peacock regards Hogg's *Life of Shelley*[3] as little better than mere caricature.

Saturday 11 March   Gabriel, who called in Euston Square, says he now feels easier about his general health, and especially about his eyes, than he had done for some years past. He has noted some alterations in my sonnet on Shelley[4]—improvements, though they don't yet quite satisfy me.

Sunday 12 March   Miss Blind has sent me her review of Swinburne's *Songs before Sunrise*; from a hasty reading I think it uncommonly good: wrote to her to say so and to come to a final understanding as to the magazine it should be offered to.

Saturday 18 March   Maria has now received a letter from Riving-

[1] G. P. Boyce (1826–97), a water-colour painter and a friend of the Rossettis.

[2] Henry Wallis (1830–1916), a painter who was much influenced by Pre-Raphaelitism: his best-known picture, *The Death of Chatterton*, is in the Tate Gallery. W. M. R. took an interest in him as he had known T. L. Peacock (1785–1866), novelist, the friend of Shelley. See *Reminiscences*, p. 158.

[3] Thomas Jefferson Hogg (1792–1862), Shelley's friend, had been entrusted with documents by Sir Percy and Lady Shelley when he was preparing a biography of Shelley, but they were bitterly disappointed with his performance and declared that Hogg had drawn 'a fantastic caricature' of the poet and had 'altered the wording of the letters quoted'. The full and authentic texts of 35 of Shelley's Letters to Hogg are given in K. N. Cameron, *Shelley and his Circle* (1961). See also the Introduction by Edward Dowden who republished Hogg's *Life of Shelley* in 1906.

[4] W. M. R.'s sonnet on Shelley was entitled 'Shelley's Heart' and appeared in the *Dark Blue* for March 1871, i. 35. It is dedicated to Edward John Trelawny who, in *Recollections*, had written: 'What surprised us all was the heart remained entire. In snatching this relic from the fiery furnace, my hand was severely burnt.' As W. M. R.'s sonnet 'Cor Cordium' is not easily available, I quote it here:

> Trelawny's hand, which held'st the sacred heart,
> The heart of Shelley, and hast felt the fire
> Wherein the drossier framework of that lyre
> Of heaven and earth was molten—but its part
> Immortal echoes always, and shall dart
> Pangs of keen love to human souls, and dire
> Ecstatic sorrow of joy, as higher and higher
> They mount to know thee, Shelley, what thou art—
> Trelawny's hand, did then the outward burn
> As once the inward? O cor cordium,
> Which *wast* a spirit of love, and now a clot,
> What other other flame was wont to come
> Lambent from thee to fainter hearts, and turn—
> Red like thy death-pyre's heat—their lukewarm hot!

ton & Co.[1] offering to consider her book about Dante, with a
view to publishing.

Monday 20 March   Christina's negotiations for the publication of
her *Nursery Rhymes* by the American firm Roberts & Co are
proceeding. Today Mr. Niles, brother of the Manager of the firm,
called on her by appointment, and received the MS. He means to
obtain from Dalziel[2] an estimate as to the cost of the necessary
woodcutting, and the question of publication will then be further
considered. Red Republic Insurrection (not to say Revolution) in
Paris notified today. I fear it will prove a bad job for the cause of
the Democratic Republic; but who shall say?

Thursday 23 March   Called to see Nettleship's[3] pictures. He has
three new ones—the chief subject being a lion and a gnu near the
edge of a precipice—exceedingly grand, and certainly a great
advance on his last year's work in solidity and merit of execution.

Saturday 25 March   Called at Pilgeram and Lefevre (Gambart's[4]
successors) to see Alma Tadema's pictures intended for the Royal
Academy: *Accession of Claudius* and a *Nubian-Egyptian*. The latter
very excellent: the former I think more showy and less substantial in general art-value than most of his work. Still very clever
of its kind. In Paris, *les Rouges* are getting on apparently: may
they prove successful, if they will only act with justice and wisdom
when the power is in their hands.

Wednesday 29 March   Called at Christie's to see Gambart's pictures,
about to be sold off. Was interested on again seeing Millais's

[1] The Rivington publishing firm was then composed of two brothers, Francis
and Septimus. Their father had published Newman's *Sermons* and *Tracts for the
Times*, Keble's *Christian Year*, and Pusey's books. See Septimus Rivington, *The
Publishing Family of Rivington*, London, 1919.

[2] The Dalziel brothers, George (1815–1902) and Edward (1817–1905), were
wood-engravers who did much work for the Pre-Raphaelites. 'We had considerable
correspondence with Miss Christina Rossetti extending over several years, she having
written some short poems which helped to adorn the pages of one or more of our
Fine Art books. We also published her charming "Sing-Song".' See *The Brothers Dalziel, A Record of Fifty Years' Work, 1840–1890, in conjunction with many of the most
distinguished artists of the period*, London, 1901, pp. 91–2.

[3] J. T. Nettleship (1841–1902), an animal painter. He appreciated the ideal and
abstract forms of art and was an admirer of William Blake. He met D. G. R. in 1868.

[4] Ernest Gambart, a Belgian who became 'the most prominent and resourceful
picture dealer in London'. He had organized an exhibition of British paintings in
America in 1857. See *Reminiscences*, p. 265 and Jeremy Maas, *Gambart: Prince of the
Victorian Art World*, London, 1975.

deplorably slovenly picture of the *Departure of Crusaders*,[1] containing as it does a portrait of Mamma painted towards 1855–6: very like and interesting, and perhaps the best thing in the picture. Three small things by Gabriel. Sandys's *Helena*[2] which was cited in connexion with the dissension between him and Gabriel is *not*, I see, founded upon Gabriel's treatment of the same subject: it is a very bad picture, about the worst thing Sandys ever produced. Legros, a *Bell-Ringer*,[3] exceedingly fine in sentiment and quality.

Friday 31 March   Called at Woolner's, to see his *Virgilia*,[4] now finished: a very fine work, as also the *Bartle Frere*[5] promises to be. The *Guinevere*[6] is the most stately and graceful of his small figures; and the *Elaine*[7] now impresses me very agreeably—and in some increasing measure the *Ophelia*[8] also. He has received the commission for the statue of Lord Lawrence,[9] in India. He says that Lady Ashburton,[10] the owner of the *Virgilia*, has, with her wonted caprice, lost now apparently all interest in the work: and it seems dubious where she will set it up, or whether possibly she will not part with it altogether.

[1] *The Departure of the Crusaders* is an oil painting, probably an early work. Mrs. Gabriele Rossetti sat for the head of the elderly woman. The picture was part of Mrs. C. E. Lees's collection in 1911.

[2] Sandys's *Helen of Troy* is now in the Walker Art Gallery, Liverpool. D. G. R. had painted the same subject in 1863. In a letter dated 1 June 1869, he complained to Sandys of the similarity of the two pictures. Sandys took it amiss and broke off relations. In 1873, D. G. R. took the first step towards reconciliation. See D. G. R., *Letters*, ii. 698.

[3] Present whereabouts unknown by Legros's most recent specialist, Mlle Geiger, Assistant Curator of the Musée de Dijon.

[4] *Virgilia bewailing the banishment of Coriolanus*: a marble alto-relief begun in 1867.

[5] Sir Bartle Frere (1815–84), Governor of Bombay, 1862–7. A marble bust was carved in 1869, then a marble statue in 1872. The latter was erected in Bombay Town Hall.

[6] A half-lifesize marble statuette. By request of Tennyson, an engraving of the statue of Guinevere was made as a frontispiece of *The Idylls*.

[7] A half-lifesize marble statuette of which three replicas were made.

[8] Also a half-lifesize marble statuette of which three replicas were carved.

[9] John Laird Mair Lawrence (1811–79), Viceroy of India, created Baron in 1869. In 1871 Lord Lawrence sat to Woolner who modelled two busts of him; the second was a marble bust which was placed in Westminster Abbey in 1880. The statue mentioned here was a bronze statue erected at Calcutta. See Amy Woolner, *Thomas Woolner*, London, 1917, p. 289.

[10] Louisa Stewart Mackenzie married the 2nd Baron Ashburton as his second wife in 1858. In 1874 Rossetti made a drawing of their daughter, the Hon. Florence Baring (see Surtees, no. 403, p. 180). Lord Ashburton's sister, the Dowager Marchioness of Bath, had for many years employed W. M. R.'s aunt Charlotte Polidori in her family as governess and later as companion.

Saturday 1 April Went by invitation to an afternoon gathering at Miss Ingelow's.[1] Re-encountered here Leland[2] (*Breitmann*), whom I had seen at Tennyson's gathering last year: his impression of Tennyson is that of extreme want of expansiveness or conversibility. He did not know Edgar Poe personally, but has a very bad opinion of his character. I was introduced to a Mrs Tennant, a handsome woman—cousin, it appears, to Hamilton Aïdé[3]. She has seen a great deal of Victor Hugo, and entertains a deep admiration of him. His kindness to children etc. most conspicuous. He delights greatly both in poring over the fire and in gazing at the sun (resembling Shelley in both these respects): the latter practice, which he holds to in quite exceptional degree, has injured his eyesight: he never, it may be said, misses contemplating the sunset. I asked why he had retired just now to Brussels, instead of coalescing with and guiding the democratic movement in Paris. Mrs Tennant thinks that the misfortunes of France during the war, and the recent death of his son Charles,[4] have broken Hugo's spirit to a great extent, and that he is not at present equal to the efforts which would be required. She says he is an extremely hearty eater; plunges into a bunch of grapes much as one may see a boy bite through an orange, rind and all.

[1] Jean Ingelow (1820–97), English poet and novelist. Christina Rossetti met her in 1864, but they saw very little of one another after that date. Jean Ingelow's poetry was introduced to Christina by Mrs. Gilchrist. See H. H. Gilchrist, *Anne Gilchrist*, London, 1887, p. 148. Though Christina greatly admired Jean Ingelow's poetry she thought it 'dismal'. In December 1864 she wrote: 'Jean Ingelow's 8th edition is also here, to impart to my complexion a becoming green tinge.' *R.P.*, p. 70. And a few months later, 'I hope that *Under the Rose* is less dismal than *The Star's Monument* and *Four Bridges* of oppressive memory.' See Troxell, *Three Rossettis*, p. 144.

[2] Charles Leland (1824–1903), American writer, considered in his day as 'one of the most picturesque figures and strongest individualities in American literature'. As a student, he spent two years in Germany which 'fascinated' him, then went to Paris during the Revolution of 1848 and played an enthusiastic part in it. After his return to the United States, he took to journalism. He became known as the author of *Hans Breitmann's Barty* [*sic*], 1869–71, composed of mock-heroic ballads burlesquing the German–American. He often visited England where he met eminent writers, artists, and political men. To the end of his life he wrote a great many books showing the wide range of his interests. As an old man he settled in Florence, where he died. Elizabeth Robins Pennell, *Charles Godfrey Leland*, Boston and New York, 1906.

[3] Charles Hamilton Aïdé (1826–1906), author and musician, son of an Armenian merchant, was born in Paris. He published some verse and many society novels, and occasionally wrote for the stage. He was a prolific musical composer.

[4] Charles Victor Hugo had died a few weeks before, aged 45.

Sunday 2 April   Dined with Brown. Somewhat to the surprise of all at table, Swinburne came in. He looks not well—but still not very particularly ill. His own statement is that he has been much afflicted with influenza that still hangs about him, but not to any serious extent now. His voice is extraordinarily changed; when in a tolerably deep key, it has a hollow rumbling husky sound: at other times it has a jarring acute tone. Whether this indicates the lung-disease that has been talked of lately I know not; I am not aware of ever having heard the like tone of voice in pulmonary sufferers. I alluded to the matter in the course of the evening, attributing his vocal pecularity to the influenza; Gabriel tells me that the same peculiarity has now existed for some while. I had no knowledge of it—not having seen Swinburne, I think, since 3 December. Brown has made a water-colour of his design to Byron's *Corsair*. Very good . . .

Thursday 6 April   Moxon called at Somerset House to ask a question about the forthcoming Milton volume: also to ask whether I would undertake to edit Tupper[1] as a volume in the series. I replied that, as I could not say that Tupper claims to be numbered among poets, it would probably suit all parties better that some other editor should be engaged. Moxon says that the series is a decided success, and promises to be so increasingly: he now has a sale of 1,000 copies per month, and is displacing Nimmo and other competing cheap editions.

Saturday 8 April   Called at Mrs Tennant's . . . Rivingtons write accepting Maria's Dante book on the system of their paying the expenses and sharing any profits . . .

Tuesday 11 April   . . . The foreign democratic bookseller near the British Museum, a Milanese, says that a copy of my father's *Dante*[2] was sold in London at a book-auction for nearly £3 . . .

---

1 Martin Farquhar Tupper (1810–89), the author of *Proverbial Philosophy* (1838). It first appeared in serial form. The first series ran through sixty editions. In a letter to Swinburne, D. G. R. said what he thought of the suggestion: 'Of course poor William is not editing Tupper. He was asked to do so and refused, and the advertisement would cause anyone but an editor of such lamb-like Galilean meekness as William to be by no means dumb before his shearers, but rather to open his mouth.' See D. G. R., *Letters*, ii. 808.

2 *La Divina Commedia con comento analitico*, vol. i, London, 1826; vol. ii, 1827.

Wednesday 12 April Went to the British Museum, to look up *Sadok the Wanderer*, a prose tale in the *Keepsake* for 1828, there ascribed (as a Mr. Campbell[1] from the Mauritius wrote me months ago) to Shelley. The Museum however possesses no *Keepsake* earlier than 1829: in that volume I find were first published Shelley's prose essay on Love, and the three poems—*Summer and Winter, Tower of Famine,* and *Aziola*: the latter has one or two variations—which I noted—from subsequent texts. Cincinnatus Miller sent me four or five sheets of his forthcoming volume of poems[2] which are full of spirit and poetic ability, and likely, I think, to make a sensation: his quietude of manner, and total absence of literary self-assertion, or even implying that he is a literary man at all, are perhaps unique in degree within my experience. I wrote him a few observations on points of detail, and said I would see about getting the book to review in the *Academy*.[3]

Thursday 13 April Gabriel tells me that Hüffer has conceived a high opinion of Miller's poems, and thinks of reviewing them in the *Dark Blue*. I told Gabriel of what happened the other day in relation to Swinburne's state of health. Dr. Chapman[4] called on me, and produced a letter addressed to him by Robert Buchanan,[5]

---

[1] J. Dykes Campbell (1838–95) was then collecting materials for his biography of Coleridge which was published in 1893 as an introduction to *Coleridge's Poetical Works*. This is what W. M. R. wrote about him: 'J. D. Campbell was a man of remarkably genial and friendly address. He was settled in the Mauritius when first he began corresponding with me relative to Shelley. He was a florid, plump man, very fresh and trim in aspect.' (Unpublished note in the Angeli Collection.)

[2] *Songs of the Sierras*, published in London in 1871; 2nd edn., 1872. See p. 45, n. 3.

[3] The review signed by W. M. R. appeared in the *Academy* for 15 June 1871, pp. 301–2.

[4] Dr. John Chapman (1822–94). After several activities as watchmaker, businessman, became publisher and bookseller in London, editor and proprietor of the *Westminster Review*, finally took a medical degree at St. Andrews and thereafter practised as physician.

[5] Robert Williams Buchanan (1841–1901), poet and novelist; wrote for the *Athenaeum* and other periodicals. He satirized Swinburne and others in the *Spectator* in 1866, and attacked the Pre-Raphaelites—especially D. G. R.—in an article in the *Contemporary Review*, 'The Fleshly School of Poetry' (1871). It was the prelude of a long and bitter controversy; he won a libel action against Swinburne (1875). After D. G. R.'s death Buchanan made the most extravagant amends in *A Note on Dante Rossetti* published in *A Look Round Literature*, London, 1887, in which he greeted him as 'a magician of the tribe of "Kubla Khan", his art expresses the inexpressible. If he was wrong, all the mystics have been wrong [p. 155]. He uses amatory forms and carnal images to express ideas which are purely and remotely spiritual and he takes the language of personal love to express his divine yearning' (p. 158). The panegyric continues for more than ten pages.

urging Chapman to see whether he could not treat Swinburne according to his spinal ice-bag system—which it seems has proved very beneficial in Buchanan's own case.

Saturday 15 April Cincinnatus Miller came in the evening. Miller tells me he was thirty last November: has a bullet imbedded in his right arm, and consequently writes with the left hand; but finds this thwarts the flow of his ideas in poetry, and then uses the right with a very illegible result. He intimates that the adventures set forth in the poem *With Walker in Nicaragua* are substantially facts regarding himself. Gabriel's *Poems* have made their way well in California: the ordinary American poems and literature of the Eastern States are not much diffused in the remote West. Miller had never read any of Whitman, though he seemed to have a general idea of his position as a poet: I gave him a copy of my Selection.[1] Byron and Poe, also Burns, seem familiar to and much admired by him. It is an astonishing fact—considering the peculiarities of style in Miller's poems, and especially the relation of *Arizonian* to *The Flight of the Duchess*—that he has read nothing whatever of Browning's save the recent ballad of *Hervé Riel*. He is a remarkable and a very interesting man. His idea now is to return to California in about a month: I suggested to him to wait here another month or so, to see how his book succeeds. He fully authorises me to use poems by him in my volume of American Selection.[2]

Wednesday 19 April Christina has received a letter from Niles, representing the American publishers Roberts & Co. They seem to anticipate a very favourable reception of her book of *Nursery Rhymes*, though they have not as yet undertaken to publish it. Dalziels, the wood-engravers, it appears are inclined to speculate in the book to some extent, in relation to the English edition. Brown and Hüffer called in the evening and want to know Cincinnatus Miller: I wrote to the latter, asking whether he can accompany me round to Brown's next Monday. Brown thinks that he, Gabriel, and two or three others, might club to illustrate Christina's book—each doing three or four designs of a simple kind. I wish this might take effect, but doubt it; the simpler the designs the better, I have always thought and said, for this particular book.

[1] *Poems by Walter Whitman.*   [2] *American Poems.*

Much discussion about the state of France etc. Brown, I find, is opposed to absolute universal suffrage: would substitute an educational franchise.

Sunday 23 April Maria has now returned her MS to the Rivingtons, after inserting the required extracts from printed translations. Rivingtons would very much like Gabriel to design a binding—one with some of his wonted emblematic circles or the like. It appears to me that a good design would be to have two wings below; and in the centre a flaming sword: thus symbolizing Paradise, Hell, and Purgatory. I made a sketch of this in the course of the evening with appropriate mottoes inscribed: also for the back cover a Florence iris, and for the back of the volume a cross atop, and at the lower end a font with bay-wreath, with 'Ed a quel fonte' inscribed: alluding to Dante's expressed wish to receive the wreath of poetry at his baptismal font. The mottoes for the front cover are 'Mentre che i primi bianchi aperser l'ali'— 'Non avean penne ma di pipistrello'—'Ed una spada nuda aveva in Mano'.[1] Wrote to Cavaliere Ferrazzi[2] in reply to a recent letter from him, sending him a few Dantesque particulars for a new edition of his *Manuale Dantesco*.

Monday 24 April Went to a gathering at Brown's, taking Miller round: the latter seemed much pleased with Brown and with some other persons he met. Karl Blind augurs no good from the present condition of things in Paris; considers the leaders of the movement not adequate to the occasion. He says that it is a well-known fact that, Blanqui[3] and others having been arrested in

[1] Most of W. M. R.'s suggestions about the binding of Maria's book were adopted. On the front cover in the outer corners are an angel's wing and a devil's wing; in the centre is the Florence iris. The spine of the volume bears the title and the name and two angels' wings, one on the upper end, the other on the lower. There are, however, no mottoes. The back cover is blank.

[2] Giuseppe Jacopo Ferrazzi (1813–87), priest and teacher at Bassano. He showed patriotic enthusiasm during the events of 1848–9, and was temporarily dismissed by the Austrians. He wrote several books on literary and historical subjects. The best known is his *Manuale Dantesco*, written between 1865 and 1877 (*Enciclopedia Italiana*).

[3] Louis Auguste Blanqui (1805–81), became early in life a member of the Carbonari and a violent opponent of the July Monarchy; he supported the dictatorship of the proletariat. After the disaster of Sedan (1870), Blanqui played a leading part in bringing about the collapse of the Second Empire. He even managed to form a provisional government for a few hours but was soon forced to withdraw. He was arrested and sentenced to ten years' imprisonment.

connexion with one of the revolutionary attempts in Louis-Philippe's time, a paper eventually came to light containing matter in the nature of King's evidence—which paper could only, according to irrefragable internal evidence, have been drawn up by either Blanqui or Barbès:[1] Barbès was wholly above suspicion, and therefore this stigma has ever since rested on Blanqui. Eudes[2] and some others are open to objections of the like class. Blind is perfectly satisfied from intimate knowledge of Alsace, that the Alsatians will, at no great distance of time, be fully reconciled to their lot as reidentified with Germany—the ties of race etc. being so strong: this corresponds with the expectations I have myself entertained all along.

Tuesday 25 April   Began writing for *Academy* the notice of Miller's poems. Christina has for some days past been suffering from neuralgia (so her doctor says), and looking very much out of condition. Dr. Jenner[3] advises her to get a change of air: she will probably therefore go to Leamington next week with Mamma.

Wednesday 26 April   Finished the notice of Miller's poems. Christina's negotiation for the publication of her *Nursery Rhymes* is progressing favourably, but with Roberts for the American edition, and with Dalziel for the English edition.

Thursday 27 April   Finished looking through Whittier's[4] poems, for the American Selection. A large proportion of them are well done, and a good percentage really fine. He ought to be better known in England.

---

[1] Armand Barbès (1809–70), also plotted against Louis-Philippe's Government. He was sentenced to death in 1839, but reprieved through the intervention of Victor Hugo. He was again imprisoned in 1849 but released by Napoleon III in 1855; however, he refused to return to France and died in Holland.

[2] E. D. Eudes (1843–88), one of the principal organizers of the burning of Paris in 1871. He was a disciple of Blanqui and took an active part in the French Commune of 1870–1 as Commander of the Commune troops. He took refuge in Switzerland, then in London where he frequented the French refugee circles in which W. M. R. moved.

[3] Sir William Jenner, Bt. (1815–98), Physician-in-Ordinary to Queen Victoria and to the Prince of Wales; regularly attended Christina Rossetti from 1870.

[4] John Greenleaf Whittier (1807–92), American poet, whose works were edited with a critical biography by W. M. R. in 1890 in the *Moxon's Popular Poets* series. See Whitman Bennett, *Whittier, Bard of Freedom*, Chapel Hill, N. Carolina, 1941.

Friday 28 April Christina unfortunately continues to suffer much, and looks wretchedly ill. She again consulted Sir W. Jenner today. He now says that she should not attempt just yet to leave town; and he connects her illness with some internal complaint (none of us knows what kind exactly) that she first felt a year or so ago. This is anything but cheering news: to hear of anything internal gives one a turn, though at present I have no reason for concluding that there is anything greatly amiss in the nature of the complaint.

Saturday 29 April Mamma gave me some explanation about the above matter of a reassuring nature up to a certain point. Gabriel says he is now advancing towards the completion of his large picture of the *Death of Beatrice*.[1] He made some improvement on my sketch for the binding of Maria's book.

Sunday 30 April Boughton[2] called to have a look at my Japanese paraphernalia. I gave him one of the finest landscape-subjects I ever saw—a drenching rain with nearer and distant trees.

Monday 1 May Brown called to enquire after Christina: he says he is now just fifty. Hüffer has resigned his sub-editorship of the *Academy*. Brown tells me that Hüffer has a great regard for me, which I reciprocate. Hüffer or some one learned from Miller that Miller's slightly illegal career is set forth not only in the poem *With Walker in Nicaragua*, but in the still more startling *Tall Alcade*. Miller it seems, is engaged to be married to the editress of a newspaper in California: his daughter, mentioned in his poems, is surmised—not known—to have been born out of wedlock, perhaps from a Comanche Indian woman,[3] as it seems that Miller once associated with that tribe. Stillman and his wife are back in London: she means to get over the two girls forth-with from America—the boy being still too ill to be moved.

Wednesday 3 May Paid a visit to the R.A. Millais's landscape[4] is certainly most excellent, but hardly so interesting or uncommon

---

[1] *Dante's Dream*. See p. 8 n. 1.
[2] George Henry Boughton (1833–1905), landscape painter and illustrator. See *Portfolio*, 1871, p. 69.
[3] The Comanche, a Plains Indian nomadic tribe, ranged from Wyoming into Texas and Mexico.
[4] *Chill October*.

as I had expected: *Moses and Hur*[1] fine: Gérôme's[2] *Cleopatra* very
fine. Barclay,[3] who does some remarkable pictures, something
midway between Moore[4] and Prinsep,[5] is new to me.

Thursday 4 May   Dalziels write to Christina, proposing Zwecker,[6]
Sulman,[7] and (for figures) Fraser,[8] as the illustrators of her book.
Christina, being still wretchedly ill and incapable of transacting
the business, asked me to attend to it. As I know nothing at
present of Fraser, I wrote asking Dalziels to show me any previous
engraved designs of his.

Friday 5 May   Christina's illness still extremely serious. I feel
more alarmed about it today than heretofore. Sir W. Jenner says
there is 'no immediate danger', and at his late visit today re-
assured Mamma a little—but only a little. He orders Christina to
keep her bed strictly, which I have thought for several days
would be the best thing; hitherto she has got up regularly, but
done little or nothing more, save lying on a sofa . . .

Tuesday 9 May   Christina is perceptibly—though it cannot be

[1] This picture illustrated Exodus, 17: 10–12.

[2] Jean Léon Gérôme (1824–1904), French painter of classical subjects. His
picture *Cleopatra and Caesar* was produced for the Paris *Salon* of 1866, then exhibited
at the R.A. of which he was made an honorary member. See Fanny Field Hering,
Life and Works of J. L. Gérôme, New York, 1892.

[3] Probably James Maclaren Barclay (1811–86), portrait painter who exhibited at
the R.A. from 1850 to 1875. But four other contemporary painters were called
Barclay and the identification is uncertain.

[4] Albert Moore (1841–93) painted religious, then classical subjects. His *Blossoms*,
in the National Gallery, shows a decidedly Pre-Raphaelite influence in the treatment
of the figure and the over-ornate setting. See Alfred Lys Baldry, *Albert Moore, His
Life and Works*, London, 1894.

[5] Valentine Cameron Prinsep (1838–1904), one of the seven young artists who
decorated the walls of the Oxford Union Debating Hall in 1857. The subject of
his composition was 'Sir Pelleas and Lady Etarde'. He became an R.A. and married
one of the daughters of Leyland, one of D. G. R.'s important patrons. He is the
original of 'Taffy' in Du Maurier's *Trilby*.

[6] John Baptist Zwecker (1814–76), German artist who resided in England from
1850 to his death. He illustrated works on Livingstone, Grant, Stanley, etc., and
contributed to important illustrated papers.

[7] Thomas Sulman was one of Ruskin's students at the Working Men's College
(founded in 1854). See 'A Memorable Art Class' in *Good Words*, August 1897, by
Thomas Sulman. Quoted by E. T. Cook in *The Life of Ruskin* (1911), p. 382.

[8] Francis Arthur Fraser, painter, exhibited in the Royal Society of British Artists
from 1867 to 1883, also at the R.A.

called greatly—better today; less pain and less fever. Dr. Fox[1] is now attending her for a while, as Dr. Jenner has had to go to Gotha.

Wednesday 10 May . . . Gabriel has now got near the end of his Dante picture. . . .

Thursday 11 May Christina still improves: but as yet there are no signs of returning appetite. It must be nearly three weeks since she ate anything even remotely resembling a meal of solid food.

Friday 12 May Maria received this evening the first proof of her book on Dante . . .

Sunday 14 May Gabriel brought round the design (not yet entirely completed) for the binding of Maria's book. It is to a considerable extent the same that I had made; modified in some respects, and made presentable by Dunn's[2] hand in all.

Monday 15 May Obtained some specimens of the wood-designs of F. A. Fraser, whom Dalziels propose for illustrating Christina's book. I don't think him, from the evidence of these designs, at all a desirable man. Wrote to Dalziels to say so, and strongly recommended that Hughes[3] should be invited. Hüffer tells me that Bismarck, of whom he knows something personally, is a singularly agreeable fascinating man: he is much addicted to reading, and Shakespeare and Molière are two of his favourite books.

[1] Dr. Wilson Fox (1831–87), appointed Physician Extraordinary to Queen Victoria in 1870; later became Physician-in-Ordinary.

[2] Henry Treffry Dunn (1838–99) had been engaged by D. G. R. as an assistant in the course of 1869; he helped him with his backgrounds, he also assumed the part of secretary and more or less managed the house in Cheyne Walk; his collaboration ceased in 1881. His *Recollections of Dante Gabriel Rossetti and his Circle* were published after his death in 1904. See also Gale Pedrick, *Life with Rossetti*, London, 1964.

[3] Arthur Hughes (1832–1915), Pre-Raphaelite painter and illustrator, though not actually a member of the Pre-Raphaelite Brotherhood. He took part in the decoration of the Oxford Union Debating Hall with his fresco, *The Death of Arthur*. He is well represented at the Tate Gallery by *April Love* (1856) and *The Eve of St. Agnes*; also in various provincial galleries. He was a successful book illustrator, illustrated William Allingham's poems in 1855 and Christina Rossetti's Nursery Rhymes, *Sing Song*. His letters to Alice Boyd, discovered at Penkill Castle in 1962, throw light on his generous and loyal character. See W. E. Fredeman, 'A Pre-Raphaelite Gazette', *Bulletin of the John Rylands Library*, 1967, pp. 5, 8, and *passim*.

Tuesday 16 May   Called at Quaritch's[1] to get some books. Had quite a long conversation with Quaritch who took me up into his private room to see some books precious in the way of binding or otherwise. Considering the splendid and costly works that are continually passing through his hands and catalogues, the show was scarcely so striking as I should have expected. He estimates his present stock of books (not taking account of volumes) at about 20,000: says that about two per cent of the books he buys pass out of his hands within the first two months; very few remain as dead stock requiring eventual sale by auction. He says the determination of the German nation to avenge themselves on the French in the last war was most deep-rooted and inexorable, though they made no noise about it beforehand. The feeling was based not so much on the invasions of Napoleon I as on the confiscation of Strasburg and Alsace long before.

Wednesday 17 May   Bought a Chinese silver and enamel ornament, of a man riding a rhinoceros and two other objects.

Thursday 18 May   Dined at Simpson's[2] with Miller, the host being his Irish friend Armstrong.[3] Professor Dowden,[4] of Dublin University, who corresponded with me some months ago as a Whitman enthusiast, was there also; likewise his brother, a clergyman, Hüffer, and a prepossessing young Irishman named Yeats,[5] whom I rather gather to be a painter. Miller says that he, like other Californians and Mexicans, is a very good rider—indeed eminently good. Hüffer does not much like Miller; thinks him too coarse and uncivilized—which I can't say I agree in, so

[1] Bernard Quaritch (1819–99), bookseller, described as 'the prince of antiquarian booksellers' by F. A. Mumby. He was of Slovenian origin, but was born in Prussian Saxony and remained in Berlin till 1842. Then he came to London and became a British subject in 1847. His bookshop was at 15 Piccadilly in 1871. It is now at 11 Grafton Street, New Bond Street, London, W.1.

[2] Simpson's, a famous restaurant in the Strand.

[3] George Francis Armstrong, Irish author of *Ugone*, a tragedy reviewed in the *Dark Blue* for April 1871.

[4] Edward Dowden (1843–1913) was then Professor of English Literature at Trinity College, Dublin, and a noted Shakespearian scholar. This was the first meeting of Dowden and W. M. R. They henceforth kept constantly in touch, both being enthusiastic admirers of Shelley and of Whitman. In his *Life of Shelley*, 1886, Dowden made use of various documents discovered by himself, R. Garnett, and W. M. R. See *Letters about Shelley*.

[5] John Butler Yeats (1839–1922), a portrait painter, father of the poet.

far as anything the least essential is concerned: says also that Gabriel did not like him when the two met lately at Brown's—but I fancy Hüffer overstates this latter point. Dowden has a very young look, and I can't suppose he is at the utmost turned of thirty: seems very sensible and agreeable. Armstrong, it seems, is the author of some dramatic poem named *Ugone*: I think I saw the name about some little while ago, but know nothing further of it. Inchbold, whom I met en route from the R.A. to Simpson's is still residing at the Charing Cross Hotel. Dalziels acquiesce, and apparently with full cordiality, in my proposal that Hughes should be employed as the illustrator of Christina's book: they even say the *only* illustrator and to this I quite assent.

Friday 19 May to Saturday 20 May   Holiday on Saturday.

Sunday 21 May   Stillman receives bad news of his boy in America: the hip-joint is ankylosed, and likely to remain moveless for life; and his general condition is very low. Stillman proposes to go over very shortly to America with his wife: not very sure whether they shall return—but, if they find it expedient to do so, thinking he had better be as quick as he can in bringing the boy over to England. Gabriel tells me Hüffer is mistaken in fancying Gabriel did not like Miller: it is rather the contrary. He and Morris are now proposing to take an old house near Farringdon, Kelmscott Manor-house, of about the time of Elizabeth: the rent is only £75, and they would take the place for a year, with the expectation of renewing in future years if suitable. It seems a very jolly old place, from what he says of his inspection of it yesterday.

Monday 22 May   The materials that I have collected for my volumes of selected American poems, are, I think, sufficient in bulk; and I am not aware of any particular writers or volumes that I ought further to consult. I shall therefore now proceed to put the book into shape, with brief summaries regarding the authors etc.

Tuesday 23 May   Began this work. I make the notices of the poets very brief indeed as yet, and shall probably continue on the same tack. Went to see Peel's pictures at the National Gallery. The *Chapeau d'Espagne*[1] is indeed a delightful masterpiece, and several other pictures are good: several also, on the other hand, of no importance, or almost worse than valueless to the Gallery. I see there are several Turners now hung beyond what used to be, and other English pictures: and the whole of the space which used to serve for the R.A., even to the Octagon Room, is now utilized, as well as the whole which used to serve for the National Gallery.

Wednesday 24 May Finished looking through the R.A. I think about the finest work is Gérôme's *Cleopatra*: among the English pictures, nothing perhaps to be preferred to Gilbert's[2] *Convocation*. To-day comes the fearful news from Paris that the Louvre, as well as several other public buildings, are in flames—purposely set on fire with petroleum by the Parisian revolutionists. A most hellish deed, if it is true, and a miserable stigma on the advanced democracy for centuries to come: I can as yet hardly credit it. But it appears to be at any rate a fact that the Louvre is burning; one awaits the event in fear and trembling.

Thursday 25 May Wrote on Christina's behalf to Roberts Bros. the American publishers; saying that she cannot entertain, nor wholly understand, an offer which they make of £25 down, and asking for more precise particulars of their other offer of 10%: adding however that no delay need ensue herefrom in the actual publication of the book in America.

Friday 26 May The horrors of Paris seem to be, in all likelihood, less disastrous to art than had been surmised: but in all other respects as atrocious and miserable as could be reported or conceived. It is a hideous blot on the name of Frenchman and of Republican: still, *in foro conscientiae*, I do not find that it abates my democratic sympathies.

[1] This must refer to the portrait of Susanna Fourment by Rubens which was part of the Robert Peel collection bought by the National Gallery in 1871. The sitter wears a Spanish beaver hat. See *Catalogue of the National Gallery*, no. 852 and *The Times*, 1 June 1871, p. 4.

[2] Sir John Gilbert (1817–97), a mainly self-taught painter who exhibited more than 355 pictures and drawings at the R.A. and the Old Water Colour Society of which he was elected President in 1871. He illustrated most of the English poets and a great number of books and magazines, *Punch* in particular. See *Portfolio*, 1871, p. 49.

Saturday 27 to Monday 29 May   Holiday on Monday.

Tuesday 30 May   Going on with, and not very far from completing, the putting into shape of the vol. of American selected poetry.

Wednesday 31 May   Continuing the above.

Thursday 1 June   Dined at Cheyne Walk with Hake, Brown, Miller, and others. Saw the beginning of Gabriel's picture of *The Blessed Damozel*, which promises to be very fine: Miss Wilding is the model. Dr. Hake has a theory that human beauty requires the absence of any features or appearances characteristic of the embryo. Thus he says that embryos have (universally, if I do not misapprehend) grey eyes: therefore in an adult face the grey eyes are the least beautiful: they improve progressively into blue, green, hazel, brown, and best of all black. Flat noses and blubber lips characterize the embryo: so also the negro, who is thus less beautiful than the European. He says he was certain a negro embryo must be white, not black, at an early stage: at last he succeeded in seeing one, and his theory was right: or rather the black tint was beginning to be deposited in patches, and the embryo was in strictness piebald. Brown seemed much impressed by these observations of Hake's. He had himself just before made a very sensible remark on the subject: that, in the art-work of each nation, the type of human beauty is a compound of—1, the average appearance of the good-looking natives of that nation, and 2, the ideal notion of beauty current in the same nation,— which ideal differs according to the general cast of mind and body of the various nations, Greek, English, French, Chinese, Turkish, etc. etc.

Friday 2 June   To-day at last Sir W. Jenner pronounces Christina free from fever. He wishes her to get out into the open air as soon as practicable: but this may apparently be some days off yet. Swinburne wrote to me proposing a demonstration in honour of Victor Hugo, on his arrival (which however I fancy is disputable, though it has been announced) in England. I replied offering £5 for such a demonstration, or £10 if any practical object were to be associated with it—such as relief to the orphans of slaughtered

Parisian republicans, or assistance to those who may be claimed for extradition.

Saturday 3 June   Gabriel left at Euston Square the design of two heads of Dante for Maria's book, thought of by himself, but executed by Dunn. He says that Howell has been speaking lately of prosecuting some person or persons for libelling him (Howell) in one way or another; and a meeting between Howell and Gabriel to talk over this matter, has been arranged for to-morrow.

Sunday 4 June   Spent the evening at Brown's, to see the last (probably) of Stillman and his wife before they go to America for a while, which is fixed for Tuesday next. I find that Brown has now a very good opinion of Stillman in his matrimonial relation. Saw Brown's water-colour *Entombment of Christ*,[1] *Corsair*,[2] and smaller *Joseph's Coat*;[3] also began oil-picture on a large scale of *Juan and Haidee*;[4] also Mrs. Stillman's *Antigone*, which looks all the better on a close view.

Monday 5 June   Finished the writing of notices etc. for the American Selection. I do not know that anything particular now remains to be done with it, beyond writing a preface.

Tuesday 6 June   The two Whistlers[5] and others dined at Chelsea. Böhm[6] gave Gabriel an interesting series of casts (reductions, I believe) from figures by N. Pisano[7] at Perugia.

[1] A replica of the 1866 water-colour. 'This is the finest piece of colour I have yet produced', Madox Brown wrote to Shields. See Ford Madox Hueffer, *Life and Works of Ford Madox Brown*, p. 266.

[2] This picture is a small water-colour replica of one of the Byron illustrations mostly done in 1870.

[3] *Jacob and Joseph's Coat* is a small oil duplicate of a large picture completed in 1866.

[4] *The Finding of Don Juan by Haidee* is a large oil picture begun in March 1871; it was sold to Leyland before its completion, which took place in 1873. There are four versions of this picture; the largest is in Birmingham Art Gallery.

[5] William Whistler, the artist's brother, had been a surgeon in the Army of the Confederates in the War of Secession. He came to London in 1866, where thanks to his brother he met the Rossettis, Swinburne, and their circle. See *R.P.*, pp. 235 and 245.

[6] Sir Joseph Edgar Boehm (1834–90), sculptor, known especially as a portrait sculptor. Whistler sat for him, and his bust by Boehm remained in the possession of Princess Louise as late as 1915. He was Sculptor-in-Ordinary to Queen Victoria.

[7] Niccolo Pisano (1204?–78), Pisan sculptor and architect. He built the basilica

Wednesday 7 June   Gabriel replied to an Italian in London—I think the name is Canini[1]—thanking him for a translation which he proposes to make from some representative passages of Gabriel's poem, 'The Last Confession'.

Thursday 8 June   Began the preface to my American Selection.

Friday 9 June   Wrote to Locker about a small bothering affair. Some while ago he asked me to hand to Stillman (who had requested to borrow it) a pamphlet by Castellani,[2] sent to Locker by Phillips the Jeweller[3]—which I did, telling Stillman by letter that the pamphlet was to be returned to Phillips. Now that Stillman is on the Atlantic, Phillips writes to Locker asking for return of the pamphlet, and Locker writes to me to get Stillman to return it. Of course I am powerless in the matter. Informed Locker that Stillman was intending to leave some of his goods at the house of Scott, who might possibly be able to lay his hand on the pamphlet —but I don't think it very likely.

Saturday 10 June   This is the most miserably chilly and lightless June I recollect. I see it stated that there is a huge spot on the sun, and probably that is the reason. Fires every evening, if not during the day also.

Sunday 11 June   Finished the preface to my American Selection.

Monday 12 June   Gabriel tells me that he understands Joaquin Miller has proposed to Mathilde Blind; who is taking counsel with some friends before returning a definite reply.

of St. Anthony at Padua. The figures mentioned here adorn the Fontana Maggiore at Perugia; they are the joint work of Niccolo Pisano and of his son Giovanni Pisano (1240–1329).

[1]   Marco Antonio Canini (1822–92), an Italian political exile who, in 1868, published *Vingt ans d'exil* (Paris) and made many translations from English or French into Italian.

[2]   Augusto Castellani (1829–1914), Italian collector who wrote a small book about gems and precious stones, *Delle gemme*, translated into English by Mrs. John Brogden, *Gems*, London, 1871. Locker had the English version in hand. The Italian original appears neither in the British Museum nor in the Bodleian catalogues.

[3]   In 1871 Joel Phillips's jewellery shop was established at 72 Regent Street. The same family business, now at 139 New Bond Street, still has Castellani's jewellery, but not the Castellani book.

Tuesday 13 June Wrote to Moxon's, saying that my American Selection is now completed, and proposing to charge £40 for this volume, and for each of the other volumes of selections— but open to discussion on their part. Proposed to call on them next Friday, to settle this matter, and about my other outstanding claims; which I have twice written about within rather more than 3 weeks past, but they have never replied. Rather a cool trick.

Wednesday 14 June My Aunt Charlotte[1] writes up saying that she would like to become the purchaser of my house 56 Euston Square, which (in consequence of the death of the landlord towards Christmas last) is shortly to be sold. I called on the agent Greenwood; and, taking as some sort of criterion the small price, £800, lately realized for the next-door house on sale by auction, I offered £1200 on my Aunt's account—Greenwood promises to let me know the result. The sale, I see, is to take place earlier than I had any idea of—Tuesday next.

Thursday 15 June Elizabeth Rovedino,[2] whom I knew all through my childhood, wrote to me yesterday that she is quite in great distress, having a law-suit pending to recover a handsome property left to her in India. Maria took round something from me in response; and Elizabeth called on us later in the afternoon. It seems her father became insane a year or so before his death, and had to be treated in Winslow's Asylum: on one occasion of maniacal violence he was near killing his wife, although when sane on very affectionate terms with her. The two brothers are Augustus, an architect, not successful and wanting in enterprise, married with four children, and Frederick in a ship-broker's

[1] Charlotte Polidori (1803–90) was the second of Mrs. Rossetti's three unmarried sisters. Like the others, she often stayed with the Rossettis, though she occupied for a lengthy period the post of governess, and then companion, in the household of the Dowager Marchioness of Bath. She had more money than the rest of the family and left £5,000 when she died.

[2] Elizabeth Rovedino was the daughter of one of Gabriele Rossetti's Italian friends, a music master who also had settled and married in London and brought up an Anglo-Italian family. The Rossettis had lost sight of her for many years when she applied to them for help which they both generously granted her. The Indian expectations mentioned here very likely formed part of the many tales told by Miss Rovedino to arouse pity in her correspondents. The following year she went so far as to forge a cheque which she drew on D. G. R.'s account at the Union Bank of London with one he had drawn in her favour. For the sake of old days, D. G. R. refused to prosecute. See D. G. R., *Letters*, pp. 1067 and 1071.

office, and of a very inventive turn, but also of restricted means, not married. He lately obtained a patent for a new form of rosined wood to light fires, and hopes to turn it to no small account. The Indian affair seems very wrong, fully contested against Elizabeth by a cousin: £10,000 is the sum that was left her.

Friday 16 June Received a note from Locker this morning, saying that Moxon's place[1] in Dover Street is shut up, and their stock transferred to Ward and Lock. Called at Dover Street in the afternoon, as prearranged on the 13th. There was no one there to respond to my appointment: but an employee of the firm told me that Payne has left the firm—that there has been great pressure consequent upon the new business arrangements—but that the name of Moxon is not to disappear wholly from the publishing trade and A. Moxon[2] would not think of neglecting or slighting my claims. I begged that the employee would ask Moxon to reply to my letter, to some effect or other, without further delay. This was promised: and I am to expect that an answer will be sent on or about Monday next. Things look a little fishy: but I am not inclined to suppose them worse than they show on the surface.

Saturday 17 June After any number of conflicting orders, my Aunt Charlotte decides not to bid for 56 Euston Sq. Her offer of £1200 down could not be accepted, as a trusteeship arrangement requires sale by auction. Dr. Jenner called with a distinguished surgeon, Spencer Wells,[3] wishing the latter to examine Christina. He reports that the case is one of a kind in which danger may result; but at the same time he does not say anything to cause

---

[1] Edward Moxon (1801–58), publisher, left a heavy burden on his widow's and young son's shoulders when he died. The firm went bankrupt in 1871. Ward, Lock and Tyler purchased Moxon's stock and copyrights, offering to pay 15 shillings in the pound and giving Mrs. Emma Moxon a large sum and an annuity of £250. John Bertrand Payne (1833–98), a clerk in Edward Moxon's business, became the manager of the firm in 1864, then a partner. He was responsible for the withdrawal of Swinburne's *Poems and Ballads* under the charge of immorality. In 1868 he invited W. M. R. to undertake a new and revised edition of Shelley's Poems and to start the series of editions of poets known as *Moxon's Popular Poets*. See H. G. Merriam, *Edward Moxon, Publisher of Poets*, New York, 1939, *passim*.

[2] Arthur Moxon, Edward's son, was now the owner of the firm, Payne remaining the manager. When Ward and partners ceased to use the Moxon title in 1877, Arthur set up as a publisher in Paternoster Row in 1878.

[3] Thomas Spencer Wells (1818–97), surgeon to Queen Victoria's household, 1863–96, created baronet in 1883.

present alarm. The two medical men agree that Christina ought not as yet to go anywhere by rail: she should shortly move off to some such neighbouring place as Hampstead, and go about in a Bath chair.

Sunday 18 June   Among other letters, wrote one to M. F. Tupper, who lately addressed me proposing some personal interview prior to my editing his poems in Moxon's series. I explained in courteous terms that the understanding is that I am *not* to edit them, and that moreover the whole affair with Moxon is at present in a very unsettled state.

Monday 19 June   Going on with the compilation of my Selection from *Poets of the Last three Centuries*; although indeed the present aspects of the Moxon affair make it a little dubious to me whether this or the other outstanding volumes will ever be published— which would be disappointing as regards the Selections.

Tuesday 20 June   Locker tells me (and seems to have some fair reason for thinking so) that Moxon's firm has gone to the dogs, and that I am not likely to get any payment, unless some dividend along with other creditors. I feel no extreme interest in the money question (though the sum actually due is not inconsiderable— £126—and more than as much again would be contingently payable): but should be annoyed if, after all my trouble with the three volumes of Selections, and getting together compilations which I consider very satisfactory, the whole affair should be burked. Locker tells me that Mr. S. O. Beeton,[1] at Ward and Lock's house, would be a proper person to obtain some information from: I therefore, in the course of the evening, wrote to Mr. Beeton, explaining my claims, and asking if he would appoint a day for me to call.

[1] Samuel Orchart Beeton (1831–77), publisher; became famous by publishing two 'best-sellers' written by two ladies: one was Mrs. H. Beecher Stowe's *Uncle Tom's Cabin* (1852); the other *Beeton's Book of Household Management*, written by his own wife, *née* Isabella Mayson (1836–64), and first published in 1861. He also founded *The Boy's Own Magazine* in 1855, *Beeton's Christmas Annual* in 1860, and handbooks on every possible domestic activity. Yet, through the failure of the Overend, Gurney & Co. Bank, he barely escaped bankruptcy, and sold his copyrights to Ward, Lock and Tyler in whose firm he became literary adviser; it was in this capacity that W. M. R. dealt with him as Ward and Lock had taken over Moxon's stock and copyrights in 1871. See H. M. Hyde, *Mr. and Mrs. Beeton*, London, 1951.

Wednesday 21 June   Mr. Beeton answers me in very civil terms, and to a purport not so wholly unsatisfactory as might have been apprehended. I propose to call tomorrow or next day.

Thursday 22 June   Called at Mr Beeton's in Amen Corner, but he had not to-day come in to business. Left word that I would probably call on Monday or Tuesday next. A letter received from Roberts Bros., Christina's American publishers, as to the arrangements, for her *Singsong* book: not highly promising arrangements, but must be taken as they come.

Friday 23 June   The great Russian novelist Turgenieff,[1] and others, dined in Cheyne Walk. Turgenieff is an older man than I had supposed—not less apparently than fifty-five or fifty-six, with abundant white hair; uncommonly tall and handsome, and very manly and prepossessing: speaks good English, though occasionally at a loss for the right word, and has a good deal of varied conversation—serious and decisive, without any parade or assumption. He seems to be very fond of animals, and took a good deal of notice of Gabriel's woodchuck (Canadian marmot). He remarked on its being a totally unsophisticated animal, whereas dogs are to some extent artificial through human association. This led him to say that he conceives prophets—Mahomet etc.— to stand in something of the same proportional relation as the domesticated dog: they have 'caught the contagion of God', and are not entirely their genuine selves. He spoke very highly of the Russian poet Lermontoff,[2] killed at an early age in a duel: thinks he had a something even beyond Byron. He thinks *King Lear* the greatest poetic-inventive work in the world (Shelley seems to have thought the same). He himself has no faculty whatever in poetry: had at one time tried to translate some of Shakespeare. Morris (*Jason*, I am not sure whether *The Earthly Paradise* also) has been translated into Russian. Looking at portraits of Swinburne (Gabriel's water-colour and three photographs) he remarked on the very peculiar character of the mouth, and made

[1] Ivan Sergeyevich Turgenev (1818–83). In 1871 he was introduced to the Rossettis by William Ralston. W. M. R. writes 'I never saw a man more impressive than Turguénief in person, and in the tone of his conversation', *Reminiscences*, ii. 339.

[2] Mikhail Yurevich Lermontoff (1814–41), one of the great Russian Romantic poets. The first English translations of his poems appeared in C. T. Wilson's *Russian Lyrics*, 1887, and in J. Pollen's *Rhymes from the Russian*, 1891.

an observation regarding it which startled us all. He says English
literature has had, for the last fifteen years or so, its turn of
predominance in Russia. I asked Hüffer about the rumoured
proposal of J. Miller to Mathilde Blind: as far as I can now gather,
nothing distinct is really known about any such event. Gabriel
is now completing the effect—glazing etc.—of his large picture
of the *Dead Beatrice*, and has made the work much more impressive in these respects.

Saturday 24 June   I find that yesterday Christina went out of doors
for the first time, being wheeled about a little in a Bath chair.
She seemed to have enjoyed it so far; but, as she now has a
cold, it seems doubtful whether the experiment will be repeated
just now.

Sunday 25 June   Replied to Roberts Bros. on Christina's behalf,
closing with their offer of 10% on copies of her book sold, after
Messrs Roberts shall have recouped their own outlay. The prospect of profit to Christina appears remote and meagre.

Monday 26 June   Called on Mr. Beeton, who entered very frankly
into the questions pending as to Moxon's firm: he seems quite
ready to accept without haggling my statement that the price per
volume (excluding Selections) was to be £21, although I have no
written agreement to that effect, but only collateral evidence, into
which he did not even ask me to go. He regards Moxon as having
been led into scrapes by Payne, of whom his opinion is not good.
I professed myself not much disinclined to accept £50 in full of
all demands (properly £126) for books already actually published;
on the understanding that prompt payment would be made for
the three volumes now on the eve of publication, and the 4th
(Cowper) thereafter to be published, and that the 3 volumes of
Selections would be brought out and paid for in due course at some
higher price—whether £40 as I had already proposed or something
else. I agreed to write shortly, stating definitely what I decide.
I see there is a certain difficulty in connexion with one of the three
Selections—that of English Poets of the Last three Centuries;
Beeton himself being compiler of a very extensive work of the
same kind, and no doubt his trade interests being rather against
than in favour of any other such volume as the one I have been

engaged upon. Perhaps however this difficulty may be surmounted: to the other two volumes, and the proposals generally,
he seems well enough inclined.

Tuesday 27 June Maria is now nearing the end of the proofs of
her book, *A Shadow of Dante*.

Wednesday 28 June Went (after an interval, I think, of about 9
months) to the Zoological Gardens. Vieillot's Pheasant a most
splendid bird—something like the Impeyan Pheasant, but with
a slaty-blue predominant, instead of a metallic green. Cormorant
or some such bird makes a sort of laugh, considerably like a horse's
neigh. Jackall with five pups, behaving much like doggies.
Leonine Monkey, and Rufous-bellied Spider Monkey. The old
Ocelot-house seems to be shut up, though a few desolate kites and
such birds still linger there in a lightless state. Lions and Tigers
very fine: one of each seems new to me—a young bright-coloured
lion, and a very large tiger. I notice that the Indian Leopard is of
a deeper orange than the African. Egyptian pussy defunct: but
there is another and smaller specimen, by no means equal to the
old one. Sea-lion went through its performances with its keeper:
very obedient to a whistle, and the word of command.

Thursday 29 June Dreadfully bad news comes to-day from Henrietta Polydore:[1] she doubts whether she will survive to the close
of the summer, and any prospect of her returning seems to be
practically given up. My Aunt Charlotte, after any amount of
vacillation, determines to buy 56 Euston Square if obtainable at
£1100, and it seems almost certain that £1000 will suffice. She
proposes to leave it by will to my Aunt Eliza,[2] then to Mamma,
and thirdly to me. Mrs Wieland's affairs are again requiring

---

[1] Henrietta Polydore, who died of consumption in 1874, was the daughter of
Henry Polydore and a first cousin of the Rossettis. Christina was attached to her
and dedicated verses to her, among them the poem, 'Next of Kin' (February 1853),
The Poetical Works of C. G. R., p. 306. D. G. R. made a pen-and-ink drawing of her
as a young child in 1848, now the property of Mrs. Imogen Dennis; then a pencil
sketch in 1863, in the Victoria and Albert Museum. Surtees, nos. 415, 416, p. 182.

[2] Eliza Harriet Polidori (1810–93) was Mrs. Rossetti's younger sister. After her
mother's death, Eliza went to Scutari as a nurse during the Crimean War.

some attention:[1] there seems a probability of Chancery proclama-
tion on her part, to compel a division of the property so as to
forestall intermeddling by Capt. Taylor.[2] I wrote on the subject
to Wieland, asking Mrs Wieland to sign a paper empowering me
as Trustee to take these steps, if so advised.

Friday 30 June   Continuing the compilation of the Selections of
Humorous and Miscellaneous Poetry: though I feel somewhat
uncertain whether the latter may not have to be withdrawn.

Saturday 1 July   My Aunt Charlotte purchased 56 Euston Square
for £1000. Theodoric[3] writes us saying that (as in the case of
Foscolo)[4] there is a project in Italy for transporting the remains
of my Father for public sepulture in that country:[5] Ricciardi has

---

[1] Mrs. Wieland was the widow of M. Warrington Taylor (1835–70), manager of
the firm Morris, Marshall, Faulkner and Co. As early as 1868 W. Taylor, realizing
that he was very ill, had asked W. M. R. to be one of the executors to his will and
a trustee for his wife on her coming into the reversion of his property. See *R.P.*,
p. 320. Very soon after her husband's death, she married Walter Wieland.

[2] The brother of W. Taylor who had called on W. M. R. on 24 February 1870
to obtain details about his brother's will. See *R.P.*, p. 499.

[3] Theodoric or Teodorico Pietrocola-Rossetti (1826–83) was a nephew of
Gabriele Rossetti. He came from Vasto in the Abruzzi. Having read Lamennais's
Paroles d'un Croyant, he refused to declare it was a bad book and was excommunicated
in 1848. He also advanced liberal theories about the political situation in Italy, was
banished, and settled in London in 1851, where he was received by his uncle
Gabriele Rossetti. He became an Evangelical Protestant in 1854, and was employed
by the S.P.C.K. 'upon an Italian work of great importance—a new edition of
Diodati's Bible'. In the same year, a translation of his *Prophecy of the Nineteenth
Century* was published in London. In 1856 Pietrocola applied for the Professorship
of Italian Language and Literature at the University of Oxford. Having failed to
obtain the post, he went back to Italy in 1857 to preach, and settled in Florence
where he took an active part in an Evangelical reform, resembling the Waldensian
creed. In 1851 he had married Isabella Steele, a Scottish girl whom he had met in
Turin. He never lost sight of his Rossetti cousins. In 1861 he wrote a biography of
Gabriele Rossetti published at Turin. In 1867 he translated into Italian, Christina's
Goblin Market under the title *Il Mercato de' Folletti*. And in 1872 he published in
London a translation of Lewis Carroll's *Alice in Wonderland*. See Carlo Zanini,
Teodorico Pietrocola-Rossetti, Alessandria, 1885.

[4] Ugo Foscolo (1778–1827), Italian writer who, because of his political ideas,
was compelled to take refuge, first in Switzerland, then in England. He was a
Dante scholar and published his *Discorso critico sul testo della Divina Commedia* almost
simultaneously with Gabriele Rossetti's *Commento analitico sulla Divina Commedia* in
1826. Foscolo died the following year at Turnham Green, and was buried at
Chiswick. His remains were taken back to Florence in 1871.

[5] D. G. R. was the only member of the family in favour of returning his father's
remains to Italy and the scheme was abandoned. But in 1926 an important monu-

also sent me a newspaper notifying the same. The feeling of every member of the family as yet available, but most especially of my mother, is wholly against this project, though of course the honour intended is a very considerable one, and gratifying in proportion.

Sunday 2 July   Replied to Theodoric to the above effect. Also wrote for the *Academy* a paragraph (long due) on electrotypes by Cavaliere G. Pellas.[1] Wrote to Mr. Beeton, saying that I would accept an immediate £50 (in full of the £126 due); provided I can depend on the early appearance of and payment for the 3 forthcoming volumes, also the 4th volume of Cowper, and the 3 Selections, to be paid at £40 each Selection. If these conditions not manageable, I would consider about it further. Gave details to show how far my Selection of Last 3 Centuries would compete with Beeton's own book.

Monday 3 July   Called on Nettleship, to see his strange picture of *The Master of the World*.[2] It is a fine invention and a striking performance: but I fear the proportions are a good deal out—especially as regards the narrowness of the shoulders and frame, contrasted with the enormous breadth of the face.

Tuesday 4 July   Mentioned to Gabriel the proposal as to transporting our Father's remains to Italy. I find Gabriel is rather inclined to acquiesce in the scheme: but the very strong objections entertained by our Mother is final in the contrary direction. Gabriel says that Jones,[3] who is now (on account of Z.[4] and other matters) as bitterly hostile to Howell[5] as he used to be

ment to the memory of Gabriele Rossetti was erected in his native city of Vasto. Gabriele is represented standing in front of a stele, each of the four sides bearing the medallions of Gabriele's four children. (From a pamphlet published at Vasto for the first centenary of Gabriele Rossetti's death in November 1954.)

[1] W. M. R.'s unsigned paragraph appeared in the *Academy* for 15 July 1871, p. 350. It mentioned: 'Reproductions made by the electro-galvanic process by the Cavaliere Giuseppe Pellas of Florence from many famous and important works of sculpture.'

[2] Whereabouts unknown.   [3] Edward Burne-Jones.

[4] See p. 37 n. 3.

[5] Burne-Jones wrote to D. G. R.: 'I can't bear the countenance you give Howell after the injuries he has done me and the miseries your disastrous introduction of him has brought about. . . . I feel that I could not endure a man who had hurt you one tenth part [illegible] and it disappoints me that you should either feel so

profusely fond of him, has taken to writing letters to Gabriel urging him to break off with Howell, if merely as an act of friend-liness towards Jones himself. Gabriel, on grounds both of feeling and of prudence, is disinclined to this, and I agree with him so far; yet, as Jones is so urgent, he intends to drop Howell as much as he can, and gradually, if possible lose sight of him altogether. His young kangaroo was found dead some little while ago: there is a suspicion—but apparently founded on no very definite reasons—that the dam had killed it in a quarrel.

Wednesday 5 July Whitley Stokes[1] is now back in England from India for a short while: he dined to-day with two or three other old acquaintances in Cheyne Walk. He lives part of the year at Calcutta, and part at Simla. Considers the Hindoos (not including the Sikhs, etc.) to be essentially inferior to the European races, on the ground of deficient physical courage: the English rule is just, and even indulgent. Allowing for a long beard, Stokes is but little changed in appearance since he left in 1862; and his character, in its refinement, simplicity, and intellectual sympathies, seems the same as ever. He expects to remain another five years or so in India, and then resettle in this country, devoting himself chiefly to philology.

Thursday 6 July Today at last Christina was sufficiently con-valescent to be moved off to Hampstead—17 Christ Church Road: the Dr. wishes her to go on to the seaside pretty soon. Brown tells me that the Stillmans have written from America, where they have arrived after a very blustering passage. Morris, with Faulkner, Magnússon, and others, goes off to-day to Iceland, on a trip that has been projected some while back. Brown and his family are about to take a holiday at Dartmouth. Much talk (Brown,

differently about our friendship or that you should look on his baseness as a matter of so little consequence.' One of the grudges that Burne-Jones bore against Howell was that the latter spread scandal about him regarding the episode with Mrs. Zambaco—cf. p. 37 n. 3. Yet this was not the only grievance. See H. Rossetti Angeli, *Dante Gabriel Rossetti: his Friends and Enemies*, London, 1949, pp. 164–7, and *Pre-Raphaelite Twilight*, pp. 165–6.

[1] Whitley Stokes (1830–1909), Irish lawyer, referred to by W. M. R. as 'the pre-eminent Celtic scholar' and by D. G. R. as 'a very good judge and conversant with publishers'. The Rossettis became acquainted with him through C. B. Cayley; Stokes greatly admired some of Christina's poems. He was also a close friend of William Allingham. See *Reminiscences*, p. 175, and *Family Letters*, p. 164.

Hüffer, and Gabriel) about P. B. Marston,[1] and other good but not first-rate poetry. Brown advocates the *raison d'être* of work of this class, as responding to the tastes of some fair proportion of the enormous total number of readers: he denounces the modern straining after 'originality' as the bane of poetic and other art.

Friday 7 July to Sunday 16 Diary interrupted on account of a press of work at Somerset House.

Monday 17 July Got a Continental Bradshaw and one or two other items, in preparation for going abroad, which I hope to do towards Sunday next. I propose going to Ravenna, if by myself: if Scott accompanies me (of which there had been some idea), it will be to Rome instead, most likely. But I don't expect him. Gabriel now at the country-house he and Morris rent—Kelmscott Manor-house near Lechlade.

Tuesday 18 July Continuing the reading of Griswold's *American Poetesses*[2] with a view to adding what may be found needful to my American Selection. This volume, and that of poor Menken's[3] poems, have been turning up since I thought the Selection in question was completed.

Wednesday 19 July Maria received the proofs of the lithographic plans to her book on Dante: the last matter outstanding with

[1] Philip Bourke Marston (1850–87), the blind poet, was Oliver Madox Brown's most intimate friend. He was an enthusiastic admirer of Dante Gabriel Rossetti: 'What a supreme man is Rossetti! Why is he not some great exiled king, that we might give our lives in trying to restore him to his kingdom!' See J. C. Troxell, *Three Rossettis*, p. 32. In 1878, D. G. R. wrote for him a sonnet entitled: 'To P. B. Marston, inciting me to Poetic Work', *Works*, p. 228.

[2] The correct title of the book mentioned by W. M. R. is *The Female Poets of America*, Philadelphia, 1849. Rufus Wilmot Griswold was the literary executor of E. A. Poe whom he shamelessly defamed in an Introduction to the posthumous edition of Poe's works. Baudelaire in his notice on Edgar Allan Poe describes Griswold as a 'pédagogue-vampire' and his introduction as 'un énorme article plat et haineux'. See Baudelaire, *Œuvres complètes*, ed. M. A. Ruff, Paris, 1968, p. 337 and ff.

[3] Adah Isaacs Menken (1835–68), an American dancer, actress, and poetess. She was married five times; her liaisons with Alexandre Dumas and later with Swinburne were notorious in Paris and in London. She was a triumphant success as 'Mazeppa' all over Europe and the United States. Her book of poems, *Infelicia*, was published in 1868 by Hotten. See G. Lafourcade, *Swinburne*, London, 1932, pp. 188–9, and B. Falk, *The Naked Lady*, London, 1934.

regard to the work. The actual publication will be deferred till October.

Thursday 30 July   Mamma and Christina returned to-day from Hampstead. Christina has certainly made some degree of progress, though still far from set-up in health. Sent Mathilde Blind (now at Lynmouth), at her request, my copy of Medwin's *Life of Shelley*[1] (which appears to be by no means an easy book to get); also the tabular statement of Shelley's life which I drew up to guide me when I was writing the Memoir. I hope—and indeed think— they will come back to me safe.

Friday 21 July   Packed up, in preparation for leaving for the continent tomorrow.

Saturday 22 July   This has been mostly a showery day, and with-out the heat which has more or less characterized the last eight or ten days. Evening however fine and rainless. Dilberoglue[2] called on me unexpectedly as I was about to clear up and dine prior to starting. He has been back from Alexandria about a fortnight, and has relinquished business, and seems bent on a life of leisure and friendly intercourse. Speaks much of the beauties of Athens and of Cairo. I started from Charing Cross Station at 8.45 p.m. for Dover and Calais. Some considerable sensation of discomfort during the passage (principally I fancy from the vibration of the screw) as I lay down at the further end of the cabin all the time of the passage: I rather expected retching to result, but it did not. This boat is vastly better than the Ostend boats I was in last year. Went on from Calais without any prolonged delay to Lille.

Sunday 23 July   Reached Lille about 4 a.m. and put up at the Hotel de l'Europe. A tolerable suggestion of the coming day is per-ceptible now as early as 2.45. The peaceful-looking country (I noticed no symptom whatever of ruin or devastation) under the calmly growing dim light looked fair and strange after what one

---

[1] Thomas Medwin (1788–1869), a cousin of Shelley. He wrote a memoir of Shelley issued in *Shelley Papers*, London, 1833, then a *Life of Shelley*, London, 1847.

[2] Stavros Dilberoglue, a Greek merchant of Turkish origin, became a naturalized English subject. He was persuaded by Stillman to try and collect funds from the Greeks in London to carry on operations in Crete in 1868. The plan failed. W. M. R. came to know him through the Spartalis. See *Reminiscences*, p. 342.

knows of France during the last year's term. Lille is an agreeable town, only in a moderate degree old-fashioned. I noticed two very curious names of streets—Rue des Os Rongés (close to the principal church, which is a Gothic building of some importance, and referring therefore, I suppose, to relics or a mortuary chapel) —and Rue des Chats Bossus,[1] close to my Hotel. At breakfast got at haphazard on the Carte 'saucisse d'oeufs', which proves to be very good—small sausages along with fried eggs, done much as my father used to have them. I hear nothing as yet of 'citoyen' and 'citoyenne'. The people look to me somewhat saddened and subdued, but perhaps it is merely an impression: certainly one sees many people in whole or partial mourning. I saw two Prussian helmets exhibited in a gunmaker's window. In the 'Tribunal de Commerce' is an effective bronze and partly gilt statue of Napoleon I, that was erected in 1854 under the auspices of Napoleon III: the statue remains untouched, but the slab inscriptions setting forth the facts in the ordinary tone of official implied adulation have been taken out of the wall—preparatory I suppose to being wholly removed. I noticed a little crib called 'Friture Républicaine'. In the 'Grande Place' is a columnar monument erected in 1842 in honour of the Lille Republicans of 1792, who are recorded, by decree of that time, to have 'bien mérité de la patrie'. Left Lille for Brussels about 3 p.m. Some heavyish showers, and a rainbow soon before reaching Brussels. Put up at Hotel d'Europe, and got a funny little room on the entresol— very low, and with a single window which touches the floor, and only extends some 3 1/2 feet therefrom. It looks sheer down on the pavement of the side-street, and no one living in this room could ever see the sky save in a recumbent position. After a light dinner went out, and found a gorgeous sunset: a few minutes however gave it its quietus. Seeing that there was a concert to-night in the Jardin Zoologique and the aquarium lit with gas, I went thither. The beautiful rock aquarium was very delightful— conger eels about the most deliciously graceful object in nature in their motions—a crocodile (or I believe American alligator) some 6 foot long from tip to tip. I touched him up with my umbrella, which roused him to some display of energy—he opened his pale pink mouth wide, and gave vent to a double outbreathing, approaching a snort or hiss. Of the instrumental

---

[1] The Rue des Chats Bossus still exists; the Rue des Os Rongés has disappeared.

concert I heard little. It was followed by some fine choral singing
by male voices. The beasts were mainly shrouded in darkness and
reclusion, but now and again one heard an owl, night-jar, or the
like, interjecting his quaint noise in the pauses of the music.

Monday 24 July   Left Brussels about 11 a.m.—too early to do
anything prior to leaving, beyond walking into the church opposite the hotel (I have not been in it, I think, since 1863): it is
a colourless building of no interest in detail. Came on to Aix-la-
Chapelle. A great deal of brisk rain, and indeed on the whole
a rainy day, though sunshine was not lacking at intervals. Went
to Hotel du Grand Monarque (I hardly think it is the same hotel
that I was in in 1854, but cannot say for certain): it is a good one,
and I am in the rare case of being on the ground floor. After
dinner went to the theatre, where *Lucrezia Borgia*[1] was the
opera: I think I must have seen this oftener than any other opera.
Marianne Brandt as Lucrezia: the whole performance appeared
to me respectable, though none of the personages was remarkable
in acting and singing combined. The fascination of this opera
(chiefly owing I think to the construction of the drama by Hugo)
seems inexhaustible, and mere questions of execution become
secondary. In the streets of Aix there seems little of antiquity or
of interest: however I require to look at them further—not
recollecting details very clearly since 1854. Evening rather cool
than otherwise: certainly no suggestion of a feeling of heat.

Tuesday 25 July   Another decidedly rainy and cool day, but fine
in the evening. Went into the Cathedral, the nave of which is in
course of restoration. The pulpit here is perhaps the most beautiful I know anywhere—a superb piece of Byzantine work, gilded
metal (or gold?) encrusted with jewels and ivory carvings. The
gardien says it is a work of the 11th century, presented by the
Emperor Henry II. The marble chair (visible in the gallery)
wherein for three centuries or so sat the corpse of Charlemagne.
His bones are now in some vault or crypt: I was ready to pay the
thaler needed for seeing them, but it proved that some priest
needed for such an operation was not at the moment available.

[1] An opera composed by Donizetti in 1833 with a libretto by Felice Romani. It
was inspired by a prose drama of Victor Hugo's performed in Paris a few months
before.

The mass was being performed at this church without any music or almost any visible sound: the congregation kneeling and following the service with motion of lips but no articulation, and a great air of simple recueillement. Came on by the rail to Bingen. One goes close by the Rhine, and I saw substantially the same view (on the opposite bank) that I saw last year, but certainly the loss of picturesque beauty caused by the rapidity and limited view from the rail is great: the gain in time however is important, if an object at all—as I did in three hours or so what took up last year the central portion of two days. At Bingen I found the Hotel Victoria full, and was referred to the Hotel du Cheval Blanc, which seems quite good enough. Took a little walk near the Rhine after a late dinner: the moon bright and waxing, more than half full.

Wednesday 26 July Walked up to the Rochusberg and Chapel, a little way behind the town, and in the onward direction. This is a celebrated view, and certainly a very beautiful one. Not advantageously seen by me however as there was not a gleam of sun all the morning: about noon a shower, and then, as I was walking back, a gleam or two. Chilliness sufficient to make me put on my underwaistcoat when I returned to the Hotel for the one o'clock dinner. My walk included also the Scharlachkopf, a height where wine is grown that I drank yesterday—about the choicest, I am told, in this vicinity. Left Bingen after dinner, and came on to Heidelberg. There was considerable delay en route through changing trains, etc.: two and a half hours at Mainz, and one at Darmstadt. At Mainz, I walked about the streets, and looked into the Barnabite[1] church, which I had not seen on my first visit. It is a fine, simple, solemn gothic interior, restored in the most severe and 'chaste' style: no doubt any quantity of extraneous accumulation has been cleared away, and now there is next to nothing to look at individually. Reached Heidelberg about 10.30 p.m. in heavy rain: put up at Hotel du Prince Charles.

Thursday 27 July The morning opens rainier than ever, and kept me in till about 1 o'clock: for, as I don't know the town, and there

[1] The Barnabites were a small religious order founded in 1530, whose name is derived from the church of St. Barnabas in Milan.

is little or nothing to be seen under shelter (so far as I am aware) an exploratory walk under a rain of cats and dogs presented no extreme attraction. At last the wet was diminishing, and I sallied out, and soon it became exceedingly fine. Went up to the castle. The grounds are in a high degree beautiful, and the castle ruins picturesque and enjoyable. Spent all the afternoon here, and then after dinner crossed the bridge, and took a walk on the opposite side of the Neckar. Went up the Heiligenberg some distance, but I suppose I did not get to the top, as I did not emerge to any summit whence a general view would be obtainable. However the walk on the hillside, covered with chestnut and other trees, and shot through with sunshine, was highly delightful. Heidelberg presents all sorts of attractions in this sort of way. Did not return to the Hotel till twilight was closing.

Friday 28 July   I am informed to-day that a house I passed yesterday in my evening walk was inhabited for some days by Luther prior to his being taken to the Wartburg.[1] It is at the entrance of the village of Handschusheim (the village following Neuenheim): is now in a very tumbledown condition, and left uninhabited for some while past. Went up to the Königsstuhl and the tower recently erected there—the highest point connected with the castle: a wide and beautiful prospect hence. Also to the Wolfsbrunnen (not far from the Neckar) the legend of which is that a princess when on tryst here with her lover, and waiting for his arrival, was killed by a wolf. There is a stream of fresh water, and tanks here where trout are bred and kept. The rushes they made to grab small fish thrown to them to eat were amusing. The Felsenmeer (so called) is between this point and the Königsstuhl, and is a remarkable agglomeration of loose boulders, lying heaped as they happen to come. I thought last evening I heard cicadas two or three times. I am now informed this is correct: I don't fancy I ever before heard them so far north: also a little Indian corn I observed growing. After dinner walked through the streets (it is pretty nearly all one street) of Heidelberg: the only house of picturesque interest I see worth noting is the one

[1] A castle in Thuringia, built in 1070. Luther took refuge there in 1521 after being excommunicated by the Pope, and remained in the castle for nine months while he translated the Bible into German.

named Zum Ritter, a hotel presumably, which is uncommonly decorated in 16th century style. The town has been wrecked by the French more than once,[1] and is thus of little architectural interest. Met in my stroll a German Yankee—born in this neighbourhood, and brought up a coachbuilder, but settled in America in 1847, and carries on a timber business at Pittsburg. He has come over on a holiday trip but finds himself solitary, and would rather be back at his business. Finds Germans and other Europeans stiff after his being habituated to American manners. Grant[2] will probably not be re-elected President, as the German votes will go against him: he disgusted the Germans by allowing the supply of arms etc. to the French during the war.

Saturday 29 July Went up into the castle grounds, and seated myself in the garden or shrubbery: there is a splendid beetle lording it here—about an inch long, green, with bright brown legs, etc. The day was most beautiful—sunny in the highest degree, and with heat to correspond but not oppressive. About 1 p.m. left Heidelberg for Augsburg: the country very agreeable generally, and from about Stuttgart to Ulm delightful. Got into conversation with a French traveller (on business) familiar both with England and Germany: he expects a new war at no very distant date and doubts the stability of the Republic: he himself is rather of a monarchical turn. He and I both put up at the Drei Mohren, an ancient inn traceable back, it seems, as far at any rate as 1364. He was in Paris during the German siege—in Brussels during the Communal siege.[3] He suffered some hardships, and ate donkey and dog, not to speak of horse—donkey is good, dog bad—of cats and rats he had no personal experience.

Sunday 30 July Augsburg is a fine old town, with some spacious as well as picturesque streets. My hotel has no very particular air of antiquity in its internal arrangements. Went to the Rathhaus,[4]

---

[1] The castle was greatly damaged by Tilly in 1622, by Turenne in 1673, and by de Lorges in 1693.

[2] General Ulysses Simpson Grant (1822–85), first elected President of the United States of America in 1868 and re-elected in 1872.

[3] After the German siege had come to an end in March 1871, a revolutionary Commune was set up in the city which was besieged for the second time by regular French troops under the command of Marshal MacMahon.

[4] The normal spelling of the word is now 'Rathaus' (town-hall).

where some decorations connected with the late war-festivities are still up, and a banquet was preparing. Here to my surprise I find three of the most splendid Tintorets to be seen anywhere out of Venice—two pictures of a siege, and a still larger one of the abdication of Charles V in favour of Philip. The two former are especially admirable and notable, and about the finest works of the sort known to me. Then to the Cathedral, which has the very ancient bronze door of which the Crystal Palace contains a copy: there are several old German paintings in uncommonly fine preservation, and good specimens of that class of work, without being exceptionally noticeable. The Fuggerei,[1] close to my hotel, is covered with recent frescoes. After dinner my French acquaintance proposed a visit to the theatre (there are at least two here), and somewhat to my surprise selected the one at which they were acting *Der Jäger bei Sedan*,[2] with a Schlacht tableau etc.[3] We went, and saw a very stupid piece of the domestic virtuous sort mainly, though the prologue Act shows the German army in France. Other strolling, etc. finish up the day, which is once again of the dull sort, particularly rainy, and cool rather than otherwise.

Monday 31 July   Got up about 5.20 a.m. and left Augsburg at 7.35. Dull when I left, and soon it became a day of persistent and soaking rain, lasting up to 3 p.m. or thereabouts. The rain then (with some slight intervals) ceased, and the day was calm, but with next to no sunshine. The Tyrol is evidently equally lovely and sublime: but the rain and mist were such as almost wholly to withdraw from sight anything beyond the nearest hills. I saw however two rather further hills of no great seeming elevation, coated with snow. Reached Innsbruck in the afternoon, and put up at the Hotel d'Autriche, which seems extremely good—clean in a remarkable degree, and otherwise pleasant. Innsbruck is truly a most splendid place: you look down a picturesque street, and see it massed with clouds above, and close over them a noble snow-sprinkled mountain-peak. Indeed I think the near association of mountain scenery and the town is closer, more constant, and grander here than anywhere else I have seen. The hills are

[1] The Fuggers of Augsburg were the greatest bankers of Europe during the first half of the sixteenth century.

[2] A play by an unknown author celebrating the military virtues of a German rifleman at the Battle of Sedan (1870).

[3] A tableau or dramatic scene representing a battle.

of some considerable elevation, but nothing extraordinary: nothing I believe beyond 8,000 feet or so at the utmost. Innsbruck itself stands at no inconsiderable height, and (to judge from to-day) is a very cool place. Went to the church containing the tomb of Maximilian which is truly a noble monument,[1] unequalled in Europe I suppose. The bronze statues are of somewhat unequal merit: the Arthur,[2] and still more especially the Theodoric,[3] are magnificent. Besides these bronze statues of which everyone has seen or heard something, I find a most astonishing series of marble alto reliefs on the tomb itself, setting forth the life of Maximilian. They are done by Colin of Mechlin,[4] and are by far the most perfect works of the kind in existence, so far as I know, with a great deal of grace and beauty, and superbly delicate and intricate in work. I should like to get a complete series of photographs of them, but am told only one (which I obtained) has been photographed: I see however one more in a shop, and shall see about the matter ere I leave. In an upper part of the church is a very curious monument of one of the magnates of this government—his effigy clad in his own real armour (say about 1530) kneeling. The figure looks more like 7 than 6 feet in height but I suppose this is deceptive. Two fine female tomb-effigies in marble, and a small series of bronze figures of the same class (but not the same figures) as those of the Maximilian tomb. Went on to the public Hofgarten hard-by—small but very lovely in its close connexion with the glorious mountains. After dinner (6 1/2) strolled out again, and ascended the clock-tower: the bell is a tocsin, only rung in case of fire. Splendid views all round: a nice quaint old man explained about the prospect, and seemed really obliged for my small fee of 20 Kr.,[5] and insisted on lighting me down with a lantern: it was indeed almost dark now, but I suppose the mere going down stairs could be performed with

[1] Maximilian I (1459–1519), Emperor of the Holy Roman Empire. The tomb here mentioned was erected by Maximilian for himself and his wife in the Hofkirche at Innsbruck. It was completed in 1584; but his remains lie in the church of St. George, at Vienna-Neudstadt.

[2] King Arthur, the central hero of the Arthurian legend. He is represented here as the Knight of Knights in medieval armour.

[3] Theodoric, King of the Ostrogoths (454–526), also represented as a knight.

[4] Alexandre Colin (1526–1612), Flemish sculptor, born at Malines, who went to Innsbruck in 1563 to work on Maximilian's tomb.

[5] Twenty kreuzer. One kreuzer was the hundredth part of the florin, the Austrian monetary unit in 1871. The florin was worth about two shillings.

little difficulty even in the dark. Went on to the bridge over the Inn stream, which was flowing with magnificent rush and energy: it is now a river of some magnitude, but I suppose more than commonly swollen by long rains. Back to Hotel about 9 3/4: the streets seem to be unlighted, but the light in the sky—although the moon was not visibly shining—was fully enough for all practical purposes. I shall certainly stay at least another day in Innsbruck though I had not contemplated doing so.

Tuesday 1 August Immediately after breakfast went up to the Berg Isel, which appears (from the statement of the *portier*) to be about the most accessible place for a walk and view. Walked along from this point up and on with extreme delight, getting the most splendid views all round, and straying in and out of glorious pine woods and the most lovely plots of grass and flowers. The stroll took up my whole time from about 9.30 to 5.30 and was I think the most enjoyable thing of the kind I ever experienced. Of course I did not reach any elevation worth speaking of, but simply strolled and basked. This has been quite a sunny fine day, wholly unlike yesterday. Many lovely butter-flies, grasshoppers, etc.—a large dull-orange butterfly, all spotted and streaked with black, is one of the most numerous hereabouts. Watched with amusement for half an hour or so the movements of two blue-black beetles, I suppose of the processionary class, though there were only two of them. One was invariably the leader, and the other the follower: they never interchanged these rôles. Sometimes the leader would tumble over a rut or other impediment, and sprawl on his back, and then the follower would be in strictness foremost: but he never availed himself of this advantage, but set himself punctually behind his fellow and went on following every movement with unfailing exactitude. At one moment I picked up the leader, and withheld him for two or three minutes. The other stopped, made some tentative false starts, stopped again, etc. On returning into the town, bought some photographs, including three (which I find to exist) of the marble reliefs in the Maximilian monument. One of these is the same composition that I got yesterday, but that, I now find, was only taken from a copy carving made in wood. I learn that the Passion-play in the Oberammergau is still being acted every Sunday for some ten or twelve weeks to come. Munich and

Innsbruck are two of the most available starting-places for going there, but the place is not accessible at all by rail, and a carriage would take a day or more getting there. If I had in time known that the performance is still going on, I would have gladly made a point of seeing it: but as it stands, the day of the week etc. are too contrary, and I shall not alter my route for Verona. Shall however stay here at Innsbruck all to-morrow and start on Thursday morning: the journey takes thirteen hours or little less. Strolled out again after dinner: going across the bridge, and then left-wards. Unfortunately sunset is always over before the dinner finishes, so that such a stroll is soon intercepted by twilight. Opposite this hotel, in mid street, is a column monument to Virgin Mary and S. Anna, commemorative of the expulsion of a Franco-Bavarian army in 1703: the first victory occurred on Mary's nativity,[1] and the second on Anna's festival day.[2] Lamps on this monument (which has some talented bas-reliefs of infant cherubs inter alia) are lighted at twilight. On going out I found a half dozen of women kneeling on the stone steps of the monu-ment in devotion—one of them repeating the 'Kyrie Eleison' etc.: all done very simply and devoutly. In a churchyard which I entered in the afternoon I saw (what I think I never saw before) little receptacles for holy water in front of many of the monu-ments, and a little brush attached thereto by a chain, to sprinkle the graves—which act I saw performed in two instances, by a woman and a small child. On numerous inscriptions it is par-ticularly specified that the deceased received the last sacraments before death.

Wednesday 2 August   Looked in again at the Maximilian tomb, and made the full tour (not a lengthy one) of the Hofgarten—then went to the Museum—pictures, designs, birds, etc. There is a certain proportion of good pictures: *S. Jerome*, with no name for reference but must be by Cranach,[3] a small *Fall of Man*,[4] I think by the same; very good small Douw,[5] *Ein Pfeifer*, small head by Rembrandt: Stichel,[6] a living or recent painter, *Moses striking the*

[1]   8 September.   [2]   26 July.
[3]   The *S. Jerome* is by Lucas Cranach (1472–1553), the famous German painter, friend of Luther.
[4]   The *Fall of Man* by Jan Van Scorel (1495–1562), Dutch painter.
[5]   Gerard Dou or Douw (1613–75), Dutch painter, of the school of Rembrandt.
[6]   'Stichel' is not the correct name. The picture mentioned here is famous and

Rock, composed with much talent, but style of painting hard and bald.[1] There is a Bubo Maximus (the same sort of owl, I think, that is called Grand Duc) of extraordinary size.—At my photograph shop there are some paintings and drawings on cobwebs: it seems that a family of peasants, from father to son, has the knack of producing these. They are not bad of their kind—especially a pen-and-ink drawing copied to look like an engraving. —Took a carriage and went to the Schönberg (the same route as yesterday at the beginning much splendid scenery, and from the Schönberg a good view of two not very remote glaciers. Dined at the inn there: its outside is painted with five or six huge figures of Saints and as many religious subjects of one kind or other: indeed crucifixes on the roads and hills, and other religious emblems in all sorts of places, abound out here. After returning to my hotel walked out again over the bridge and some little way up the hills beyond, getting seemingly within no very great distance of the snow patches on the loftier ranges: goats and cattle returning to the valleys. Finished the evening by returning a little to the Hofgarten, where some music was being performed.

Thursday 3 August   Was travelling all day from Innsbruck to Verona. Whether it arises from the mode of travelling by rail, or from whatever other cause, the crossing of the Brenner Pass seems a trifle in comparison with S. Gothard, the Simplon, etc.; there is neither the same awful grandeur of scale and view, nor the same apparent exertion in reaching the summit. One scarcely indeed knows where this is past, though the fact soon becomes manifest by the greatly enhanced rate of speed. The scenery however, with whatever drawbacks, is still very fine, and the Italian Tyrol, about Trento and Rovereto, is of luscious and enchanting prodigality of beauty. The heat also becomes great, and I found I had committed a great mistake in putting on my under-waist-coat as a protection against possible cold (none actual) in crossing the mountain-top. On getting out at the frontier station of Ala[2]

was painted by Franz Strecher (1814–53), an Austrian painter who spent some time in America, where he decorated the Jesuits' Church in Philadelphia and St. Canisius's Church in Buffalo. See Martha Reinhardt, *Franz Strecher*, Vienna, 1957.

[1] These five paintings are now in the Tiroler Landesmuseum Ferdinandeum at Innsbruck.

[2] Ala was then on the old frontier between Austria and Italy; by the treaty of

to have my baggage examined for the Customs, I find my baggage is not in the train, though I did everything required for it at Innsbruck: it is guessed to have remained behind there. A vile nuisance: and as I write (about noon) I remain still without any news of it. What effect this will have on my proposed trip remains as yet uncertain to me. Telegraphed about the matter from Ala (no time for receiving a reply), and did what I could in Verona by speaking to the omnibus conductor at the Railway station. Reached past 9 and put up at my old quarters, Due Torri.[1]

Friday 4 August Went into S. Anastasia[2] and the Duomo. Then into a little Orto Botanico, which I think I never entered heretofore. The Veronese notion appears to be that, if botany will take care of itself, there is no objection to it: but that any sort of pains bestowed upon it, beyond hanging a label on a bush here and there, would be excessive. Took a cab, and went about the principal streets, stopping only at the churches of S. Zeno[3] and S. Fermo.[4] At the former I see the crypt has been fully opened out[5] (which I fancy was still only in progress when I was last in Verona), with a marked improvement in the aspect of the church. Looked also at the fine old cloister, which perhaps I had not seen before. After dinner walked out over the Ponte Garibaldi, and watched a lovely calm sunset, and the motions of many bats, succeeding in seeing the actual look of these more clearly than I ever did before. Sometimes they almost skim the ground or water, but not any of them seems ever to rest definitely. The luggage not appearing all the afternoon, I thought it best to dispatch a commissionnaire to Ala, and on returning past 9 from the Piazza dell'Erbe and Caffè Dante had the satisfaction of receiving the blessed effects: they had been most improperly taken out at Trento instead of coming on to Verona. I happened to mention to the

St. Germain (1919), the Trentino and the Alto Adige as far as the Brenner Pass were ceded to Italy, so Ala is now some 100 miles south of the Austrian frontier.

[1] Still a famous hotel in Verona.

[2] The church in which the fresco by Pisanello (1377–1458) of St. George setting off to free the Princess of Trebizond from the Dragon could be seen when W. M. R. visited it. It has since been removed to the Palazzo Bevilacqua.

[3] S. Zeno Maggiore is one of the finest Romanesque churches in Italy.

[4] S. Fermo Maggiore consists of two churches superimposed, eleventh century below, and thirteenth century above.

[5] The crypt, built in the tenth century, was restored in the thirteenth and sixteenth centuries and again in 1938.

Commissionnaire the robbery of my money in 1868, suggesting that it must possibly have been done at the Verona station, and he says this is extremely probable, as it was found that some of the railway men here possessed false keys. My watch unfortunately begins to-day its old bad habit of stopping suddenly at intervals: this may prove a trouble henceforth.

Saturday 5 August   Gave my watch to be mended, and am told the chain had broken: I trust the thing may now be set right. Strolled about the Piazza dell'Erbe, Porta dei Borsari, and Arena, which I once more inspected under the guidance of an inevitable cicerone who utilized me by asking how to turn certain Italian words into English—such as stretto, perchè, lavoro, etc. Looked through the Church of S. Eufemia, which I do not remember entering before. There is a well-executed able picture by Brusa-sorci[1]—*Virgin in glory with Sts Roch, Sebastian,* etc. I see the street leading straight down from the statue of Dante is now named Via Dante Allighieri—name written up with record of municipal vote for this name in 1865. Most of the street inscriptions seem to be newly written—well and clearly like those in Venice: I suppose this is a sign of the national energy revived since the departure of the Austrians.[2] Left Verona at 2 p.m. and came on to Padua. I have linen to get washed, that I could not conveniently do without; I find that this will keep me in Padua up to Monday evening, as, to-morrow being Sunday, they will not undertake to give it me earlier. I would rather not be delayed so long; but perhaps there is no great harm done, as at the worst I can on one of the days take a return ticket for Venice. I find in this region, Verona and Padua, that contrary to what seems the general experience in Europe, there has now been a long period—6 weeks or so—of drought and extreme heat. Yesterday was hot by dint of much sunshine, but with a good deal of air: to-day at last the drought seems to be closing: for there has been no sun, but a souring loaded sky, and in the afternoon rain comes on pretty freely. There don't seem to be many travellers hereabouts: in Verona only five or six were at the table d'hôte and here only two, myself included. Took a rainy but agreeable walk after

---

[1] Domenico del Riccio, alias Brusasorci (1516–67), a Veronese painter. The picture can still be seen in the church.

[2] The Austrians left Verona for good in 1866.

dinner straight out leftwards from my hotel, and got out of Padua through the Borgo Saracinesca. I had been told that the mosquito demon did not haunt this place, but find it incorrect. Hums and flittings afflicted my night (the actual bite, fortunately for me, I appear never to feel): at last I had to light the candle, I saw some eight or ten of the monsters, of which I succeeded in killing three or four. I slept sounder after this: perhaps the advancing dawn tended to close their reign of terror. These mosquitoes, I see, have not got those combed or brushlike antennas which I had always hitherto supposed to be the mark of the beast.

Sunday 6 August A lovely sunny day again after the rain: heat more than sufficient, but nothing really exceptional. I again, as in 1862 with Scott, feel a strong liking for Padua: it has such an old, uncared-for, and yet undecrepit look, and its picturesqueness, while indisputable, depends (save now and then in the conspicuous instances) on such simple undemonstrative elements and combinations. Went to the Arena Chapel: there is much scaffolding inside the church, and the custode says the object is to clean the pictures: he strictly denies that they will be retouched, but I fear their future is threatening.[1] There is one spot at any rate where the ornamental work has been conspicuously retouched, and I am not quite clear but that repaintings are discernible on the noble *Pietà*, but the painting is higher up than would allow me to speak with decision. To the Eremitani,[2] where I looked at the Mantegnas the better part of an hour: only some of them have as yet been photographed. To the Carmine.[3] To the Duomo and its baptistery: the frescoes in the latter, by Giovanni and Antonio di Padova,[4] are among the finest extant works of the school of Giotto, and uncommonly well preserved: the

[1] The Arena Chapel, also called 'la Cappella dei Scrovegni', contains the famous fourteenth-century Giotto frescoes. The chapel appears to be constantly under repair. The frescoes are on the whole in very good condition and the attendant, pressed with questions, answers exactly in the same way as the one questioned by W. M. R. and denies all repainting.

[2] The church (thirteenth century) was almost completely destroyed by an American bombardment in 1944, and rebuilt with its own materials. But the Mantegna frescoes, with the exception of three or four, and these in a very poor condition, have been ruined.

[3] A Romanesque church of the thirteenth century.

[4] The frescoes of the 'battistero' are now generally described as the masterpiece of Giusto de' Menabuoi, painted between 1376 and 1378.

Paradise, with endless saints seated in rows, painted on the vaulting, is truly beautiful and impressive. To the Palazzo della Ragione,[1] where I stayed a longish while. To S. Antonio,[2] another long stay. Then dined at Pedrocchi's,[3] and afterwards walked out to the Prato della Valle, and looked with some degree of care at the numerous statues forming the inner line, and a few of those on the outer.[4] I had an impression that they were simple rubbish, but find this is not the fact: several are quite up to a fair average in force of conception and of work. A new public building[5] hard-by has under its arcade a statue of Dante and another of Giotto, both erected in 1865. Done by Vela,[6] and telling figures in their skilful way. Got a look at 'Antenor's Tomb'[7] on my way homewards. A street fruit-seller had encumbered its base with some of his litter, to which there may be small or no objection: a photographer's advertisement ought not however to be allowed to be pasted on the tomb.

Monday 7 August   Went to the Church of S. Giustina, where, between the late church and the ancient one, there is a good deal to be seen. The Veronese is a very beautiful one,[8] especially the central portion with flying cherubs; but it is at such an elevation that one can hardly estimate its excellences of detail. To the interesting little Botanic Garden, the oldest in Europe: some splendid magnolias, and a superb 'araucaria excelsa' (the custode says the finest in any collection) the growth of which with fanlike fronds growing at all angles, is very beautiful. To the Church of

[1] The Law-courts of Padua during the Middle Ages. It is a huge building begun in the twelfth century and enlarged in 1306.

[2] The famous Byzantine basilica dedicated to S. Antonio of Padua.

[3] This well-known café, established in 1831, was the favourite meeting-place of students, intellectuals, artists, and patriots during the troubled years of the Risorgimento. Stendhal celebrated its famous 'zabaione' in the *Chartreuse de Parme*. It is still a popular café.

[4] There are seventy-eight statues, representing professors and students of the University of Padua. They were erected towards the end of the eighteenth century.

[5] The Loggia Amulea, built in 1861 in a neo-Gothic style.

[6] Vincenzo Vela (1822–91), an Italian sculptor born in Switzerland, and famous in his day.

[7] Antenor of Troy, according to the legend, was supposed to have landed in the north of Italy and founded Patavium (Padua). In the centre of the town, one can see the funeral monument built in 1283 which is called 'Antenor's Tomb'.

[8] This fresco represents the martyrdom of S. Giustina and was painted by Paolo Veronese in 1575.

S. Giorgio, with valuable but damaged frescoes by Avanzo[1] doomed to restoration. To the Scuola di S. Antonio, with the Titian frescoes.[2] The two in the further corner are in a bad state. To the Palazzo Pappafava,[3] to see the curious carving of the Fall of the Rebel Angels,[4] all cut out of one block (so it is said, and so it seems) with unaccountable dexterity. Then went to the Prato della Valle and walked out of Padua in that direction—dined at Pedrocchi's on my return, and again walked out through the Northern exit of the city, and round to the Prato della Valle, and so back. I think I have now seen almost every street in Padua. Had in the morning also looked at the courts of the University,[5] picturesque with a crowd of carved and painted heraldic shields. The heat these two days is considerable without being excessive, nor yet sultry, as there is a moderate movement of fresh air most of the day. There seem to be no landscape views of any importance in the circuit of the town, yet plenty of agreeable strolling by the Bacchiglione and its canals.

Tuesday 8 August Came on from Padua to Ravenna. One sees the Euganean hills as soon as one gets out of Padua and at no very great distance. Several of them are noticeable for their strictly conical shapes. Passed Este, another Shelleyan locality, but saw nothing of it from the rail-station. The country between Padua and Bologna is mostly flat, and not particularly interesting. Beyond

[1] Jacopo Avanzo or Avanzi was the pupil of Altichiero da Zevio (1330–85), with whom he collaborated in the decoration of this small church or oratory with frescoes. They have been restored since W. M. R.'s visit.

[2] The 'Scuola' is a fifteenth-century building adjoining the basilica. The chapter hall on the first floor is decorated with eighteen frescoes by different painters. Only four of these are by Titian; they were executed in the early part of the fifteenth century.

[3] This 'palazzo', built in 1763, is still owned by Count Papafava dei Carraresi (this is the present spelling of the name). It can be visited with his permission.

[4] This is an extraordinary piece of virtuosity by a little-known eighteenth-century sculptor, Agostino Fasolato, who carved sixty figures entangled one into the other out of one block of marble. It is mentioned by Herman Melville who visited Padua in 1857: 'On April 1st, to the private palace to see "Satan and his host". Fine attitude of Satan. Intricate as heap of vermicella.' See Herman Melville, *Journal of a Visit to Europe and the Levant*, ed. Howard C. Horsford, Princeton, 1955, and Leo Planiscig's article, 'Fasolato's Satan and Melville', in *Art News and Review*, no. 50, January 1952.

[5] Padua University was founded in 1222, the oldest in Italy after Bologna. St. Albert the Great and Galileo taught at Padua. The present building was built in 1501 and is familiarly called the 'Bo' as it stands on the site of an inn, the sign-post of which represented an ox. Recent buildings have been added to the old one.

Bologna it is a rich fine country most of the way to Ravenna. Put up at the 'Spada d'Oro'. Went out to see first of all the Tomb of Dante: what I had seen of it on prints etc. gave me quite a different notion of its aspect. It is a little roofed shrine, in a street-corner, with an iron grating[1] through which you clearly see the interior and with nothing to prevent every passer-by in the street from doing this. You look through the grating, and opposite you is the Sarcophagus, with Dante's own (so it is said) inscription in rhymed Latin,[2] surmounted by the half-figure of him in bas-relief done by Pietro Lombardo,[3] a creditable work. The outline of the nose was shattered, as I am told, by some mischievous boys a century or two ago: this led to the putting up of the iron-grating, the monument having previously been wholly unenclosed. The shrine abuts on a dead wall, painted in 1865 with some slight imitation columns etc. (mere housepainter's work); this wall turns an angle, and a hole has been (also in 1865 as I understand) cut through it, and then on the ground comes a new tomb marking the spot wherein the bones of Dante, preserved by a friar, were actually reposited and found: these have now been removed to the sarcophagus in the shrine.[4] I mean to return to-morrow, and have the door opened: but believe I shall see practically nothing beyond what I now have looked at. Opposite the shrine is a corner house inscribed as having belonged to the Polentas,[5] and been the dwelling-place of Dante, and one room (or rather one site of an old room long gone) is pointed out as the one where Dante died. Entered the Baptistery, with important and almost unaltered

[1] The iron grating has now disappeared and one has free access to the inside of the mausoleum, built in 1780.

[2] The inscription was composed by Bernardo Canaccio, one of Dante's disciples, in 1357.

[3] Pietro Lombardo (*c.* 1435–1515), sculptor and architect. He is the most famous of the four Lombardi. He built the Palace of the Doges in Venice. The bas-relief mentioned here was done in 1483.

[4] After Dante's death in Ravenna in 1321, his body was buried under the portico of the Church of S. Francesco; in 1483 Pietro Lombardo carved the bas-relief representing the poet. About 1500 the Franciscan friars, having heard that Florence would claim the remains of the poet it had banished, secretly opened the urn which contained the bones, placed them in a small wooden box and hid them in a wall. In 1780 Cardinal Gonzaga had a mausoleum built to shelter the sarcophagus. It was only in 1865, however, that a bricklayer found the casket: the bones were identified and placed in the sarcophagus.

[5] The Polentas were the rulers of Ravenna from the thirteenth to the fifteenth century. Guido Novello da Polenta received the banished poet with great honour, and gave him a house where Dante completed the *Divina Commedia*.

mosaics of 6th century. Whilst I was there a christening party came in (people of a humble grade), and it was curious to see the same ceremony performed in this same building appropriated to the purpose for 1200 years. Went to the Cathedral: building entirely renewed towards 1680 or so: but there are some beautiful fragments of carved work and mosaic paintings—two astonishingly massive sculptured tombs of 5th and 6th cent. to two of the archbishops—two elaborately carved ambones about same time —statue of S. Mark by Pietro Lombardo, fine—etc. Saw Byron's house:[1] this also is so altered interiorly that the actual rooms used by him and Shelley would not, I am told, be traceable. After dining went out again to small public garden, and the walk by a canal from the sea which finally leads to the sea itself. This some 5 1/2 miles off, and of course I did not propose to reach it.

Wednesday 9 August Wrote to Theodoric, saying that I propose to go hence to Pistoia, whither he might write to fix either Florence or Via Reggio as the more convenient for us to meet at. On going to the Post, I find letters from home which show that Theodoric himself is not now available: I therefore altered my letter into one to Isabella, who is still at Via Reggio, saying that I expect to be there towards Sunday next. Went to see the ancient episcopal chair in the Duomo, and one or two other things there additional. To S. Vitale,[2] where are some magnificent mosaics and tombs. Returned to and entered the tomb of Dante: the custode also opened the outside cenotaph, which is a new erection, containing now merely bricks and earth, amid which the bones were found in 1865, and transferred thence to the monumental sarcophagus: it seems visitors are addicted to picking out bits of these bricks etc. when the cenotaph is opened, and it is intended to put up a grating inside to prevent this. Afterwards to the tomb and sepulchral chapel of Galla Placidia,[3] with other

[1] This was the Palazzo Guiccioli where Byron came to stay with the young Contessa in 1819. Byron remained at Ravenna for two years but in 1821 the Contessa's family (the Gambas) being expelled from Ravenna, Byron wrote to Shelley asking him to come at once and made him write a letter to Contessa Guiccioli to dissuade her from going to Geneva with Byron as she had suggested. See Shelley *Letters*, ii. 316, 325; also Iris Origo, *The Last Attachment*, 1949, p. 269.

[2] This church was built in the sixth century and is one of the finest specimens of Byzantine architecture in Europe; its mosaics are one of the marvels of the Western world.

[3] Galla Placidia (d. 450), the sister of the West Roman Emperor Honorius; she governed the Western Empire for a time after his death. Her mausoleum is said to

very fine mosaics, and three remarkable tombs: that of Galla
Placidia herself is of vast size and mass. Then took a 'vettura',
and went to S. Apollinare in Classe[1]—a beautiful simple interior
(that of S. Vitale also very beautiful, but much more complicated)
and the mosaic of the dome exceedingly grand: *Transfiguration,
S. Apollinaris preaching to the faithful represented as sheep*, etc. Here
also a good number of fine sarcophagi of archbishops. To the
sepulchre of Theodoric, severe and impressive: scarcely any
traces of decoration now perceptible, though I believe the monument was once very rich. Then to the Pine Forest,[2] which is
beautiful and enjoyable: but what I saw of it (and I am told the
rest is similar) more open than I expected—not any great closeness
or gloom of trees. Finished the day by going into the little
Giardino Pubblico.

Thursday 10 August   Went to see the buildings I had not yet
examined, S. Giovanni Evangelista,[3] S. Agata,[4] S. Apollinare
Nuovo,[5] with the great series of male saints adoring Christ, and
female saints and the three Magi adoring the Virgin and Child:
besides a great number of separate figures of saints and comparatively small Bible subjects, all in mosaic. Palazzo of Theodoric:[6]
only the outside (which however was not originally the outside)
has any antiquity. S. Maria in Cosmedin,[7] mosaic vault. S. Maria
in Porto, 17th century church[8] with some goodish pictures[9] (or

have been decorated with sumptuous mosaics during her life-time. The two other
tombs are not identified.

[1] Another church of the sixth century. It stands outside Ravenna on the site of
the old Roman port of Classis.

[2] The famous 'Pineta' celebrated by Dante in the XXVIIIth canto of *Purgatorio*
and by Byron in *Don Juan*, and where Byron and Shelley used to ride.

[3] A basilica founded by Galla Placidia in the sixth century, restored in 1921 and
badly damaged during the Second World War.

[4] A church built in the sixth century.

[5] The basilica built by Theodoric in the sixth century was for some time in the
hands of the Arians. Its round campanile is typical of the Ravennese towers of the
tenth century, when it was added to the main building.

[6] Theodoric, King of the Ostrogoths, conquered Ravenna and ruled the city till
his death. His so-called 'Palazzo' is little more than a ruined front wall.

[7] S. Maria in Cosmedin is a very small sixth-century octagonal church decorated
with magnificent mosaics, and was in fact the baptistery of the Arians.

[8] W. M. R. is mistaken as to the date of the construction of the basilica. It was
begun in 1553 and completed in 1561. The front was finished in 1784 by Camillo
Morigia.

[9] There are twelve pictures in the side chapels, six in each, all by different
seventeenth-century painters.

rather I think these were in Apollinare Nuovo) which nobody seems to know anything about, painting being in this city almost nullified by mosaic and remote antiquity. One of the pictures represents the Japanese martyrs. Another shows the body of a female saint (looks like the Madonna), and a young man dead or fainted, with both hands lopped off. To the Library where there is the codice principe of Aristophanes written in 10th or 11th century. Here also is a glass case containing the wooden box wherein the Franciscans had deposited the bones of Dante, there found in 1865. Also a few other things connected with the same matter, such as a wire mould which was used for keeping in proper shape the bones united into skeleton form—which form, as I am told, they still retain now in the sarcophagus. This Library was visited in 1857 by the Pope, [1] who wrote in the visitors' book the terzina from Dante about the transiency of fame ending (something like) 'Che muta . . . perchè muta sito'. It is a large offhand rather rough handwriting. There are various good ivory carvings etc. in the little museum connected with this Library, and a curious circular object termed a Turkish table—made of leather, I take it, with a good deal of patterning, and I think I never saw any such thing before. Then to the Museum of Sculpture (chiefly casts) and painting. There is an extremely fine sepulchral figure, Guidarello Guidarelli,[2] a Ravennese captain named Braccioforte[3]—indeed I scarcely know where else a sepulchral effigy uniting such accomplished art with such a fine simplicity is to be found. The face is that of a handsome man, still almost young, slightly leaned aside—eyes closed in death, and mouth lightly opened with the teeth just showing (a thing almost invariably offensive to my eye in art, but not so here): the form clad in full armour, with no accessories whatever,

---

[1] Pius IX (1792–1878), Pope from 1846 to 1878.

[2] Guidarello Guidarelli (1468–1501), a soldier in the service of Caesar Borgia. He is said to have been murdered in a brawl. His name became famous, thanks to the beautiful recumbent figure executed for his tomb by Tullio Lombardo in 1525 and described here by W. M. R. Originally, Guidarello's sepulchre was in the Church of San Francesco at Ravenna; it was transferred to the Accademia di Belle Arti, now located in the Loggetta Lombardesco, via di Roma, Ravenna.

[3] Braccioforte was not the name of Guidarello Guidarelli; it refers to some vague legend according to which some warrior in distress had appealed to Christ, in these terms: 'O tu che hai il braccio forte, ajuta mi!' What is now called 'l'arco di Braccioforte' contains anonymous sarcophagi in the immediate vicinity of Dante's tomb. This is, at least, the information I gathered on the spot.

such as dogs at the feet or the like. This effigy comes from the immediate neighbourhood of the Dante monument: author unknown. There are some creditable and other curious pictures, but nothing very memorable. Then went to the photographer's (Ricci) and bought several photographs of Ravennese monuments. These include two stereoscopic views of the Dante monument: he has done a larger one of the work, and is to send me a copy tonight if he can get it printed in time. He has also a very curious small stereoscopic photograph taken surreptitiously (for no such copies were or are now permitted) of the bones of Dante as they were exhibited in 1865. One sees the enclosed place close by the Dante shrine: in this the glass case now in the museum, and therein the bones of Dante arranged in skeleton form (the ribs seem scantily represented), and a dozen or so of people crowding round to look. The bones, as seen on the photograph, are black. This would be a great prize for any Dantean to secure: I offered 10 francs, and would willingly have gone further, but Ricci seemed quite resolved not to part with it at any price. He seemed willing to take from this photograph another photograph which I could purchase: but this will clearly not be manageable within the short remainder of my stay in Ravenna. There is no photograph of the house wherein Dante is said to have died. Ricci seems to think that the alterations to which it has been subjected deprive it of historical interest, and very likely he is not far wrong, were it not for the feeling of association so potent in all such cases. Dined early, and then went out again to S. Maria in Porto fuori, an ancient church whitewashed and uncared for, but containing some frescoes by Giotto, among the finest things I know of his.[1] The vault gives in four compartments the four Evangelists and four Fathers of the Church—one Evangelist and one Father in each section—beautiful and noble, and fairly preserved. The only Evangelist represented as an old man is Mark: the others young and beardless. Then on the walls there are the *Nativity of Virgin*—Her *Presentation in the Temple*: here the furthest figure to one's right is said to be Dante, and the attribution seems to me at least a possible one: age perhaps forty-five, a fine head muffled as usual: it ought to be made accessible by

[1] S. Maria in Porto fuori stands three and a half miles out of the city. The frescoes of the fourteenth century are not now attributed to Giotto, but to various artists of Romagna.

photographs or engravings. *Christ appearing to the Apostles and Women* seems to have formed one picture now divided by a window, and that closed by some ordinary altar-piece, *Massacre of the Innocents, Calling of Matthew*, very expressive. *Christ giving the Eucharist in both kinds to Apostles*, a dignified treatment of the semi-symbolical kind. *A Saint converting or evangelizing a King*, very expressive again. Two subjects which I suppose on reflection (the priest in attendance presumes them to be Apocalyptic subjects) to represent 'Herod causing the two Disciples to fall by the sword' (as in Acts) and then himself struck by Angels, one of whom cuts at him with a sword. Many figures or heads of female Saints, of more than common beauty and completion—and several other matters, some of them, almost effaced, not to speak of the general body of the church totally whitewashed. The priest takes an interest in them, and has applied himself with no mean success to bringing out some of the heads and draperies. He is rather of the unshaved and squalid order of ecclesiastics, but with a very vivid intelligent face. Finding me to be *un dotto* (as he said), he begged my acceptance of a small drama he has printed about S. Vitale, and he contemplates similar popular dramatic narratives of the chief matters of interest connected with Ravennese monuments—a very good idea if he has any corresponding faculty of execution. In this church is the tomb (originally of very early date—say 4th century) of Petrus Peccans,[1] enrolled in Dante's *Paradise*. Went from this church down to the Adriatic, skirting the Pine forest: a beautiful early evening, and blue sea much less tame than at the Lido. Many bathers and bathing machines. This finishes my stay at Ravenna, which I have much enjoyed. Saw on the road the Capanna di Garibaldi,[2] where he lay in hiding some

[1] 'Petrus Peccans' appears in Dante's *Paradiso*, Canto XXI, lines 121–3:

> In quel loco fu' io Pietro Damiano,
> e Pietro Peccator fu' nella casa
> di Nostra Donna in sul lito adriano.

All commentators agree that already in Dante's time there was a confusion between two Peters: S. Peter Damiano (1007–72) who was a monk, then a cardinal, and the other Peter, also a monk, who may have been Pietro Onesti who founded the Church of Santa Maria in Porto and died thirty years after Pietro Damiano and may have called himself 'Peccatore' out of humility. As to the genuineness of the tomb, there is room for doubt. There are many ancient tombs in Ravenna from which legends seem to have grown.

[2] Giuseppe Garibaldi (1807–82). His personality appealed greatly to the English liberal intellectuals of the day. W. M. R. in his diary, 23 April 1867, wrote: 'I am

days after the fall of the Roman Republic. I bought a photograph of it in the morning. My valet de place was with him in Rome, and admires him much: he was, I am informed, a tenor singer for some years, but now reduced to this means of livelihood. Garibaldi's wife Anita[1] was 'molto simpatica'. I asked my guide what was the cause of Garibaldi's separation from his second wife: he does not know, but seems to think that Garibaldi was not easily to be satisfied with any wife after Anita.

Friday 11 August   Sleeping and waking to the music of a mosquito. I rose about 4 1/2 (supposing it to be 5, but my watch though very satisfactorily set right in other respects, seems to go uncommonly fast now), and started for Pistoia. Silver seems to have wholly disappeared from ordinary circulation in Italy: and indeed one franc that I had in silver was refused by one of the Railway officials, though accepted by another: the former said that these coins had been called in. Had to get out of the train at Bologna, with a stay of full 2 1/2 hours, most of which time I spent in the Accademia. There is a fine Perugino here that I did not specially remember from my previous visits: 'Virgin with John Evangelist (the finest figure of all), Michael, Catherine, and I suppose Agatha.' Two of the Guidos[2] are fine works: the 'Samson with jawbone of ass' (a duplicate I saw and admired in Turin), and an enormously tall votive picture for Bologna with colossal figures of 'dead Christ, Virgin and Angels above, and Petronius and other saints below'. A 'Virgin in heaven' by Ludovico Caracci[3] is a remarkable work of luminous effect—

surprised to hear (from Howell) that Lord Houghton was most demonstrative towards Garibaldi when the latter was in London two or three years ago. Houghton having actually, on being introduced to him, knelt down and kissed his knees, not much to Garibaldi's satisfaction.' See *R.P.*, p. 230.

[1] Anita Garibaldi (1821–49), a Brazilian by birth, married Giuseppe Garibaldi when the latter went to Brazil to lead a rebellion of the southern provinces. She met him at Laguna in 1839 and fought as one of his soldiers. She followed him to Italy when he returned to fight the Austrians in 1848, took part in the war and died, pregnant, near Venice. In 1859 Garibaldi had her remains taken to Nice, his birthplace. But, in 1932, at the order of Mussolini, they were transferred to the island of Caprera, seat of the Garibaldi family.

[2] Guido Reni (1575–1642). The 'Samson Drinking from the Jawbone of an Ass' mentioned here is considered one of Reni's masterpieces.

[3] Lodovico Caracci (1555–1619), Bolognese painter, perhaps the most talented of the three Caracci. The article on the Caracci in the *Encyclopaedia Britannica*, 11th edn., v. 298, is by W. M. R.

also his 'Jerome' fine. I do not know that there is any other Caracci I much care for, and the Domenichinos[1] I continue to dislike very decidedly. The Raphael 'Cecilia' I admire more than heretofore, but not fervently—a Francia[2] with very tender and pure 'Madonna in heaven', the other figures moderate—indeed I think the Baptist very bad. A Guercino,[3] some military saint and a number of other figures is among his most surprising works of manual power, though some surpass even this. The Montanina, a circular way laid out with trees, shrubs, and grass, must look very grand on a fine sunset day. This day however has been dull— almost wholly sunless till towards 6 p.m., and to some extent rainy. The country between Bologna and Pistoia, crossing the Apennines, is splendid: I question whether I have ever seen an equal space so intensely and beautifully Italian: had the sun been shining, the effect would have been doubled. There is an extra-ordinary number of tunnels that cut up the views provokingly: at times half a dozen or more will come together—no sooner out of one than into the other, and at least three of the series are uncommonly long ones. Though I had been from Bologna to Florence twice, I never saw this country before, as I then travelled by diligence, and through the night (1860 and 62). Put up at the 'Locanda (so called here) di Londra', which seems fully up to the better average of Italian comfort. Got a dish of lentils at dinner which reminded me of my father: I doubt whether I had ever before met with them in my travels. Arriving at 5, and then dining, there was no time to look at the monuments of the city: so I took a walk—perhaps 2 1/2 miles out—to the nearest hill named Giaccherino, with a convent and row of cypresses. Caught many charming glimpses en route, though there is a long suburb of Pistoia which stretches nearly the whole distance. By the time I reached the convent it was turned of 8, which now means dark. This is a Capuchin convent and there are still many friars there, though I scarcely understand why. One sees a few friars still about in various places: before Ravenna however, I saw none. One of my informants about these matters was a little girl of some

[1] Domenico Panfieri known as il Domenichino (1581–1641), worked with Annibale Caracci.

[2] Francesco Raibolino known as il Francia (c. 1460–1517), painter and goldsmith in Bologna.

[3] Giovanni Francesco Barbieri Guercino (1591–1666), painter, was born at Cento, near Bologna.

10 or 11 who goes 'cercando la limosina'[1] and picking up a living
as she can. Her parents are dead, the 'babbo'[2] about two years
ago, leaving four children. One of them is 'maggiore' than this
little wench, another is 'piccina piccina'. She seems a diligent
small damsel, as she was pleating a mat of rush, and her fingers
never ceased a moment all the time she was talking to me, and
mounting the hill, steep enough to make me pant ere I was atop.
One sees women with distaffs and spinning wheels about here.
There *are* mosquitoes in this house, as I found by personal experience at night, though I had been told to the contrary.

Saturday 12 August   Pistoia is a fine old place, with much massive
and vigorous house architecture, and some remarkable churches.
As I write I have only made a discursive stroll about the streets,
and most of the churches I wanted to enter were shut. S.M.
dell'Umiltà,[3] a good Renaissance interior—Cathedral not very
large: highly picturesque campanile,[4] and a beautiful Robbia[5]
over the portal of the church, Virgin and Christ with Angels and
flower and fruit work most exquisite—The Baptistery is ornate
and elegant outside, it seems there is nothing inside. S. Barto-
lommeo ancient (12th century or so): several sculptured lions
about preying on men and animals with considerable force of
expression—S. Giovanni black and white marble very picturesque
—S. Francesco, 1294, imposing though simple almost to bare-
ness—The Palazzo Civile is a grand simple building, decorated
very systematically in its cortile etc. with heraldic helms and
scutcheons—mostly painted, some carved, others in Robbia ware.
They are very excellent work of their order—the painted one
perhaps the finest that I know: the great majority of them were
indeed restored in 1844 in a very thoroughgoing style, and their
artistic and picturesque value is, of course much abated, but on
the whole the restoration seems to have been done in a spirit of
faithfulness and painstaking. Two bears are the supporters of the
Pistoiese arms, and figure quaintly on many buildings. Palazzo

[1] That is, 'searching for alms'—'la limosina' being the girl's version of
'l'elemosina'.   [2] The 'daddy'.
[3] Santa Maria dell'Umiltà, which is at once original and imposing, was built by
Ventura Vitoni (1442–1522). The great cupola was finished by Giorgio Vasari
(1511–74).
[4] The campanile was built in the thirteenth century.
[5] This terracotta frieze is by Andrea della Robbia (1435–1525).

del Commune[1] opposite, also fine. Very picturesque market Della Sala, with an old figured fountain with a lion, as is the general market-place in the Piazza del Duomo. Ospedale del Ceppo:[2] the famous frieze of works of mercy by G. della Robbia and two others of the family, highly coloured, and very talented and in parts admirable: also various medallions of sacred subjects etc. After dining went out again, and saw the interior of the Duomo, with monument to Cino da Pistoia:[3] another monument to Cardinal Forteguerri,[4] partly by Verrochio,[5] has great excellence. S. Paolo,[6] half flayed to death by restoration, and the interior now so dark that one can scarcely see the noted picture by Fra Paolino. S. Andrea,[7] with the celebrated pulpit by one of the Pisani, much like the one at Pisa. One of the basal figures, a lioness with two sucking cubs and a rabbit, is singularly fine and true: one can hardly suppose but that the sculptor had seen the animal, though where I cannot guess. S. Domenico[8] with a fine but repainted Ghirlandaio[9] of S. Sebastian, etc., and other pictures and monuments worth inspecting. This church is attached to a convent of nuns: and I saw (what I think I had never seen before) the Parlatorio, with large and small gratings for the nuns to appear at. Finished by going to the Theatre, Arena Matteini, open to the sky. The play was 'Le Mosche Bianche', about a ballerina of suspected but severe virtue—full of moral sentiment, like almost all the Italian plays I have seen, the acting highly respectable.

Sunday 13 August Finished up with Pistoia. Entered the Baptistery,

[1] The Palazzo del Commune was begun in 1294, rebuilt in 1345, and several times enlarged. The principal architect was Simone di Ser Memmo da Siena.

[2] The Ospedale was probably founded in the thirteenth century and the frieze s by Giovanni della Robbia (1469–1529), son of Andrea.

[3] This sepulchre was executed in 1338 by Cellino di Nese in honour of the poet of the 'dolce stil nuovo' (1271–1336).

[4] Cardinal Niccolo Forteguerri (1419–73), who later became Pope Pius II. The monument mentioned here was begun in 1477.

[5] Andrea di Michele Verrochio (1436–88), Florentine painter and sculptor.

[6] San Paolo is a thirteenth-century church and the picture by Fra Paolino da Pistoia (*c.* 1490–1547) represents a Madonna with Child and Saints painted in 1528.

[7] Sant'Andrea is a twelfth-century church with a Romanesque façade of 1166. It is attributed to Gruamonte, sculptor and architect. The pulpit is by Giovanni Pisano (*c.* 1240–1329).

[8] A fourteenth-century church much restored after 1944.

[9] Ridolfo Ghirlandajo (1483–1561), Florentine painter.

which has a richly panelled ancient font, and various panels of like class are standing, propped up against the wall. Ascended the Campanile, with a fine view all round, Florence discernible. Entered S. Giovanni, rich carved 13th century pulpit by an uncertain master.[1] The figure certainly quite as correct as those of the Pisani, though perhaps there is less genius. One of the chapels contains, instead of a picture, a very beautiful marble group of the Visitation, Elizabeth kneeling before Virgin and embracing her, entirely simple and pure, and executed with perfect accomplishment.[2] It is not mentioned in Murray.[3] I feel rather uncertain about the date, but inclined to think it is recent— say towards 1700, though so different in style and spirit from the barocco work of that time. Started at noon for Pisa: a superb country on the road especially the earlier half. Passed two Shelleyan localities: the Serchio at Ripafratta (seems a very quiet stream there now) and the Baths of S. Giuliano.[4] After Ravenna, even Pistoia looked an observably civilized place, and Pisa's air is one of smug decorum. Put up at Hotel della Vittoria, which is highly clean and well kept, with carpet in bedroom. Here again there seem to be next to no travellers, and one is referred to a neighbouring café for meals. After dining there went to the Campo Santo:[5] as before, I like the very old pictures the best, and, save for simple figures not unfrequently recurring, am no great enthusiast for the Gozzolis.[6] This whole group of buildings—

[1] S. Giovanni Fuorcivitas was built towards the end of the twelfth century. The marble pulpit was executed in 1270 by Fra Guglielmo da Pisa, a pupil of Niccolo Pisano.

[2] The group is in glazed white terracotta; it is attributed to various artists, and principally to Andrea della Robbia.

[3] John Murray's famous guide-books. The one used by W. M. R. was *A Handbook for Travellers in Central Italy*, pt. i, London, 1857.

[4] In October 1820 the Baths of San Giuliano, where the Shelleys had taken a house, were flooded by the River Serchio; they then moved to a house at Pisa on the Lung' Arno. The story is told by Mary Shelley in her 'Note on Poems of 1820'. See also Shelley, *Letters*, ii. 240.

[5] The Campo Santo is a cemetery like a vast cloister decorated with a series of frescoes by important fourteenth-century artists including Giotto, Orcagna, and Gozzoli. In 1828 the Campo Santo superintendent, Carlo Lasinio, had their subjects engraved and published at Florence. This book came into the hands of Millais in 1848; he invited his friends Holman Hunt and D. G. R. to examine it. W. M. R. declared: 'Mr. Holman Hunt considers that it was the inspection of the Campo Santo engravings at this special time, which caused the establishment of the Praeraphaelite Brotherhood.' See *Memoir*, p. 125.

[6] Benozzo di Lese, known as Benozzo Gozzoli (1420–97), famous for the frescoes he painted in the Campo Santo.

Baptistery, Cathedral, Tower, and Campo Santo—have now been strenuously restored—no doubt with deplorable and irreparable loss in some respects, but one cannot deny that there is some compensation in their general sightliness and orderliness of aspect. Went into the Cathedral at late sunset, vespers I suppose. There was a huge congregation in the vast and beautiful edifice, including (what is exceptional) a large minority of men—most of the people kneeling on the marble floor, and singing with vigorous and sweet sonority. The hatred of priests among all Italians one talks with is something extraordinary. The headwaiter here, or perhaps part proprietor of the Hotel, speaks like a moderate and conservative person on general politics, and has the air of a highly respectable old gentleman of the middle class. But he would like to see a war break out between Italy and France. Why? Because then there would, all over the country, be a Sicilian Vespers of the Priests.

Monday 14 August   If I remember right, Shelley is said to have lived, during a portion of his Pisan stay, in the Palazzo[1] opposite the one that is inscribed 'alla Giornata'. This would appear to be a large mansion (now broken up into four shops on the ground floor, and containing a Fire Insurance office named 'La Nazione'). A little East of this however is another Palazzo, still apparently such, numbered 322: the house first mentioned is still partly let out in lodgings. Casa Lanfranchi,[2] where Byron lived, and I think also Shelley at one time is on the same North bank of the Arno as 'alla Giornata', and to the East of that house. Ponte a Mare[3] is the bridge to the extreme West, having by it the Torre Guelfa, which Shelley supposed to be the Torre della Fame.[4] It is Browning who says Shelley made this mistake. As I stand near the Ponte a Mare,

---

[1] The Shelleys lived in Pisa from January 1820 to April 1822, in the Palazzo Galetti, described by Shelley in a letter to Clare Clairmont, 29 October 1820. See Shelley, *Letters*, ii. 242.

[2] When Byron decided to move from Ravenna to Pisa, the Shelleys found the Palazzo Lanfranchi for him; they were frequent visitors, but never lived there.

[3] W. M. R. was trying to find the bridge which Shelley mentions in the short poem *Evening: Ponte al Mare, Pisa* (1821). The Ponte a Mare stood near the Porta a Mare; it has not been rebuilt but replaced by the Ponte di Ferro.

[4] La Torre della Fame is mentioned as such by Dante in *l'Inferno* (Canto XXXIII) as being the place where the tyrant of Pisa, Ugolino, and his sons were starved to death in the thirteenth century. It inspired Shelley's poem, *The Tower of Famine* (1820).

I observe on the North bank, further within the city, another
very ancient and bare-looking tower: it strikes me that Shelley
may have meant this latter, as he seems to speak of a tower standing in a piazza or street, whereas the Torre Guelfa, though not
wholly isolated from buildings, is close by the river side, and
quite at one end of the city. This other is called Torre Beniforti,[1]
if I catch the name aright. On going up to what I have termed
above the Ponte a Mare, I find it is not that, but a railway bridge
impassable to foot passengers. The Ponte a Mare stood close by
however, and one can see in the Arno a trace of its foundations:
it got destroyed years ago, perhaps in 1827, and is to be rebuilt.
S.M. della Spina[2] is now being reconstructed: they have taken
off the upper gables, but intend, I am told, to put everything on
again. A great deal also has been done of late, and is still being
done, to the quay or embankment of the Arno—raising it higher
as protection against inundation, as there was a severe one some
few years ago. Saw while at breakfast a number of the Fratelli
della Misericordia, perhaps 25 to 30, conveying a corpse to be
buried: one of them entered the caffè, and rattled a little box
marked 'Elemosina per la povera Defunta' (whether for burial
or purgatory I am not clear); most of the persons present gave
something. My watch is again beginning to stop and go on again
and some mess will result. Went on from Pisa to Via Reggio,
a short hour's journey. Found Isabella[3] fairly well, and expecting
Theodoric to-morrow, probably in the evening. She has been
learning swimming at the baths here, and appears now to be
quite expert. I took and enjoyed a bath. Raffaelli (Lorenzo) the
owner of this lodging-house, 37, Via della Vignita, looking now
not less than 65 at any rate, saw (as Isabella had told me) Shelley's
corpse when cast up on this shore, and afterwards saw the
burning; he seems impressed with the large amount of disfigure-
ment of the corpse—one eye and legs particularly injured by
fishes. Isabella pointed out to me on the shore the actual spot
where the burning took place, and that where the corpse was

[1] From the position described by W. M. R. the tower he saw was probably the
Torre Ghibellina.

[2] The tiny church S. Maria della Spina was built in the fourteenth century so
near the river that it was constantly threatened by the rising waters; so in 1871 it
was taken down and rebuilt where it now stands.

[3] Isabella Pietrocola *née* Steele, Teodorico's Scottish wife, who, after his death,
married an English Waldensian and became Mrs. Cole.

thrown up: one sees a tower or pier-light which is not the Tower of Migliarino. Enquiries made by Raffaelli after the spy-glass found on the *Don Juan* and kept here by the town till 1860 have not resulted in tracing it: if my recollection serves me, I have been told that Captain Roberts[1] possesses it. Mrs. Jarves[2] and her sister, Miss Haydon are here. Jarves in America, and has some idea of seeing Japan before he returns. Took a walk with Isabella in the Pinewood. Her father died somewhat suddenly; a bursary is about to be founded in his name. The place of Shelley's burning is where the Piazza Paolina has now been built, but more especially in a space there still unoccupied, and containing sand and litter of whatever sort. Raffaelli, I learn, was born in 1805, and was consequently about seventeen at the time.

Tuesday 15 August Mosquitoes are abundant here, and my night was disturbed. Took another bath. Many of the bathers not only have to do with the water, but roll themselves about in the sand, or one sees a sand-potted baby with his head sticking out: indeed I learn that Isabella is using also the sand-treatment, but only locally for the feet. A large proportion of the bathers have little medals or the like consecrated trifles hung round their necks. It is curious to see a priest in his robe and shovel-hat, and then splashing about in the water with a pair of drawers on. The only one I distinctly identified among the bathers in the water (there are however many priests who frequent the same bathing establishment with myself) had on a waistcoat as well as drawers: possibly this is the correct, but not universally observed thing for the clerics. Theodoric arrived in the middle of the day, and was most cordial. He expects to visit London with his wife next year: of course I told him to come to us, which was already his intention. He would have been minded to settle in England when last there; but the scale of living was too high for his income, without some addition thereto which he did not find forthcoming—as to teaching, he had made up his mind not to resume that 'noja'.

[1] Captain Daniel Roberts, R.N. (1780–1870), an old 'naval friend' of Trelawny's, living at Genoa, who supervised the building of Shelley's boat, the *Don Juan*. After the shipwreck, Trelawny commissioned Roberts to recover the foundered boat, which he did. He then wrote to Trelawny: 'Pisa, Sept. 1822. We have got fast hold of Shelley's boat, and she is now safe at anchor off Via Reggio. Everything is in her, and clearly proves that she was not capsized.' Trelawny, *Recollections*, p. 97.

[2] Mrs. Jarves, *née* Isabel Kast Haydon, was the second wife of James Jackson Jarves (1818–88), an American art critic and collector who had settled in Florence.

He tells me that Ricciardi, having strong provincial (Neapolitan) sympathies, is not greatly in favour of the transfer of my father's remains to Florence, but rather to Naples: the conflicting feelings on this auxiliary question among members of the committee, proposing subscribers, etc, have created a certain amount of complication. I asked Isabella about an 'aziola'[1] (Shelley): she does not know that name, but thinks it must probably be a small owl known hereabouts, and called 'chiù'—that being the sound that it emits, in a gentle voice.

Wednesday 16 August   Took another bath. Called on Mrs. Jarves, who is staying with a Mr. Monti, American Consul at Palermo, and his wife, a sister of Parsons,[2] the translator of Dante. This is a very loud-voiced woman, and not a favourable specimen of American feminine manners, though I find Isabella has a very good opinion of her character in essentials.

Thursday 17 August   Raffaelli the landlord has been making further enquiries about the spy-glass that used to belong to Shelley. It is now in the possession of the widow of Simoncini— Silvia Triverina, Vedova Simoncini, living in Lucca. She would not part with it (so at least it said) under £40, which seems a very high price. A good deal of stormy rain, with thunder and lightning, came on last evening, and lasted mainly through the night, and as I write (9 1/4 a.m.) the rain is still coming down very heavy and steady, and the storm not quite finished otherwise. Mrs. Jarves told me last night that a sister of hers used to tend the wounded of the American War in one of the Hospitals that Whitman frequented. He was sincerely liked by the patients, but had a habit of kissing them, and also of asking whether they would like to hear poems, and thereupon reading *Leaves of Grass*—both which habits were a little formidable to the patients—who would accordingly, on the approach of Whitman, all affect to be sound asleep. Possibly there is a mythical element in this anecdote. At noon I went on from Via Reggio to Spezia: country still very fine, passing the Carrara quarries, which reach to a considerable height up big hills. Put up at Croce di Malta, and forthwith

---

[1] The 'aziola' (a local Venetian name) is a small owl. It inspired Shelley's poem 'The Aziola', published by Mary Shelley in the *Keepsake*, 1829.

[2] T. W. Parsons (d. 1892). His translation of seventeen cantos of the *Inferno* was published in Boston in 1865.

sallied out in a boat to see Shelley's house between S. Arenzo[1] and Lerici: as my boatman said, it might be better described as being the last house (detached from any others) in S. Arenzo. About 1 1/2 hour takes one there from Spezia: we had contrary wind, and were a little longer. The house is no longer known as Casa Magni,[2] but Casa Maccarani—or for tourist purposes the Casa di Shelley: I have made a very rude sketch of it at the end of this book. It is of very considerable size outside, set in beautiful and picturesque scenery—may be termed the inner end of a semi-circle, the extremities of which are the castles of S. Arenzo and of Lerici, both striking objects. Both these villages must, I suppose, be a good bit bigger than in Shelley's time, for even S. Arenzo, much the smaller of the two, has an inn, café etc., and there could now apparently be no occasion for sending to a distance (as Mrs. Shelley records)[3] for ordinary necessaries. The house is now tenanted for six months in the year by a Colonel Cross. I asked whether I could be allowed a sight of the rooms: but the proprietario, who appeared and was very civil, said that Colonel Cross does not permit this. He pointed to the rooms facing one's right (as one stands with back to sea) as being those which Shelley occupied. I saw a kitchen-garden within, just beyond the entrance hall, and the fine background of trees up the hill spoken of by Mrs. Shelley.

Friday 18 August　　Went on from Spezia to Sestri Levante. I had no idea this journey was so long. I did it by an omnibus-diligence, and it occupied from 9 a.m. to 5.30 p.m. It is a most magnificent country, and I saw it to the greatest advantage, being up on the 'banco', perhaps 10 ft. above the ground, and with nothing at all to intercept my view. A splendid sunny day at first: as we got towards the summit, clouds chequered or obscured the sun to a great extent: but the beauties of the views, with their vast and unexpected variations of sun and shadow, were hardly diminished: I don't think I ever saw any mountain scenery in Italy to greater

---

[1] The correct name is San Terenzo.

[2] The Casa Magni where the Shelleys lived in 1822 is described by Mary Shelley in her 'Note on Poems of 1822'. See Shelley's *Poetical Works*, O.U.P., 1921, p. 670.

[3] 'We could get no provisions nearer than Sarzana at a distance of three miles and a half off' wrote Mary Shelley in the 'Note on Poems of 1822'. In the same note, she also describes the trees planted by the insane proprietor of the house and mentioned by W. M. R.

advantage, nor any that is in itself finer. Aloes are seen in considerable plenty, bordering roads etc., soon before reaching Sestri. Five horses, or once only four, draw the omnibus: some of them are partially covered with chestnut-leaves. I notice that the cries of one driver are wholly different from those of another. One is perpetually saying something like 'Isai' and never 'Ourri'. The next is vice-versa. Reached Genoa soon after 10 p.m. and put up at Hotel Feder. I am not sure that I was ever in any Hotel here save the Gran Colombo once; as, though often passing a longish while in the city, I have mostly visited it as a stopping-place for the steamer.

Saturday 19 August Beyond strolling through a few streets near the Hotel, and changing a little money, did nothing in Genoa. Left at noon, and came on to Turin: some parts of the scenery, towards Villafranca and thereabouts, have rather an English air to my eye: Moncalieri, the last station before Turin, with a large fortress (I suppose it is)[1] is striking. Went to Hotel Trombetta, which I know of old to be very good. Here also there was only time for dinner, a few steps out of doors, seeing the statue of Gioberti[2] etc. and then to bed about nine, having to be up before four to-morrow morning.

Sunday 20 August Got up accordingly and went to Susa, and thence by the rail over M. Cenis. Two women in the train got sick, as if at sea. I suppose in consequence of the rapid and frequent veering-round of the train as it goes down in a zigzag or semicircular direction. The stations at Susa and S. Michel[3] are not now abodes of such total misery as when I passed their ordeal in 1869. The delays of the train between S. Michel and Culoz were however great: I had taken my ticket for the latter place only, so it was no great consequence to me: other travellers going to Marseilles and Paris lost, or were left in expectation of losing, the trains which ought to have met them and taken them on. No reason

[1] The fortress is the castle of the Dukes of Savoy, built in the thirteenth century and restored in the fifteenth century.
[2] Vincenzo Gioberti (1801–52), 'Torinese' philosopher and liberal politician, one of the leaders of the romantic Risorgimento. His book *Il Primato degli Italiani* (1845) helped to prepare the Revolution of 1848. He was considered dangerous and was banished in 1833.
[3] St. Michel de Maurienne in Savoy.

for this is particularly apparent, but I suppose it must be due to the traces of disorganization remaining from the war. The country, as long as light lasted for seeing it, is truly beautiful, with the Savoy mountains all about. This evening I see the moon again—a growing crescent: did not once see it all the time I was in Italy. Put up at the Hotel opposite the Culoz station, not finding any names of Hotels in any book, and being told by a loud-voiced porter that they are 'tous bons', and that, if this one does not answer his description, I am to tell him so to-morrow. I got here a very savoury omelette, and coffee in what I had supposed to be a soup-dish: the old lady of the house put into it three lumps of sugar with her own fingers.

Monday 21 August   This notebook is running short. Got up about 5 a.m. (full two hours earlier than needed, as I distrusted my watch) and took a little country walk. Then on to Tonnerre which I reached about 10 p.m.—even earlier than the appointed time and no delays worth speaking of en route. Prussian soldiers still at Dijon: a broken railway bridge close by, etc. The French converse freely about them of course with plenty of animus: almost all Frenchmen and women in some sort of mourning. One with whom I talked between Mâcon and Tournus (a little heated with wine) was full of brag. In two years Thiers[1] will give France an invincible army: Bismarck will get up some pretext of quarrel, and they will smash up every one on Prussian soil. Bazaine[2] was a traitor. Gambetta[3] a patriot, but ought not to have read lessons to Aurelles[4] who if left to himself would have kept the Germans out of Orléans, and finally conquered. To think that

[1] Louis Thiers (1797–1877), French historian and politician, elected President of the third French Republic in 1871, signed the first Treaty of Versailles which brought the Franco-Prussian war to an end.

[2] Achille Bazaine (1811–88), French Marshal who, without apparent justification, surrendered Metz to the Germans in 1870. He was tried and sentenced to death. The sentence was commuted to solitary confinement on the isle of Sainte Marguerite, off Cannes. He escaped, and went to live in Spain where he died.

[3] Léon Gambetta (1838–82), French politician of Italian origin. As Minister of War after the collapse of the Second Empire, he organized desperate resistance to the Germans. Extremely popular after the war, he devoted all his energy to the establishment of the Republic.

[4] General Louis d'Aurelles de Paladines (1804–77) took an active part in the conquest of Algeria, won a few battles during the Franco-Prussian war, but could not avoid ultimate defeat.

a beer-drinking nation should beat a wine-drinking nation! etc., etc. Put up at Hotel des Courriers.

Tuesday 22 August   There is a pretty little house here belonging to the Ducs de Bourgogne of old—now to my landlady, who would like to sell it, or (as usual) let it. The Prussians were quartered on her, and paid for no ordinaries—only for extras. Officers and men used to get tipsy, but she seems to have no particular feeling against them. One (Baron Pettenwerf or some such name) she lauds most affectionately for all sorts of good and courteous qualities. Her husband had a long almost mortal illness from his excessive labour in cooking, etc. Came to Paris. Before reaching the inside of the city, I saw no traces worth mentioning of the damages of war etc.: inside of course the drive from station to Meurice's Hotel showed much as regards particular buildings, and something of a battered look in the city generally.

Wednesday 23 August   Went about chiefly to look at ruins— Tuileries, Finances (the worst), Cour d'Escomptes [*sic*], Luxembourg and Arc de Triomphe slight, especially the former. Jardin des Plantes; beasts seem much as usual. Elephant and camels and no doubt some others were eaten: monkeys not, but most of them died of hunger. Saw Theresa last night in the 'Chatte Blanche': she is certainly a woman of talent of a coarse kind.

Thursday 24 August   To Folkestone from Boulogne.

Monday 28 August   Trelawny[1] wrote me some days ago, saying that he is in town, and would like to see me. I replied on Saturday, and called this morning, but find he is now back at his country residence at Sompting, and may remain there an indefinite while.

[1] Edward John Trelawny (1792–1881), the friend of Shelley who organized the burning of Shelley's remains on the beach of Viareggio. W. M. R. had seen him once in 1843 when Trelawny called on Gabriele. In 1869, when W. M. R. was engaged on work on Shelley, he asked Barone Kirkup for an introduction to Trelawny. Then began a long series of visits and of letters exchanged about Shelley. W. M. R. himself published in the *Athenaeum* some papers entitled *Talks with Trelawny*, which consisted of extracts from his own diary referring to their conversations about Shelley. See *Reminiscences*, p. 367.

Trelawny had published *Recollections of the Last Days of Shelley and Byron* in 1858. He enlarged and recast the volume and published it in 1878 with the title, *Records of Shelley, Byron and the Author*. See also R. Glynn Grylls, *Trelawny*, London, 1950.

Friday 29 August Stillman and his wife have been back from America these few days, bringing the three children over with them. Mrs. Stillman is staying with her mother at Shanklin: her father ignores her, and, on meeting her lately at a railway station, gave no sign of recognition. Stillman is looking out for a house in which to settle. His son, it is now thought, may prove curable so far as the affection of the hip-joint is concerned: but of late a serious enlargement of the liver has come on, causing some anxiety.

Wednesday 30 August Hewitt of the Baker St. Bazaar had written to me while abroad, to say that he has several Japanese books newly arrived. I called this afternoon, and bought a considerable number, including various parts of the Huxi Series.[1] the blocks of these are unfortunately almost worn out now.

Thursday 31 August to Wednesday 11 October Very busy with office work.

Thursday 12 October I am now apparently very close indeed to finishing the long-lingering compilation of my three volumes of poetic Selections. The American one awaits nothing beyond the ascertaining of one author's date. The Humorous one (which Beeton would like to get out early) seems to be finished, unless *Hudibras* be included—which I have proposed to Beeton as the best mode of gaining bulk, supposing that to be desired. The general Selection may be considered finished when I shall have read through Ebenezer Jones,[2] whom I began upon this evening: though no doubt casual accessions to that volume might continue accruing up to the very eve of publication. The prefacing etc. of the two last-named volumes remain still to be done.

[1] No 'Huxi Series' exists. The curator of the section of Japanese prints in the British Museum has suggested that 'Huxi' may be a misreading for 'Hoxi', a contraction of the name of the Japanese artist Hokusai (1772–1862). C. A. Howell had given W. M. R. his first Japanese book in 1866, and since then W. M. R. had collected Japanese books and prints.

[2] Ebenezer Jones (1820–60), poet. Author of *Studies of Sensation and Event* (1843). D. G. R. thought him a 'neglected genius'. He wrote in *Notes and Queries* of 5 February 1870: '. . . I was much pleased to hear the great poet Robert Browning speak in warm terms of the merit of his (Jones's) work; and I have understood that Monckton Milnes (Lord Houghton) admired the *Studies*, and interested himself on their author's behalf' (reprinted in *Works*, p. 614).

Friday 13 October   Called to see the Stillmans at their new house, 100 Clarendon Road, Notting Hill (first time). Stillman has been writing to *The Times* etc. on the question of Anglo-American copyright:[1] he considers the chief obstructives to be the English (rather than the American) publishers—who fear lest, if English authors were entitled to copyright in America, the American publishers would bid higher for their works than the English, and thus the latter would have to pay higher also than they now do. There seems to be some reason in this: and Macmillan the publisher, it seems, sustains Stillman's general assertion in the matter. Some copies of Maria's book on Dante, fully completed and bound, reached her this evening: we do not however as yet know whether the book is actually published.

Sunday 14 October   Maria's book is likely to be out at the end of next week. I have now set the finishing (I *believe* the finishing) touch to the American Selection, and to the compiling of the Humorous Selections, and have begun with the prefacing, etc. of the latter.

Sunday 15 October   Called on Mathilde Blind, and left her some Shelley books she wants in the compilation of her Shelley Selection for Tauchnitz.[2] I advised her to get in *Prometheus*, if possible,

---

[1] In *The Times* of 27 September 1871 a letter to the editor signed 'A traveller' and entitled 'American Piracy' complained of the fact that American publishers republished English books without any remuneration. The sum taken out of the pockets of English authors amounted, he alleged, to between £50,000 and £100,000 a year.

In *The Times* of 29 September W. J. Stillman answered that: (i) American writers have no more rights in England than English writers in America, (ii) no work by recent English authors published in America goes under the same arrangement as the one made in England for American authors, (iii) the English publishers are those who have the chief interest to oppose an Anglo-American copyright for if American competition is allowed, some authors would get much more than they do now from any English publisher. In the course of the correspondence which went on for two weeks in the columns of *The Times*, Mortimer Collins declared that unless he was misinformed, 'England is ready at any moment for an international copyright, and America is not'. Stillman concluded by writing: 'I notice as a psychological phenomenon that a large class of English writers (mainly anonymous) seem to regard America and the Americans as their natural butts. Since my first letter, I have seen two London publishers both of whom approved its assertions.'

[2] The book was published by Tauchnitz: *Selection from the Poems of P. B. Shelley, edited with a Memoir by Mathilde Blind*, Leipzig, 1872. Miss Blind followed W. M. R.'s advice and included the first and fourth acts of 'Prometheus', but did not sacrifice 'Adonais', nor the choruses from 'Hellas'.

and to sacrifice for this purpose *Alastor*, *Adonais*, and *Hellas*, which she had proposed to insert; also to sacrifice some minor poems, which I marked with her concurrence. She is not very sure however as to the proposed substitution of *Prometheus*. She tells me that R. Garnett informs her that Shelley, when he first left England with Mary, and went to the Lake of Lucerne etc. wrote thence to Harriet, proposing that she should join them; also that, on his return to England soon afterwards, being in want of money, he asked Harriet for some. I must confess I think this last alleged fact very little to his honour: Garnett and Miss Blind however, cite it rather as proving that Shelley had reason to consider Harriet well off, and so as relieving Shelley from any odium on the ground of abandoning her to straits or destitution: and no doubt this is not an untenable position, so far as it goes.

Stillman called in the evening. His wife found her mother, when she visited her last Friday, painfully cold and unsympathetic: this had so distressing an effect on poor Marie that she cried incessantly till past midnight, and almost fell into convulsions. Stillman thinks that the father is now coercing the mother into this harsh line of conduct, and that total alienation may probably ensue: I fear he has some good reason for his opinion.

Monday 16 October   Received at the Union Bank the £50 due from Moxon, for which I consented some while ago to compromise my claim of £126. Burns was also lately paid for in full. The claims for Campbell, Milton, and Cowper, remain to be met in due course —also those for the 3 volumes of Selections.

Tuesday 17 October   Gabriel called. He is displeased with Appleton in regard to a small paragraph which appeared in the last *Academy*[1] objecting to the virulent attack on Gabriel's poems published in

---

[1] The offending paragraph appeared in the *Academy* for 15 October 1871. It reads thus: 'A curious instance of the obsolete vituperative style in criticism appears in the October number of the *Contemporary Review*, a periodical happily less known for such eccentricities than for very respectable services in the field of latitudinarian Christianity. The paper in question, called *The Fleshly School of Poetry: Mr. D. G. Rossetti*, by a Mr. Thomas Maitland, shows more acrimonious personal discourtesy, founded on more grotesque literary misapprehension than it would have been easy to suppose possible. Until the writer has learned to correct his manners he cannot expect a hearing for his opinions.' See p. 127 n. 1.

the *Contemporary Review*. It appears that Colvin[1] and someone else had each proposed to write in the *Academy* on the subject in a more complete and decisive manner, and Gabriel had sanctioned this, but Appleton demurred: the present paragraph has been put in by Colvin on his own authority, he being temporarily in charge of the paper during Appleton's absence. I do not myself see any great ground for complaining of the discretion which Appleton exercised. Gabriel speaks of the isolated situation of the country-house which he and Morris have lately taken at Kelmscott near Lechlade, and where Gabriel passed the summer. When the weather breaks, the whole country is under water; and he used of late to be going in a boat over the meadows whereon he had previously been walking. All sorts of things—even to victuals in many instances—have to be sent for to a railway station some way off, and a carrier has to make a special journey for the purpose, costing six and sixpence in each instance. The population of Kelmscott is only about 180—all of them the merest villagers.

Wednesday 18 October   Poor Lucy Brown has been very ill of late—having abscesses in or by the ear. This has been going on some while—supposed to have been caused by exposure in landscape painting, or other climatal cause, at Lynmouth, where she passed a portion of the Summer. She passed five nights without sleep just now: but to-day Maria, on calling, found that the abscess has at last broken, and she is somewhat relieved.

Thursday 19 October   Brown called. I showed him the proofs of Christina's *Sing-Song*, with Hughes's illustrations. He was singularly pleased with both; going so far as to say that the poems are about Christina's finest things, and Hughes the first of living book-illustrators.

Friday 20 October   Going on with the annotating, etc. of my Selection of Humorous Poetry.

[1] Sidney Colvin (1845–1927), then a Fellow of Trinity College, Cambridge, was already beginning to be known as an art and literary critic. He had contributed a long article to the *Westminster Review* of January 1871 on D. G. R.'s *Poems* and was on friendly terms with the two Rossettis. In 1872 he applied to W. M. Rossetti for a testimonial in view of his candidature for the Slade Chair of Fine Art at Cambridge. See S. Colvin, *Memories of Men and Places*, London, 1921, *passim*.

Saturday 21 October Gabriel has been informed by Ellis, who hears it from Locker, that the writer of the article in the *Contemporary Review* attacking Gabriel's poems, signed Thomas Maitland, is in fact Robert Buchanan. Gabriel is minded—partly through not relishing the attack, and partly for the fun of the thing—to write and print a letter castigating Buchanan, and he read me tonight a few sentences of this letter. However, my advice to him is to print nothing—and generally to leave the whole affair to take care of itself.

Sunday 22 October Having had a cold hanging about me since Monday last I breakfasted in bed to-day. and did not rise till about 2. This is (to the best of my recollection) the first time I have breakfasted in bed since in or about 1852, which is certainly a very handsome account to be able to give of one's health at the age of 42. Even to-day there was not the least necessity for my doing this: I indulged in it rather as a lazy luxury condonable under the circumstances. Stillman tells me that his wife's confinement is expected in January next: she has gone on extremely well hitherto. He is getting Hare, a photographic machinist, to execute, with some modifications, the plan of a camera which he sent me over from Crete 3 or 4 years ago, and which he himself executed some while afterwards: he thinks of patenting or at least registering this invention. He tells me that he finds, in this and other instances, the English workmen strangely inapt at anything of a constructive kind.—Having occasion to write to J. Tupper,[1] whose brother George finds his sight failing at his present lithographing work, I suggested that a good thing for George or some one to compile would be a reprint of contemporary reviews of famous books or pictures, especially abusive reviews: as the *Quarterly* on Keats and Shelley, etc., etc.

---

[1] John Lucas Tupper (*c.* 1826–79), one of the early enthusiasts for Pre-Raphaelitism. His father, who ran a printing firm in the City, undertook the printing of *The Germ* (1850) and even financed the last two numbers to give the new publication 'a fair trial'. John Lucas contributed two articles to *The Germ*: 'The Subject in Art' (no. 1 and no. 3) and a poem (no. 1). He was a sculptor, then became an anatomical designer at Guy's Hospital and, later, drawing master at Rugby School. 'He had a real gift for poetry', wrote W. M. R. It was only in 1897, long after J. L. Tupper's death, that W. M. R. edited a selection of his poems, issued by Longmans and Green. See W. M. R., *Praeraphaelite Diaries and Letters*, p. 257, and *Reminiscences*, p. 161.

Monday 23 October   Dined with the rest of the family (including my Uncle Henry, now on a visit with us) in Cheyne Walk. Gabriel's picture of the *Death of Beatrice*—in the carved frame designed by himself, which is a very fine piece of decorative work, excellently executed by Ford and Dickinson—looks very impressive and beautiful:[1] he has worked on it vigorously of late, with a view to general strength and harmony of effect, and has advanced it noticeably. Something still remains to be done, but apparently very little.—His deer is now dead; one kangaroo alive; the two armadilloes have disappeared, and are supposed to have burrowed into some neighbour's premises. They are said to have been very destructive to pigeons etc—but whether this is a well-ascertained fact I am not clear.

Tuesday 24 October   Met Dr. Heimann[2] in the street: the first time I have seen him since he underwent in the summer a severe operation for hemorrhoids. He looks to me pretty nearly as usual, and seems to feel so: but says his powers of mental application are diminished. His daughter Golde, now Mrs. Möller, is just back from her wedding-tour. They saw the husband's family, living in Stralsund: Dr. Heimann reports the family to be very agreeable people, mixing with the best society of the place. I believe there is nothing Hebraic in the Möllers.

Wednesday 25 October Demetrius Spartali[3] called at Somerset House, wishing me to certify (which I did) my belief that his father is a naturalized British subject. It seems that news has been received of a very dangerous illness of his sister Christine,[4] now in Naples; and Demetrius and his mother are starting off to-day to see her. The certificate was wanted as a preliminary to including Mrs. Spartals in Demetrius's passport.

Thursday 26 October   Christina, whose health continues unsatis-

[1] The picture, in the Walker Art Gallery, Liverpool, remains in its original frame. See Surtees, no. 81, p. 43.

[2] Dr. Adolf Heimann, Professor of German at University College, London, after 1848; became a friend of the Rossetti family as early as 1840. He taught German to the four children in exchange for Italian lessons from the father. It was through him that Dante Gabriel was acquainted with Bürger's *Lenore*, the *Nibelungenlied*, Hoffman, and other German writers. See *Memoir, passim*.

[3] Demetrius Spartali, brother of Marie Spartali (Mrs. Stillman).

[4] Christine Spartali, a younger sister of Marie Stillman, married Comte Edmond

factory (though much less bad than during the Spring and Summer), consulted Dr. Fox to-day. He says that the circulation is out of order and prescribes digitalis.

Friday 27 October A Dr. Duncan called on us, introduced by Burcham.[1] He has done rapidly, in intervals snatched from business, a translation of the whole *Divina Commedia*, and wished to consult Maria about it (knowing her book of Italian Exercises). He seems to have a certain sharpness and aptitude; but is evidently quite ignorant of the laws of verse—his lines being of all sorts of lengths, and many of them in all probability quite unmetrical: the difference of such work from blank verse seemed never to have occurred to him. He knew Munro; and tells me that (so he understands) the mortal illness was found, by a post-mortem examination, to have been cancer in the liver. He also knew Ciciloni[2] very lately (I suppose it may be 30 years since I saw him): thinks Ciciloni is most probably dead now—if living, would be about 86 years old.—A large new set of bookshelves for my room was set up to-day: the room will now, I think, positively admit no more.

Saturday 28 October Going on with the annotating etc. of the Humorous Selection.[3] One great difficulty in this volume, lessening its bulk and restricting the area of selection, is the frequent grossness of poems of a humorous character—especially such as are not of modern date. In reading up for the volume I had included the two poems of Scottish kings, 'Peebles to the Play', and

de Cahen. In 1864 Whistler painted her as *La Princesse du Pays de la Porcelaine* (Freer Gallery of Art, Washington, D.C.).

[1] Robert P. Burcham (d. 1894), a neighbour of the Rossettis in Albany Street. He was a chemist by profession, but also an able amateur water-colourist. William Hunt painted his portrait which was bequeathed to W. M. R.; now in the possession of Mrs. Imogen Dennis by descent. See *Reminiscences*, i. 111.

[2] Ciciloni, another Italian refugee from Vasto who taught Italian in London and sometimes took up Gabriele Rossetti's work when the latter was prevented from doing it through illness or otherwise. See *Memoir*, i. 48.

[3] The two poems mentioned here were omitted in the Selection. In the Preface, W. M. R. explains the motives for which they were excluded: 'And, lastly—without, I hope, lapsing into utter and unmanly squeamishness—I have carefully avoided poems which are gross or indecent in general drift or even in particular expressions; for the present volume . . . [is meant] for all readers. This precaution entails many exclusions . . .; for the British humourist has been a personage the reverse of mealy-mouthed.' *Humorous Poems* (*Moxon's Popular Poets*), 1872.

'Christ's kirk on the Green'; but, in the more minute perusal I am now giving to the selected works, I find there are in both these poems indecent expressions which will entail their exclusion. It would not, I think, be fair to the publishers to admit any poems open to this objection, as to do so might greatly limit their sale: on the other hand, I totally object to missing out anything that I find in my text, and am so reduced to total exclusion.

Sunday 29 October   Gabriel called—also Brown and Hüffer. I told Gabriel that, according to Swinburne's last information from S. Solomon,[1] Buchanan is not the writer of the hostile article against Gabriel in the *Contemporary Review*. Gabriel however inclines to believe that Buchanan really *is* the author; and that the present denial, following after a previous admission, is a mere subterfuge to avoid unpleasant imputations or consequences.— Lucy Brown is now well again.

Monday 30 October   Scott and others dined in Cheyne Walk. Gabriel tells me that he lately received a request from Virtues[2] the publishers to write a book on English Sculptors: not having any inclination for such a job, he has referred the publishers to Scott. Gabriel now thinks that perhaps the publishers had intended to address, not himself, but me: I see no particular reason however for thinking so, and would rather Scott did the work than I. Jones was this year in Orvieto and other parts of Italy: is greatly enthusiastic about Italy and Italians, the beauty of the Romans, men and women, etc.: and vows he would live altogether in Italy, could he but get certain friends of his to adopt the same resolve. Scott told us a singular incident. There is an old rhyme (perhaps centuries old) saying that when the last leaf falls from a certain ash-tree, well-known locally, the Boyds of Penkill

---

[1] Simeon Solomon (1840–1905), a young Jewish painter attracted by the Pre-Raphaelite ideals; his picture *Moses* made him famous in 1860; exhibited fifteen works at the R.A. in 1858–72. Burne-Jones introduced him to Swinburne who exerted a great influence on him, and gave him access to the works of the Marquis de Sade. In 1872 and 1873 he was convicted of pederasty and imprisoned; he soon lapsed into utter degradation, actually becoming a pavement artist. In 1879 Swinburne, hearing that Solomon was trying to make money by selling some disreputable letters of his, wrote: '[Solomon] . . . is now a thing unmentionable by men and women, as equally abhorrent to either—nay, to the very beasts.' Solomon died in St. Giles's Workhouse, London. See Swinburne, *Letters*, iv. 107.

[2] J. S. Virtue and Co. printed the *Fortnightly Review*.

will be extinct. Miss Boyd is now concerned to find that recently, in the building of a farmhouse, this ash has been cut down: and certainly there is at present every prospect of the early extinction of the Boyds, for she herself is the last of the stock.—Gabriel read, with great and general applause, and some little skirmishing as to details (especially with Hüffer), some of his recent poems: 'Rose Mary',[1] a poem of wings[2] (relative to the starlings at Kelmscott), a sonnet,[3] etc.: also the plan (in prose, with a few stanzas as well) of his proposed poem of 'The Orchard Pit',[4] and of another story[5]—very well invented, I think—of a King who resigns to a friend a peasant-girl they both love, and the final reunion of the King in death with the woman's spirit. Gabriel rather thinks of publishing as a Christmas book his old translation (done perhaps in 1847) of *Der Arme Heinrich*,[6] which he has lately been revising in some details. I think it would be quite reasonable to do so.— As to his poem of 'Rose Mary', the only objection I suggested (or sustained), is that the death of the heroine, after shattering the magic beryl, is not sufficiently accounted for or led up to. To me it seems that the *prima facie* inference from the narrative is that the duration of her life is magically co-extensive with that of the beryl—an incident in which I see no rationale. Gabriel denies that this is intended: the death being in fact consequent on the breaking of the spell, and the convulsion of nature and supernature accompanying that. He does not admit that this more reasonable *motif* is not already adequately indicated: I should not be surprised however if eventually he were to add some touches to make the idea more patent to the reader.

[1] In a letter to W. B. Scott, dated 15 September 1871, D. G. R. called this poem 'The Beryl Stone'. See W. B. Scott, *Autobiographical Notes*, ii. 157. The poem was first published under the name of 'Rose Mary' in 1881. See *Works*, p. 119.

[2] It was called 'Sunset Wings', first published in 1873. See *Works*, p. 220.

[3] Most probably the sonnet 'After the German Subjugation of France'. *Works*, p. 217.

[4] D. G. R. generally called it 'The Orchards Pits'. See *Family Letters*, ii, p. 214. W. M. R. refers to the poem as 'The Orchard Pit'. The prose narrative and the poem were probably composed at Penkill in 1869; the poem was first published in 1886, then in *Ballads and Narrative Poems* in 1893. Both poem and narrative appear in the 1911 edition, p. 239 and p. 607.

[5] (The story entitled 'A Cup of Water'. W. M. R.) See *Works*, p. 615.

[6] (No such publication ensued. W. M. R.) But after D. G. R.'s death the translation was included in the 1886 edition of *The Collected Works of D. G. Rossetti*. It appeared in the second volume under the title 'Henry the Leper by Hartmann von Auë'. It was republished in the 1911 edition, p. 507, with a sub-title: 'Henry the Leper, A Swabian Miracle-Rhyme by Hartmann von Auë (A.D. 1100–1200)'.

Tuesday 31 October   Geo. Tupper seems inclined to take up my idea of a reprint of old reviews:[1] but would not be able to see to such work for the present. I find the same idea had just been occurring to Gabriel.

Wednesday 1 November   Christina received £10 for the little poem, 'A Christmas Carol',[2] which, at Stillman's request, she lately sent to *Scribner's Magazine* (American): this is liberal payment.— Gabriel has not now done any more to his proposed epistle to Buchanan, though he still has some hankering after it. He has some thoughts of exhibiting at the next Royal Academy his picture of the *Death of Beatrice*. Would like all the advances towards that result to come from the Royal Academy and has consequently some idea that it might suit him to invite Stephens[3] to see the picture, so that Stephens may write an account of it in the *Athenaeum*; but Gabriel would not wish this to be done, unless Stephens's article were to be such as Gabriel thinks adequate to the importance of the work. (Stephens had lately written to me, expressing a wish to insert a notice of anything there might be to see at Gabriel's studio). Gabriel says that if at any time he were invited to become a R.A., he would decline, because it would not suit him to take his turn in superintending the students, late in the evening with gas, etc.—nor on the other hand would he like to occupy the post without discharging its ordinary duties.

Thursday 2 November   Dined with the Stillmans. Marie looks very delicate, and to some extent anxious. Met here Miss Thackeray,[4]

---

[1] See the entry for 22 October, p. 117.

[2] Christina Rossetti wrote several poems entitled 'Christmas Carol'. The one mentioned here appears in *The Poetical Works of C. G. R.* (1904), p. 246, with the following note by W. M. R. 'This was first published in *Scribner's Monthly*, January 1872'. Ibid., p. 476.

[3] Frederic George Stephens (1828–1907), art critic. He was one of the original members of the Pre-Raphaelite Brotherhood in 1848, when an art student, but gave up painting. He contributed to *The Germ* and was art critic to the *Athenaeum* from 1861 to 1901. He published a monograph on Dante Gabriel Rossetti, 1894, and was described by W. M. R. as 'the kindliest and most persistent of friends'. See *Reminiscences*, pp. 67–8.

[4] Anne Isabella Thackeray (1837–1919), elder daughter of the novelist, later Lady Ritchie. Her sister, Harriet Marian, was Leslie Stephen's first wife. The rivalry and differences between Dickens's and Thackeray's supporters never flagged, but in 1863, shortly before his death, Thackeray declared it was 'ridiculous' that he and Dickens should be at enmity. They met at the Athenaeum Club, shook hands, and

and saw more of her than I had ever done before (met her some years ago at the Prinseps'). She seems much bound up in her sister's children, and very kindly: speaks in strong terms of reprobation of people who used to tell ill-natured tales of Dickens to Thackeray, and vice versa. Stillman feels that his campaign (in *The Times* etc.) against English publishers, in their relation to authors and American publishers, has set the former class against him, and will trammel his career as a writer for publication here: and I fear this apprehension is too well founded.[1]

Friday 3 November Maria's book is very favourably reviewed in the *Athenaeum*: I think, from the details of the article, there is no doubt of its being written by Dr. Barlow.[2]

Saturday 4 November Going on with the Humorous poetry volume.

Sunday 5 November Dr. Wilson Fox called to see Christina, who has been particularly unwell these two days. He does not seem to consider her state different from what it was before, but has made some modification in the digitalis medicine. He says that the external swelling in her throat (he does not define it by any particular name) is a sort of thing prevalent in some parts of England—as for instance Derbyshire: also that it has nothing to do with the difficulty in swallowing, which is now one of the most troublesome details of Christina's illness. This, he says, depends upon spasmodic nervous action. He says nothing as to the probable duration of the swelling.

Tuesday 7 November John Burroughs,[3] the friend of Whitman, who has been of late in London on a short trip, called on me for

the hostility between them was over. See Gordon N. Ray, *Thackeray, The Age of Wisdom*, London, 1958; pp. 310, 404, and *passim*.

[1] See p. 114 n. 1. An article on the question entitled 'International Copyright' was published in the *Athenaeum* for 9 March 1872, p. 306.

[2] William Hagger Barlow (1833–1908), Cambridge scholar and specialist on Dante. See *R.P.*, p. 86.

[3] John Burroughs (1837–1921) was one of the first American critics to acknowledge Whitman's genius. In 1866 he had written an enthusiastic and sensible article on 'Walt Whitman and his Drum-Taps' (*Galaxy*, December 1866) and in the following year a book which is still of interest: *Notes on Walt Whitman as Poet and Person*, New York, 1867.

the third time. I asked him several details about Whitman. Whitman has two brothers living (another died in the war), and two married sisters: the latter not known to Burroughs. His Mother also is still alive. Whitman lives with his Mother, and with one of his brothers, who is a carpenter: this is the same Brother that was a Colonel in the war. Burroughs has sometimes suggested to Whitman to marry: but Whitman seems to have no particular views in that direction, and Burroughs thinks it likely he may die unmarried. Some American ladies write to him from time to time in an enthusiastic strain: One was a poetess (Miss Beech,[1] I think, the name), and a little poem by Whitman relating to some such cordial recognition of him refers to this lady. Whitman sells perhaps 300 copies of his poems per annum. He has a fine, rich, powerful voice, whether for speaking or singing. Burroughs has sometimes suggested to him to become a Lecturer (more of a recognised vocation in the States than it is here), and Whitman seems not averse from the idea. His present salary is not large, and he would have no claim to a pension were he to leave (he is in the Office of the Attorney General: does copying work, and some précis writing). His official chiefs are not very well affected towards him (Burroughs is in the same office): he might therefore not improbably be leaving at some early date, but would have no difficulty in obtaining some other post of the like kind. Sumner[2] is a great admirer of his—partly influenced thereto by English criticism. Whitman has no inclination to enter into political life. He dresses simply: the chief peculiarity being that he wears the shirt open at the throat: never covers the throat, considering his present plan the healthy one. He always spends a good deal of time in the open air—perhaps five hours a day. Does not, and Burroughs understands never did, pursue any

[1] This certainly refers to an anecdote told by Emery Holloway in the introduction of *Uncollected Poetry and Prose of Walt Whitman* (1921), by Clara Barrus in *The Life and Letters of John Burroughs* (1925) and most definitely refuted by Clifton H. Furness (*American Literature*, January 1942). The story went that Whitman had been in love with a married woman, Mrs. Juliette Beach, and composed for her the poem 'Out of the cradle endlessly rocking'. See R. Asselineau, *L'Evolution de Walt Whitman*, Paris, 1953, p. 190. The story, started by one of Whitman's closest friends, was circulating as early as 1871. It is evident that W. M. R. knew nothing of the facts related by the various biographers or critics after 1921.

[2] Sumner Jones (b. 1818), a brother of the poet. He wrote his brother's obituary notice which appeared in the reprint of Ebenezer Jones's poems *Studies of Sensation and Event*, London, 1879, together with a preface by Richard Herne Shepherd and *Memories*, by W. J. Linton.

hunting, sporting, or athletic occupation of any sort—boating, wrestling, or the like. Is however fond of some amount of muscular activity, and keeps at his office a biggish stone, which he is used to throw up and catch at intervals of official leisure: also sings lustily at such moments. He is passionately fond of the opera: has often composed verses while there. Among his more cherished companions are two or three car-drivers (corresponding, as Burroughs himself observed, to omnibus-drivers): one of these more especially is viewed with predilection by Whitman.— Whitman has read Shelley with pleasure; has no great liking for Milton. He is not unprepared to regard his own works according to a *literary* standard, or to take into consideration such questions as those of rhymed or unrhymed, regular or irregular, metre: but he would take little interest in any work of his own, if it had not some aim and scope apart from executive attributes of this kind. He is at times quite ready to engage in discussions of this sort, and maintains his positions stoutly.—I received a cheque for £7 odd from my Dante translation published several years ago:[1] the first I have seen or heard of that matter for a long while.

Wednesday 8 November   There is a good deal of sickness in the house now. Christina bad as usual, and must moreover go to the dentist tomorrow; Mamma has a troublesome sore-throat and cough, of a bronchitic character; Maria also a somewhat violent cough. My uncle, who is still with us, suffers from various maladies: one of the chief is constriction of the chest and it is feared that the spine is in some way affected.

Thursday 9 and Friday 10 November   Going on with the volume of Humorous Poetry.

Saturday 11 November   Having now bought Southey's Selection from the Later English Poets,[2] I shall have to explore that also before finally settling my Humorous volume.

[1] *The Comedy of Dante Alighieri—The Hell.* Translated into blank verse by W. M. R., London, 1865.

[2] *Specimens of the Later English Poets,* ed. Robert Southey and Grosvenor Bedford, Longmans, London, 1807. Jack Simmons in his *Southey*, London, 1945, p. 113, declares that this is 'the only really unsatisfactory piece of work with which Southey is associated'.

Sunday 12 November   Gabriel tells me that the illness which has for
some months afflicted Andrew Johnson (of the Bank Bullion
Office) has taken a very peculiar and distressing turn as regards
his mental faculties. He cannot at all remember proper names, nor
can he read anything—nor attend to reading very long together.—
In other respects his faculties are much the same as before. The
doctors who attend him say however that his case is curable.—
Swinburne consulted Gabriel lately as to how he had better treat
a very gross attack made upon Swinburne in some novel recently
published by Mortimer Collins,[1] who makes Swinburne (under
the thinnest disguise) one of the personages of the tale. Gabriel
said (and indeed it was the only thing to say) that there is nothing
to be done, under the circumstances.

Monday 13 November   Brown's family and Hughes dined at
Cheyne Walk: Lucy seeming to be pretty well again now, but not
very strong. Hughes says that the illustrating of Christina's book
took up his whole time for a while. At first he worked tolerably
leisurely: but after a certain time Dalziels asked him to furnish
ten designs per week: he furnished twenty the first time.—
Garnett, the Asst. Sec. for Taxes, informs me that he is married
to a lady of the Pilfold family—the same to which Shelley's
mother belonged.[2] He knows the Medwins and Cattys;[3] but, as
far as I gather from his remarks, not the Shelleys. I am not aware
that he is in any way connected with Richard Garnett, who wrote
the *Relics of Shelley*.[4]

Tuesday 14 November   Dr Wilson Fox, who is now (in Sir W.
Jenner's absence) attending Christina, and pursuing the plan of
keeping up the system as much as possible by frequent glasses of
wine, etc. throughout the day (solid food not so much), considers

---

[1] Mortimer Collins (1827–76). The novel is *Two Plunges for a Pearl* which appeared
in *London Society* from January to November 1871, and was published in three
volumes in 1872. The name of the character representing Swinburne is Reginald
Swynfenn. The details of this affair are told by Swinburne to D. G. R. in a letter
dated 10 November 1871. See Swinburne, *Letters*, ii. 167.

[2] Timothy Shelley, the poet's father, married Elizabeth Pilfold of Horsham in 1791.

[3] Sophia Stacey a ward of Shelley's uncle, Robert Parker, who had married a
sister of Timothy Shelley. She met the Shelleys in Florence in 1819 and a pleasant
relationship began. On Christmas Day, 1819, the poet handed her the verses he
addressed to her: 'Thou art fair and few are fairer.' Later, Sophia Stacey married
Captain J. P. Catty. See H. Rossetti Angeli, *Shelley and his Friends in Italy*, and the
Athenaeum, 18 April 1908, for an article by C. S. Catty, Sophia's son.

[4] *Relics of Shelley*, ed. Richard Garnett, London, 1862.

her a little better today. He does not attach any particular importance to Mamma's cough: she however continues suffering from the cough itself, and from considerable depression. Maria pretty well again.

Wednesday 15 November   Stephens having lately addressed Gabriel direct about his picture, Gabriel proposes to write to him in the sense before noted (1 Nov.): he is also writing to Locker to enquire further about Buchanan's alleged authorship of the *Contemporary* article,[1] as a recent letter from Locker to Swinburne reaffirms said authorship—without apparently any cognizance on Locker's part of the denials recently bruited.

Thursday 16 November   Poor Christina continues in a very deplorable state. Besides her two standing maladies, both of which seem for the time to be kept tolerably in abeyance, she has the external lump on the throat, which shows no sign of going, and of late a sort of fluttering at the heart, (*not*, it would seem, regular palpitation of the heart, or other definite heart-disease) which incommodes her, producing a kind of stifling or fainting tendency from time to time, compelling her to desist from any occupation, and lie down. She often passes bad nights, which seldom befall her heretofore. Frequent headaches of a very aggravated kind are another trouble: these she thinks are mitigated by the early tea with brandy which Dr. Fox makes her take. He calls the heart symptoms 'accelerated circulation'. As regards appearance, she is a total wreck for the present, and I greatly fear this change may prove permanent: her hair also comes off in a distressing way, and she expects to have to take to caps almost immediately. I urged her to try some hair-wash, which she proposes doing. With all these disasters—and she is fully alive to every one of them— her spirits are not so bad as might have been expected: she shows

---

[1] The article had appeared in the *Contemporary Review* for October 1871. It was entitled 'The Fleshly School of Poetry', and signed Thomas Maitland. This is how Swinburne describes it in a letter to Frederick Locker, dated 11 November 1871: 'I did see with a sense of nausea the article signed Thomas Maitland in the *Contemporary*, but on hearing that this signature was a mask behind which a pseudonymous poetaster was cowering and making mouths, I found that I was even yet capable of astonishment (as well as disgust) at the baseness of certain professional dogs-of-letters.' Two days later he wrote to D. G. R.: 'I send you a note from Locker guaranteeing as you will see the identity of R. with T.', that is of Robert Buchanan with Thomas Maitland. See Swinburne, *Letters*, ii. 169, 170; also above, p. 115 n. 1.

a really admirable constancy, and the worst shafts of Fate find her their equal. Another of Christina's troubles now is the continual shaking of her hands. This has quite spoiled her handwriting, which is so shaky now that it might be the work of a woman of 75.[1]

Friday 17 November Called on Beeton the publisher, at his request, to talk over some details of the Moxon series of Poets. 1. Humorous volume. He wishes this to contain American as well as English humorous poems: I will therefore transfer from the American to the Humorous volume all appropriate poems, such as those from the *Biglow Papers*,[2] etc. Beeton has an idea that, at any rate in the Volumes of Selections, it will be better not to have any illustrations: I entirely agree, considering the sad pass to which the illustrations to other recent volumes have come, and said indeed that I think *all* future volumes, will be better without them. As to this matter, it seems that Beeton thinks of substituting woodcuts for steel-engravings; also of reissuing in a 5/- form the volumes already published, with larger and better paper, and more skilful *printing* of the illustrations: Byron (if not other volumes) has been already thus treated, and looks well. Beeton asks me to take my own time about the Humorous volume. I suppose it may be ready towards the end of the year.— 2. Cowper.[3] I am to send details as to the edition to be printed from, and then this volume can at an early date be proceeded with. 3. Pope[4] and Thomson.[5] Beeton seems to have paid no attention to—or to have been unaware of—the arrangement made long ago by Moxons, reversing the original proposal of including these two volumes in the series. I shall therefore in due course do what is requisite for these two poets. 4. Beeton has an idea that the Queen is not unlikely to die pretty soon; and that, when that event happens, a volume of selected poems concerning her, issued during the course of her life, would, if launched forthwith upon the public, have a fine chance of success: I conceive he is

[1] Christina was suffering from Graves's disease which often causes general unsteadiness in movements and alters the expression of the face.

[2] *The Biglow Papers*, written by J. R. Lowell in 'Yankee dialect', were published in two series, one in 1848, and the other in 1864–6.

[3] *The Poetical works of William Cowper* ed. W. M. R., London, Moxon, 1872.

[4] *The Poetical works of Alexander Pope* ed. W. M. R., London, Moxon, 1873.

[5] *The Poetical works of James Thomson* ed. W. M. R., London, Moxon, 1873

quite right in this notion as to such a book. He would therefore wish to get the materials all in readiness, and asked me whether I would undertake to make the compilation. I have not the remotest idea of doing so, for such a farrago on such a subject would be the last thing I would dream of connecting myself or my name with. However, not to seem uncivil or sarcastic, I said I would consider the proposal, and write to Beeton as to my decision. It might perhaps be a good piece of work to get into the hands of Geo. Tupper; to whom therefore I think of writing before I send my reply to Beeton: but of course it may be that Beeton would not transfer the commission to Tupper.

Saturday 18 November   Christina's book *Sing-Song* was sent to her to-day. The general publication of it will take place, I understand, within two or three days. It ought to be a great selling success, and even perhaps *may* be. She is to get 10 per cent upon every copy sold: it seems there is no stipulation as to any conjecture at which this arrangement would terminate, and therefore, even if fifty editions were called for, the agreement would be equally binding upon her (I suppose) for the fiftieth as for the first.

Sunday 19 November   Replied to Beeton declining the offer as to a volume of selected poems concerning Queen Victoria. I said that, if he would like, I shall name a person likely to do such a job well; but on reflection I have not felt justified in mentioning the matter beforehand to George Tupper, as Beeton might very likely object to any divulging of the project. Wrote also to Macmillan, to correct the date of Christina's birth (1827, which should be 1830) given in Martin's *Handbook of Contemporary Biography*.

Monday 20 November   Locker writes to Gabriel that, after the notice of Gabriel in the *Contemporary Review* was in print, the editor of the *Review* informed him that Buchanan was the writer: Solomon also writes some details scarcely less positive. After this, it certainly seems difficult to doubt Buchanan's authorship. Solomon shows that Swinburne must have misunderstood him in supposing (as Swinburne wrote to me a little ago) that Solomon had received information disproving the previous assertion made to him, that Buchanan was the writer. However, Gabriel does not now feel any great ardour for completing his proposed pamphlet to Buchanan, though he has not wholly relinquished the idea: I continue of opinion that it were best left undone.

Tuesday 21 November Wrote to George Tupper proposing the Selection about the Queen for him to attend to, Beeton having written in terms which authorize my doing this.

Wednesday 22 November Mamma is still unwell with the cough caused by irritation of the windpipe. Has been confined to her room various days, though not continuously for more than two or three: to-day again she is thus confined, and I fear she ought not to come downstairs for some few days to come. At the same time, the Dr continues to say that it is not a matter of any serious importance. Long fits of coughing, keeping her awake at nights, are the most vexatious symptoms.

Thursday 23 November Going on with work on the Humorous Selection.

Friday 24 November G. Tupper called in Somerset House, and I sent him in the evening a note of introduction to Beeton.— Dr. Fox, having called again to see Mamma, entered into some details regarding Christina's illness. The thing that is essentially the matter with her now is connected with the heart (as previously indicated), though not amounting strictly to heart disease. The swelling outside the throat and other symptoms depend on this same malady. It is a very rare one: so rare that Dr. Fox has seen only two cases of it (one of which he treated successfully), and Sir W. Jenner, as I understood, had also only seen two cases. Sir William has concurred in the treatment of Christina as conducted as yet by Dr. Fox. Locker called at Somerset House, and gave me some details bearing on Buchanan and the *Contemporary Review*. He says that Tennyson censures the spirit in which the article on Gabriel was written (though mainly in Tennyson's own interest), and speaks of some of Gabriel's sonnets as the finest in the language. If this is literally true, the praise is high indeed, coming from Tennyson, as I know him of old to be a most intense admirer of Shakespeare's sonnets. I remember he told me many years ago (1858, at Freshwater) that he had at one time maintained Shakespeare's sonnets to be greater than his dramas—but of course he had then long ago receded from this *fanatical* phase of admiration. My uncle returned to-day to Gloucester.

Saturday 25 November Dalziels sent Christina £25, being an anticipative payment of her percentage on the sale of the first 1000 of *Sing-Song*. Maria's book is handsomely reviewed generally, and has so far attained a success: as to sale, we don't know as yet. —Sir W. Jenner (just back from Balmoral) visited Christina, and gave minute attention to her case. He confirms what Dr. Fox said about the complaint, and adds that there is a change in the colour of the skin pigment: this indeed is sufficiently evident, though I had not noticed it as going beyond what might be ascribed to Christina's extreme thinness now, and depressed condition of health. Jenner clearly regards the case as a serious one, and says Christina ought not to go up and down stairs, in the present state of her heart, but should be confined to one floor. She has for this fortnight or more been sleeping in the same room with Mamma, the back drawing-room. She will now therefore restrict herself to the back and front drawing-rooms, and we shall regularly dine, and probably take tea in the latter. Just at present she is pestered with a bad tooth (Sir W. J. doesn't allow her to take decisive measures with it), and something of an ear-ache, and a recurrence (not very bad as yet) of the gathering in the nose.

Sunday 26 November Authorized Miss (or Mrs?) Biggs,[1] at her request, to put me down on a newly-formed London Committee for Female suffrage. Told Ricciardi that I would probably at some time, but not now, review a book of his he has just sent me, about S. Marino:[2] I must confess I would much rather not have been asked to do this: but Ricciardi seems to think one is bound to do something in connexion with every book he issues, and, when he asks me, I can hardly do other than submit.

Monday 27 November Stephens announces to me his mother's death. She must have been, I think, little if at all less than 80 years of age.

[1] Miss Biggs worked with Mrs. Taylor on the Committee for Women's Suffrage.
[2] *La Repubblica di San Marino e l'Italia*, Studio storico-critico, Napoli, 1871.

Tuesday 28 November   Wrote declining an invitation which has come to me (partly through Aldam Heaton)[1] to lecture on Art at Bradford, with prospect of repeating the lectures at Halifax. I feel no incitement towards lecturing, and the frequent absences from Somerset House would be inconvenient—if not next to impracticable. Mentioned Scott, Stillman, and J. Tupper, as suitable persons to be addressed for the same purpose.

Wednesday 29 November   To-day Mamma got out (in a cab) for the first time since her cough came on: she passed a good night, and may perhaps be near convalescence. Gabriel has seen a letter written by Knowles, Editor of the *Contemporary Review*,[2] saying point-blank that the article on Gabriel is by Buchanan: so this matter is finally set at rest. The letter raises some objections to the article, and favours the idea of a counter-article to be inserted in the *Contemporary*; a bungling and sneaking sort of compromise. Gabriel has now finished his letter to Buchanan, and has had it partly printed; but considers on the whole he had better withhold it. This view I have upheld from the first: though I confess, on hearing the thing as a whole (especially the more serious part, which replies to the substance of the objections raised by Buchanan), I think the letter such a successful performance that its suppression will be in some measure a pity after all. Ellis doubts whether it would not be open to a charge of libel: to me this seems scarcely possible. Gabriel troubled me not a little by telling me that he spat blood to-day; and this not for the first time, as the same thing had occurred while he was staying at Kelmscott. He feels also a sort of chilliness in the chest, and bobbing of the heart. I can scarcely think that (contrary to all appearances hitherto) there is anything of a consumptive tendency about him: at the same time I urged him to lose no time in consulting a Doctor. But for this, his health has of late seemed to be very reasonably fair—much better than two or three years ago.— Simcox,[3] who writes in the *Academy*, had proposed to Gabriel

[1] John Aldam Heaton was a manufacturer in Yorkshire, later a decorative artist in London. In 1861 D. G. R. had painted a portrait of Mrs. Heaton with the title *Regina Cordium*. See *Family Letters*, p. 169; *Memoir*, p. 401, and Surtees, no. 323, p. 166.

[2] James Knowles (1831–1908), editor of the *Contemporary Review* from 1870 to 1877 when he founded the *Nineteenth Century*. 'Signed writing' was his main editorial principle.

[3] The review, signed G. A. Simcox (1841–1905), poet, critic, scholar, librarian

an amusing form of retaliation on Buchanan; i.e. Simcox is to review in the *Academy* Buchanan's new poem, *Drama of Kings*, and he thought of signing his review, 'Thos. Maitland', the pseudonym adopted by Buchanan himself: of course the review would be not highly complimentary. This would have been fair enough, I think, as turning the tables on Buchanan: but it properly occurred to Gabriel that Gabriel himself would be suspected as the real author of such a review, and it would not be possible to clear himself by breaking confidence with Simcox. He has therefore dissuaded the latter from carrying out his idea.

Thursday 30 November There seems to be some *little* improvement now in Christina's health, and perhaps even in her appearance also. It would appear at any rate that Doctor Jenner's order restricting her to living on one floor of the house was judicious, and conducive to her comfort.

Friday 1 December Lucy Brown having called, I mentioned to her about the Bradford lecturing proposal; and, she having then named the matter to her father, he looked round later, and said he would be somewhat disposed to undertake the work himself. He thinks it might suit his interests to come forward in connexion with art, in some fresh position, and that this would furnish an opening. I, of course, am only too glad to second any such scheme: therefore wrote again to Miss Lambert mentioning Brown, and saying that I consider him so desirable a man to secure for the purpose that I might, had I then known of his inclination, have mentioned him *alone* in the first instance. Maria hears that Rivington is about to print a second 500 of her book on Dante. This looks as if the sale were prosperous—decidedly more so in fact than could have been anticipated as likely: it seems also that a republication in America is projected, and Rivington proposes to look closer into this. Macmillan sent Christina £4 odd, accruing from sales of *The Prince's Progress*: only 25 copies of that book are now in stock, but 250 (I think) of *Goblin Market*, second edition.

of Queen's College, Oxford, appeared in the *Academy* for 1 January 1872. It was indeed not 'highly complimentary'. The writer summing up the poetical career of Buchanan wrote: 'some rejoiced that the coster-mongers had found their Wordsworth'. He continued: 'The volume is three times too long for its ideas', and concluded: 'The main faults are incurable.'

Saturday 2 December   There is a paragraph in the *Athenaeum*[1] saying that Colvin will answer Buchanan's article (they name him as the author) in the *Contemporary*. This seems a bungling way of putting the thing; and Gabriel tells me that Colvin is not at all obliged to the writer of the paragraph. Gabriel has had the offer of a young penguin to buy—very tame and apparently very amusing: price £10 or thereabouts. Gabriel is not prepared to pay all this; but I have offered to go shares with him to the extent of £3, and probably some bargain may be struck. I greatly fear, however, that the penguin, living in so unnatural a condition, will die almost as soon as bought.

Sunday 3 December   Furnivall has asked me to undertake some more Chaucer work—Collation etc. of the *Clerk's Tale*. I am not at present prepared to engage for this. Wrote him to say so—adding that, if he makes no other arrangement meanwhile, I might renew the subject towards the beginning of March, and say yes or no.

Monday 4 December   Scott called. The Bradford people applied to him to deliver the proposed lectures: but he declined, being much engaged on etchings for the Bible, and other work. He at the same time suggested, a man who is my aversion, Beavington Atkinson:[2] however, my letter about Brown must have reached before Scott's letter about Atkinson, so I hope nothing will have occurred to thwart Brown's views. The latter has not yet heard from the Bradford people, and indeed I think there has not yet been time to admit of his hearing. As he and Hüffer came round whilst Scott was with me, much discussion ensued as to the proper way to set about lecturing. Scott is strongly in favour of thorough getting up of the lecture, and complete writing of it, and then reading it to the audience: Hüffer (who also has had some experience) says the first lecture ought, under any circumstances, to be written, but, if the lecturer then finds himself unembarrassed and fluent, he should try to trust increasingly

---

[1] Sidney Colvin's answer to Buchanan's article in the *Contemporary Review* was announced in the *Athenaeum* for 2 December 1871, p. 724.

[2] Beavington Atkinson was an art critic; he contributed articles to *Fraser's Magazine*, the *Saturday Review*, the *Portfolio*, and the *Art Journal*. In 1873 he published *An Art Tour to Northern Capitals of Europe*, and in 1874 *Studies among the Painters*. See *Blackwood's Magazine*, March 1883, pp. 393–411.

afterwards to extempore speaking: Brown wants to speak extempore, having only such notes or jottings as will serve to remind him of his topics (with accurate particulars of names, dates etc., at which he is notoriously bad), and of the order in which they should be treated. I think myself that this is what he, with his special personal adaptabilities, should *aim at*; but whether he is up to carrying out the scheme must remain for experience to test.—Scott gets £40 for each Bible-etching (from some Scotch publishing firm). He has done the book on sculpture[1] which Virtues (on Gabriel's suggestion), asked him to undertake, and is to have £52.10.0 for it. His *Half-hour Lectures on Art*[2] continue to improve in sale as the years go by: the last annual payment that he received, £39 odd, is the largest of all.

Tuesday 5 December Dined at Cheyne Walk, with the Browns, Hake and his son, and several others. Marston has seen various phenomena in spiritualism, and is satisfied of the genuineness of some of them; but, as far as I gather, has no very distinct opinion as to whether the agency of spirits is really concerned in them or not. Hake thinks of establishing his sons at Brindisi to avail themselves of the probable great openings which that port presents for commercial enterprise etc.; and he himself might pass this coming winter there, or in some other part of Italy. Gabriel read his poem of *Rose Mary*—and afterwards, to a diminished audience, his pamphlet in answer to Buchanan. The penguin has been sold to some one else—surmised to be the Zoological Society at Antwerp. Saw for the first time one of the armadilloes. The deer that Gabriel used to have (now dead) one day saw the peacock making a great display of his train. The deer followed him about; and, though not displaying any peculiarly marked ill-will, systematically trampled out all his train-feathers, one after the other. Shortly after this, Gabriel gave the peacock away.

Wednesday 6 December Christina is considered to have decidedly gained *somewhat* in health and strength since she took to living entirely on the first floor: Dr. Fox, who called again to-day, confirms this. The choking sensation in her throat, however (said to

[1] W. B. Scott, *The British School of Sculpture*, London, 1872.

[2] Idem, *Half-hour Lectures on the History and Practice of the Fine and Ornamental Arts*, 50 illustrations by the author, engraved by W. J. Linton, London, 1861. There was a second edition in 1866 and a third in 1874.

arise entirely from nervous contraction, and not from any internal lump), threatens to cause trouble from time to time. She nearly choked to-day at dinner, while swallowing some potato; and seemed, at the moment and afterwards, more scared and upset than I think I ever before saw her at any moment of pain or distress.

Thursday 7 December Looked into a concluding volume of Ferrazzi's *Manuale Dantesco*, which he sent me yesterday. I see he has inserted particulars regarding English translators of Dante etc. etc., being the substance of what I wrote him at his request 3 or 4 years ago. There are various inaccuracies of detail, however.

Friday 8 December Very bad news to-day as to the Prince of Wales's health:[1] indeed the universal impression appears to be that to-morrow morning's papers will announce his death. It is interesting to note the sort of family feeling with which the event is regarded. The newspaper-woman at the corner of Wellington Street, from whom I bought a *Standard* going home, spoke of the Prince as 'poor dear'. G. Tupper writes me that he has arranged with Beeton as to making a beginning with the proposed Victorian Selection.

Saturday 9 December Received a confidential letter from Aldam Heaton about the proposal of Madox Brown as a lecturer.

Sunday 10 December Answered this letter, saying that I consider Brown likely to make a very interesting lecturer, the best of all who have been proposed (not taking Scott into account), so far as the value of his lectures to serious persons who understand the subject would be concerned: in other respects, experience would show how the facts stand. Mentioned also Cave Thomas,[2] and gave my opinion as to Atkinson, proposed by Scott, and

[1] The Prince of Wales (1841–1910), afterwards King Edward VII, was seriously ill with typhoid fever.

[2] William Cave Thomas (b. 1821) was a friend of Madox Brown. The Rossettis met him for the first time in Brown's studio in 1848. He exhibited several times at the Royal Academy. See *Reminiscences*, p. 138.

Scharf[1] and Burges[2] and Stephens, whose names are started by Heaton himself.

Monday 11 December   Swinburne came round to me with Brown; the latter having just found for Swinburne a lodging in some hotel close by me. I am rather afraid this vicinity, combined with Swinburne's unruly habits, will entail some inconveniences upon me at no distant date: for the present evening, Swinburne, though not absolutely unaffected by liquor, was well enough, and perfectly pleasant in demeanour. He complimented Maria very warmly on her book upon Dante, and is (as a letter of his had shown us some days ago)[3] most enthusiastic about Christina's book.[4] Has some idea of making and publishing a collection of lyrical poems by various authors: as he expressed some hesitation as to this, on the ground that it might interfere with *my* Selections, I strongly urged him to persevere. Indeed I don't consider the books would clash to any serious extent.

Tuesday 12 December   Moxons ask me to settle the text of the Cowper volume,[5] in preference to any other work on the series of Poets. I therefore began looking into this matter. I should like to include the translations from the *Iliad* and *Odyssey*, but suppose they would make the book too bulky. Must leave Moxons to decide as to this.

Wednesday 13 December   Wrote to Moxons on this subject.— Mamma has now got fairly rid of her cough, but is troubled with a cold, and at times considerable depression of strength and energy. Dr. Fox called to-day, and advised her to stay in bed, to the extent at any rate of breakfasting there for some few days— which indeed has been my advice often renewed.

[1] George Scharf (1820–95), painter. He illustrated Macaulay's *Lays of Ancient Rome*. He was appointed Secretary and later Director of the National Portrait Gallery.

[2] William Burges (1827–81), architect and designer. He designed Cork Cathedral (1862); his work shows a Pre-Raphaelite fondness for detail.

[3] Swinburne's letter mentioned here does not appear in the Lang edition of Swinburne's correspondence.

[4] After many hesitations and delays, Christina's 'Nursery Rhymes' were published by Routledge in November 1871 with the title *Sing-Song*; it was illustrated by Arthur Hughes. See pp. 116, 129 above.

[5] *The Poetical Works of William Cowper*, edited with a Critical Memoir, by W. M. R., illustrated by Thomas Seccombe, London, Moxon, 1872.

Thursday 14 December   Stillman called. His wife's sister, Christine, is again very ill (a cataleptic habit); and this and other matters weigh heavy upon poor Marie, making her very miserable at times: her cough also persistent and severe. Mr. Spartali, it seems, has under these afflicting circumstances written to Christine, and that quarrel may be considered in course of healing: I should hope that the quarrel with Marie, much less well-grounded in its essence, may also be healed at no very distant date.—Dr. Fox saw Christina again to-day and pronounces her progressively and even considerably improving. To-day indeed—for the first time to any serious extent—she strikes me as looking decidedly not quite so miserable in the face. There seems some little diminuation [*sic*] of the thinness, starting eyes, etc.

Friday 15 December   Going on with work on the Humorous Selection.

Saturday 16 December   The *Athenaeum* of to-day contains a communication from Gabriel, being the more serious portion of the rejoinder which he had written to Buchanan.[1] It also contains a glaringly untruthful letter on the subject from Strahan,[2] the publisher of the *Contemporary*, and another from Buchanan,[3] avowing the authorship of the article, and saying he means to republish it in a separate form.

Sunday 17 December   Gabriel tells me that, on Buchanan's making

[1] D. G. R.'s communication to the *Athenaeum* is a long letter entitled 'The Stealthy School of Criticism' in which he refutes Buchanan's accusation of 'extolling fleshliness as the distinct and supreme end of poetic and pictorial art' by quoting from 'The House of Life', the 'Last Confession', and 'Jenny', poems in which 'all the passionate and just delights of the body are declared to be as naught if not ennobled by the concurrence of the soul at all times'. This was only an extract from a longer reply which was withheld as the publisher was advised that it might entail an action for libel. The *Athenaeum*, 16 December 1871, pp. 792–4.

[2] Strahan writes in the same issue of the *Athenaeum*, p. 794: 'In your last issue you associate the name of Mr. Robert Buchanan with the article "The Fleshly School of Poetry", by Thomas Maitland, in a recent number of the *Contemporary Review*. You might with equal propriety associate with the article the name of Mr. Robert Browning, or of Mr. Robert Lytton, or of any other Robert.'

[3] On the same page, Buchanan declares: 'I cannot reply to the insolence of Mr. "Sidney Colvin", whoever he is . . . I certainly wrote the article on "The Fleshly School of Poetry", but I had nothing to do with the signature. Mr. Strahan . . . can corroborate me thus far, as he is best aware of the inadvertence which led to the suppression of my own name.'

the above-named re-issue, Gabriel will probably forthwith issue the whole of his pamphlet as it originally stood (and this, I think, will be reasonable enough), with any slight addition which Buchanan's re-issue may demand. He has meanwhile asked Ellis the publisher to consult his Solicitor, as to the question (heretofore raised) whether anything in Gabriel's pamphlet would be liable to action for libel.—I settled the text of the Cowper volume, and wrote about it to the printers, Messrs Sanson.

Monday 18 December   Aldam Heaton writes me that the Bradford people have not availed themselves of Brown's offer to lecture, but have applied to Mr. St. John Tyrwhitt[1]—a gentleman regarding whom my notion is very vague. I fear Brown will be a little annoyed at this upshot of the matter—more especially as it seems Tyrwhitt is in some way under the wing of Ruskin, to whose position as an authority in art-matters Brown supremely objects.

Tuesday 19 December   Called on Brown, and explained this matter to him. He doesn't seem ruffled; but shows also no disposition to send in any notification (as Heaton had proposed) of his readiness to deliver lectures, available at some future opportunity.

Wednesday 20 December   I am now just at the end of the writing of notices etc. for the Humorous Selection; leaving nothing to be done beyond writing some few pages of general introduction, with index etc.—Gabriel urges that Christina, with Mamma, should occupy the house at Kelmscott for a while, and no doubt this might be beneficial to Christina's health in some respects. The country gets flooded in the damp season, but Gabriel says that the house itself is not damp.

Thursday 21 December   Sir W. Jenner, just back from attending the Prince of Wales, called and considered Christina to be sensibly better. He does not however countenance any going out of doors for any purpose.

Friday 23 December   Finished the Preface to my Humorous Selection.—Jack Tupper writes me that he is about to marry Miss

[1] Richard St. John Tyrwhitt (1827–95), art theorist and painter. Some of his paintings were exhibited at the Royal Academy. Ruskin wrote a preface to Tyrwhitt's book on *Christian Art and Symbolism*, reviewed by S. Colvin in the *Fortnightly Review* 1 July 1872.

Annie French, one of his pupils near Rugby (whom probably I saw in 1869, though I do not remember with any distinctness). Tupper's age must be 46 or 47, I think.

Saturday 23 and Sunday 24 Dec. lead up to *Monday 25 December* Christmas day. Dispatched a letter to Beeton, telling him that the Humorous Selection, and the books out of which it is compiled (no less than 64 volumes) are now at his disposal whenever he likes to send for them; also the American Selection, which however he will no doubt leave over for a while. I began looking up some dates for the Miscellaneous Selection (last three Centuries), prior to putting in final order the materials that I have collected for that— as these also seem to be completed, allowing for any little extras that may drop in *passim*. Gabriel tells me he has placed at Colvin's disposal, for publication if he likes in the *Pall Mall* or elsewhere, his burlesque verses about Buchanan—*The Brothers*[1]—being a parody of Tennyson's *Sisters*. The verses are a very good hit, but I am sorry on the whole that they are offered for publication : should rather infer however that they will not pass the editorial ordeal.

Tuesday 26 December   Began writing the notices of poets etc. for the Miscellaneous Selection. Swinburne called, and showed interest at some of my compiling work, more especially for the Humorous Selection. He is now lodging close by me, 12 Upper Woburn Place.

Wednesday 27 December   Stillman called at Somerset House. He says his wife's sister is now better. His own youngest child, Bella,[2] has had some symptoms of brain-disease lately, which of course adds to his anxieties.

Thursday 28 December   Going on with the notices for the Miscellaneous Selection.

Friday 29 December   D°.

[1] *The Brothers* was written in 1871; first published in 1911 in *Works*, p. 273.
[2] Bella Stillman was the youngest child of Stillman by his first wife. She married John Henry Middleton (1846–96) who became Art Director at the Victoria and Albert Museum.

Saturday 30 December Brown and Hüffer called on me.—Hüffer does not think Gabriel's letter in the *Athenaeum* about his poems (replying to Buchanan) very successful (to me it appears quite so, though I should still have preferred if Gabriel had held aloof from all publishing in the matter): indeed, Hüffer thinks that Gabriel's prose is never quite satisfactory, and that he should write little or nothing save poetry. Hüffer has a project of purchasing half the proprietorship of the *Fortnightly Review*, for £1500: he has already started the subject with the publisher Chapman.[1] Hüffer would thus become part proprietor, and also editor. Chapman seems quite willing to entertain the proposal; but wants first to ascertain how the present editor, Morley,[2] would feel about it. It seems that Morley receives £600 a year as editor. Besides this, Chapman hands him £100 per month, out of which Morley satisfies the contributors, at the rate (mainly) of 10/- per page: if this payment does not exhaust the £100, Morley retains the balance, in his own character of contributor. This seems handsome remuneration. Chapman says that the *Fortnightly* fully pays its expenses: I suppose it does not do much *more* than that. Brown tells me that Scott has lately had a little unpleasantness with Appleton, editor of the *Academy*—in which paper Scott acts as art-editor and writer: Appleton having asked Scott to resign for this year to Robinson[3] the reviewing of the Old Masters at Burlington House. Scott, it appears, resents this (he himself liking this particular work better than what else falls to his share); but is not inclined to refuse.[4]

[1] Frederic Chapman (1823–95), publisher, became the head of the firm Chapman and Hall after 1864, and started the publication of the *Fortnightly Review* in 1865.

[2] John Morley (1838–1923), politician and literary critic, the editor of the *Fortnightly Review* from 1867 to 1882. He was also editor of the *English Men of Letters* series. He had started the campaign against Swinburne's *Poems and Ballads* by his articles in the *Saturday Review* for 4 August and 17 November 1866. He denounced 'the feverish carnality of the schoolboy over the dirtiest passages in Lemprière'. G. Lafourcade adds: 'It was to a great extent Morley who created the immorality of *Poems and Ballads* by pointing to relevant passages in the lexicon.' See *Swinburne*, London, 1932, p. 137.

[3] George T. Robinson, architect and art critic, became a friend of W. M. R. after 1876. He made a water-colour drawing of D. G. R.'s drawing-room in Cheyne Walk, which is now in the possession of Mrs. Imogen Dennis.

[4] Despite this assertion, an article entitled 'Exhibition of pictures in water-colours at the Dudley Gallery' and signed by W. B. Scott appeared in the *Academy* for 15 February 1872.

Sunday 31 December   Called on Brown, to see his recent pictures. Water-colour of *Sardanapalus*[1] (the composition engraved in Moxon's *Byron*): fine in many respects (especially the flesh-painting of Sardanapalus), but I fear Myrrha, more particularly her arms, is not very well drawn, and the effect somewhat too open and uniform for lamplight. The water-colour of *Don Juan cast ashore*[2] I had seen, but perhaps never by daylight. He has begun the same subject on a large scale as an oil-picture. Lucy has nearly finished her water colour of *Surrey and Geraldine*: very good indeed in several respects, and as a whole greatly more satisfactory than I had (from what Gabriel had told me) expected to find it. There is something harsh and startling in the way Geraldine shows in the Magic Mirror—very large, and the effect of open air background, etc. unsubdued: yet after all this may be the best—as it is certainly the most unmistakeable—way of expressing the fact pictorially. Cathie's portrait—subject of Mrs. Tadema[3]—is also nearly finished: a pretty little dog was sitting to her for its likeness in this work. Mellow fine colour, and otherwise very successful. Nolly's picture, water-colour, from *Silas Marner*—the Miser with the baby finding the mother dead in the snow—realizes its subject very expressively and tellingly, and is good in style: in details of execution—texture, object-painting, etc.—both the girls seem to excel Nolly: perhaps this is only in proportion to his fewer years.[4]

[1] There are three versions of the subject: the water-colour mentioned here; a large *Sardanapalus* painted in 1874 and another large one begun in 1873 and finished in 1891: *Sardanapalus' Dream*. See F. M. Hueffer, *Ford Madox Brown*, p. 255, and *passim*.

[2] The full title of the picture was *The Finding of Don Juan by Haïdee*. It was first executed as a design to illustrate Moxon's edition of Byron's *Poems*, then as a water-colour commissioned by Craven and later as a large oil-painting which was finished in 1873 and is now in the Birmingham Art Gallery. See F. M. Hueffer, op. cit., *passim*.

[3] The wife of the artist. See p. 45 n. 7.

[4] See p. 10 n. 6.

Monday 1 January   A nasty little affair seems beginning to-day. Keeping as I always do some change in a pocket of my great-coat which hangs up at home in the passage, accessible to all servants and others, I had in it yesterday a six pence which happened to get incrusted with mud yesterday. This morning the coin is gone. I cannot suspect any one of the three servants in the house: there are at present two charwomen besides, Mrs. Stephens and Mrs. Pride; also George Catchpole (whom again I would not willingly suspect) is continually in and out. Late at night, after everyone is in bed, I count the money now in the pocket, and find it 8/–.

Tuesday 2 January   This morning the money is only 7/–. I mentioned the matter to Mamma, and she to Betsy; and, as it turns out that Mrs. Pride was not in the house between Monday evening and Tuesday morning, there is no doubt strong reason to suppose Mrs. Stephens is in fault.

Wednesday 3 January   It now appears that the statement made to me, that Mrs. Pride was not in the house, was incorrect: She *was* in as well as Mrs. Stephens. This morning however there is nothing further amiss. Miss Holmes, with Miss Wynn Jones, called in the evening to take tea with my sisters. Miss Holmes being sister of the Holmes[1] whom I knew at the British Museum, and who is now Librarian at Windsor Castle. He likes his post there, and the royal family. Gives some instruction in drawing to the children of the Prince of Wales, and likes the eldest boy[2] particularly, as intelligent and agreeable—more so than his

[1] Sir Richard Rivington Holmes (1835–1911) was Assistant Keeper at the British Museum from 1854 until he became the Librarian of Windsor Castle. He tried his hand at water-colours, and designed stained glass and bookbindings. It is supposedly his head which appears in Rossetti's 1859 water-colour *Writing on the Sand*. See Surtees no. 111, p. 67.

[2] Prince Albert Victor, Duke of Clarence (1864–92).

younger brother.[1]—Maria was talking the other day to her surgical friend Mr Curgenvan about Christina's illness. He says that he quite understands what it is, from the various statements he has heard about it. It is the malady called Dr. Graves's disease, or exophthalmic bronchocele—very rare. A Dr. Cheadle has treated some cases successfully. The disease is (as we had been previously told) in the circulation of the blood: some congestion hence arising causes the swelling at the throat—which is not (as Dr. Fox had intimated) the same sort of thing that is prevalent in parts of Derbyshire: this latter being caused by the quality of the water. Mr. Curgenvan agrees in saying that going up and down stairs would be most noxious to Christina.

Thursday 4 January   Called at 12, Upper Woburn Place (which is a handsome house, apparently quite equal to those in Euston Square, of which indeed it forms a corner) to see Swinburne. I find he has been out of these lodgings for two or three days past. Saw the landlady, a well-bred person; and found, as I expected, that Swinburne had relapsed into his horrible drinking-habits, and had caused so much trouble in the house that he had to leave. This lady and another younger one who was in the sitting-room with her, had evidently no small liking and regard for Swinburne, but had found him impossible as a lodger. It seems he is now with (or *probably* with) Powell—whose acquaintance has, if what I fear is correct, been a very disastrous thing for Swinburne, confirming him in the drinking-habits he was already too prone to. The landlady says that a Dr. Duncan (88 Gower Street) was in attendance on Swinburne, and got him to give his word of honour that he would drink no more spirits. This was only two or three days ago. Swinburne has now implored the Dr. to release him from his promise, but the Dr. refuses. So much the better—though I am afraid not even such an obligation as this would or could prove a safeguard for long.

Friday 5 January   Gabriel tells me that just before Swinburne left Upper Woburn Place, Brown found him there in bed in the back kitchen, with all the house bells just above his bed, and con-stantly on the ring. Apparently he had been transferred to this

---

[1] Prince George, afterwards King George V (1865–1936).

ineligible site by the people of the house, on some occasion of his being incapable of taking care of himself.

Saturday 6 January Dined with Scott: Mrs. Bodichon the only guest besides myself. Scott showed me some of his recent etchings to the Bible, also interesting water-colour of the *Birth of Burns*. He has presented to Mrs. Bodichon (as a gift, I understand) the cartoon drawings for his various painted windows in S. Kensington:[1] Mrs. Bodichon means to bring these into use; at once for decoration and instruction—in the Ladies' College[2] which she and others have founded—I believe, in Cambridge. Scott is going to write for Virtues a book about Spanish Art.[3]

Sunday 7 January Spent the day with Trelawny, at his invitation; arrived at 2, and remained till 11, Trelawny keeping up, without ever flagging, a conversation about Shelley, Byron, and several other matters: he told me a number of interesting details. He must now be seventy-nine, I think, (if not even eighty): he thinks Mrs. Hogg[4] is much the same age. I started the question whether she was ever really married to Hogg (as I have been told not): his answer appeared to me to be a negative, but I think he was disposed to give the question the go-by. Her two children by Williams, and daughter by Hogg, are all commonplace uninteresting persons. Williams's son was in some Government-office, and retired not long ago on a pension. His daughter married a son

[1] W. B. Scott's stained-glass windows were in the Ceramic Gallery of the South Kensington Museum. They disappeared during the Second World War. The gallery has now been entirely altered and redecorated. Scott's designs for the windows ('cartoons drawings') are now in the Print-Room of the Victoria and Albert Museum: two coloured designs executed in 1867, one in 1868, and sixteen others in 1870, illustrating the history of earthenware and porcelain.

[2] Girton College.

[3] W. B. Scott, *Murillo and the Spanish School of Painting. Fifteen engravings on steel and nineteen on wood. With an account of the School, and its great Masters*, London and New York, 1873.

[4] Mrs. Hogg was 'the Jane Williams to whom Shelley had addressed some of the latest and not the least graceful of his poems'. See *Reminiscences*, ii. 337. After the tragedy of the 'Don Juan', in which Williams had been drowned, his widow Jane Williams was introduced to Hogg by Mary Shelley; they soon fell in love, but it was only in 1827 that they decided to live together. In a letter to R. Garnett, dated 2 June 1878, W. M. R. wrote that, after having consulted Hogg's letters, he came to the conclusion that the lady could not have married either Hogg or Williams, as she still had a first husband living—who had deserted her—at St. Helena. See *Letters about Shelley*, p. 62.

of Leigh Hunt, the husband being, according to Trelawny, a bad lot, who infected his wife with venereal complaints more than once. Trelawny showed me a bit of Shelley's jawbone which he snatched from the funeral pyre: charred white, with the teeth-sockets showing; his features were almost gone when the burning took place. I described to Trelawny the spot shown to me last Summer at Via Reggio as being the site of the cremation: he thinks my information must have been inaccurate, the true spot being farther away from the town, and only 'seven yards' from the sea. Miss Clairmont continues corresponding with him: there is an idea of her forwarding her reminiscences for publication. Trelawny says he would perhaps offer £50 for them, and I expressed a strong opinion that he or a publisher would far more than cover this outlay by the actual publication. He has himself also written down some anecdotes and reminiscences, which I read: valuable and interesting, but possibly (I fancy) a little dressed up in some details—mostly what he had before told me. Trelawny's spelling is singularly faulty for a man of so many literary associations: this struck me the more in connection with the points of a like kind so much debated in the Tichborne trial[1]—though Trelawny does not make any such utterly *vulgar* blunder as 'i ham' etc. Trelawny feels perfectly certain the claimant is the real Tichborne.—He wrote down on Byron's coffin a number of details of Byron's last hours given him by Fletcher:[2] these have never been published,[3] nor did Fletcher so freely relate the real facts to members of the Byron family. Byron had a habit of keeping by his bedside a Bible[4] and two pistols. Near his end, he made some remark, in a spirit of resignation, to Fletcher: who being of a 'canting' turn (according to Trelawny), availed himself

[1] Roger Charles Doughty Tichborne (1829–54) was lost at sea; his mother, Lady Tichborne, could not be convinced of his death and advertised for him. An impostor, Arthur Orton (1834–98), the son of a butcher, presented himself in 1868 and claimed the heritage. The other relatives stood against such a claim and the case was brought before the Court of Common Pleas on 11 May 1871. The trial lasted for months and was one of the great events of the time. Orton lost the case and, in a subsequent trial, was condemned to fourteen years' penal servitude.

[2] Fletcher was Byron's 'trusty servant'. After Byron's death he returned to England, visited Lady Byron and told her that her husband's last intelligible words were: 'My wife! My child! My sister!'

[3] (The narrative appears in Trelawny's *Records of Shelley, Byron and the Author*, W. M. R.)

[4] The Bible by his bedside had been given to him by his half-sister the Hon. Augusta Leigh.

of the opportunity to open the Bible, and began reading from it to Byron; but Byron stopped him, saying: 'Shut it up—that is all weakness, weakness, weakness'—striking his hand hard on his forehead.—Byron had no palate: Trelawny could mix his gin and water as weak as he chose without Byron's taking any notice of it whatever, and once purposely missed out the gin altogether, and Byron seemed struck by it only after several sips. Byron's left leg and foot were much worse than the right. The toes of both feet were perfectly well formed, and Byron used to wear linen pantaloons with straps in bathing. (Trelawny says this is quite common, especially with seafaring people.) Hence it is that, although Trelawny had often seen Byron bathing, he did not accurately understand the condition of his legs and feet till he examined Byron's corpse: this is a point that has struck several people (myself included) as not accounted for in Trelawny's book. Trelawny considers that Shelley would have joined him and Byron in the Grecian expedition, had he survived, but would not have made a good soldier. Neither did Byron show the least faculty that way, or as a political leader (Moore[1] gives a contrary idea). Had Byron survived, a movement would have been started to make him King of Greece, and Trelawny thinks the thing would have been achieved. Trelawny's notes of conversations with Byron in the Grecian expedition disappeared: he suspects Emerson Tennent (who went out there as reporter to the *Chronicle*) of having filched them. Shelley was utterly fearless in every way—standing on the edge of precipices, etc. Trelawny thinks also he had no sensation of horror as connected with the idea of death—only ideal feelings in relation to it, and mostly even aspirations towards it. I did not care to discuss the point minutely, but myself consider there is ample evidence in Shelley's poems of a very intense horror and shrinking from whatsoever has a disgustful physical aspect in death.

Monday 8 January　I learn that Stillman called in Euston Square yesterday. His wife has just been confined of a girl, after rather a difficult labour: she wished for a boy. Before the event happened, her father had sent her a message of 'forgiveness': it is not even

[1] See p. 254 n. 4.
[2] Sir James Emerson Tennent (1804–69), traveller, politician and author. He visited Greece in 1824.

yet clear however that he will be on affectionate terms with her henceforward—still less with Stillman.

Tuesday 9 January   Dined with Stillman: his wife is now going on well, but it is questioned whether she will be able to rear the baby[1] herself—though both she and Stillman are very reluctant to hand it over to a wet nurse. Stillman entertains strong views of the influence that the nurse-milk produces on infants or animals: he knew in Crete a girl who, having been reared by a goat, had the jumping habits of a goat, and was so shy and skittish as to fall into convulsions on going into company: also a young man reared by a cow that wholly consorted with cattle, and never with sheep. Stillman went round in the evening to the Photographic Society in Conduit Street, where he is to explain the construction of a new camera and dark chamber of his invention: he has some considerable expectations of the success of this invention, if patented. His boy Russie has, within these few days, begun tentative efforts at walking about the room: he looks to me rather less miserably invalided than heretofore.

Wednesday 10 and Thursday 11 January   Great pressure of business at Somerset House.

Friday 12 January   Troubled with a cold these few days, and now sore throat. Put on a mustard poultice.—Harrison (. . .[2] London Central) showed me a pamphlet about Darlows Skenasma Belts—magnetic (not galvanic). It professes that these belts cure a number of diseases: and one testimonial speaks of curing in three days a long-standing bronchocele—the disease (or one part of the disease) that Christina suffers from. I should myself be a little disposed to see what this belt might do; but on showing the notice to Mamma, find her quite opposed to the idea. So I suppose it may as well be set aside—at any rate for the present.

Saturday 13 January   Spent the evening, with others, at Mrs. Bodichon's—the first time I have been in that house for several

---

[1] Euphrosyne Stillman, sculptress, married William Ritchie, the nephew of Lady Ritchie (Thackeray's daughter).
[2] Illegible in MS.

years. She showed us the plans drawn up by Waterhouse[1] for the Ladies' College at Girton, near Cambridge. She continues painting landscape a good deal, evidently not without a feeling that her uncommon talent does not receive its due meed at exhibitions, etc. The chief hitch appears to be that her works are not considered sufficiently finished; while she, on the other hand, objects to attempting any finish—and considers it detrimental in her own practice—beyond the point at which she has succeeded in hitting the mark she aimed at.

Sunday 14 January Maria saw lately a notice from the 'Christian Knowledge Society' inviting literary contributions of a particular aim. This induced her to look up a series of short addresses to girls, in class, relative to Bible topics, which she wrote about eleven years ago, and then used practically. The Society has entertained the offer, and publication seems not unlikely.[2] I looked through the earlier section of these Addresses, and think them up to a high standard in their kind, and likely enough to obtain a large sale.

Monday 15 January Called again by appointment on Trelawny, who treats me most kindly, and I might almost say with affection. He is about the most remarkable instance I know of force of body, character, and mind, in the same person. He says he has never once had a regular illness: has been shot through the lungs (I think this is narrated in his Byron and Shelley book), and had lock-jaw for some while, but his iron constitution and temperate habits carried him through. He gave me a copy of the original unpublished *Queen Mab*: at least I *believe* this is the original edition,[3] and he affirms it to be so, but is, I am sure, under some

---

[1] Alfred Waterhouse (1830–1905), architect. He studied in France, Italy, Germany, and built many neo-Gothic buildings at Oxford, Cambridge, Manchester, London, etc., one of the best known being the Natural History Museum at South Kensington.

[2] This is the first mention of a book which was entitled *Letters to my Bible Class on 39 Sundays*, published by the S.P.C.K., London, 1872. The first 'letter' is dated 1860.

[3] *Queen Mab* was privately printed in 1813 in an edition of 250 copies, seventy of which had been distributed by Shelley himself before finally leaving England for Italy. Eight years later, in 1821, when at Pisa, Shelley was informed that a 'piratical' edition of *Queen Mab* was being published by a certain Clarke, 'one of the low booksellers in the Strand, against my wish and consent', Shelley wrote to Gisborne. This Clarke edition was followed by numerous pirated editions by Richard Carlile, another 'arch-republican publisher'. See H. Buxton Forman, 'The Vicissitudes of Queen Mab', *The Shelley Society's Papers*, 14 April 1888, pp. 19–31.

mistake in saying (in an inscription to the volume), that the edition consisted of thirty copies. Must compare this copy with the one that Tebbs[1] possesses, or Locker. He also showed me two letters from Shelley to Godwin (copies) written just before he left England in 1816. They show that Shelley was then raising £300 to give to Godwin, although not on good terms with him.[2] He considered Godwin to have wrongly objected, contrary to God-win's own principles, to the connection between Shelley and Mary; while Godwin, it might appear, considered Shelley to be alienated from him by aristocratic birth, etc. Trelawny has also lent me three or four more letters of Shelley, copied out by Miss Clair-mont, relating, I believe, to the marriage with Mary. These I shall read at home, at my leisure. Shelley never smoked, but tolerated any amount of smoking in Trelawny, etc. Byron also could not smoke. Shelley may, as Hogg and Peacock intimate, have cared about babies at one time, but took no interest in children: once stepped over his own child Percy and his nurse, without recog-nizing them, in Trelawny's presence. He was as clever with his legs as other people are with their arms: these were comparatively weak in Shelley.

Tuesday 16 January Gabriel tells me that the article lately pub-lished in the *Quarterly*[3] is very abusive against himself, and still more perhaps against Morris; against Swinburne more measured. I looked at the Shelley letters lent me by Trelawny, and kept a note of their contents: one of them—(not Shelley's own writing) is of much importance, showing how difficult it was to get Shelley to marry Mary Godwin.[4]

[1] Henry Virtue Tebbs, an art-collector.
[2] This refers to a letter dated 3 May 1816 from Dover, in which Shelley promises to give Godwin £300 to be taken from the sum allowed him by his father to pay for his debts; but on 2 October 1816 Shelley wrote 'I cannot send you £300 because I have not £300 to send'. See Shelley, *Letters*, i. 471, 509.
[3] The article which appeared in the *Quarterly Review* for January 1872 attacked Rossetti and Swinburne; it was reputedly written by Courthope. The critic com-plained of the obscurity of *The House of Life*, describing the sonnets as 'vain en-deavours to attach a spiritual meaning to the animal passions' and summed up the whole work as 'emasculated obscenity'.
[4] Mary Godwin had been living with Shelley as his mistress ever since they left England in July 1814. Within a month of Harriet's death, William Godwin insisted that they should be married in the most conventional form. The marriage took place in London on 30 December 1816, in spite of Shelley's attachment to the principle of free love.

Wednesday 17 January Attended at the Langham Hotel a meeting of the Central Committee for Women's Suffrage, which I lately joined. Saw for the first time Jacob Bright[1] and Miss Becker.[2] Bright, in his speech, intimated that he does not expect a very *early* success for the movement. Mr. Pochin,[3] Mayor (or late Mayor) of Salford, does. I am quite of the same opinion as Bright. Remember writing last year to Mrs. Peter Taylor[4] that I thought, if suffrage for women-householders (not to speak of any larger question) were to be carried within 20 years from then, it would be fully as much as I expect—the revolution herein involved being in fact one of almost unprecedented scope.

Thursday 18 January Going on with the editorial work on the Miscellaneous Selection of Poems.

Friday 19 January Had occasion to call at Hotten's. He told me that there has of late been some degree of revival in the demand for the Whitman Selection; this may perhaps be attributed to the articles in the *Westminster*,[5] and more particularly in the *Dark Blue*.[6] I don't perceive that Hotten feels any sort of grudge against me on account of anything that took place in connexion with Swinburne's leaving him for Ellis as publisher.

Saturday 20 January Obtained and read the article against

[1] Jacob Bright (1821–99), M.P. for Manchester. After John Stuart Mill's defeat in 1868, Bright took charge of the Women's Suffrage Bill which he introduced in 1870, 1871, and 1872. Each time Gladstone opposed it, declaring that it was 'a practical evil of an intolerable character'.

[2] Lydia Ernestine Becker (d. 1890), one of the leaders of the Women's Suffrage movement. Thanks to them, the Women's Disabilities Removal Bill was introduced and so began the forty years' Parliamentary struggle. She edited the *Women's Suffrage Journal* from 1870 until her death.

[3] Mrs. Pochin and Mrs. Jacob Bright drafted the first Married Women's Property Act in 1870; it was passed in 1872.

[4] The wife of Peter Alfred Taylor (1819–91), M.P. for Leicester, a friend of Mazzini and chairman of the Society of Friends of Italy. Mrs. Taylor was, with Miss Becker, one of the fighters for the Women's Suffrage Bill. She had organized the first petitions presented to Parliament by J. S. Mill in 1867 and formed in London the first Women's Suffrage Society which held public meetings. See M. G. Fawcett, *Women's Suffrage*, Edinburgh, 1911, and Sylvia Pankhurst, *The Suffragette Movement*, London, 1931.

[5] In the *Westminster Review* for July 1871, pp. 33–68, appeared a long article entitled 'The Poet of Democracy: Walt Whitman'.

[6] 'A Study of Walt Whitman, the Poet of Modern Democracy', by the Hon. Roden Noel, *The Dark Blue*, October 1871, pp. 241–336.

Gabriel, etc., in the *Quarterly*, It does not seem to me to amount to very much beyond saying that the reviewer doesn't particularly like the poems, nor care for the class of work to which they belong. There is however a distinct statement that either Gabriel or Morris (which of the two is not clearly defined) avows himself an atheist: this might deserve some attention. I am sure Gabriel has made no such statement, and do not at all think Morris has.

Sunday 21 January   Sent Mrs. Bodichon £22 (as offered the other night) for her Ladies' College.

Monday 22 January   Gabriel tells me that Brown has sold to Leyland for £420 (a small price, which may possibly be raised in the long run to £500) his large picture, now in progress of *Don Juan found by Haidee*.

Tuesday 23 January   Had to call on Rose,[1] in connexion with the Trusteeship for Mrs. Wieland; as it seems that a Chancery cause for partitioning the property will probably be needed. Rose is a little nettled at some observation made by Wainewright's firm, implying that the difficulty arises from the wording of the marriage-settlement; whereas in fact, as the Wielands themselves have had to acknowledge, the difficulty arises from the mortgage-deed. I hope I may be able to keep on easy terms with both these legal authorities; but I certainly think Rose is in the right so far, on the essential point of this debate.—Went on afterwards to Trelawny's, to return him the Shelley letters he had lent me. He was not in, but his niece, Miss Taylor,[2] kept me the rest of the evening, partly in expectation of his return. I find she has more conversation than had appeared in my previous interviews with

[1] James Anderson Rose, a London solicitor, who purchased some of D. G. R.'s pictures and drawings in the sixties. He was Whistler's lawyer. See *R.P.*, *passim*.

[2] Miss Taylor was Trelawny's housekeeper whom he introduced to his friends as his niece; she looked after him, in the house he had bought at Sompting, for the last eleven years of his life. See R. Glynn Grylls, *Trelawny*, 1950. A letter of Miss Taylor to W. M. R., dated December 1886, throws light on her character and on that of Mrs. Call (Trelawny's daughter): 'Your letter has caused me the most intense astonishment, Mrs. Call's statement that you "had once proposed marriage to me" is false . . . I most solmly [*sic*] declair [*sic*] that you never made me an offer . . . One or two persons did joke me about your coming so constantly to the Crescents, but I always knew it was to see Mr. Trelawny and not me and always said so' (unpublished letter in the Angeli Collection).

her, and a very fair share of sense and spirit in talk. Trelawny
bathes every morning without exception in cold water, and at the
seaside bathes in the sea in addition at all seasons. This past
November, however, being unusually cold, he did not go
through with the sea-bathing. He often takes Turkish baths also.
His longstanding habit of wearing no stockings was principally
with a view to keeping a healthy heat in the feet; this used to be
deficient while he wore stockings, and he set the matter right by
leaving them off.[1]

Wednesday 24 January Stillman called. His wife is not yet up,
but has done very well ever since the birth of the child. Her
father has now relented so far as to have two interviews with her,
which passed off satisfactorily. Mrs. Spartali is very urgent that
the Stillmans should come and live in a vacant house abutting
upon the 'Shrubbery' grounds. Stillman has written a conciliatory
letter to Spartali, and there seems a fair prospect of his replying
in such terms as to make some sort of intercourse between them
possible henceforward. Assuming this, the projected housetaking
will be effected—Mrs. Spartali furnishing all or some of the funds
for the requisite furniture etc. Stillman, in his letter to Spartali,
said expressly that he would not under any circumstances expect,
nor even accept, a dowry or other money provision for Marie.
Spartali is very kind to Stillman's two girls, who have been
staying at the 'Shrubbery' ever since the confinement began.
Russie is, to some appreciable extent, improving in health and
power of motion.[2]

Thursday 25 January At Miss Blind's request, I posted her (for
the second time) Mary Wollstonecraft's *Rights of Woman*,[3] and sent
for her perusal the abstract I had made of the Shelley letters lately
shown me by Trelawny.

Friday 26 January Wieland and I met at Rose's for further discussion of Mrs. Wieland's affairs: and it was agreed that Rose

[1] See the *Athenaeum*, 15 July 1882, p. 79.
[2] Stillman had three children by his first wife: one boy, Russie, and two girls,
Lisa and Bella. From his earliest years the boy was an invalid; his death at the age
of 13, in 1875, was a terrible grief for his father who cherished him. W. J.
Stillman, *Autobiography, passim*.
[3] The full title was *A Vindication of the Rights of Woman, with Strictures on Political
and Moral Subjects*, London, 1792.

should in the first instance take the opinion of Counsel as last suggested by Wainewright. Wieland is indignant with Wainewright for drawing up the mortgage-deed in such form as to create this difficulty as soon as its provisions get tested: and, though reluctant to think ill of Wainewright, I must confess I do not well understand why he directed or allowed the deed to be so drawn up. Mrs. Wieland has been much out of health of late—and even dangerously so, I fear, from what her husband says.—Gabriel hears that the poem, 'St. Abe and his Seven Wives', is probably by Buchanan.[1] Can this be true? It is Hepworth Dixon[2] who expresses a conviction to that effect; and he, I believe, is intimate with Buchanan. Hotten expressed to me the other day the opinion that the poem must be by Lowell:[3] at any rate, the present is the first suggestion I hear of its being by any other than an American.

Saturday 27 January   I have now advanced a good way with the Selection of Miscellaneous Poems; having got on as far as the authors who belong chiefly to the 19th century. There will be also the anonymous poems still to attend to; and a good deal has to stand over till the material for the Humorous Poems (needed also for these Miscellaneous Poems) shall be returned to me.

Sunday 28 January   Wrote to Wainewright asking for information about Mrs. Wieland's affairs; also to Moxons claiming the £21 for the Campbell volume and on other details.—Christina, while quietly reading to herself towards 9 p.m., had an alarming sensation at the heart, as if it suddenly swelled almost to bursting: this, in a much minor degree, recurred once some few minutes afterwards. We sent for Sir W. Jenner, who advised a change of

---

[1] 'St. Abe and his Seven Wives: A Tale of Salt Lake City' was published anonymously in 1872 by Strahan. It was linked with H. W. Longfellow's 'Divine Tragedy' by the reviewer in the *Athenaeum* (23 December 1871) under the heading 'American Poems' and commented upon as follows: 'The irony of the Saint is enhanced by the dexterity with which he uses the American–English language.' The reviewer was probably W. M. R.

[2] William Hepworth Dixon (1821–79), historian, traveller, editor of the *Athenaeum* from 1853 to 1869.

[3] James Russell Lowell (1819–91), American poet and critic. He edited the *Atlantic Monthly* and associated with C. E. Norton in editing the *North American Review*. He was a Dante scholar. In W. M. R.'s American Selection, he is represented by fifteen poems. In 1880 W. M. R. published a comprehensive edition of Lowell's poems, published by Ward and Lock, but in the series *Moxon's Popular Poets*.

medicine. He was not very communicative about the matter; but assured Christina, in reply to an enquiry from her, that there is nothing in this occurence rendering it probable that she may be overtaken by instantaneous death. Still, the symptom seems both startling and alarming. In other respects Christina has continued of late not deteriorating, but of the two rather less bad than she was a couple of months ago.

Monday 29 January   Christina has gone on all today without any recurrence of this attack.

Tuesday 30 January   Called again on Trelawny, and as usual had much interesting chat about Shelley, etc. He says that both Shelley and Byron spoke good Italian (Trelawny himself, as far as a very restricted experience guides me, speaks it very badly): when they spoke English, they heedfully avoided interlarding it with foreign words or phrases, and Lady Blessington's book[1] about Byron is unfaithful in giving the contrary idea. Shelley never got angry, though sometimes in discussion he was vehement. Trelawny disbelieves Mrs. Stowe's[2] story about Byron, and considers that he knows the real reason of the separation from Lady Byron. He has some thought of publishing it before his death, or at any rate leaving it on record: it would vindicate Byron against that grave imputation, but would show him to have fallen into 'other weaknesses'. Trelawny possesses a very capital piece of Japanese

[1] Countess of Blessington, *née* Margaret Power (1789–1849) was born in Ireland; at the age of 18 she was sold by her father into marriage to Maurice Farmer (d. 1817) whom she left after three months. She was offered a home by a Captain in Dublin, then in Hampshire. In 1818 she married Charles John Gardiner, Earl of Blessington. From a first marriage, the earl had a daughter who married Count Alfred d'Orsay in 1818 (from whom she was separated by deed in 1838). In 1823 the Blessingtons met Byron in Genoa and for ten weeks before his final journey to Greece, Byron enjoyed Lady Blessington's conversation and company, to the great displeasure of Teresa Guiccioli. After her husband's death in 1829 Lady Blessington produced novels, reminiscences, edited magazines, became bankrupt in 1849, and fled to Paris to Count d'Orsay with whom she had been living for some years. See *Conversations of Lord Byron with the Countess of Blessington* which she published in 1834. A second edition with a Memoir appeared in 1893.

[2] Harriet Elizabeth Beecher Stowe (1811–96), author of the famous novel *Uncle Tom's Cabin* (1852). She started the scandal about Byron and his half-sister, the Hon. Augusta Leigh, in *Macmillan's Magazine*, 1869, pp. 377–96. She asserted that she had received the information from Lady Byron herself. See H. Beecher Stowe, *Lady Byron Vindicated, and History of the Byron Controversy*, Boston, 1870; *The Stowe–Byron Controversy: a Complete Résumé of all that has been written and said upon the subject*, by the editor of *Once a Week*, London, 1871.

painting, given him by the Chinese traveller Lay. It forms one long strip several yards long, and represents various animals—more particularly monkeys and frogs—racing and otherwise engaged. Full of fun and spirit.

Wednesday 31 January   Last November was unseasonably cold; but, since the early days of December, the weather has been uncommonly mild, and the season now seems to me considerably more advanced than I ever recollect it before. Numberless shrubs are in green bud; and in some the leaves are expanded to no small extent—the beginning of the bud must certainly have been eight or ten days back at least.—Called on Wainewright. I gather from what he says that the mortgage-deed was drawn up in a form which he still considers quite correct; and under it the power of leasing, partitioning, etc., could have been exercised by Mrs. Wieland's trustees etc. with the concurrence of the mortgagee: therefore what creates the difficulty is the fact that the marriage-settlement, while it recites and affects the powers contained in Taylor's will, does not do the like as regards the mortgage-deed—and in this sense it is the settlement, not the deed, that has created the difficulty. He cannot understand how it is that, in the instructions and information he received prior to prefacing the settlement, Rose remained (it would seem) unaware of the mortgage. Neither can I understand this well, the instructions were given to Rose by me, and I am morally certain I must have told him of the mortgage. Wainewright hopes that the course suggested by him to Rose may stave off the difficulty: but, if not, I fear from his tone that the difficulty will be a serious one, and cause a deal of trouble.—Read with great interest some further Shelley letters handed to me by Trelawny yesterday: explanation of the *Stanzas, April 1814*, etc.: shall keep an abstract for my own satisfaction.—Brown called: he is going to paint Fawcett, M.P.,[1] and his wife, for Dilke.[2] Hüffer's idea of buying a share in the *Fortnightly* has

[1] Henry Fawcett (1833–84), Professor of Political Economy at Cambridge, Liberal M.P. for Brighton, later became Postmaster-General in the second Gladstone government. At the age of 25 he had been totally blinded by his father in a shooting accident. The portrait of Professor and Mrs. Fawcett is now in the National Portrait Gallery. See F. M. Hueffer, *Ford Madox Brown*, p. 271.

[2] Sir Charles Wentworth Dilke (1843–1911), nicknamed 'the Republican Baronet', was a prominent radical politician whose career was to be ruined in 1885 after he had been cited as a co-respondent in a divorce case. He published several works about British and imperial policy. His grandfather having restored the *Athenaeum*'s

fallen through: the publisher had had no notion of selling merely a share, though he might have entertained the question of selling the whole. Hüffer is writing for Longmans, a book on living English poets,[1] including Gabriel.

Thursday 1 February Christina troubled with a sty in the eye these 2 or 3 days. One of them burst to-day, and gives less trouble: the other, not apparently likely to be so troublesome, is still coming on. There has been no recurrence as yet of the attack of Sunday last.

Friday 2 February Got to the end of the anonymous poems for my Miscellaneous Selection. Thus the general framework of this volume is completed; though a good deal remains over, to be done when the books for the Humorous Selection come back to me. Showed Gabriel the remarkable poem *Weddah and Om-el-Bonain* by B.V.,[2] in the *National Reformer*, sent to me (no doubt by the author) a few days ago. He quite agrees with me as to the uncommon merits of this poem: I must write and endeavour to trace the author.

Saturday 3 February Dined with Mrs. Gilchrist in her new house,

fortunes in 1830 and founded *Notes and Queries* in 1849, Sir Charles became proprietor of both journals after his father's death in 1869. At the time of the D. G. R.–Buchanan controversy he was meanly attacked by the latter as editor of 'the leading organ of the Fleshly School'. See Roy Jenkins, *Sir Charles Dilke, A Victorian Tragedy*, London, 1958, *passim*, and also O. Doughty, *A Victorian Romantic, Dante Gabriel Rossetti*, p. 493.

[1] The book was never published.

[2] B. V. was the pseudonym of the poet James Thomson (1834–82). These initials stand for Bysshe (Shelley) and Vanolis (Novalis). James Thomson was a friend of Charles Bradlaugh and was an active propagandist in favour of free thought. On receiving numbers of the *National Reformer* W. M. R. wrote 'I had never heard (of his name or initials) until in February 1872 I received by post a copy of his pathetic oriental poem *Weddah and Om-el-Bonain*, in a number of the *National Reformer*. I read it, and so did my brother immediately afterwards, and we both agreed in deeming it remarkable. I then wrote to B. V. to say as much . . .' On 8 February 1872 Thomson replied: 'No living writer can have less reputation than myself who am simply known to some readers of the *National Reformer* as B. V., the author of many pieces and scraps in prose and verse which have appeared in that periodical during the last seven years or so. And I am bound in honesty to confess that some of those pieces were among the most wicked and blasphemous which even Mr. Bradlaugh ever published' (unpublished letters in the Angeli Collection). B. V.'s most famous poem, *The City of Dreadful Night* also appeared in the *National Reformer* in 1874. See H. S. Salt, *The Life of James Thomson*, London, 1889, and W. M. Rossetti's 'Reminiscences of James Thomson' (unpublished papers in the Angeli Collection).

50 Marquis Road, Camden Square. It is an uncommonly low rent, £35. Her health is now good, though less strong than before her severe illness: what tries her most is prolonged application of any kind—as to writing or reading. Her son Herbert is studying drawing at Cary's, and is a very nice intelligent boy: he showed me some of his drawings, in which I don't observe any signs of *superior* aptitude, but no doubt he is too young for one to form a very decisive opinion.

Sunday 4 February   Made an abstract (somewhat lengthy) from the Shelley letters last shown to me by Trelawny.—Wrote to B.V. and to Sumner Jones asking authority for inserting in my Miscellaneous Selection some of the poems of Ebenezer Jones.[1] Looked at the first specimen page, now printed, of the *Troilus–Filostrato* work that I finished about a year ago.

Monday 5 February   Howell has written to Gabriel, saying he has found a portrait of a boy, purporting to represent Shelley at the age of ten, painted by Hoppner:[2] he good-naturedly suggests a subscription to present it to me. There seems to be one serious objection—the eyes are brown, and ought to be dark blue. However, I must see the picture (a magnificent find, if genuine) before adopting any settled opinion. Wrote a few words to the *Athenaeum* à propos of certain communications, in their last two numbers,[3] concerning Hotten's *Shelley*.[4]

[1] In a letter dated 8 February 1872, answering W. M. R.'s request, Sumner Jones wrote as follows: 'I am heart and soul with those who can appreciate Eben's early work . . . Never was book a more genuine outcome of the man—a boy-man—turned out, faults and all, with beating heart and working brain between the covers; to be kicked into Lethe very quickly as you know . . . Ebby brought it out on savings of his salary for the purpose, 1838–1843' (unpublished letter in the Angeli Collection).

[2] John Hoppner, R.A. (*c.* 1758–1810), portrait painter, was Lawrence's chief rival. The portrait mentioned by W. M. R. was supposed to have been painted by Hoppner in 1805. Walter De La Mare included it in *Early One Morning* (1935), p. 492, as 'Shelley aged 13' by Hoppner. It also appeared in the catalogue of the sale of H. G. Marquand's collection, New York, in 1903. This attribution now appears doubtful and it has been suggested by some art critics that it may be the work of Raeburn (1756–1823).

[3] In the *Athenaeum* for 27 January 1872, p. 114, appeared a very critical paragraph on Hotten's edition of Shelley. It was unsigned, but written by Mathilde Blind who acknowledged it later. She disputed Hotten's claims to have published new material. W. M. R.'s answer appeared in the *Athenaeum* for 3 February 1872, p. 147.

[4] *The Poetical Works of P. B. Shelley, now first given from the author's original edition, with some hitherto unedited pieces.*

Tuesday 6 February Howell brought me round the supposed portrait of Shelley. It is a pretty fair workmanly sort of picture, with no very salient qualities. The face does not look to me like Shelley, to any extent worth mentioning; though the hair, I think, might very well indeed be his, and the forehead is of noticeable development. The eyes (to judge by candle light) are brown— Howell thinks they may be violet-blue discoloured; the features are of a rather blunt English type: the upper lip long rather than otherwise, and the mouth—considered proportionately as that of a child—I should call large—both of these points being quite contrary to the recognized portrait of the adult Shelley. The writing at the back, 'Percy B. Shelley, born 1792—Hoppner' is in an accurate printing sort of hand: I can form no particular inference from it, but should not much suppose it to be written by Hoppner himself. A letter from the owner Symmons says that a Mr. Doble now in a Lunatic Asylum (otherwise I do not know who he is) saw the portrait hanging up, and said it must be Shelley; and only then they took it down, and found the confirmatory inscription. This is noticeable, if accurately true. I recommended Howell to take back the picture to his own house: invite Allingham to look at it, as he knows a portrait of Shelley in early childhood belonging to the family; and then (unless Allingham can unqualifiedly pronounce it spurious) to obtain—through Allingham or possibly through Garnett—the opinion of Shelley's sisters. It would appear naturally presumable that, if the portrait (a life-size half-length, the boy lying with arm over sofa) is genuine, the sisters, or some one of the three, would not only recognize it as portraying Shelley, but would remember it as an actual family property. Howell will act on this suggestion. We spent all the evening talking together on the many complicated activities to which Howell has been giving himself up these three or four years, and the messes of all sorts into which these have brought him. I spoke very frankly, but in a friendly spirit. He admitted his serious misdeeds; but insists that the many accusations of slipperiness in money affairs are cruel untruths, and indeed, according to his own account, some of them can be nothing less than wilful malicious calumnies. He wants to get up an art-buying Society, of which he would be secretary. Gabriel had given him a written testimonial: and I drew up (after he had left) another—in which I don't enlarge on character, but on capacity.

Wednesday 7 February   Looked by clear morning light at the eyes in the Shelley portrait: they are an indistinct brown, and, I should say, have, from the first, been that same colour. Called on Mathilde Blind, to leave her my abstract from the Shelley letters last shown to me by Trelawny. She clears up a point I have been stupidly puzzling over for some while past—who 'Fanny Godwin' was: no doubt (as M.B. says) she was Mary Wollstonecraft's illegitimate daughter by Mr. Imlay,[1] and her legal name would have been Fanny Wollstonecraft. I mentioned to Miss Blind the fact (appearing in these Shelley letters) that Miss Clairmont was staying at Lynmouth for some time in 1815: this, she thinks, must be the explanation of something that she (M.B.) heard at Lynmouth last year from an old servant who had known Shelley there, about some relative of Shelley's being likewise there. I think so too: but whether this might furnish a clue to any further local enquiry, of interest to a Shelleyite, may be more than dubious.

Thursday 8 February   Called again to see Trelawny, but he was out. In going along, met Millais. He tells me that his wife has been a great invalid for about a year and a half past, very seldom leaving the house; the illness, it seems, is in some way connected with her last confinement. Millais says he gets more and more devoted to his art. Miss Taylor, Trelawny's niece, tells me that Trelawny's mother died at the age of 90: this seems to be the only conspicuous instance of longevity in the family.

Friday 9 February   I am now looking through the new volume of Ferrazzi's *Enciclopedia Dantesca*, with a view to noticing that and another Dante compilation in the *Academy*.[2]

Saturday 10 February   The Shelley information that I have lately obtained through Trelawny is of such importance as to require additions or revisions to my memoir in various particulars: this I am now seeing to. The more essential points however—such

[1] Captain Gilbert Imlay, American officer and author, met Mary Wollstonecraft in Paris; they lived together for two years in Paris and Le Havre, where their daughter Fanny was born in 1794. Very soon afterwards he deserted her. See R. Glynn Grylls, *Mary Shelley*, p. 5.

[2] The review of the 4th volume of Ferrazzi's *Enciclopedia Dantesca* by W. M. R. appeared in the *Academy* for 1 April 1872, together with a notice on the *Bibliografia Dantesca*, ed. Julius Petzholdt, Dresden, 1872–80.

as details regarding the elopement with Mary, and the subsequent marriage to her—have not been placed at my disposal for use, nor should I feel justified in even asking for this to be done: these matters therefore I shall not introduce in a positive form, though they may entail some alteration in a phrase or two that I had used here and there. The Memoir and Notes[1]—done though they were with indefatigable painstaking and minute particularity—have indeed become already to some extent obsolete, through new information received, new readings announced, etc. Moxon ought to see to their being issued, at the earliest opportunity, only in the revised form which I have given to them, and am yet engaged in giving. This point I mentioned to him many months ago: but everything in that firm seems to be conducted on a remiss and happy-go-lucky footing, and I have no expectation of getting the thing set right—unless possibly I take it up warmly myself at some future time.[2]

Sunday 11 February   Wrote to the Editor of *Notes and Queries*, bespeaking, at the request of Sumner Jones, admission for an article[3] he wishes to write about his brother Ebenezer; to Garnett, mentioning the Shelley portrait now at my house, etc.

Monday 12 February   Began writing a notice of the two Dante Bibliographical books for the *Academy*.

Tuesday 13 February   Called again on Trelawny. He seems to be increasingly inclined to publish the further Shelley Memoranda supplied by himself and Miss Clairmont, at his own expense, if needful: on this point he will probably give me his decision next Tuesday. He agrees with me that several details in the Clairmont correspondence are too confidential for publication. I asked whether he thinks that Shelley, had he lived to the age of sixty or seventy, would have gone on writing poetry as his chief occupation, without taking up any other vocation in life. He says yes— poetry and prose. Trelawny and other friends had especially

---

[1] *The Poetical Works of P. B. Shelley, with Notes and a Memoir* by W. M. Rossetti (Moxon, London, 1870). The two volumes were dedicated to Trelawny. A second edition appeared in 1871, but without Notes.

[2] The third edition with revised Notes and Memoir was published in 1872, a few weeks later.

[3] I have not been able to trace this article in *Notes and Queries*.

encouraged Shelley towards dramatic writing: and Trelawny
thinks that, if he had once had any public (more particularly
stage) success as a dramatist, he would have taken up that line
of writing, 'filling up the gaps left by Shakespeare', more especially
in English or other great historical subjects. Shelley once spoke
of his poems as 'alms for oblivion';[1] and Trelawny believes he
really did not regard them as destined to live for generations or
ages. He never recited or read them out, within Trelawny's
experience; but may from time to time have shown a new stanza
or so to his wife. Trelawny knows nothing either way about any
portrait of Shelley by Hoppner. A good deal about the profusion
and hospitality of American living, and means of life.—Sir C.
Napier, the General[2] (whom Trelawny knew well, and admired
intensely). Napier, on being appointed Commander-in-Chief in
India, was required to dine with the Queen—a sort of thing he
had always held aloof from. He mustered black trousers of his
own, and put on a black coat and dress-boots belonging to his
valet. Trelawny believes (and I am greatly of the same opinion)
that, were war to break out between America and England (as
now half apprehended by some people in connexion with the
'Alabama' claims,[3] etc.), England would suffer a downfall com-
parable to that of France last year in real damage: while, even if
England were continuously victorious in naval engagements,
America would be damaged to no extent worth reckoning practically.

Wednesday 14 February Finished the notice of Ferrazzi's and
Petzholdt's Dante books.

Thursday 15 February Allingham has replied to Howell, saying
he could not give any decisive opinion about the Shelley portrait:

1   'Time hath, my lord, a wallet at his back,
                           Wherein he puts alms for oblivion',
                                         Shakespeare, *Troilus and Cressida*, III. iii. 146.
     2 Robert Cornelis Napier (1810–90), created Baron Napier of Magdala in 1868
Commander-in-Chief in 1870, Field Marshal in 1883, after a long career in India
and China.
     3 The *Alabama* had been built and armed by English firms for the American
Southern States in 1862; she sank or captured a great number of North American
cargo-boats and was herself sunk in 1864. The United States claimed damages,
and by the Treaty of Washington the difference was referred to arbitrators; but
the tension was such that a rupture was feared.

probably (as Gabriel reminded me the other evening) Allingham really objects to go to Howell's house, being intimate with Burne-Jones.—I sent to Sumner Jones a note from the Editor of *Notes and Queries*, consenting to insert the article which Jones proposes to write concerning Ebenezer Jones.

Friday 16 February Hüffer called with Brown, and asked Christina's authority for setting to music, and so publishing, two of her poems—'When I am dead' and another. Christina of course consented. Brown intimates that it might be desirable for Hüffer to make a certain position as a musical composer, and then to give singing lessons: he thinks that the latter occupation would not be *infra dig*, if enjoined with the reputation of a composer, but otherwise would be so. Hüffer has also received either a position offer, or at any rate a practical invitation, for him to become a Professor at the University of Strasburg—Professor of Modern Literature, Brown infers: but Hüffer seems to consider that his prospects in England are so far good as to make it undesirable that he should sacrifice them for any such position in Germany. Hüffer is now doing the notice of Gabriel prefatory to the proposed Tauchnitz edition of Gabriel's Poems: the same notice, it seems, will be incorporated in the book on *Living English Poets* which he is to do for Longmans.[1]

Saturday 17 February Going on with the revision of Shelley Memoir.

Sunday 18 February Reading with a view to some extension of the Introduction of my *Troilus–Filostrato* work,[2] the *Roman de Troie* by Benoît de Ste More edited by Joly[3]—said to be the first mediaeval form of the Troy legends. I find here what I think the undoubted explanation of a point that has always hitherto puzzled me in Dante, and which no commentator (certainly none of those I have had occasion to consult) has ever elucidated in detail, though probably some of them imply it—viz: why Dante places Achilles among the lustful, 'che la ragion sommettono al talento'. Benoît gives nothing about the quarrel with Agamemnon leading

[1] (No such book appeared W. M. R.).

[2] W. M. R.'s introduction is cited by Professor L. Constans in his book *Le Roman de Troie par Benoit de Sainte-Maure*, Paris, 1912, vi. 338.

[3] *Benoît de Sainte-More et le Roman de Troie, ou Les Métamorphoses d'Homère et de l'épopée gréco-latine au Moyen-âge*, by Aristide Joly, Paris, 1870–71.

Achilles to withdraw from the Grecian host: but he makes such a withdrawal consequent on Achilles's falling in love with Polyxena, and negociating to obtain her in marriage on condition of his thus violating his military duty. Benoît professes to follow Dictys and Dares,[1] so perhaps the same incident appears in those authors, whom I never yet read. This is an interesting Dantesque point, and I shall publish it in some form—perhaps as a note to the Chaucer affair. There is also an important matter as to Courtesy-book questions (John of Salisbury) raised in Joly's preface: this I notified by letter to Furnivall, who as far as I know, has not as yet turned his attention to this item.

Monday 19 February Having sent in the morning to Professor Beesly[2] a contribution to relieve French Communals in distress, I received a call from him in the evening: he is a fine tall man, still youngish as far as I saw by a very dim light. He is not himself a Communist, but a Positivist: believes few of the Communals were properly Communists. Some of them have now obtained some sort of employment, in the way of conversational lessons that Beesly suggested in the *Daily News*. As a rule, they seem *désorientés* in this country, and hardly apply themselves so much to picking up the English language and so on, as in prudence they should. Beesly seems to believe that the conflagrations in Paris arose partly from the operations of the Versailles troops, partly from intentional firing by the Commune—the latter being for strategic purposes, and (in his view) more or less defensible. He has conceived a good opinion of Ferré[3]—setting aside as unproved the charges against him of ordering the shooting of hostages, and firing of buildings. One of the Communals, to whom he spoke about Ferré said—'Ah! c'était un homme.'

[1] Benoît de Sainte-More (or de Sainte-Maure), a *trouvère*, composed his poem, *Le Roman de Troie*, between 1155 and 1160. There appeared for the first time the episode of Troilus and Briseida which developed into Boccaccio's *Filostrato*, Chaucer's *Troilus and Criseyde*, and Shakespeare's *Troilus and Cressida*. Benoît named his alleged sources as Dares of Phrygia and Dictys of Crete, mythological figures who were supposed to have written two short narratives, declaring that they were present at the siege of Troy.

[2] Professor Edward Spenser Beesly (1831–1915). He was influenced by the positivist philosophy of Auguste Comte. Beesly wrote *Religion and Progress* (1879), *Comte* (1883), and *Comte as a Moral Type* (1885).

[3] Charles Theophile Ferré (1845–71) took an active part in the disorders of the Commune, and was sentenced to death and executed in September 1871. See Lissagaray, *Histoire de la commune de 1871*, Bruxelles, 1876.

Tuesday 20 February Called again on Trelawny. He says that Shelley had an uncommon faculty of abstracting himself from anything going on about him in which he took no interest. If he met thoroughly stupid commonplace persons, this faculty came into play: in miscellaneous company, he would get into talk with such people as he felt disposed towards, of which he would judge mostly by the look of the face. He was a good judge of character. His voice was not to be called disagreeable: in the high notes it was somewhat unpleasant, but he generally spoke in a low tone, very earnest and distinct. Trelawny does not recollect his ever saying anything funny: he 'never laughed'[1] (this, I suppose, is not *literally* true). Trelawny knew Mrs. Godwin, whom he thought an ordinary sort of person: was concerned in obtaining her a pension after her husband's death, and Rogers[2] very handsomely lent his assistance. Trelawny knows nothing as to the sale of his book on Shelley and Byron: Moxon did once (some years ago) send him an account, but he did not look into it.

Wednesday 21 February Maria tells me that Garnett called yesterday, and looked at the portrait said to be Shelley: he is not disposed to believe in it, but will, as before proposed, write to the Shelleys to make enquiry.—Dined at Chelsea with Brown, Leyland, and the two Whistlers.[3] Gabriel is now chiefly engaged on two pictures:—1, a lifesized half-figure (Miss Wilding the model) of a woman, who listening to a bird, is going to try some like notes on a 'viol d'amore';[4] 2, two women playing (Miss Wilding is to sit for the second as well as the first), and two others in the middle dancing.[5] This is done of the old background that

[1] (Trelawny himself did not like laughter: I doubt whether I ever saw him laugh, and he but seldom smiled. He certainly did not object to that heartiness of character which goes with genuine laughter, but a mere conventional laugh and especially a female 'giggle' were his aversion. Possibly his own feeling in this matter led him to some degree of overstatement regarding Shelley. W. M. R.)

[2] Samuel Rogers (1763–1855). His poem 'Jacqueline' was printed in the same volume as Byron's 'Lara' (1814). Famous as a poet in his day, he was a generous patron of the arts, was acquainted with the most eminent men of the period. In 1822 he spent some weeks with Byron and Shelley at Pisa; hence the interest of *Recollections of the Table-Talk of Samuel Rogers*, ed. Dyce, 1856.

[3] The painter and his brother William.

[4] *Veronica Veronese*. See Surtees, no. 228, p. 128.

[5] *The Bower Meadow*. See Surtees, no. 229, p. 128 and also p. 205 n. 2. (The painting was done in Knowle Park, Kent,—Holman [Hunt] and Stephens being there, but not Millais. W. M. R.)

Gabriel painted years and years ago (1851, I suppose) in Surrey or Kent, in company with Millais and Hunt—representing the skirts of a wood in the distance against the sky. No. 1 is for Leyland—who, it seems, has suggested to Gabriel to paint a good number of similar half-figures for him to buy. Gabriel seems to have rather an inclination now to get to Italy at no very distant date, and perhaps stay there some while—painting these works for Leyland if convenient. He would want Dunn to accompany him, speaking highly of the use Dunn's assistance is to him: he also speaks in extremely laudatory terms of a picture Dunn is now himself painting, from the old ballad of *The Two Sisters*.[1]— Whistler, it seems, has proposed to Miss Lizzie Dawson, a sister of Mrs. Leyland, and his suit is believed to be prosperous: she is only about 20 years of age.[2]

Thursday 22 February   Further conference with Rose about Mrs. Wieland's property: he is to take the opinion of Mr. Joshua Williams.[3]—Our servants at Euston Square, Betsy and her mother, have given notice to leave. Betsy has been with us, I think, 9 years, and has suited us most thoroughly, and their departure is not a little vexatious, especially considering Christina's ill-health etc. Betsy can't be got to say distinctly *why* they go, although it was 2 or 3 weeks ago that she first started the question, and she has had the interval to think the matter over. There seems to be some sulking over something or other, but why or what remains very imperfectly accounted for.

Friday 23 February   A change in Christina's medicine was ordered the other day, and seems to have had some appreciable good effect: she looks rather more natural in the face, and the difficulty (of late often vexatious) in swallowing is diminished.

Saturday 24 February   Louisa Parke[4] called. She is looking better

---

[1] 'The Two Sisters', an anonymous fifteenth-century ballad, also called 'Binnorie'. See *The Oxford Book of English Verse*, p. 444, no. 386 (ed. 1939), also *The Oxford Book of Ballads*, ed. A. Quiller-Couch (ed. 1910), p. 104, no. 23.

[2] The engagement was broken. 'The lady was pretty, but not the wife for him', so thought E. R. and J. Pennell in *The Whistler Journal*, p. 101. Whistler was then 38.

[3] Joshua Williams (1813–81), legal author, barrister, Professor of law of real and personal property.

[4] A friend of the family, mentioned by D. G. R. and Christina in their letters and again in this diary, p. 245.

than she often has done of late years, and says she has been free from cough this winter.

Sunday 25 February Mrs. Bodichon having sent me a letter addressed to her by Lewis Morris[1] (author of *Songs of Two Worlds, by a New Writer*) who would like me to write a review of him somewhere. I replied expressing (as indeed I have done before) a good opinion of the poems, but saying I would rather not write the review—for the poems, though well executed, have nothing, so far as I have yet noticed, noticeably original or distinctive.

Monday 26 February The new information I have lately obtained concerning Shelley[2] appears, from communication I carry on with Garnett, to be open to discussion or doubt in many particulars. I shall therefore for the present hold over any further revision of my Memoir.

Tuesday 27 February Went to the Zoological Gardens after a long interval. Sumatran Rhinoceros, Penguin, 2 Lynxes, new tiger-cat, young polar bear presented by a brother of Mrs. Bodichon.—In the evening called again on Trelawny, and again had much interesting conversation—more, perhaps, about Byron today than Shelley. I mentioned to Trelawny two principal points in which Garnett has contested statements made by Mrs. Godwin in the Shelley correspondence (sent over by Miss Clairmont). Trelawny attended to what I said, but did not enter minutely into details: in fact, as he told me, once before, he does not make himself closely, and sometimes hardly at all, acquainted with the contents of the missives he receives from Miss Clairmont. These last two times I have seen him he has hardly (today not at all) started the question of publishing the correspondence; and I incline to think he won't take any definite steps—for some while to come, at any rate. To my intense satisfaction, he gave me a little piece (not before seen by me) of Shelley's skull, taken from the brow: it is wholly blackened—not, like the jawbone, whitened, by the fire.

[1] Lewis Morris (1833–1907), poet and Welsh educationist. His *Songs of Two Worlds* was published anonymously in 1871.

[2] The details of this information are given in two letters from W. M. R. to Garnett, dated 18 and 25 February 1872; they concern Shelley's marriage or marriages—one in Scotland, one in London—to Harriet and his relationship with Fanny Godwin who, according to Claire Clairmont, was madly in love with Shelley. See *Letters about Shelley*, pp. 45–61.

He has two such bits of the jawbone, and three (at least) of the skull, including the one now in my possession. I must consider how best to preserve it. I enquired whether he had any of Shelley's hair: answer, no, the scalp having, with the hair, been all eaten off the corpse when recovered: this point, I think has never yet been notified. Shelley was not good at reciting poetry (this I have seen, however, stated otherwise); nor yet Byron,—whose voice was full and melodious, but he had an affected twang in reciting, probably acquired at Harrow.—Trelawny possesses the velvet cap (blue, now much faded) which Byron wore for about the last three years of his life,—making little use of a hat. Byron's head is known to have been small (Shelley's still more so); I tried on the cap and, though it is just a little tight, I consider that, with a few days' wear, it would be a very adequate fit for me. Byron's head went up sloping to the apex: the shape of Shelley's head could not be discerned owing to the thick growth of his hair. Byron's last words to Trelawny, as they parted after landing in Greece, were:—'Now Trelawny, it depends upon what you do whether I put you into the next canto of *Childe Harold* or into the next of *Don Juan*' (a capital anecdotic touch this). He projected, after leaving Greece, going to Naples, and there writing a fifth canto of *Childe Harold*: as to *Don Juan*, he had no fixed plan, but would have continued it indefinitely—'as long as Murray pays the £1000 a canto', he said to Trelawny.[1] He enjoined Trelawny, in the event of his death, to have him buried in a desert islet near Maina—'don't treat me as you did Shelley': and showed him the islet in the course of the voyage, saying it was the one he had had in view in *The Corsair*. However, Trelawny did not find an opportunity of complying with this request. Byron had no religion at all, though a goodish deal of superstition: had *not* any superstition as to ill-luck on Fridays. Shelley had no superstition of any kind whatever. Trelawny says the book about Medora Leigh[2] is true, but not that she was Byron's daughter: the belief that she was so however was the impelling cause of Lady Byron's separation. (This is a matter I have never looked close into as yet.) I observed that I supposed a good deal of Trelawny's own

[1] (Byron can hardly have said this. All the later cantos of *Don Juan* were published by John Hunt, not by Murray. W. M. R.)

[2] Charles Mackay, ed., *Medora Leigh. A History and an Autobiography, with an Introduction and a Commentary on the charges brought against Lord Byron by Mrs. Beecher Stowe*, London, 1869. See p. 155 n. 2.

early career was set forth in *The Adventures of a Younger Son*;[1] he assented, but did not seem to encourage further enquiry as to details. The person there named De Ruyter[2] really existed; he was of Dutch extraction, named Senouf (as I understood the name), and had a commission from Napoleon as a privateer. Byron was in a marked and extreme degree indifferent to ruins, said (on one occasion of an introduction proposed by Trelawny) that he wished to know no men under thirty, nor women beyond it. Was to some extent jealous of Shelley; startled at the evidence of dramatic power in *The Cenci*. Trelawny says positively that *Epipsychidion* was printed in Italy, in a version of Italian poetry written by Shelley himself for Emilia (Viviani) to read.[3] I think he says that he himself saw it: scarcely gather whether or not he implies that there was both the Italian and English (suppose so), but he is very decided as to the Italian. This is an entirely new point. Spite of Trelawny's positiveness, I should almost suspect some treachery in his recollection—tempered, however, by the consideration that there certainly is some inherent probability in the notion that Shelley would have put the poem in such form as that Emilia could read it. Mrs. Shelley, as he says, avoided writing anything about the Italian version: and in fact (as I reminded him) preserved equal silence with regard to the English poem itself. Trelawny thinks he could have saved Shelley from the storm,

[1] The book was published in 1831. It was considered as largely autobiographical until Lady Anne Hill, by a close study of muster-books kept in the Public Record Office, London, discovered that Trelawny had told the story 'not of his life, but of his day-dreams'. He never deserted from the Navy, and was discharged on 18 August 1812 at the age of 20, having sailed for seven years on board eleven different ships of the Royal Navy. 'The proportion of truth to fiction in *The Adventures* turns out to be no more than one tenth.' Anne Hill, 'Trelawny's Family Background and Naval Career', in the *Keats–Shelley Journal*, v, Winter 1956 (The Keats–Shelley Association of America). I am indebted to Lady Mander (Miss R. Glynn Grylls) for kindly drawing my attention to this article, condensed from Anne Hill's study published in 1956 at the Mill House Press, Stanford Dingley, Berks.

[2] De Ruyter was supposed to be a French privateer of Dutch origin, whose real name was De Witt. But Anne Hill, after inquiry from the various authorities concerned, could find no trace of the names of De Ruyter or De Witt. She states, however, 'It is impossible not to believe that Trelawny encountered somebody very like De Ruyter . . . though no trace of such person has been found.' See ibid., p. 22.

[3] Richard Garnett wrote: 'The first draft of *Episychidion* existed some time before Shelley met Emilia Viviani in 1820, but his meeting with her supplied the needful impulse to perfect and complete that piece of radiant mysticism and rapturous melody' quoted by R. S. Granniss in *A Descriptive Catalogue of the First Editions of the Writings of P. B. Shelley*, New York, 1923, p. 65. No allusion is made to an Italian version in this Catalogue.

had he been able to accompany him. The oar found under rather suspicious circumstances after the wreck he believes to have really come from Shelley's boat,—it being after an English pattern, though made in Italy: he has not, however, the slightest suspicion of intentional foul play. Roberts saw little of Shelley. Mavrocordato[1] was not a genuine patriot. Shelley never walked out with his wife in Trelawny's time: was out almost all day, and would sleep under a tree or so when he felt inclined. Dreamed much. Retained the habit of lying down before the hearth (recorded by Hogg), and often sat on the floor, as readily as on a chair. Had no longer the habit of propelling pellets of bread: nor of launching paper boats, though he did this once at Trelawny's request. He would look a great deal at falling Autumn leaves, or leaves drifting on a stream. Fear was positively unknown to Shelley (this Trelawny has said to me more than once): The 'Madam, I never saw fear' was just a phrase in Nelson's mouth, but would have been strictly true of Shelley.

Wednesday 28 February   Betsy and her mother (see 22 February) have finally decided to leave, after further discussion and considerations; so there is nothing to be done now but look out for other servants.

Thursday 29 February   A party at Brown's. I talked most of the evening to Mathilde Blind, about Shelley, etc., and found several people interested in contemplating the fragment of Shelley's skull which I took round for inspection. Mathilde Blind is a very intense admirer of Christina's *Sing-Song*: had written a notice of it, which she offered to the *Academy*, but Appleton seemed to think it too fervently expressed, and Colvin wrote an article instead.[2]

[1] Prince Alexander Mavrocordato of Greece (1791–1865) and his cousin Princess Argyropoli met the Shelleys in Pisa in 1820–1. Shelley dedicated *Hellas, a Lyrical Drama* in these words: 'To His Excellency Prince Alexander Mavrocordato, The Drama of *Hellas* is inscribed as an imperfect token of the admiration, sympathy and friendship of the author.' See E. Blunden, *Shelley*, London, 1946, p. 247, also 'Alexander Mavrocordato, Friend of the Shelleys', *Keats–Shelley Memorial Bulletin*, xvi, 1965, pp. 29–38.

[2] The article appeared in the *Academy* for 15 January 1872. Colvin wrote: 'The volume written by Miss Rossetti and illustrated by Mr. Hughes, is one of the most exquisite of its class ever seen, in which the poet and artist have continually had parallel felicities of inspiration.' In the same notice appears a review of Lewis Carroll's *Through the Looking-glass*.

Garnett tells me that Charles Clairmont[1] (Godwin's step-son) was a scamp—though in what precise aspect he doesn't say: he died only some few years ago; also that Godwin's son, William,[2] grew up and wrote some book. He has already begun some enquiry of the Misses Shelley, with regard to the portrait that Howell placed in my hands. He asked whether, in any mention he may make to the Shelleys of the Clairmont correspondence belonging to Trelawny, I would object to his naming me as the source of his information on the subject: I replied that I see no objection. Swinburne, who knows what swimming is, maintains that Trelawny's printed assertion[3] that Byron had both feet clubbed and both legs withered to the knee, cannot be accurate: a man so formed could not swim. Swinburne's attention was particularly called to this view of the matter by Browning, in a conversation they had last autumn.—It was curious to observe the different feelings with which the sight of the fragment of Shelley's skull was received by different people. Mathilde Blind changed countenance in a moment: her eyes suffused, and she put the fragment reverently to her lips. Next to her, Scott seemed the most impressed, and interested in a very marked degree. Lady Hardy[4] much interested—also Marston, Brown and his family, and some others in varying degrees. Swinburne, to my surprise, paid next to no attention to the matter. Gabriel passed it off jokingly, but was interested nevertheless.

---

[1] Charles Clairmont (1795–1868), Godwin's stepson, and brother of Jane (Clara, Clare, Claire) Clairmont. In 1819 he stayed with the Shelleys in Italy, and on several occasions borrowed money from them, then went to Vienna where he was English tutor to the Archduke Ferdinand Maximilian, later the Emperor Maximilian of Mexico. See *Keats–Shelley Memorial Bulletin*, viii, 1957, pp. 9–19.

[2] William Godwin, Jr. (1803–32), was the son of Godwin by his second wife, Mrs. Clairmont. He tried his hand at commerce, engineering, and architecture without success; became a journalist, writing in the *Morning Chronicle*, the *Mirror of Parliament*. He wrote essays, an opera based on the legend of Robin Hood, a tragedy about the fate of Regulus, and a long novel in three volumes: *Transfusion or the Orphans of Unwalden*, published posthumously with a Memoir by his father, 1 May 1835 (the above note is taken from this memoir).

[3] When Trelawny went back to Missolonghi, after Byron's death, he was taken into the room where 'lay the embalmed body of the Pilgrim—more beautiful in death than in life . . . I uncovered the Pilgrim's feet; both his feet were clubbed, and his legs withered to the knee—the form and features of an Apollo, with the feet and legs of a sylvan satyr'. See Trelawny, *Recollections*, London, 1906, p. 149.

[4] The wife of Sir Thomas Duffus Hardy (1804–78), archivist, deputy-keeper of the Public Records from 1861.

Friday 1 March   Christina very unwell these 3 days—though Sir W. Jenner, on Wednesday seemed to think her better rather than otherwise; weakness, loss of appetite, much trouble in swallowing, and bad nights with difficulty of breathing at whiles. This evening, though not light-headed (as she was at times last Spring), her thoughts were evidently somewhat flighty and unsettled.

Saturday 2 March   Gabriel tells me a singular circumstance—the only thing, he says, having the appearance of a supernatural visitation, that ever occurred direct to himself (this would be apart from occurrences of the kind proper to 'spiritualism'). Something like two years ago, he was sitting up in his studio towards midnight, after everyone else had retired, when he heard most distinctly, as if the passage outside the studio leading between its side-door and the garden-door, the sound of a continuous whining or whimpering of a child. The noise advanced and retreated, as if the child were going up and down the passage, but he is not confident that he heard anything like a sound of feet. This continued for about 5 minutes, and ceased. He then went to the passage, to see what it could be, and found nothing. Says the sound was unmistakeably such as he described it—no caterwauling, or the like sound producible by any animal in his possession. (It has subsequently occurred to me that this noise might have been produced by the Racoon, which got shut up, unknown, in a drawer in that passage. I mentioned the surmise to Gabriel but he still affirms the noise was not such as the Racoon could have produced.)

Sunday 3 March   Finished reading Elze's *Life of Byron*[1] (English version) for review in the *Academy*. It closes with a translation of some German verses: this translation being introduced with some words pretty clearly identifying the translator of them with the translator of the volume generally, and being signed R.N.— Trelawny had asked me to find out, if possible, who the translator of the book is—he himself being somewhat scurvily treated therein by the translator, as apart from the German author.

[1] Karl Elze wrote a biography of Byron, published in Berlin in 1870. The English translation was published by John Murray in 1872. A review of the book appeared in the *Athenaeum*, 17 February 1872, p. 209.

(I apprehend that R.N. is in all probability Richard (or is it Robert?) Napier, who was, I believe, or perhaps now is, Editor of the *Quarterly*. It happens too that Trelawny himself told me that, on asking the attendant at his Club (the Reform) whether any one read the book there, he was told that only Mackay and 'Mr. Richard Napier' had asked after it: this seems in no small degree confirmation of my surmise.)

Monday 4 March   Bought a Shelleyan curiosity—a poem on *The Weald of Sussex* written by Miss Hitchener, the 'Brown Daemon'.[1] It is poor tedious stuff, containing a fulsome tirade about Princess Charlotte etc., and seems to show that Miss Hitchener had by this time (1821) kept her infidelity etc. in the background.—There is however a tooth-and-nail attack on soldiering. Several quotations etc. from authors, but not a single word referable to Shelley.

Tuesday 5 March   Called again on Trelawny. His niece informs me he is not so old as I had supposed—seventy-nine or eighty, but perhaps seventy-five or seventy-six: she is not certain of the exact age. I have a strong impression that, in some book about Shelley, I found that Trelawny was of much the same age as Shelley, who would, in the August of the current year, be 80. According to Miss Taylor's statement, Trelawny was full four years younger, and must have been quite youthful—only about twenty-four—when he first met Shelley.—I asked Trelawny whether Shelley had (as Medwin intimates) any of the prepossessions of an aristocrat—whether, for instance, he would have had any preference for a well-bred intelligent man of good family over a like man of no family. Trelawny says Shelley had no such feeling; nor, indeed, does he think that even Byron had much of

---

[1] Elizabeth Hitchener (1782–1822), the daughter of a Sussex innkeeper, was a schoolmistress at Hurstpierpoint when Shelley, aged 18, first met her and began with her an important correspondence in which he endeavoured to enlighten her mind by developing his own ideas on philosophy, politics, religion, and poetry. The intellectual enthusiasm was great on both sides and Shelley called her the 'sister of his soul', but when, on Shelley's suggestion, she came to live with the Shelleys at Lynmouth and at Tanyrallt in 1812, disillusion soon set in, and Shelley wrote to Hogg: 'She is an artful, superficial, ugly, hermaphroditical beast of a woman' (Shelley, *Letters*, i. 336) and designated her as 'the Brown Daemon'. After four months the Shelleys asked her to leave with a promise of £100 per annum. Later she married an Austrian officer and left England. She published a poem, *The Weald of Sussex* in 1822.

the aristocratic feeling in this particular direction—his disagree-
ments with Hunt were not assignable to any such cause. Colonel
Leigh[1] squandered his means on the turf, for which he had an
infatuation, and his son does the same on a smaller scale. Mrs.
Leigh was a person of full average intelligence: she was not the
least like Byron in person, nor was any one of her children so,
as far as Trelawny can say. Trelawny did not know Lady Byron,
but seems to have a regard for her character—or at any rate the
natural direction of her character.—Trelawny wears no under-
clothing, at any season, even at his present advanced age; and
even a light great-coat is the exception with him. Does not
accurately know what became of Whitcombe, the man who
attempted to assassinate him in Greece. He disappeared from
society, and is no longer alive. Leicester Stanhope[2] was a weak-
minded man. He imported a lot of Bibles into Greece (about the
time of Byron's expedition there), for diffusion among the people:
they came into Trelawny's hands, and he tore them up for
cartridge-paper.

Wednesday 6 March   Wrote to Miss Taylor, recommending Mme
Filopanti[3] to read Dante with Mrs. Morison (as yesterday mentioned to me by Miss Taylor) and talk Italian with her.

Thursday 7 March   Having received back from the printers my
text giving the framework of the Humorous Selection, I made
the necessary addition of a few extra poems found since I first sent
in the MS; also began making, in the Miscellaneous Selection,

[1] The husband of Byron's half-sister.

[2] Leicester Fitzgerald Charles Stanhope, fifth Earl of Harrington (1784–1862),
went to Greece as agent of the English Committee in 1823. He met Byron, but they
totally disagreed about the measures that ought to be adopted in Greece. Stanhope
wished to establish hospitals, schools, post-offices, and to set up a printing-press
for the publication of Greek newspapers. Byron thought this premature, especially
the printing press, since the people could not read. Stanhope brought home Byron's
remains; contributed to W. Parry's *Last Days of Lord Byron*, 1825. See Roden Noel,
Life of Lord Byron, 1890, pp. 191–2.

[3] Madame Enrica Filopanti was the wife of an Italian revolutionary who had
adopted this name to express his opinions without danger; his real name was
Barile. She earned her living by giving Italian lessons in London. Christina Rossetti
composed a short poem, 'Enrica, 1865', in which she contrasts Enrica's genial
Southern behaviour with that of English women: 'She summer-like and we like
snow'. See C. G. R., *Poetical Works*, p. 377 and *Reminiscences*, p. 135.

such additions as are dependent upon the notices etc. in the Humorous Selection.

Friday 8 March Called by invitation to see Nettleship's picture, for the International Exhibition, of a *Lion and Hyaenas* on the lookout: they are supposed to have caught sight of a man. Very able, and I think the lion's head and mane may be the best piece of painting that Nettleship has yet produced: A certain want of texture and solid form in large foreground objects is perhaps the greatest technical difficulty that he now has to contend with. Saw also a very capital picture (lately at the Dudley Gallery) of two rival stallions, with several mares and some pigs; one of a bull in heat, also very good. Various designs: a very finely invented Caliban in the subject where Prospero reproaches Caliban with having once tried to deflower Miranda; *Jane Eyre and the maniac*; the *Trapper's Marriage* (partly suggested by a passage in Whitman, but carried far in dramatic invention as to the dominant and waning races); *Passion and Death*; the *Black Panther*, from a story by Dumas, a great design in force and rush. Also a picture of a black panther and two puff adders—very telling, but execution not so good as in some others. The great picture of the *Master of the World* has been considerably benefited by turning his head slightly to one side. O'Shaughnessy[1] came in while I was with Nettleship: he says that no paper save the *Athenaeum*[2]—which gave a review he considers depreciatory—has noticed his *Lays of France*.

Saturday 9 March Finished what I can for the present do in piecing-in the material of the Humorous and Miscellaneous Selections.

Sunday 10 March Called by invitation on Stillman and his wife

[1] Arthur William Edgar O'Shaughnessy (1844–81), poet, was married to P. B. Marston's eldest daughter. He published *Epic of Women and Other Poems*, illustrated with designs by J. T. Nettleship in 1870, and in 1872 he published *Lays of France* adapted from Marie de France, a French poetess of the twelfth century who was born in Normandy, lived in England, and dedicated her poems to an unknown king later identified as Henry II of England.

[2] The book was reviewed in the *Athenaeum*, 6 January 1872, p. 8. The praise was limited. 'Mr. O'Shaughnessy exhibits greater power than we were prepared for by his *Epic of Women*.' Edmund Gosse reviewed it favourably in the *Academy*, 1 November 1872, and commended its 'liquid numbers'.

at their new house, 8 Altenburg Gardens, and thence on the Spartalis. The small garden of the Stillmans' house abuts on the extensive grounds of the 'Shrubbery', and an opening will be broken so as to give access from one to the other. Mrs. Stillman is now looking well again, and cheerful, though a little delicate: Stillman anxious, the Dr. having lately pronounced that the little boy Russie has dropsy, and there seems very little prospect for him now save death after a lingering illness. Mrs. Stillman seems now quite reconciled to her father again: I saw them together— myself the only third party—and there seemed to be no strain nor distance between them. Stillman tells me he is not as yet on any confidential footing with Spartali: but they meet on terms of mutual tolerance and concession. I saw Mrs. Stillman's baby, Euphrosyne, who seems a more than commonly well-looking and well-grown infant. Mrs. Stillman is 28 years old to-day. Stillman's book about Crete is all in print.[1] The English pub- lishers are as yet Smith and Elder: but Stillman finds them rather inclined to interfere with passages expressing his opinions: and he thinks that Smith and Elder are in fact now the reverse of cordial to him—the copyright controversy in which he lately took a part having had the effect of seriously hampering their sale of advance sheets (*Cornhill Magazine* etc.) in America, as (following the advice given by Stillman) the authors themselves are now put in the way of securing the profits in this form. On these grounds Stillman is disposed to transfer the book to another publisher, if practicable.

Monday 11 March By an arrangement made through Furnivall, I was allowed to call and see Mr. Fuller-Russell's old Italian and other pictures:[2] permission was granted me to call with Scott at some future time, if he would like to see the so-called Dürer etc.

---

[1] *The Cretan Insurrection of 1866–7–8*, New York, 1874.

[2] In *Treasures of Art in Great Britain*, London, 1854, ii. 461–2, Dr. Waagen wrote: 'So richly are Mr. Russell's walls adorned with Italian specimens of the 14th century that the spectator feels as if transported into a chapel at Siena or Florence.' There were forty-three early Italian pictures among which were thirteen religious subjects by Ugolino da Siena. There were also some early Flemish and German pictures. Three pictures belonged to the school of Albert Dürer and two others long attributed to him were in fact the works of two different artists: *Christ taking leave of his mother before the Passion* is by Albrecht Altdorfer (1488–1558), *The Crucifixion* by Michael Wohlgemuth (1434–1519). The whole collection was dispersed at Christie's on 18 April 1885. See Christie's Catalogue of that date.

It is a homogeneous and interesting collection, with several good works, and a few that may even be regarded as first-class specimens. Spent the evening at Furnivall's, re-encountering the Japanese Sanjo: had not however much opportunity for conversing with him.

Tuesday 12 March Sir W. Jenner pronounces the swelling on Christina's throat sensibly diminished. Certainly however, of late, there has been no improvement in the general tone of her health—rather the reverse. Her voice too has considerably altered, within these three or four weeks more especially wanting body and distinctness. I suppose the state of the throat may account for this.

Wednesday 13 March Went to Trelawny's for the purpose more particularly of meeting Mrs. Hogg (Williams). She is an upright old lady of fine height—getting on towards eighty, Trelawny says: with the remains of a well-made face and figure: eyes dark purplish blue, still noticeable though without brilliancy (brilliancy lost only very lately, I am told): dark and plentiful hair, which I suppose must be false, but did not venture to look sharp enough to be sure. Mrs. Hogg is slightly deaf, or at any rate seems to have a certain unreadiness in catching at first hearing what is said; and I am rather afraid that every now and then she said 'yes' or 'no' to my enquiries without fully apprehending them. Trelawny says her mind is now beginning to get enfeebled—health also bad: I should not have said so from anything I noticed myself. She entered readily and kindly into talk with me on any Shelleyan subject I started, though she did not continue of her own accord to dilate on any such matter. She seems to preserve still a deep and tender feeling for Shelley, says she has never re-visited Italy since 1822[1]—the memories too painful. Shelley could not be called handsome or beautiful, though the character of his face was so remarkable for ideality and expression: his voice decidedly disagreeable. She was cognizant of his suffering from spasms, but not in any very frequent or alarming degree. Has heard him read passages from *Prometheus Unbound* or other poem, though he did

---

[1] The year of the tragedy of the *Don Juan* when Shelley and Lieutenant Williams were drowned.

not make an ordinary practice of this. Hogg's *Life of Shelley* was continued beyond the two published volumes (whether *finished* or not she did not distinctly say): she has not read the latter portion, the reminiscences being painful. She related to me unsought the same anecdote that Trelawny has told me ere now—about Shelley's going out in a boat with her and the children, and suddenly asking her whether she and Shelley should forthwith 'try the great Unknown'. She replied (as she tells me, for I think Trelawny gives greater detail) 'Hadn't we better land the children first?'—which was conceded. After this, she did not again venture out on the water with Shelley. Trelawny tells me that her maiden name was Cleveland (whether or not related to the poet Cleveland[1] he knows not). She has a daughter, Prudentia,[2] by Hogg—now married. A nephew, of weak mind, lives with her, or at any rate is very generally with her, and is very attentive to her requirements. Millais and a few other guests were also with Trelawny this evening. Millais's eldest son is 16: neither he nor his next brother shows any turn for painting.[3] Millais thinks it highly advantageous for a painter to show his pictures about to all sorts of people, so as to keep himself right in the proportion, etc: even a stupid remark has generally *some* sort of truth in it, and public criticism of the present day is of very fair quality on the whole. Millais is a perpetual smoker now, mostly of pipes: began towards the age of twenty-eight, prompted by A. J. Lewis.[4] He smokes throughout his painting hours, and even when he has ladies or others sitting for portraits. Mrs. Hogg says she has no idea what career Shelley would have liked his son Percy to adopt. She thinks Shelley might have returned to England at some time or other, had his life been prolonged: but he had no direct intention of doing so as long as she knew him.

Thursday 14 March   Rivingtons inform Maria that the first edition of her *Shadow of Dante* is now exhausted—exactly six months after

---

[1] John Cleveland (1613–58), Cavalier poet.

[2] Prudentia Hogg married first, Thomas Jones Arnold, a London magistrate, and secondly, James John Lonsdale, Recorder of Folkestone. She died in 1897. R. Glynn Grylls, *Mary Shelley*, p. 196.

[3] Millais's eldest son (1856–97) Everett Millais, 2nd Baronet, introduced the basset hound into England. The second son, George, died at the age of 21.

[4] Arthur J. Lewis, painter; he was an exhibitor at the Pre-Raphaelite Exhibition, Russell Place, in 1857. See W. M. R., *Ruskin, Rossetti, Pre-Raphaelitism*, p. 172.

date of publication: 500 copies sold in England, and 500 in America. They propose therefore to bring out a second edition. This may be regarded as a not insignificant success.

Friday 15 March Replied to Garnett as to a most disgusting blunder he has pointed out in my two volume Shelley (repeated in the cheap edition)—*Cenci*—'This deed is *done*',[1] which (as all readers of the poet know) ought to be 'none'. Also replied that I give up the alleged Shelley portrait as Helen Shelley wholly disbelieves in the existence of any such work.[2] Mrs. Hogg, by-the-bye informed me the other day that she possesses a portrait of Shelley: this, Trelawny says, is the one that Clint[3] executed after a drawing done by Lieutenant Williams.[4]

Saturday 16 March Christina is miserably exhausted now, as to all such matters as appetite, strength, etc., causing us all grave anxiety: yet it seems that the lump outside the throat has diminished, and the spasmodic difficulty in swallowing is also less.

Sunday 17 March Wrote to Howell, informing him that the Shelley portrait is given up; to the printers Sanson, asking various questions, with the view of learning whether and when I could introduce requisite corrections into the Memoir and Notes to the two volume Shelley, etc.

Monday 18 March Brown called. He says Nolly has, to the astonishment of everybody, and without consulting anybody,

---

[1] *The Cenci* iv. 4. 46. The reading 'The deed is done' was adopted by T. Hutchinson in the Oxford edition (1904) of Shelley's poems as corresponding to that of the 2nd edition (1821). See the letter mentioned here in *Letters about Shelley*, p. 53.

[2] See entry of 5 February. Helen Shelley was one of the poet's sisters.

[3] George Clint, A.R.A. (1770–1854), portrait painter. His portrait of Shelley was made after Shelley's death from descriptions given by Miss Amelia Curran, who had made an oil portrait of Shelley in Rome in 1819, and by Jane Williams whose husband had made a water-colour drawing, now lost, of the poet. From this portrait by Clint derived most of the alleged portraits of Shelley.

[4] Edward Elleker Williams (1793–1822) and his wife met the Shelleys at Pisa in 1821 and henceforth both couples lived in close intimacy: they tenanted the same house and in April 1822 they moved together into Casa Magni at Lerici. Williams helped her refit the *Don Juan* in which he and Shelley lost their lives after her sinking. See *Maria Gisborne and Edward E. Williams, Shelley's Friends: Their Journals and Letters*, ed. F. L. Jones, Oklahoma Press, 1951.

written a prose tale of passion, of extraordinary power:[1] it drew tears from Mathilde Blind. He wishes Gabriel, myself, and perhaps Morris, to meet soon at Miss Blind's to hear the tale read by Lucy, and to offer opinions as to its merits, and chance of success. It seems that some little while ago Nolly burned a lot of sonnets that he had written.—Brown talked to me confidentially about various details of the complications that have been going on of late years between Jones, Howell, etc. and his own family as related thereto: he is by no means in a friendly or indulgent frame of mind towards Jones—as indeed Gabriel had told me some while ago.

Tuesday 19 March   Swinburne called—chiefly to be steered through an answer in Italian which he wishes to return to a letter a certain Chiarini[2] has addressed to him from Italy, very enthusiastic as to his poems, and asking some details to serve for a biographical notice. I suggested to Swinburne to write his reply in English (which he did before leaving me), and I would afterwards turn it into Italian. As regards the purely poetic faculty, Swinburne will only acknowledge two directions of it—the lyrical and the dramatic. Thus he will go so far as to say that Byron was not a poet, although heartily recognizing his greatness in some form of writing in the poetical shape: he considers energy to be Byron's great excellence, and would, as a single work of his, soonest preserve *The Vision of Judgment*.[3] Thus Swinburne also objects to my having (in short notice of Shelley) classed Chaucer along with Shakespeare, Milton, and Shelley, as forming the greatest quatuor in English poetry. Swinburne has for the last two months or more been living at 12 North Crescent, Bedford Square.—Professor Beesly writes me that one Lefèvre[4] has called on him, professing (falsely) to be sent by me, and asking for assistance as connected with the Paris Commune: Beesly infers that Lefèvre may be in league with a certain Laatsch,[4] whom I was lately assisting on the same ground, but whom, from recent correspondence with Beesly,

[1] *Gabriel Denver*, later published in 1873; it appeared in its original form with its first title, *The Black Swan*. See J. H. Ingram, *Oliver Madox Brown*, 1883.

[2] Giuseppe Chiarini (1833–1908), scholar, critic, and editor of Leopardi. For the letter mentioned here, see Swinburne, *Letters*, ii. 175.

[3] This counterblast to Southey's poem *A Vision of Judgment*, in which the 'Satanic School of Poetry', was stigmatized, was first published in the *Liberal* on 15 October 1822.   [4] Not identified.

I now perceive to be a slippery customer, and perhaps worse. I am to call on Beesly to-morrow morning, to settle the question as regards Lefèvre.

Wednesday 20 March   Told Beesly that Lefèvre is an impostor. He had already convinced himself of this fact, and had made arrangements for giving Lefèvre into charge should he reappear, as he had fixed to do this morning—(I do not as yet know the upshot). Beesly asked me also, if Laatsch reappears (he is now presumably in Lyons) to refer him also to Beesly who would apply the same rule of treatment to him, in respect of a recent cheating application for 10/–, falsely said to be on my authority. I should not scruple to do this if the occasion arises; though I would on the whole drop Laatsch altogether rather than bring him to justice.—Garnett sent me a transcript he has lately made from the journal of Lieutenant Williams, as copied out by Mrs. Shelley,[1] covering about the whole period of his acquaintance with Shelley: the entries are of a summary kind, and without much matter of positive novelty, yet highly interesting for a lover of Shelley to read. One entry purports that my uncle Dr. Polidori[2] poisoned himself with a very potent poison *of his own making up*: I don't know whether this last detail has appeared elsewhere, or is authentic. Mamma does not confirm it—saying simply that the poison was prussic acid.

Thursday 21 March   Sir W. Jenner called again. He told Maria that the disease Christina suffers from, exophthalmic bronchocele, is one from which the patient more generally recovers: the chief danger is exhaustion. Of this unfortunately there have been very distressing symptoms lately in Christina: almost total want of appetite, prostration of strength, and very frequent vomiting. The last was particularly bad yesterday: today she has of a sudden

[1] Richard Garnett edited and published the *Journal of Edward Elleker Williams* in 1902.

[2] Dr. John Polidori (1795–1821), W. M. R.'s maternal uncle. He accompanied Byron on his Continental tour in 1816 as his private physician and secretary. While associated with Byron and Shelley, he wrote a diary which W. M. R. published in 1911: *The Diary of Dr. John W. Polidori, 1816.* Dr. Polidori also wrote two volumes of verse and two prose tales, one being the *Vampyre* (1819), which has been wrongly attributed to Byron, who had written the beginning of another tale, also named *The Vampyre.* Dr. Polidori committed suicide at the age of 26, as a consequence of a gambling debt.

bettered to some appreciable extent, having had a good night (Wednesday), more appetite and liveliness, and throughout the day no vomiting—though this came on again towards bed-time.— Gabriel came, and says he is now going to see to the republication of his *Early Italian Poets*, altering the arrangement somewhat, so as to give greater prominence to Dante. With Gabriel also there is now some complication concerning Communals or other refugees—Karl Blind having written to him regarding a certain Marnowski[1] who seems rather a suspicious personage, and connected somehow with a subscription to which I contributed a trifle lately, on the understanding that it was for a Spanish artist. The details wholly vague to me as yet. Miss Losh,[2] Miss Boyd's aunt, is dead of bronchitis: only three or four weeks ago she underwent the operation for cataract.

Friday 22 March   The apparent slight improvement in Christina's condition is not maintained today: she passed a good night however.—Sir W. Jenner will now be going to Baden with the Queen for a fortnight or so, and Dr. Wilson Fox will take his place in looking after Christina.—Called on Rose to see the opinion Mr. Joshua Williams has offered on Mrs. Wieland's case. Both Williams and Rose consider that the only proper and conclusive course is to get a decree in Chancery. In this therefore I expressed my full concurrence: but, as Rose is going to-morrow to start for a fortnight or so in Italy, it is proposed that his clerk should meanwhile send a copy of the opinion to Wieland, and that any ulterior steps should await Rose's return. I am sorry to hear that poor Rose has some form of kidney disease, liable, if not checked, to lead to deposit of gravel.

Saturday 23 March   Passed the proof of the notice of Cowper, for the *Popular Poets*.

[1] In a letter to Karl Blind, dated 19 March 1872, D. G. R. describes the 'suspicious personage' and presumes that his name might be known in the refugees' quarters, as in October 1871 he had subscribed to a 'Communalist Benevolent Society' in London. See D. G. R. *Letters*, iii. 1046.

[2] Alicia Margaret Losh (1801–72) was Miss Boyd's cousin, not aunt. She met D. G. R. at Penkill in 1868 and was fascinated by his personality; she offered him a 'loan of money to prevent him using his eyes (which were then causing him anxiety) in painting or any other trying occupation'. After her death, an I.O.U. from D. G. R. was found but 'destroyed by a friendly hand'. See *Memoir*, p. 267, also Troxell, *Three Rossettis*, pp. 80–7.

Sunday 24 March Finished a review, for the *Academy*, of Elze's *Life of Byron*.

Monday 25 March Dr. Fox called on Christina, and considers that the action of the heart has improved since he saw her last: she also does not now suffer from the feeling of perpetual heat which she had not long ago. In other respects there is no good to be recorded—Mathilde Blind consults me as to the fittingness of her lecturing at the anti-religious Hall of Science, on women's suffrage or other matters. I reply that I think she would be wholly *right* in doing so; but that, as a question of prudence affecting her literary and other position, there may be something to consider per contra.

Tuesday 26 March Went with Scott to see Mr. Fuller-Russell's pictures—more particularly the *Crucifixion* attributed to Dürer. Scott has now about seceded from the *Academy* (review); not entirely liking the treatment he receives from the editor Appleton, and finding the reviewing of exhibitions etc. a considerable inter-ference with the time which he might otherwise get for painting. He says the death of Miss Losh (see March 21) was almost sudden. It is believed she has not left anything to Miss Boyd, but that the bulk of her property has passed to another lady, a niece.[1]

Wednesday 27 March Received the first proof of the Chaucer work—*Filostrato–Troilus*—which I did some while ago for the Chaucer Society.—Christina having lately asked Dalziels how her *Sing-Song* has sold, they reply that the sale has fallen far short of their expectations.—Still, more than 1,100 copies have now gone off (beginning about 18 November): 1000 up to the close of last year, and the rest since—and this cannot certainly be regarded as a crass failure.

Thursday 28 March Resumed looking at Benoît de Ste More, to guide me in what has to be done with the Chaucer proofs.

[1] Miss Losh's principal legatee was Frances Elizabeth Pennell, wife of Follet Walrond Pennell; she died on 8 April 1900 and left Miss Losh's will unadministered. Miss Losh left about £16,000. D. G. R. was not mentioned as a beneficiary (from the transcription of the original will kept in the records of Somerset House).

Friday 29 March Mr. Geo. Browning, Secretary to the Society for Promotion of the Fine Arts, called, asking me to act as chairman at a lecture on Modern Art to be shortly delivered at that society by a Mr. Thomas—who, as I understand, is a gold medalist of the R.A.—such work is not much in my line, so I declined. It is only a fortnight or so ago that I had declined a previous invitation to deliver, myself, a lecture or lectures at the same place.

Saturday 30 March Bad news of Henrietta Polydore: extreme weakness, failing sight etc.

Sunday 31 March Wrote at some length to Whitman, in reply to an interesting letter he sent me at the end of January.[1]—Informed him that I had dedicated to him my Selection of American Poetry.

Monday 1 April Called by invitation to see Boughton's[2] pictures for the R.A.—three subjects of human life in symbolic relation with birds, and among his most successful work, but ought to have more positiveness of truth and of realization. To two of them he has given mottoes from Christina's poems: he professes the most unbounded admiration for Gabriel's large picture—which with others now at his studio, he has lately seen. An American named Armstrong came in—a friend of Whitman's: I asked him to give Whitman my love when he sees him again. Armstrong is said to be extremely like Home the spiritualist[3]—so much so as to have been not unfrequently mistaken for him: he has no faculty as a medium.

Tuesday 2 April Saw Nettleship's interesting picture of a *Tiger in the Jungle, and Impeyan pheasants*—grandly felt and expressed, and

---

[1] In this letter, dated 30 January 1872, Whitman declares that 'my poetry remains yet quite unrecognized here, in the land for which it is written. The best established magazine and literary authorities quite ignore me and it. It has to this day failed to find an American publisher.' See H. Traubel, *With Walt Whitman in Camden*, 1953, pp. 58–61.

[2] George Henry Boughton (1833–1905), painter and illustrator. See *Portfolio*, 1871, p. 69.

[3] Daniel Dunglas Home (1833–86), born at Currie, near Edinburgh. His father, William Humes, was said to be the natural son of Alexander, the tenth Earl of Home, though no real foundation appears for this assertion. He became famous as a medium all over Europe and was termed 'the celebrities' celebrity'. See Jean Burton, *Heyday of a Wizard*, London, 1948.

in various respects ably executed, though I rather fear that this work also will fail to find favour in the eyes of the R.A.—Was introduced to Nettleship's mother, who I see is a widow. Whether the loss of her husband is recent or not I know not: but at any rate her look is that of a person who has seen a good deal of trouble.

Wednesday 3 April Some degree of improvement has been perceptible in Christina's health these five or six days past. There is some decided (though still but faint) revival of appetite, greatly diminished tendency to nausea, and generally less exhaustion and prostration. As to looks, she continues as bad as possible. Gabriel called. I asked him whether he has had any recurrence of the blood-spitting of which he told me some weeks ago, and I am sorry to learn there *was* a recurrence within these few days—and has occasionally been at other times after a fit of coughing. Gabriel seems to attach little importance to it: I think however he should consult a doctor and so told him.

Thursday 4 April I have obtained a copy of my two volume Shelley to present to Thomson, author of the poem *Weddah and Om-el-Bonain*; and have given the better part of these two evenings to noting in it such corrections and added information as required notice.

Friday 5 April Continuing this work. Roberts the American publishers write to say that the American edition of Christina's *Sing-Song* has not yet covered its expenses—one obstacle being that it reached the country too late: 800 copies sold. They ask for 250 more copies of Maria's book on Dante.

Saturday 6 April Admiral Swinburne called on me at Somerset House wishing to learn any news of his son. He had called at his lodgings (12 North Crescent, Bedford Square), and could only learn that Swinburne had not been in-doors the preceding night. I was unable to afford any information, beyond suggesting that Powell or Brown might possibly be worth enquiring of. The Admiral says that the family, as a measure of precaution, drink no wine when Swinburne is with them.

Sunday 7 April   Sent Ferrazzi a copy of the no. of the *Academy* containing my notice of his book on Dante.[1]

Monday 8 April   Thomson[2] and Pope were originally set down to be published among *Moxon's Popular Poets*; were afterwards withdrawn by Payne; but have now for some while past been restored by Beeton. I took up and completed the notes which I made long ago for the biographical notice of Thomson.

Tuesday 9 April   Mamma has been unwell these three or four days with a cold and cough. She passed a very bad night, (Monday), and had to remain in bed in the morning, and to see Sir W. Jenner in the evening.—He finds some degree of fever, and of bronchial affection; but does not seem to attach (nor indeed do I) more importance to this indisposition than to others that have preceded it of the like kind.—I left the copy of Shelley for Thomson at his house, 240 Vauxhall Bridge Road.

Wednesday 10 April   Sansons the printers write asking me to send them the material for my Poetic Selections. I suppose what they want first is the Humorous volume (as previously decided) and I shall send this accordingly: have now dedicated it to Madox Brown. Lucy and Nolly came in in the evening, and I regret to learn that Brown is laid up with a sharp attack of gout. This is, I think, the first for some considerable while past that has caused him much inconvenience; as a remedy indicated to him by certain young ladies from Corsica, whose acquaintance he made perhaps two years ago, has ever since then been found markedly efficacious.

Thursday 11 April   Called to see Brown: he is up to-day, after two or three days, in bed. Does not suffer any particular pain as long as the gouty foot remains unused, but can't put it to the ground, nor does he expect to do so yet awhile.—Met poor Andrew Johnson in the street: his mind remains in the same deplorable state as for months past—cannot read a book, nor remember any proper names. In other respects, nothing very definite amiss.

[1] W. M. R.'s notice appeared in the *Academy* for 1 April 1872.
[2] James Thomson (1700–48), author of the *Seasons*, not to be confused with B.V. See p. 128 nn. 4 and 5.

Friday 12 April A most troublesome hacking cough, with scarcely any intermission, plagued Christina last night, and all to-day. Sir W. Jenner came to see her: he does not seem to attach special importance to the cough and has ordered some appropriate remedies. It does not pain Christina to any extent worth mentioning, and seems to arise from some slight local irritation consequent on unexpelled phlegm: the persistency of the small iterated cough is however most remarkable in degree. Happily she passed this Friday night well.—There is nothing in the house now but coughs and colds: Mamma's cough still to some extent violent, but decreasing: Maria painting her throat with glycerine; myself steeped in the nuisance of a cold in the head; Betsy (to-morrow will be her last day in our house), with a very bad cough.

Saturday 13 April Christina's cough better, but not by any means gone.

Sunday 14 April Sent to Ferrazzi, as he had requested, photographs of Maria, Gabriel, and myself; and began noting down from his volume 4 a few needful corrections which I will forward to him, as I had previously proposed.

Monday 15 April Bought some silk handkerchieves and a few other things at Hewitt's. He tells me that the sale of Japanese articles continues largely on the increase; much more, for instance, sold now than three years ago. I noticed in his stock one of those boxes of Delhi work—minute cubes of ivory etc. put together in patterns—in which a considerable portion of the pattern had fallen out, and required refitting. I asked Hewitt whether he could get this done in England, and was surprised to learn that he could: he says however that there are not more than a couple of men who could perform the work satisfactorily.

Tuesday 16 April Maria says that, having to-day seen Christina's throat uncovered, she was agreeably surprised to find how very much the external swelling (once so large) has diminished: one might now almost take the throat for its natural shape: the discoloration also is less marked. Better news come from Henrietta Polydore: she had almost lost her sight, and had destroyed various letters etc. in preparation for death, but has now once again taken a comparatively favourable turn. She has lately had some English beer to drink and finds it salutary.

Wednesday 17 April Called on Rose regarding Mrs. Wieland's affairs: the chief question now is whether we should take the initiative in the required Chancery suit, or whether we should leave Captain Taylor to do so—Rose being in favour of the former course. Further consultation with the Wielands will be needed.— Rose, when lately in Florence, found that Isabella was almost dead of diphtheria: in the course of the evening however a letter reached me from Theodoric, to say she has now surmounted the crisis after extreme suffering, and still remaining very prostrate. Rose tells me he got rid, as soon as he went abroad, of the kidney-disease (see 22 March), but is now troubled by stricture: he looks better decidedly.—He also tells me that Legros is in debt to the extent of £10,000 (which seems a surprisingly large sum under the circumstances): Rose has been trying to arrange matters with the creditors, but they seem resolved to make Legros bankrupt.— Teodorico informs me that the Municipality of Florence have, subject to the approval of the Government, ordered that a tablet to my Father's memory shall be set up in the cloister of Santa Croce—not in the church. This, according to Teodorico, is a very minor affair in point of honour: however, it appears to me not despicable, and one must take what one can get. Besides this, the movement for a monument at Vasto[1] is being pushed forward.— Gabriel called in the evening, and he and I began talking about our earliest recollections: neither of us being well able to say whether or not he remembers matters of so remote an age as 2 or 3. Gabriel thinks that these are two of his very early reminiscences:—1., that when we lived in 38 Charlotte St., a Punch show used to perform opposite our house, but for the benefit of our opposite neighbours—the consequence of which was that the back of the show only was visible from our windows, much to Gabriel's disgust. He used to want to walk out into the street, and face round towards the show, but this was objected to as *infra dig.* 2. our grand aunt having sent a rocking-horse, Gabriel set to at drawing its portrait in the passage of the house, and was seen thus occupied by the milkman, to the latter's no small astonishment.

[1] Gabriele Rossetti was born at Vasto in the Abruzzi on 28 February 1783.

Gabriel thinks he was then probably only four.[1] Of each of these incidents I also have some indistinct but still actual recollection. It seems to me that one of my own earliest reminiscences is that, in some infantile malady (if I recollect right, it was teething), I used to sit on a stool or little chair with its back to the wall, and with my hands drooping in front of me like a Kangaroo's—suffering in silence. This seems to me a very early affair—perhaps at the age of three.

Thursday 18 April   Mathilde Blind asked me a short while ago to attend a lecture in Seymour St., by a Mr. Macdonell,[2] regarding Women's suffrage, and to be one of the speakers. I staved off this latter suggestion, not wishing to feel tied in the matter, but promised to attend. Did so: a very scanty audience. Though I had not from first to last offered to speak, I found myself announced by the Chairman to second the final vote (thanks to Chairman, as and occasion for some general observations) and I therefore made my speech—some 8 to 10 minutes long, I suppose—being the first time (if I except an occasion in 1857 connected with the Exhibition of English Arts in America) that I ever addressed an audience in public. I found no particular trouble in getting through the speech; and, had I thought over its subject-matter beforehand, might perhaps have done pretty tolerably. At any rate I spoke my opinions out in an uncompromising form (going further than any of the preceding speakers)—saying that I would advocate Female Suffrage on the general ground of liberty and justice, even apart from the question whether or not it would produce better government, and that the right final upshot would be universal suffrage for both sexes. Met at this lecture Mrs. Orme,[3] her daughter Blanche (Mrs. Holland Fox), and her grand-daughter Flora Masson,[4] who has a very sweet and well-formed

---

[1] (I still possess a childish drawing by my brother of a rocking-horse. Our Mother had marked it with the date 1834, when he was at least five years of age. If this is that very earliest drawing of his, it is a good deal less bad than one would have expected. W. M. R.) This is D. G. R's earliest recorded drawing.

[2] James Macdonell (1842–79), journalist. He was then on the staff of the *Daily Telegraph*.

[3] Mrs. Orme was the sister of Coventry Patmore's first wife. She was a beautiful woman and liked to entertain writers and artists. Her husband was a distiller in London. *Reminiscences*, p. 89.

[4] Flora Masson was the daughter of Mrs. Orme's eldest daughter and of David Masson (1822–1907), Professor of English Literature, first at University College,

face, and is now just about grown up. Mrs. Orme was as usual
exceedingly cordial, though sarcastic as to my neglect of ever
calling at her house—which of course I had to confess and ward
off as best I could—I shall have to go there soon, Masson being
about to come up.

Friday 19 April Christina is still troubled with the cough which
began on 11 April though to a much smaller extent than at first;
frequent attacks of vomiting are extremely vexatious; and her
appetite is exceedingly bad, though not so almost null as it was
three or four weeks ago. To-day, we sent for Sir W. Jenner to see
her. He tells Maria that Christina's life is 'in jeopardy' but that the
case is most decidedly not hopeless. He finds her pulse better than
it has been for an indefinite while past.—The proofs of my Humorous Selection are now beginning to come in.

Saturday 20 April Attending to these proofs, and to those of
the Chaucer work.

Sunday 21 April Early this morning poor Christina had a tor-
turing attack of neuralgia across the chest and arms—a new symptom—with hurried action of the heart. Dr. W. Fox was sent for;
and in the course of the day he attended twice, and Sir W. Jenner
once. The attack soon subsided; and, up to Monday morning
when I write, has not recurred. The doctors recommend Christina
to keep her bed (which, indeed, I have frequently thought and
said would be the better course); and, as she can't take natural
nourishment at ordinary times, they direct that, every two hours
day and night, (unless she is asleep) she shall take some small
modicum of food.

Monday 22 April My cold and cough are not yet subdued. The
cold in the head (one of the most violent I have had for years) is
indeed today as good as gone; but the cough (which is a very
uncommon form of illness with me, frequent as my sore throats
have been) does not seem inclined to go. Today, more especially
judging from the rumbling sound of my voice, I fancy the cough
has the character of bronchitis, and that it may possibly turn out

London, then at Edinburgh, and for thirty years an intimate friend of Carlyle.
See *Reminiscences*, p. 487; and J. A. Froude, *Thomas Carlyle*, London, 1885.

a worse affair than I have been used to. I put on a mustard poultice before dinner.

Tuesday 23 April The poultice seems to have done me a considerable amount of good; also Mr. Roberts (Somerset House) is getting me to take a draught of some composition in the nature of muriatic acid. To-day I have finished at Somerset House looking through an old MS book of my father's which I first set aside some 11 years or so ago, when I was making a selection of his poems: soon afterwards, it was shown to Keightley[1] at his request, and he said it was merely material for the unpublished portion of the *Comento Analitico*[2] on Dante. This conclusion, I find, is not correct. A good deal of the MS does belong to the *Comento*; but other substantial sections either do not belong to that at all, or at any rate are in the nature of general disquisitions, such as might form part of the *Amor Platonico*,[2] or of the *Beatrice di Dante*.[2] Some portions, I fancy, will on investigation be found to have been utilized in the *Amor Platonico*; whatever has not been so utilized may be regarded as valuable material, according to my father's system of interpretation, and would deserve to be offered for publication in Italy, in some form or other.—My co-trustee for Mrs. Wieland, Mr. Thompson, attended with me at Rose's and we signed an authority for the firm to begin the Chancery suit required in her case. The person Mrs. Wieland has proposed as her 'next friend' (who will also have to figure in the suit, but, as Rose tells me, with little more than a mere technical connexion therewith) is Sidney Wieland, her husband's brother. Thompson says that Sidney Wieland is not a desirable person to put forward for such a purpose, and that he will represent as much to Mrs. Wieland.—He says that S. Wieland was courting Mrs. Taylor (as she then was) on his own account; but, having introduced his brother Walter to her, the latter saw his own opportunity, and cut out Sidney. C. E. Read, my co-trustee under Taylor's will (not under the marriage-settlement) was also in consultation with Rose to-day, and will, it seems, concur as a party to the Chancery suit.

[1] Thomas Keightley (1789–1872), classical scholar, a friend of Gabriele Rossetti whose theories about Dante he supported with great enthusiasm. He himself wrote a book on *The Secret Societies of the Middle Ages*, published anonymously in 1837.

[2] The *Comento Analitico* had been published in London in 1826–7; the *Amor Platonico* in 1840 and the first part of *La Beatrice di Dante* in 1842; the manuscript of the remainder of the work is in the Biblioteca del Risorgimento, Rome. See R. D. Waller, *The Rossetti Family*, 1932, p. 301.

Wednesday 24 April   Gabriel says that his re-edition of *The Early Italian Poets* is not likely to come out quite yet, as the publisher Ellis says it is not the right season. His armadillo has been making himself highly obnoxious by killing ducks, chickens, and anything it could lay claws on, and by sinking all over the garden pits sufficiently deep to incommode those who walked there. At last, in desperation Gabriel has had prussic acid given to the armadillo, in the corpse of a chicken that it had slaughtered. Since then, the chicken and the armadillo have both disappeared; and the latter is surmised to be lying dead in some one of his own pit-holes.

Thursday 25 April   Dined at Brown's with Leyland, Bodley,[1] and a few others. Brown is still suffering from gout, but can now put his foot to the ground. Saw his cartoon-drawing for the portrait-group of Fawcett and his wife[2]—very expressive and satisfactory. I hear that young Charles, the son of Mrs. Stephens by her first husband, has been lost at sea. Lucy Brown tells me that Jameson (the dentist) had told her that my short speech the other day about Women's Suffrage—he being present at the meeting—had thrown all the other speakers into the shade. As I told Lucy, I had really no clear idea as yet whether the auditors may have considered or not that I had made a fool of myself. Is Jameson's account of the matter in any degree a reasonable one?

Friday 26 April   A new scheme sanctioned at Somerset House whereby my business will probably be lightened henceforth (though indeed for the last two or three months it has altered in this respect, and been quite moderate in amount), and I shall be less tied to daily attendance, whether or not I have something of my own to look to which would make a holiday convenient. I have not, I think, taken a single casual holiday since I was appointed Asst. Secretary in July 1869, nor allowed myself to lie by for health's sake, nor ever taken my full annual leave.

Saturday 27 April   I had overlooked a second but smaller volume of my father's MSS (see 23 April). Shall now attend to it.

[1] George Frederick Bodley (1827–1907), architect; first exhibited at the Royal Academy in 1854. He designed (1860–70) many churches and private houses, worked at Oxford and Cambridge for various colleges and chapels. He published a small volume of verse in 1899, and was a friend of Morris, Burne-Jones, Madox Brown, and the Rossettis.   [2] See p. 265 n. 3.

Sunday 28 April Wrote to Beeton, claiming the money due to me from Moxons: this matter has now been hanging over since late in January. Gabriel says that his armadillo has after all not succumbed to the prussic acid: the beast has not been seen again since that plot was laid for his life, but new pits sunk by him are found in the garden. He also says that Buchanan's pamphlet[1] on *The Fleshly School of Poetry* is advertised for immediate publication; and that Colvin has in some way or other (Gabriel has but an imperfect knowledge of the details) provided for its being hostilely reviewed in the *Saturday Review, Pall Mall, Athenaeum, Daily News,* and *Fortnightly.* The late depreciating review of Gabriel and others in the *Quarterly* was written, he is told, by Courthope,[2] who recently published some poems (I believe talented) of his own.

Monday 29 April A platform-ticket for a Women's Suffrage Meeting at St George's Hall was lately sent me, with a request that I would attend. I went round this evening, punctual to the appointed hour; but found that at some earlier time the Hall had been filled to overflowing, and the doors were now closed. Waited about some while, but to no purpose, and therefore had to return home. There must have been mismanagement somewhere.

Tuesday 30 April Dr. Fox called to see Christina, who has complained these two days of unpleasant sensations at the heart— a feeling as if it were ceasing to act. He speaks in very decided terms of her being improved since he saw her last (21 April), and sees no reason why she should not surmount the illness, which, however he admits to be a serious and dangerous one. I asked him about the chance of her recovering flesh, and some proportionate amount of the good looks she used to have (for in both

[1] Buchanan, incensed by the articles which appeared in the *Athenaeum* on 16 and 30 December 1871 in answer to his own article in the *Contemporary Review,* October 1871, decided to continue the war with a pamphlet of about 100 pages, *The Fleshly School of Poetry, and other Phenomena of the Day,* published by Strahan and Co., 1872. It aggravated and enlarged the 1871 article.

[2] William John Courthope (1842–1917), Professor of Poetry at Oxford and literary critic. He was the supposed author of the article in the *Quarterly Review* (January 1872) which was unfavourable to Rossetti, Morris, and Swinburne. Buchanan counted on the support of Courthope and other critics in his own attacks. The article in the *Saturday Review,* 24 February 1872, was entitled 'Coterie Glory'.

these respects she is at the lowest ebb, and seems only to deteriorate progressively): he says there is no reason why these should not revive with reviving health. Her appetite, though still below any normal standard, is very markedly improved of late. She has remained in bed (with two or three brief intervals) ever since 21 April. No recurrence of the neuralgia of that morning.

Wednesday 1 May   Christina's illness seems to have taken a rather peculiar effect on her mind. It necessarily reduces her powers of continuous attention; but appears to have disposed her in some increased degree to reading books conveying some sort of positive knowledge, such as history—all of which class of reading has been almost wholly neglected by her all her lifetime. She has just got Mamma to read through to her Southey's *Life of Nelson*, and is herself reading Goldsmith's *History of Greece*—neither of them certainly a work of arid or profound learning, but still the sort of thing that Christina has hitherto mostly steered clear of as yet. She thinks also of reading Herodotus.

Thursday 2 May   Going on with proofs of the Humorous Selection. This is the only work, in connexion with Moxon's series, that I am doing at present, or that I feel inclined to attend to until my claim on past volumes shall be properly settled.

Friday 3 May   Gabriel tells me that Swinburne has been writing a pamphlet about Buchanan, and other hostile reviewers of the 'School of Poetry' with which Swinburne is associated.[1] He has read the pamphlet to Gabriel, but I infer that there is little or no real idea of publishing it. Gabriel thinks it talented, but its tone somewhat exceptionable, as showing too intimate an acquaintance with the minutiae of the hostile writings.

Saturday 4 May   Brown called on me—being now just well enough with his foot to walk that short distance. He says the various works sent by his family to the Royal Academy have been turned out, save Cathie's portrait of Mrs. Tadema, and that is hung over a door. Of course, this does not improve his opinion of Royal

---

[1] The pamphlet, *Under the Microscope*, was published in July 1872 by F. S. Ellis. See Swinburne, *Letters*, *II*, 163 (Letter to W. M. R.).

Academicians. Nolly has done something in the way of revising details in the prose story he wrote (and which I have not read anything of—see 18 March), and has now begun another story. Andrieu,[1] the Parisian Communist, now here in exile, is in great straits. He has written an account of the Commune, and Brown wishes to see about getting it published by subscription, in a translated form; thinks also of getting Cathie to make the translation.

Sunday 5 May Wrote to old Kirkup,[2] after too prolonged a silence: he has been very ill again, but yet once again his vitality has prevailed.

Monday 6 May At last the money—£42—for the Campbell and Milton volumes has been sent to me by cheque. The payers purport to be Ward, Lock, and Tyler; and they ask me to sign documents by way of assignment of copyright to them. To this I have no particular objection; but, as I think some previous authorization should be forthcoming from Moxon and Co. (with whom my bargain and all negotiations hitherto have been made) I wrote to Ward and Co to say as much.

Tuesday 7 May Gabriel called, and spoke of his receipts and expenses, both of which are large. On looking into household bills lately—merely those of butcher, baker, and other such purveyors—it was found that the annual expenditure on these accounts exceeds £1000. Startled at this enormous amount,

[1] Jules Andrieu (1837–84), French writer of minor importance, who, as an active member of the Commune, was banished from France. He came to London where he gave French lessons. Oliver Madox Brown was one of his pupils. He probably introduced Verlaine and Rimbaud into Madox Brown's literary circle as both poets seem to have taken an interest in Oliver's artistic and literary career. See V. P. Underwood, *Verlaine et l'Angleterre*, Paris, 1959.

[2] Seymour Stocker Kirkup (1788–1880), English painter. He was acquainted with William Blake, and present at the funeral of Keats in 1821 and of Shelley in 1822. He settled in Florence and was made 'Barone' by the Italian Government in recognition of the discovery he made in 1840 of the portrait of Dante by Giotto in the chapel of the Podestà in the Bargello of Florence under the whitewash of three centuries. He was a correspondent of Gabriele Rossetti, whose theories about Dante he greatly admired, and a friend of Trelawny. W. M. R. met him in Florence in 1860 and henceforth they exchanged letters mostly about Shelley and his circle. Kirkup wrote to W. M. R. 'I met Mrs. Shelley, but I did not like her, she was worse than blue, she was masculine.' (Unpublished letter, 16 August 1870, in the Angeli Collection.) See also W. M. R., *Gabriele Rossetti*, pp. 144 ff. for a letter from Kirkup to Gabriele Rossetti in which he relates the details of the discovery.

Gabriel now hands over to Emma £5 per week: she is expected to defray everything out of this sum, and keeps accounts accordingly with Dunn—sometimes a little within the £5, and sometimes a little beyond. Provision for F.[1] Gabriel has now designed the next large picture he proposes doing—illustrating Dante's sonnet *Guido, vorrei* etc.[2] Maria received this morning a handsome letter from Longfellow[3] regarding her *Shadow of Dante*. I signed and returned the documents sent me by Ward & Co.—the assignment being (at their suggestion) now made to Moxon & Co., rather than themselves.

Wednesday 8 May   Daldy[4] the publisher called on me, thinking of including Blake in his Aldine Series of Poets; and he asked me whether I would undertake the editing—including a memoir of some 30 to 100 pages. He does not wish to insert the *Prophetic Books*, but only a complete set of the poems of an ordinary cast. I replied that I would undertake the work for £50, on the understanding that I am not to be controlled in anything I may see fit to say; also that I might not find it convenient to commence the work for some six months or so to come. Daldy took leave, saying he would consult with his partner Bell. He had in the first instance proposed for either Gabriel or me as editor; but, as I told him, it is practically certain that Gabriel would decline.

Thursday 9 May   Going on with the proofs of the Humorous

[1] The abbreviation F. appears several times in W. M. R.'s diary. It refers to Fanny Cornforth (1824–1906). This was the professional name of Sarah Cox. In 1858 she became D. G. R.'s model. In 1860 she married a Mr. Hughes who died in 1872. After Lizzie's death in 1862, D. G. R. moved to Chelsea and Fanny was his model, mistress, and housekeeper. She sat for some of D. G. R.'s best-known pictures. She became Mrs. Schott in 1879, and she and her husband commercialized the pictures of Rossetti that were in their hands. See *Dante Gabriel Rossetti's Letters to Fanny Cornforth*, ed. Paull Franklin Baum, Baltimore, 1940.

[2] Dante's sonnet appears in *Canzoniere*, Rime LII (edition of La Società Dantesca Italiana). Its first line runs: 'Guido, i' vorrei che tu Lapo ed io'. The picture inspired by this sonnet had been in D. G. R.'s mind as early as 1850; it was called *The Boat of Love*. The oil picture mentioned here was abandoned in 1881. It is now in the Birmingham Art Gallery. See Surtees, no. 239, p. 136 and no. 239 A, B, C, D, F, G, pp. 137–8.

[3] The American poet Henry Wadsworth Longfellow (1807–82) had translated Dante's *Divine Comedy* in 1867.

[4] F. R. Daldy joined George Bell in 1856 and formed the firm Bell and Daldy. They took over the Aldine Poets from Rivington's but their partnership was dissolved in 1872 and W. M. R.'s volume *The Poetical Works of William Blake* was published in 1874 under the sole imprint of George Bell.

Selection. Our cat (a smallish tabby cat that we have had two or three years, in no way remarkable) seems to be a very unnatural mother. Some while ago she had a brood of kittens: one was kept, and fed by the mother for some days, but she then refused it any further sustenance, and it died. Now there is every reason to think that she has had another brood: but no trace of them remains, so the mother is surmised to have devoured them.

Friday 10 May   Went for the first time to the R.A. Looked through the first two rooms and got something of a general glance round the others. About the finest thing is Walker's[1] picture of *An Asylum for Aged Poor*: one of Millais's two land-scapes—*Flowing to the River*[2]—very excellent, I think at least as good as the greatly admired *Chill October*[3] of last year. Brett's[4] seapiece with gulls is very masterly.

Saturday 11 May   Troubled with a recurrence of cold in the head, after it had been got rid of about a fortnight.

Sunday 12 May   Christina this morning had another bad attack of neuralgia, more diffused than that of 21 April over the whole person. Fortunately it did not last long. In other respects, she is now excessively low, and confined to bed.

Monday 13 May   Finished looking through the second of my father's MS volumes. It contains the *Comento* on the *Purgatorio*

[1] Frederick Walker (1840–75), painter, exhibited many oil-paintings and water-colours at the R.A. and elsewhere between 1863 and 1875. This picture, generally known as *Harbour of Refuge*, shows his generous tendencies to social observation; it is in the Tate Gallery, London.

[2] *Flowing to the River*. I have been unable to locate this picture.

[3] *Chill October* was painted in 1870 from a backwater of the Tay near Perth. W. M. R. alludes to the laudatory articles of *The Times* for 29 April 1871 and of the *Athenaeum* of the same date. Millais sold it in 1871 for £1,000; it was bought by Agnews in 1910 for £5,040; it now belongs to a private collection. See M. Bennett, *Catalogue of Millais's Exhibition*, 1967, pp. 49–50.

[4] John Brett (1830–1902), a painter influenced by the Pre-Raphaelites whose principles he tried to put into practice in landscape and marine painting. He was a regular exhibitor at the R.A. Christina Rossetti's poem, 'No thank you, John' (1860) refers to John Brett. In one of her marginal notes, she wrote: 'The original John was obnoxious, because he never gave scope for "No, thank you".' See *The Poetical Works of C. G. Rossetti*, p. 483. In 1872 Brett exhibited two pictures at the R.A.: *A Morning amongst the Granite boulders* and *A North-West Gale off the Longships Lighthouse*.

(completed, with the exception of a few of the early cantos), and but little else besides.

Tuesday 14 May   Late this evening, towards 9.30, poor Christina, being out of her bed for a few minutes, fell down to the floor in momentary insensibility—the result, as far as we can trace, more of extreme weakness and exhaustion than anything else. Sir W. Jenner was sent for, and came: he did not say anything to lead us to suppose that stoppage in the action of the heart, or other such serious symptomatic result of her malady, had led to the fall. I picked her up, and we got her at once into bed again.

Wednesday 15 May   We felt very uneasy about Christina all the earlier part of to-day; as, although she had slept well in the night, she was in a terribly low condition, accompanied with frequent vomitings. Sir W. Jenner called again, without saying anything very particular: in the later part of the evening Christina had revived to some extent, and seemed pretty much at her usual level, and she again passed a good night. I have great apprehensions as to the result however—perhaps at no very distant date: for there seems to be no real rally of physical energy now for months past, and the process of exhaustion proceeds with fatal and frightful steadiness. What shows least trace of disease in Christina is her voice (which had indeed altered some time ago, but that passed off); she speaks with much the same tone, animation, and general manner, as of old, and with equal readiness on any subject that is uppermost; and her strength of mind continues to maintain an admirable triumph over all physical suffering and prostration.—Gabriel came, bringing round Buchanan's book on *The Fleshly School of Poetry*. He seems sufficiently untroubled by it—save as regards one phrase on page 1, 'cowards', which is intended to apply to him more than any one else. As to this he had scribbled a denunciatory letter to be sent to Buchanan, which he showed me. I advised him not to send it: indeed I consider that this word 'cowards' has, where it comes, almost as little meaning as relevancy, and cannot be understood to convey any substantial charge of want of courage, physical or even moral.—Gabriel left, intending to consult Brown also. This little book of Buchanan's seems likely to create a good deal of hubbub—many reviewers coming forward (it may be foreseen) to champion its views, and others to controvert them. I now all the more regret that Gabriel ever came forward with his letter in the *Athenaeum*; for that first step might almost require him to take a second and third (which, however, he is not minded to do, in any public way), while on the other hand I think it most highly desirable that he should hold utterly aloof from controversy, and leave it to wrangle itself out as best it may.

Thursday 16 May   The other day, Petruccelli della Gattina[1] called on me (when I was out) with a letter of introduction from Ricciardi: to-day I returned his visit. I find him an energetic agreeable man, whom I shall be pleased to see from time to time: he knew my Father in 1852. Has for years past had his regular home in Paris, and was there during the Prussian and the Communal sieges. Soon after the entry of the Versailles troops, he was expelled, being supposed to have been mixed up with the Commune: he does not allow this to be true, but at the same time does not disguise that to a considerable extent his sympathies were and are with the Commune. He says that at starting, their government was most mild and tolerant—they only put to death one person, a Versaillist spy: but, when they set up a Committee of Public Safety, and began (as he says) 'aping 93', his approval of the movement ceased. He saw, from his lodgings (in the Rue de Bourgogne, I think) two hundred Communists shot in a courtyard 'come i caprioli':[2] stacked up to be shot at (without any sort of trial), and fired into as they ran about the place. Many were only half dead, and went on groaning throughout the night: next day they were flung in lumps into the dead-carts, and carted off.— Petruccelli professes himself a Republican, but this seems to be rather a theoretic than a practical opinion with him: he knows the prominent men of the Republican party in France, and does not believe in any of them—has no regard for Gambetta. He wrote a History of the Franco-German War, and has offered it for publication here in England: he showed me a letter from Chapman and Hall, declining the work—the public interest in the subject having, as they say, gone off to such an extent that there would be a very inconsiderable sale.

[1] Fernando Petrucelli della Gattina (1815–90), Italian revolutionary and writer; one of the many Italian refugees and exiles in London. He wrote *Gli Incendiari della Commune o le Stragi di Parigi*, Milano, 1871, and *Le Notte degli Emigrati di Londra* in 1872.   [2] 'Like so many kids.'

Friday 17 May Dined with some others at Brown's—principally for the purpose of meeting Andrieu of the Paris Commune: He is a one-eyed thick-set man, of rather uncouth exterior; but has much readiness of conversation, and considerable acuteness—having seemingly paid uncommon attention to questions of physiognomy, and to semi-mystic mediaeval writings such as those of Paracelsus. I asked him about various members of the Communal Party—Rossel,[1] Grousset,[2] Dombrowsky,[3] Cluseret,[4] etc: He appears to think little of any of them; and is especially severe on the negligence and disingenuousness displayed by Rossel as War Delegate. Raoul Rigault[5] seems to be one of those he liked best, and more especially Delescluze.[6] He says he himself was one of the few members of the Commune who wished to renew hostilities against the Germans. Raoul Rigault is undoubtedly dead, whatever rumours may appear to the contrary from time to time.—Wallis was here, apparently recovered from the distressing failure of sight from which he was suffering some months ago.—Saw Lucy Brown's picture of *Margaret Roper receiving the head of her father Sir Thomas More*;[7] a satisfactory work

[1] Louis Nathaniel Rossel (1844–71) had fought against the Prussians. When the Paris Commune began, he was given an important post. Arrested in May 1871, he was executed at Satory on 28 November 1871. His memoirs and letters were published in Paris in 1908 with a preface by Victor Margueritte. See *Westminster Gazette*, 16 December 1871.

[2] Paschal Grousset (1845–1909), a member of the Commune. In September 1871, he was banished to New Caledonia. In 1874 he escaped and went to London where, together with F. Jourde, he published *Récit de deux évadés*, 1874.

[3] Iaroslaw Dombrosky or Dombrowski (1838–71) had fought in the army of Garibaldi; appointed general by the executive commission of the Commune, he was killed on a barricade.

[4] Gustave Cluseret (1823–1900), member of the Commune. In March 1871 the Commune put him in charge of the Department of War, but he was found incompetent and charged with treason. The entry into Paris of the Versailles troops enabled him to escape to London. He contributed articles to *Fraser's Magazine* (July 1872, December 1872), and to the *Fortnightly Review* (1 July, 1 August, 1 September 1873), all about his experiences as a Communard.

[5] Raoul G. A. Rigault (1846–71), another Communard. He advocated the burning of the Palais de Justice, the Tuileries, and the Palais Royal. On 24 May 1871 he was caught in a street and shot.

[6] Louis Charles Delescluze (1809–71), member of the Commune; he held an authoritative position. He was in charge of the Department of War and fought with great courage. He was killed while fighting on a barricade. For further information about these men, see Lissagaray, *Histoire de la Commune de 1871*, Brussels, 1876, and Paris, 1896.

[7] Presented by the late Mrs. Helen Rossetti Angeli to the Burford Roman Catholic church in 1965.

in point of invention etc., and seems an improvement, in the management of oil-colour, over the *Tempest* picture she had previously done. I dare say however, by day-light, defects of execution would be sufficiently noticeable. Andrieu does not appear to have any definite view for the present as to the publication of his book about the Commune.

Saturday 18 and Sunday 19 May   Whitsuntide.

Tuesday 21 May   Scott called in the morning, having just seen Miss Boyd off to Penkill. Hennessy[1] the American painter now rents the studio in his garden. Gabriel came in the evening; somewhat perturbed by an article which (as he tells me) has appeared in *The Echo*, reviewing Buchanan's book.[2] Without exactly adopting Buchanan's views, it restates them with enhanced unpleasantness of phrase, and says that, if Swinburne and Rossetti do not take some notice of the attack, they must be 'mere *simulacra* of humanity.' I strenuously urged Gabriel to think and see as little of these matters as he can; and above all to take no steps at all in the matter—whether by writing anything for publication, treating the attacks as libels, or otherwise. He tells me that Brown has drawn up a letter to the Editor of the *Athenaeum*, with some view of sending it for publication: the gist of it being that the whole affair on Buchanan's part is a matter of personal spite, founded on my having called him (in the *Criticism* of Swinburne which I published in or about 1865) 'a poor and pretentious poetaster'.[3] I would myself much rather that Brown should not send this letter;

[1] William John Hennessy (1839–1917), American painter and illustrator of Irish origin. In June 1870 he came to England where he settled for five years. He exhibited several paintings at the R.A. See *Dictionary of American Biography*.

[2] The review appeared in *The Echo*, no. 1,072 of 18 May 1872. D. G. R. seems to have been unnecessarily 'perturbed' as the article, entitled 'Fleshing the Fleshly', insists on the fact that Buchanan's criticism is 'uninstructed as well as unjust, offensive', mentions Buchanan's 'rudeness and violence of manners' and declares that what in the poems 'may be censured as sensual becomes filthy in Mr. Buchanan's handling'. The very words of the passage quoted by W. M. R. were: 'In order to bear tamely the charges and insults hurled pell-mell at the heads and hearts of Mr. Swinburne and Mr. Rossetti, they would really need to be the very aestheticized simulacra of humanity.'

[3] *Swinburne's Poems and Ballads, A Criticism by W. M. Rossetti*, London, 1866. It begins thus: 'The advent of a new great poet is sure to cause a commotion of one kind or another; and it would be hard were this otherwise in times like ours, when the advent of even so poor and pretentious a poetaster as a Robert Buchanan stirs storms in teapots.'

First because I consider it to be one more symptom of that camaraderie or coterie-feeling which Buchanan especially denounces, not without some reason, and as such impolitic; and second because it would tumble me willy-nilly into the fray. However, rather than thwart Gabriel in case he should finally favour Brown's idea, with a view to his own part in the controversy, I said nothing about these counter considerations.—I incline to think (and so informed Gabriel) that, if Swinburne makes up his mind to publish the pamphlet he has been engaged on—expressing some general critical views, and taking up Buchanan's attack as well, but without saying anything directly or in detail about Gabriel—this would be a good move: it would be the latest word in the dispute, and would give reviewers something to talk about more novel than Buchanan's *rechauffé* and at least as pungent. Gabriel seems to agree in this opinion to some extent: he has himself enjoined Swinburne to say little or nothing about Gabriel himself.

Wednesday 22 May   Moxons sent for the MS and books needed for printing the Selection of American Poems—the printers having asked for these, as the Humorous Selection is now pretty nearly done with.—Gambart wants to engrave Gabriel's large picture of *The Death of Beatrice*: he would entrust the work to Blanchard.[1] What he proposes is that Gabriel should paint a smaller replica of the picture, which Gambart would buy for 1000 guineas, and get engraved, retaining all ensuing interest in the copyright: he says he would have to pay £1600 to Blanchard. Gabriel would not accept the proposed £1000, but would probably take £1500, subject to making proper enquiry to ascertain whether the terms demanded by Blanchard are really such as to preclude Gambart from leaving to Gabriel any interest in the copyright. He is to some extent disinclined to close with the offer, having lately come to a strong resolve to do no more duplicates of any kind from his pictures.[2]

[1] Auguste Blanchard (1819–98), French engraver, one of the best engravers of his time. He was in demand in London almost as often as in Paris. He often worked for Gambart and was Alma Tadema's particular engraver.

[2] A smaller replica of the picture was done in oil by D. G. R. in 1875 for William Graham; two predellas were added later and the final version is dated 1880 (Dundee City Museum and Art Gallery). See Surtees, 81 B, R2, p. 46.

Thursday 23 May   Gabriel called again. He had been round to Swinburne's wishing to know what he might be doing with regard to his pamphlet; but learned that Swinburne is again very unwell (through the usual cause), and not capable of attending to any business. I had heard much the same yesterday from Solomon, whom I met in the street. Gabriel understands that Swinburne's father is at present in Italy, where Swinburne ought to be joining him soon.

Friday 24 May   Christina has received a very pretty present, from some American admirer, of American foliage, in autumnal tints, mounted on paper: Colonel Higginson brought it over. Maria is looking over the little Religious Addresses written by her which the S.P.C.K. think of publishing. The Society have had them put into print, with a view to their being further considered and they wish Maria to make some alterations here and there. She is not minded to make *all* that they propose.

Saturday 25 and Sunday 26 May   Forgot this journal for F.

Monday 27 May   (To-day at last is very like summer: almost the first day that I have done without a fire at home. The spring has been very shifting and characterless: fine days from time to time, but hardly anything so marked and continuous as to make up a season of the year.)[1] Brown called, somewhat crippled by gout, wishing more particularly to consult with me as to the Buchanan pamphlet. He was thinking of writing a letter to the *Athenaeum*, vindicating Gabriel from attack, on general grounds: as I told him, it seems to me that these are the very arguments that ought to be put forward, not by personal friends, but by outsiders— while on the other hand I deprecate anything like a personal defence by friends, which would only the more go to confirm one of the more substantial heads of Buchanan's attack, viz: that Gabriel, Swinburne, etc. hang together as a coterie for mutual support. Brown seems to acquiesce in my views to a certain extent; though he is evidently much displeased at what he regards as a dead set at all the artists and men of our connection, and thinks that 'something ought to be done' if they are not to be scouted out of society etc.: all which, in my opinion, goes

[1] This paragraph appears in W. M. R.'s typescript, but not in the MS.

considerably beyond the real conditions of the case. Much serious talk about matters connected herewith. Gabriel also called in the evening; he has not yet succeeded in seeing Swinburne, but learns that the latter is again about as usual. If Swinburne resolves to produce his pamphlet, Ellis, it seems, is not willing to be the publisher: but he would put Swinburne in the way of publishing with some one else. Brown does not (and, as far as I can trace, never did) propose to write to the *Athenaeum* to the effect referred to under 21 May.

Tuesday 28 May   Went to Mrs. Orme's and was received with surprising cordiality by all, considering my manifold neglects in that quarter. The members of the family I saw were—Mr. and Mrs. Orme, Masson and his wife and daughters, Bastian[1] and his wife, the two unmarried daughters, and Mr. Howard Fox who (as I learn from Mrs. Orme) is connected with the Dr. Wilson Fox who attends Christina from time to time. Miss Masson, aged I believe 16, is certainly a very pretty girl, and has very uncommon force and continuity of conversation for one so extremely young: as regards aplomb of demeanour and range of talk, she might be a married woman of 25. This was a characteristic of the Orme girls in the remote days when I remember them very young, and markedly of Mrs. Masson: but I incline to think the daughter has still bettered the lesson of the mother. She says she wishes to adopt a profession: not medicine, but would be disposed for law, were that career open to women. The *Scotsman* published some verses of hers, parodying the passage in Shakespeare about 'she never told her love' in the sense of the exaggerated female fashions of the day.[2] Masson spoke of his studies regarding the Parliamentary Army, etc, in connexion with his *Life of Milton*.[3] He says the army constituted an immense 'peripatetic debating society' as well as a fighting body, and that its discussions show it to have embodied the most advanced mind of the nation. All kinds of modern speculative or subversive questions were mooted in those days, and in some instance doctrines of the most unmodified toleration were upheld.—Bastian wholly scouts the pretensions of phrenology.

[1] Dr. Charlton Bastian was a son-in-law of the Ormes. See *Reminiscences*, p. 89.

[2] I have been unable to trace these verses in the *Scotsman* of the period.

[3] The first volume of Professor Masson's *Life of Milton* (6 vols.) was published in 1859 and the last in 1880.

Wednesday 29 May   Passed the last proofs of the Humorous Selection.

Thursday 30 May   Attended with Brown and Lucy, by Brown's request, at Miss Blind's, to hear the story which Nolly wrote some little while ago, *Gabriel Denver*: the only other person present was Ralston.[1] Certainly the tale is very remarkable (considering that Nolly is now only seventeen) in point of sustained literary competence, keeping together of the various requirements in a naval narrative, and other points of this sort, and shows indisputable gift and power. In point of originality, thrill of passion, etc. (the matters which Brown had more especially dwelt on in referring to the story) I think it is perhaps scarcely so uncommon as he supposes: though in this way also noticeable, and for such a youth as Nolly very much so.—Ralston thinks that the moral twist in the story would be much against its general acceptance, were it to be published; and in this I agree to a considerable extent: in other respects Ralston is very favourably impressed. The whole of the story was not read to us, but the main connecting chapters. I think many things are given at too great length, and that the quality of the story is rather questionably balanced between that of a full-sized romance with very few incidents, and that of a condensed tale of passion narrated with some excess of scale.

Friday 31 May and Saturday 1 June   Holiday on Saturday.

Sunday 2 June   Was all day with Gabriel at Chelsea—a day of extreme distress and anxiety on account of the nervous and depressed condition into which Gabriel has allowed himself to get worked. Scott came round, and as usual acted in a spirit of the truest and kindest friendship. In the morning Gabriel completed the sale, to Pilgeram and Lefèvre, of his picture[2] of two

[1] William R. S. Ralston (1828–89), Russian scholar and official of the British Museum, where W. M. R. met him. He translated some of Turgenev's novels and introduced him to the Rossettis. See *Reminiscences*, ii. 339 (wherein the name is spelt Turguénief, which was the current spelling).

[2] The oil painting mentioned by W. M. R. is *The Bower Meadow*. The following letter of J. Pilgeram and Lefèvre refers to the transaction:

London 22 April 1872

Dear Sir,

Please find enclosed cheque for £367.10.0—half the purchase money of *The Bower Garden* [*sic*]. This is rather an expensif [*sic*] picture for us (beginners) and we hope you will please finish it well. By doing so you will greatly oblige, dear Sir, /

women playing music, and two dancing—the background being that which he painted in the summer of (I think) 1850 or 51. Price £735, which is truly very large.

Monday 3 June   Again with Gabriel, so far as office attendance allowed: Scott, Dunn, F., also about him: and in the evening he and I went round to Brown's. Some table-turning in the evening rather earlier at Chelsea:[1] the table moved very considerably but not violently, and some messages came, purporting to be from Lizzie.[2] Nothing very marked in these, unless one can so consider the answers that she is happy, and still loves Gabriel.— Initials, for her younger brother, H.S.,[3] given correctly. Gabriel was, I fancy, the only person at the table who knew of the 'H': I did not—or rather had wholly forgotten.

Tuesday 4 June   Mr. Walter Besant[4] brought me round the MS. (belonging to Mr. Campbell, of the Mauritius, who has written me letters on the subject) containing the originals of writings published in *The Keepsake* for 1828. One of these is a 'poem' named *Sadok the Wanderer*, notified in the Index to the MS. as being by Shelley. I am quite certain it is neither the composition nor the handwriting of Shelley, and pretty certain that it is not the handwriting of Mrs. Shelley. Garnett (Somerset House) does not suppose it to be Medwin's.

Wednesday 5 June   This diary-work is becoming too painful now if important matters are to be recorded,[5] and too futile and

Yours very truly, / Pilgeram and Lefèvre. (Unpublished letter in the Angeli Collection.)

Pilgeram and Lefèvre were mistaken in calling it *The Bower Garden* which is a different water-colour picture painted in 1859. See Surtees, no. 229, p. 128 for *The Bower Meadow* which is now in the Manchester City Art Gallery, and no. 112, p. 68 for *The Bower Garden*.

[1] D. G. R. and W. M. R. had been interested in spiritualism for several years. Between 1865 and 1868 they used to attend frequent seances. See *R.P.*, pp. 153–61.

[2] Lizzie Siddal, Rossetti's wife, had died in 1862.

[3] Harry Siddal; according to W. M. R. he was 'somewhat weak-minded'. See *Memoir*, p. 172.

[4] Sir Walter Besant (1836–1901), novelist and literary critic. He taught for some time in Mauritius, was a good French scholar, and from 1872 published novels which called attention to the miserable existence of the very poor in London. See Walter Besant's *Autobiography*, London, 1902.

[5] D. G. R. had, for some time, been showing distressing signs of a serious nervous strain. He was subject to delusions and hallucinations. His severe condition led

irritating if the unimportant are made to take their place. I shall therefore drop it. Perhaps a great change may have come over the face of things when—or if—I next resume it: or there will have been, as Swinburne says, 'An end, an end, an end of all' and no resumption of it.

Sunday 3 November I resume this diary under much less gloomy circumstances than when I left it off, although all causes of distress and anxiety are by no means removed.—Gabriel is now at Kelmscott, and inclined to settle somewhere near but not in London; Christina not so wholly incapacitated as when I discontinued writing. I have lately returned from Kelmscott and have done the work needed for including Mrs. Hemans[1] in Moxon's series.—Wrote to-day to Benham and Tindell, the Solicitors of J. B. Payne, who wish me to sign an affidavit in a cause in Chancery pending between Payne as defendant, and Moxons. It seems that Payne claims a sort of royalty on the profits of the *Popular Poets*, as being the projector of the series: while Moxons decline to pay this, and allege that J. S. Roberts was the originator of the idea. Certainly, as far as I know, Payne is in the right here, whatever may be his other misdeeds. I settled the form of the affidavit, and reposted it to Benham and Tindell, saying that I would rather not sign it as a matter of personal convenience —my business connexion being wholly with Moxons now, and not with Payne,—but would further discuss the matter if their clerk calls to-morrow as proposed. Wrote also to Appleton, offering to review in the *Academy* the book on Shelley by MacCarthy,[2] of which I have received from Hotten an advance

W. M. R. and his friends to take him from Cheyne Walk to Dr. Hake's house at Roehampton where on 8 June 1872 he took an overdose of laudanum. Then he stayed with Madox Brown who showed him in his own terms 'brotherly lovingness'. Later, he went to Scotland where William Graham, M.P., his friend and patron, had placed two houses, Stobhall and Urrard House, at his disposal. These are the 'painful' circumstances referred to by W. M. R. and which led him to interrupt his diary from 5 June to 3 November 1872. See W. E. Fredeman, 'Prelude to the Last Decade: Dante Gabriel Rossetti in the Summer of 1872', *Bulletin of the John Rylands Library*, 1971.

[1] *The Poetical Works of Mrs. Felicia Hemans*, ed. W. M. R., with a Critical Memoir, London, Moxon, 1873.

[2] The book was entitled *Shelley's Early Life, from Original Sources, with Curious Incidents, Letters and Writings now first published or collected by Denis Florence MacCarthy* (Hotten, London, 1872). 'This book relates . . . chiefly to the sojourns of Shelley in Dublin.' *Reminiscences*, 388. MacCarthy had written an account of Shelley's stay in Ireland in the *Nation* (Dublin), 1846.

copy. There are some things I should like to say about it, on my own personal account.

Monday 4 November   After some discussion, I consented to make and did make the affidavit applied for by Payne—explaining to the lawyers' clerk that I did so from a sense of fair play, and contrary to my own apparent interest and convenience.—Lyster[1] gives me a melancholy account of the state to which poor old Keightley is reduced in mind and body—the recent very sudden death of his sister Frances by apoplexy having contributed to his present total break-up: he is hardly expected to survive to-day.—I resumed the annotating etc. needed for my selection of Miscellaneous Poems, being very near the end of that job.

Tuesday 5 November   Scott dined with Dunn and me at Cheyne Walk (Dunn being for the present settled in the house); Howell also called along with Brayshay,[2] who is connected with him and Heaton in art-dealing matters at Bradford. Scott told me various particulars about the edition of Burns on which he is now engaged: it is to contain everything written by Burns, prose or verse, save only the indecent poems. Virtue & Co. want Scott to continue writing, for them to publish, books about various forms of art: one subject would be Venetian painting, and Scott thinks he may have to revisit Venice, with a view to this work. Howell still talks (as he began doing about a couple of months ago) of his intention of going out to Japan for a year or two, to buy up works of art, etc. He [Howell] is now acting as general purchaser, or purchasing agent, of the pictures etc. executed by Gabriel, under an arrangement very lately settled between him and Gabriel:[3]

[1] Alfred Chaworth Lyster was Thomas Keightley's nephew and a colleague of W. M. R. at the Inland Revenue Office, Somerset House. Like his uncle, he was a spiritualist and took part in seances in which he played the part of medium. See *R.P.*, pp. 165 ff.

[2] Howell introduced W. Hutton Brayshay to Madox Brown as 'a rich man in Bradford, a friend of mine who likes to see pictures, and sell pictures, and exchange pictures, in fact a man who seems to like to be damned for the fun of the thing'. See Helen Rossetti Angeli, *Pre-Raphaelite Twilight*, p. 122.

[3] This arrangement had been laid down in a very detailed form by Howell in a letter to Rossetti dated 3 October 1872: 'I wish to have your pictures, and to extend your market for your and my sake, but in this case, I think you would have to leave Pilgeram and go out of the market. Of course all offers you will refer to me', and further 'your market is splendid, paint what you like and there will be five men for each picture.' Part of this letter is quoted by Mrs. Angeli in op. cit., p. 87; otherwise the letter is unpublished (Angeli Collection).

Brayshay came round to see about the drawings which Gabriel has offered in exchange for the drawing named *Silence* (Mrs. Morris)[1] which was sold in the summer on Gabriel's behalf, to Murray Marks, along with the collection of blue china. Gabriel offers *La Donna della Fiamma*,[2] and a circular Head of Mrs. Morris;[3] and besides, if wanted, a few pencil drawings. Brayshay and Dunn looked out six of the latter, and Dunn will write about the details to Gabriel before any such exchange is concluded. Brayshay says that he himself is an excellent facsimilist of art-objects—as for instance of Turner water-colours: Howell says the same of himself: and each of them, it appears, has been pronounced in writing by Ruskin to be the best facsimilist in the country, barring Ruskin himself.

Wednesday 6 November Lyster informs me that Mr. Keightley died, placidly and unconsciously, on the night of the 4th: since the death of Mr. Potter[4] a year or two ago, he must have been about the earliest friend I had living. Steps are being taken in the hope of securing to his sister Eliza the whole or a part of the literary pension which he received.—I began writing for the *Academy* a notice of MacCarthy's book on Shelley.[5]

Thursday 7 November Called by invitation to see Chapman's[6] pictures, portraits, subjects from his recent tour in Egypt, etc. Some of the portraits are full of grace and sprightliness of motive, and have very respectable qualities of execution: the other works appear to me not generally satisfactory, though Chapman himself

---

[1] See p. 41 n. 1.

[2] Coloured chalks; Manchester City Art Gallery. See Surtees, no. 216, p. 122.

[3] Probably the one in the Manchester City Art Gallery. See Surtees, no. 224 C, p. 126.

[4] Philip Cipriani Potter (1792–1871), Principal of the Royal Academy of Music and a talented pianist. Godfather to W. M. R., his family was the only one with which the young Rossettis were familiar. He helped Gabriele Rossetti on one occasion by giving him forty pounds for a libretto. See *Reminiscences*, p. 11.

[5] W. M. R.'s notice appeared in the *Academy* for 1 December 1872. It gives a good account of the book but questions some of the points set forward by Mac-Carthy.

[6] George R. Chapman (d. *c.* 1880), painter, who greatly admired D. G. R. and saw much of him in the sixties; and in 1866 he painted a small picture inspired by C. G. R.'s sonnet 'A Triad'. See *Family Letters*, p. 185. D. G. R. himself had illustrated his sister's poem in 1865 with a pencil sketch called 'Three Sang of Love Together'. See Surtees, no. 184, p. 107.

is especially pleased with a subject of an Egyptian boy munching a melon, in an effect of after-glow. He is living now at the house of one of his brothers, 30 York Place, a very handsome mansion: he says he is very fairly well off for commissions. Alfred Hake[1] called in Euston Square. He says that the project of completing at an Italian University the education of his brother Henry[1] is not likely to be further mooted just at present, but may be revived next year.

Friday 8 and Saturday 9 November   Holiday on Saturday.

Sunday 10 November   Going on with the editorial work on the Miscellaneous Selection of Poems.

Monday 11 November   Called by arrangement at Scott's; but he had gone out, having apparently forgotten his engagement with me. Saw his picture of *The Nativity*, which is in several respects well invented and put together; also a sketch he did of the exterior view and garden of Stobhall House (rented by Graham M.P. in Perthshire) where he was staying this last summer with Gabriel—an interesting-looking old place.

Wednesday 13 November   Finished the ordinary compiling work on the Selection of Miscellaneous Poems—the writing of a brief Preface remaining to be done. I am almost certain, unfortunately, that the mass of material I have put together is more than can be got into a volume, and that I shall have the bother and disappointment of considerably cutting it down again. However, I propose to send it off to the printers as it stands.

Thursday 14 November   Went round with Dunn, by appointment, to Boyce's, there to meet Brown; the latter being interested in a subscription exhibition which is to be got up for the benefit of the widow and family of a Manchester artist named Holding,[2] and

---

[1] Alfred Egmont Hake was Dr. Hake's fourth son and author of *Paris Originals* (1878), *Flattering Tales* (1882), and *The Story of Chinese Gordon* (1883). Henry Wilson Hake (1851–1930) was the youngest of Dr. Hake's five sons.

[2] Henry James Holding (1833–72), a Manchester landscape painter known to Ford Madox Brown. He was commissioned to go and paint some scenery round Paris; hardly had he arrived there than he died of typhus. Ford Madox Hueffer, *Ford Madox Brown*, p. 275.

having got Gabriel to present two drawings for sale at this exhibition, and wishing Boyce to do the like.—Boyce consents, and gave a water-colour of Llyn Idwal. Brown says that the widow of Mason,[1] the admirable landscape-painter lately deceased, will receive from the R.A. a pension of £100 per annum, as widow of an Associate. There is also some smallish estate belonging to her in right of her husband, and a half-built house thereon of no practical value: on the whole, the provision for herself and six children appears to be very meagre. Lowes Dickinson[2] tells Brown that Mason, when he resided in Rome years ago, was most notoriously impecunious, and any one rambling with him through the streets was liable to have a long round to make, so as to save Mason from passing sundry 'trattorie' etc. where bills had been run up against him. He frequently passed days without any tolerably adequate meal, and no one at that time expected him to take any distinguished position as a painter.

Friday 15 November   Gabriel having been summoned to attend as a Grand Juryman at Common Pleas, I wrote to the Summoning Officer, explaining that Gabriel is out of town, and offering to procure a medical certificate if needed.

Saturday 16 November   The weather is now cold, though not extraordinarily so: I don't as yet hear from Kelmscott that the floods prevail to that troublesome extent which is customary there in the late autumn and winter.

Sunday 17 November   I have looked further into the question of space for the Miscellaneous Selection of Poems, and fear the materials, as they now stand, must be more like the thickness of two volumes than of one: shall probably have to cut them down before sending the work off to the printers—though I am by no means *inclined* to do this.

[1] George Heming Mason (1818–72), a painter; visited France, Switzerland, lived in Rome ten years and when he returned to England, painted mostly landscapes.
[2] Lowes Cato Dickinson (1819–1908), portrait painter, one of the founders of the Working Men's College (1854) where he taught drawing. He was a steady friend of the Pre-Raphaelites, more especially in the fifties. He was the son-in-law of William Smith Williams, who persuaded Smith and Elder that *Jane Eyre* was worth publishing. See *Reminiscences*, p. 96.

Monday 18 November   I have again examined this matter, with the aid of the notes as to space occupied that I took months ago during the compilation of the Selection: and it appears to me that after all those notes show the amount of material collected to be not at all excessive for one volume, so I shall for the present proceed on that assumption. Began the Preface to this volume.

Tuesday 19 November   Dunn tells me that George Hake[1] was in town the other day from Kelmscott, whither he has now returned. He says that Gabriel had a sharp attack of diarrhea lately, but it had ceased by the time Hake was in town. Mrs. Morris is likely to return to London pretty soon, but Gabriel seems still disposed to remain at Kelmscott. He has some thoughts of closing with an offer made by Mrs. Bodichon, to let her house, at Scalands for the winter half-year, at the very moderate rent of £40.

Wednesday 20 November   Received a copy of my Selection of Humorous Poems.

Thursday 21 November   Dr. Heimann has heard from his son Horace, who recently started to emigrate to New Zealand: he writes from the Cape of Good Hope in excellent spirits. It seems that he has met on board the son of a Brewer, who offers to share his purse with him: what the contents of his purse may be, or the prospect of any practical result from such an offer, I know not.

Friday 22 November   Completed the Index of Contents to my Miscellaneous Selection of Poems.

Saturday 23 November   Lyster tells me that half of Mr. Keightley's pension has now been granted to his surviving sister—£50. Gladstone personally managed these grants (so Lyster is told by Mr. West, one of the Commissioners here, who was lately Gabriel's Secretary and has interested himself very kindly in the matter).

[1] George Gordon Hake (1847–1903), was the second son of Dr. T. Hake. 'He had been so good as to accompany Madox Brown and my Brother to Scotland, at Pitlochrie in June 1872. He took all sorts of care of Rossetti for a long while ensuing. After a time, he accepted a regular engagement as my Brother's secretary, lasting up to the early months of 1877 or thereabouts.' (Unpublished note by W. M. R. in the Angeli Collection.)

Sunday 24 November   I finished the Preface to my Miscellaneous Selection of Poems. There is now nothing at all to do with it further except that I ought to get a day at the British Museum, and look up one or two dates etc. that my materials as yet have not enabled me to supply.—Nolly Brown tells me that the novel (*Belladonna*)[1] that he is now writing has been shown to Stephen,[2] Editor of the *Cornhill Magazine*, who thinks very well of it, and is not indisposed to accept it at some convenient opportunity for the magazine; but he has made various suggestions as to alterations etc., which Nolly Brown is not much inclined for, but would submit under pressure. I suspect that the Editor's chief object must be to shorten the immensely full scale at which Nolly develops every character and incident, large or small: and in this view I should quite agree with him.[3]

Monday 25 November   Called on Rose with regard to a Grand Jury summons recently served on Gabriel: Rose says he will set the matter right. I am sorry to find he was a great sufferer during the summer from stricture etc: however he now seems well, and his Dr. tells him the cure is permanent. He showed me some of the recent documents in Mrs. Wieland's case: it rather seems that the result of the Chancery suit will not be a partition of the estates as between Mrs. Wieland and Captain Taylor, but a sale of them to rid of the various complications between different mortgages etc.; though the Wielands would rather have the partition, and so indeed would Taylor. Rose possesses a very fine Japanese work, showing the conflagration of a lot of houses etc.; the fire etc. most admirably represented. The work was in a dark part of the room. To me the colouring appeared to be mostly (or all) by hand, and

[1] *Belladonna* was one of the titles Oliver Madox Brown considered for the second novel he was then writing. But he found that there already existed a novel with that name and decided that it should be called *The Dwale Bluth* which is a Devonian name for Deadly Nightshade. It was published after Oliver's death with the following title: *The Dwale Bluth. Hebditch's Legacy and Other Literary Remains of Oliver Madox Brown*, ed. W. M. Rossetti and F. Hueffer, 2 vols., London, Tinsley, 1876. These tales were preceded by a 'Lament' by P. B. Marston. See Ingram, *Oliver Madox Brown*, Ch. VII.

[2] Sir Leslie Stephen (1832–1904), the famous critic and man of letters, was editor of the *Cornhill Magazine* from 1871 to 1882.

[3] Oliver Madox Brown did comply with Leslie Stephen's suggestions and sent him the revised manuscript which was returned after some time without a word. Ingram, op. cit., p. 178.

perhaps the designing also; but Rose says it is an engraving.—
Uncle Henry came up from Gloucester on a visit to my Aunt
Eliza: Henrietta has improved in a rather remarkable degree under
the treatment (Congreve's) that she is now pursuing: I am not
however so sanguine as to believe in any permanently beneficial
result.

Tuesday 26 November   Called on Scott, and there met Linton[1] the
wood-engraver, lately back from America on some land-selling
business. He intends to return to America, but prefers England to
live in. He has met President Grant various times, and has a very
low opinion indeed both of his intellectual capacity and his
character. Considers him 'the stupidest man in the company'.
I don't readily acquiesce in any such view. Linton does not believe
he now possesses any unpublished poems by Ebenezer Jones.

Wednesday 27 November   Was unexpectedly subpoenaed this
morning through Rose to give evidence in a case in the Queen's
Bench this same day. Harding versus Baxendale. The question
turns upon the value of two gouache pictures which I happened
to see at Rose's office on Monday: they are elaborate battle-pieces
ascribed to Van Bloeremberg senior or junior, and were damaged
by seawater while in transit to Paris, and the carriers Baxendale
(or Pickford), although they had insured the works for £1050,
now turn round and say they are mere copies and of no substantial value. I am convinced this plea is not correct; and, having
said as much to Rose, he now asks me to testify my belief in court.
I attended, and did so. Had to leave the court immediately afterwards, to resume work at Somerset House.

Thursday 28 November   I see by the newspaper that the plaintiff
gained his cause. Holman Hunt called in the evening—He intends
to go back pretty soon to Jerusalem, and to take his son with him:
finds that the boy is kept too sheepish by the Waughs[2]—no noise

---

[1] William James Linton (1812–97), wood-engraver, also a poet and political
reformer whom D. G. R. had met in the early fifties. Linton was a friend of Mazzini,
of G. H. Lewes and of Thornton Hunt. He founded several periodicals, the *Leader*
in London, the *English Republic* at Brantwood on Coniston Water, which in 1872
he sold to Ruskin from America for £1,500. See W. J. Linton, *Memories*, London,
1895, and E. T. Cook, *The Life of Ruskin*, London, 1912, ii. 219.
[2] Cyril Benone Hunt was born in 1866, his mother Fanny Waugh dying in

or rough exertion allowed: indeed he finds that Mr. Waugh is in all respects too dictatorial and too much resolved to rule the roost with all people, Hunt included, and therefore he keeps to some extent aloof now from the family. Mr. Waugh suffers a good deal from gout, and from seizures of something of an apoplectic character. Hunt shows himself by no means indisposed now to marry again, if he can find a suitable person: he did not say so, but I should not be at all surprised if he already had some one in his eye. Meanwhile he thinks of engaging Wentworth Monk[1] (the 'Prophet'), now in England, as a sort of personal guardian for his son; so that, when Hunt himself in the East is taken away from keeping the boy under his own eye, Monk may be there to do so constantly.

Friday 29 November   Reading up for the Prefatory notice I have to do to the volume of Pope in Moxon's series. This is the last volume now outstanding in that series, though very likely something else will be added to it in course of time.

Saturday 30 November   Brown writes me that he intends to try for the Slade Professorship at Cambridge. He does not particularly want testimonials. I did some few weeks ago give a testimonial to Colvin, who is also a candidate, but told him at the same time that I should not hold myself precluded from doing the like for some one else in case the occasion were to arise: so I am free to act in Brown's behalf as circumstances may suggest.

Sunday 1 December   Wrote to Moxon asking for payment (£40) for my Selection of Humorous Poems; also for £40 for the American Selection, in case that volume also is now published—which I believe may be the case.

childbirth. In 1875, Holman Hunt married his sister-in-law Edith Waugh in Switzerland to evade the Deceased Wife's Sister Act. For further details about the Waughs, see Diana Holman Hunt, *My Grandfather, his Wives and Loves*, London, 1969. See also p. 273 n. 3.

[1] Henry Wentworth Monk (1827–96), a Canadian whom Holman Hunt had met in Palestine towards 1855. He entertained special views as to the millennium, preached the abolition of war. He stayed in England for some years during which he was taken in charge by Holman Hunt. The painter made a very fine portrait of him in 1858, now in the National Gallery of Canada, Ottawa.

Monday 2 December   Called on Brown, who is busy writing to people likely to influence the Cambridge election.[1] This, it seems, lies in the choice of seven persons, one of whom is the president of the Royal Academy.—Brown does not mean to forward or solicit any testimonials: but to reprint such articles of importance as have appeared regarding his paintings etc., along with the *Catalogue* of his own exhibition, and an address to the electing body. He does not know of any rival candidate other than Colvin, and probably Digby Wyatt[2] (for re-election), but it seems not unlikely that Cave Thomas may compete.—Brown tells me that Dr. Hake is now down with Gabriel at Kelmscott along with George Hake: Henry, the youngest son, has gone to Germany, and will go on into Italy, and Dr. Hake will probably join him at no very distant date.

Tuesday 3 December   Scott called at Chelsea. He has been invited by the *Art Journal* people to do a series of articles (about two pages each) on certain engravings from Italian Masters of which they have bought up a stock at Paris; but is not inclined to do this, especially as he is likely soon to do the text of another gift book on Italian Art,[3] similar to the recent one on Spanish Art. He has an idea of getting to Venice and Rome next year, and I should be well inclined to accompany him, if the conditions are propitious. He is likely to go down on Saturday to Kelmscott for four or five days.

Wednesday 4 December   MacCarthy wrote me about his recent book on Shelley,[4] and my review of it in the *Academy*, expressing a hope that he had done nothing to annoy me. I replied in the negative, and in cordial terms, intimating at the same time (what I think is strictly correct) that his treatment of me had not been particularly handsome, considering the accommodation I afforded him

---

[1] For the Slade Professorship of Fine Arts at Cambridge University.

[2] Sir Matthew Digby Wyatt (1820–77), architect and writer on art, Slade Professor of Fine Arts at Cambridge University (he was the first occupant of the chair) from December 1869 to December 1872.

[3] W. B. Scott wrote the book suggested by W. M. R.: *Pictures by Italian Masters, with an introductory essay and notices of the painters and subjects engraved*, London, 1874.

[4] See p. 207 n. 2.

regarding Shelley's *Declaration of Rights* etc., and the correspondence belonging to Mr. Slack.

Thursday 5 December   MacCarthy writes again, giving me valuable information as to the library wherein a copy of Shelley's *Poetical Essay on the Existing State of Things*[1] is affirmed to exist. This is truly very handsome on his part: I wrote acknowledging the obligation, and promising to keep the information to myself.

Friday 6 December   Began a new catalogue of my books: the old one is becoming too unhandy, by the scattering of the works by the same author, giving away of certain volumes, etc. Since the troubles that encompassed me round in June last I have advisedly discontinued book-buying; but, if matters remain tolerably satisfactory, may probably, at no very distant date, resume purchasing on the like small scale as of old.

Saturday 7 December   Got a copy of the Humorous Selection to send to Locker, who has shown a marked disposition to oblige me in numerous instances.

Sunday 8 December   Mathilde Blind, who reviewed in the *Athenaeum* MacCarthy's book about Shelley, told me about the same time that the Editor would be glad to obtain from me some publishable communications on the subject: It would appear that his object partly is to wipe out the impression of the hostile review of my two volume Shelley (written, it is believed, by Buchanan) which appeared in the *Athenaeum* at the beginning of 1870.[2] I would willingly assent to the Editor's wish; but had in

[1] 'No copy of this pamphlet is known to exist. Owing to the discoveries of D. F. MacCarthy and W. M. Rossetti, we know that it was announced in the *Oxford Herald* of March 9, 1811, as just published "by a gentleman of the University of Oxford, for assisting to maintain in prison Mr. Peter Finnerty, imprisoned for libel"; that Shelley subscribed to a fund for Finnerty and that the *Dublin Weekly Messenger* stated on March 7, 1812, that the proceeds of a "very beautiful poem" written by Shelley for Finnerty's benefit were said to amount to nearly £100. One or two early allusions to the *Posthumous Fragments of Margaret Nicholson* as having been printed for the benefit of Finnerty, made some authorities think that the two are one and the same thing.' R. S. Granniss, *A Descriptive Catalogue of the First Editions of the Writings of P. B. Shelley*, p. 18.

[2] This review appeared in the *Athenaeum* for 29 January 1870. Its tone is exemplified by the following quotation: 'We prefer the text of the original with all its inaccuracies and irregularities to Mr. Rossetti's untrustworthy version.'

the first instance to await the appearance in the *Academy* of my own notice of MacCarthy's book.[1] That notice is now published, and I have thought over anything that I might find to say about the book to the *Athenaeum* : but really don't discern that there is any particular opening for any such communication, and must therefore notify this to Miss Blind, for the Editor.

Monday 9 December   Uncle Henry returned to Gloucester to-day. The accounts of Henrietta continue to some appreciable extent improved.

Tuesday 10 December   Passed the evening at Chelsea with F., Dunn, and Boyce. Dunn is now halfway through the copying of Raphaël[2] (a half of the cartoon of 'Charge to Peter') that he is doing in a competitive scheme. He has been at it about three weeks, and five weeks still remain.

Wednesday 11 December   Going on with the catalogue of my books.

Thursday 12 December   A letter received from Gabriel this morning shows that he is likely to remain at Kelmscott an indefinite while yet, and that Dr. Hake and Scott have left him. Nothing is said as to George Hake, who will therefore, I presume, remain domesticated with Gabriel for the present.

Friday 13 December   I see in the newspaper that Ch. Justice Bovill[3] imposed a fine of £10 on the several Jurymen (special) who failed to attend at Common Pleas. I hope Gabriel is not included in this penalty : he ought not to be if Rose carried out the arrangement made on 25 November, but I confess to feeling a little timorous on the subject.

Saturday 14 December   Christina seems to be gradually picking up

---

[1] W. M. R.'s moderately favourable review of *Shelley's Early Life* by D. F. MacCarthy appeared in the *Academy*, 1 December 1872, p. 441.

[2] The South Kensington Museum, now the Victoria and Albert Museum, contains seven of a series of ten cartoons designed by Raphael in 1515–16 as patterns for tapestries intended for the decoration of the Sistine Chapel. The cartoons were discovered at Brussels by Rubens in 1630 and sent to Charles I. After his death, Cromwell bought them for £300.

[3] Sir William Bovill (1814–73), Chief Justice, was judge during the first Tichborne trial. He ordered Orton to be indicted for perjury.

a little in health and strength: though still very far back indeed, if compared with what she was up to March 1871 or thereabouts.

Sunday 15 December Mathilde Blind called—wishing to see a figure of a tarantula which I have in one of my books, as she is writing some story on the tarantula superstition. She spent the evening with us, and showed a good deal of interest in Japanese engravings. The very severe headaches she used to suffer from have vanished entirely within the last year or so: this she attributes to her having resumed the practice of dancing as she found immediate relief to ensue the first time she did so.

Monday 16 December Wrote to Howell, enquiring about the tiresome affair of the Botticelli picture belonging to Gabriel.[1] This was entrusted to Howell in the summer, with a view to sale; during his absence from town, taken away to Italy by his semi-partner Pinti, with the like view; ordered back; notified some weeks ago to have been despatched back to London; but as yet not received, nor (so far as I know) heard of further.

Tuesday 17 December Scott called at Chelsea. He gives a very good account of Gabriel at Kelmscott, whom he has just left. Virtues the publishers have for some while past intimated to Scott that, when Hall[2] ceases to edit the *Art-Journal*, they will ask *him* to undertake that office: the salary is £5 or £600 a year. This is strictly confidential for the present.—Luckily I do not find at Cheyne Walk anything to indicate that Gabriel was fined at Common Pleas (13 December).

Wednesday 18 December Brown called: symptoms of asthma or

[1] On 11 September 1872, Howell wrote to W. M. R.: 'As regards the Botticelli, I must inform you of a mistake made by Pinti respecting it. During my absence, I entrusted him with it for sale and of course said nothing respecting it being Gabriel's, he is buying for the king of Italy, and having leave to do with my pictures always as he pleases, deeming this one mine, and without consulting me, sent it off to His Majesty last Friday by passenger train.' Helen Rossetti Angeli, *Pre-Raphaelite Twilight*, p. 64. In the end, the Botticelli returned to Cheyne Walk. It is now in the Victoria and Albert Museum, and is attributed to the 'School of Botticelli'. Salvini in *All the Paintings of Botticelli*, 1963, calls it a 'Portrait of Esmeralda Bandinelli', which D. G. R. appears to have retouched.

[2] Samuel Carter Hall (1800–89) as a young man had been literary secretary to Ugo Foscolo; he became editor of the *Art Journal* from 1839 to 1880, and was among the critics who wrote a notice when *The Germ* appeared in January 1850. See *Memoir*, p. 154, and S. C. Hall, *Memoirs of Great Men and Women*, London, 1871.

bronchitis have troubled him a little of late. He is going down to Kelmscott on Saturday, to return on Monday.—He understands that Ruskin's re-election to the Slade Professorship at Oxford is dubious: Ruskin having himself notified as much to Brown, speaking civilly at the same time of Brown as a candidate for the Professorship at Cambridge. Brown feels a little doubtful under these circumstances whether it might not have been as well for himself to set up for Oxford rather than Cambridge, but considers himself now too far committed to the latter to make any change—and herein I quite agree with him—Moreover, my own belief is that Ruskin will not miss his re-election.[1]—Brown has got nearly ready for printing the materials for his address etc. in connexion with his candidateship. Dr Hake called at Somerset House, after returning from Kelmscott: he considers Gabriel to be now well, decidedly beyond even his old average, in strength and spirits. Hake is intending to sell or let his house at Roehampton, so that he may be set free to winter in Italy, and he will also have some accommodation in London, in chambers taken by his sons Edmund and Alfred. George's eyesight has now so far improved that he thinks he shall be able to read three hours per day, and to be in the way of taking up his degree at Oxford.

Thursday 19 December Called on Pinti, 46 Berners Street, to enquire about Gabriel's Botticelli picture. He showed me a document dated 30 November showing that certain goods had then been shipped to London (precise date of *shipping* not specified). Pinti says that the picture is among these goods, that the transit will occupy 45 days; and that this lengthy method of carriage was adopted, to avoid some rather serious custom-house difficulties which beset works of art leaving Italy through the French frontier. Assuming the shipping to have taken place on or about 30 November, the picture should be here towards 14 January.—This is a vexatious delay, after so much other antecedent delay: let me at least hope that the picture will really arrive about then.—Pinti

[1] Ruskin was re-elected and kept the chair of Fine Arts at Oxford till 1878, when he resigned in consequence of the action for libel brought against him by Whistler. The latter was awarded one farthing damages. Ruskin had to pay £400 costs. On 28 November 1878, he wrote to Dean Liddell: '. . . the result of the Whistler trial leaves me no further option. I cannot hold a chair for which I have no power of expressing judgment without being taxed for it by British Law.' See E. T. Cook, *The Life of Ruskin*, ii. 430.

professes utter ignorance of any negociations (of which Howell had told me much) with the King of Italy for the sale of this picture.

Friday 20 December   Called at Hewitt's to see about Japanese screens, which Gabriel is enquiring about; and in the evening wrote the result to Gabriel.

Saturday 21 December   Very mild weather just now. Rain falls at some time or other about every day, and the season, taken as a whole, has been extremely and even disastrously rainy: the quantity of rain per day is often however not considerable.

Sunday 22 December   Dunn called, showing a telegram from Gabriel, intimating that he is likely to be in London *before* Tuesday.—Dunn wishes to get up the techniques of distemper-painting, as, if he obtains the work on Raphael's cartoons for which he is now competing, he would like to execute his copy in distemper, as the method of the original, rather than in any other mode. I sent him Cennini[1] and one or two other books. What he is doing now is a half of the cartoon of the 'Charge to Peter', including the figure of Christ: The man who is doing the other half of this cartoon is, he says, the best among his competitors.

Monday 23 December to Thursday 26   Away from Somerset House from Tuesday. Gabriel up from Kelmscott.

Friday 27 December   Gabriel has been making a list of his pictures, sketches, etc., at Chelsea; so as to know exactly what is there, and be able at an advantageous opportunity to take up anything that may require completion. He, George Hake, Dunn, and myself, spent the evening at Scott's where Miss Boyd is now, having returned recently from Penkill. She thinks Gabriel much altered, and also spoiled, by his beard.

Saturday 28 December   Gabriel returned to-day to Kelmscott, and no definite time is fixed when he is likely to be again in town.

---

[1] Cennino Cennini (*c.* 1360–1440), Florentine painter who wrote an important treatise on the art of painting. It was published at Rome in 1821 under the title: *Trattato della pittura*, annotato dal Cavaliere G. Tambroni. This edition was translated into English by Mrs. Merrifield in 1844 under the title *On Painting*.

Sunday 29 December   Replied to a letter which Theodoric recently addressed to me relative to the various projects now going on in Italy in honour of my Father. Asked him for twelve copies of the medal which has been struck[1]—or, if the price is inconsiderable, twenty. Sent him photographic copies of the two portraits Gabriel did of my Father, to be used as authorities for the proposed monument at Vasto, and medallion in the cloister at Santa Croce; and explained that Gabriel thinks these may probably supply all that he can give by way of authority, although he would personally be willing to design (as Theodoric suggests) the figure for the two memorials. Also that I approve the Santa Croce project—a tablet with medallion portrait in the cloister, as the body of the church is not sanctioned for the purpose by the authorities; but that Gabriel thinks this minor honour unimportant, and would as soon see the project dropped.—Called on Brown who has now printed his address as a candidate for the Slade Professorship at Cambridge: the proof has been returned to the printer so I have not seen the address in any of its stages.

Monday 30 December   Stillman and his wife called. The former finds no real outlet for his energies here in England, and thinks he may soon be going to America, to see about a projected Art-Journal there of which he would be appointed editor. He would go alone: but, if the scheme takes shape, would settle in America and take his wife and family over. Joaquin Miller also called on me at Somerset House, looking uncommonly well. He has been back here from America two or three weeks now: speaks with some bitterness of the publicity given by the American press to his domestic affairs—a divorce (I believe) having lately taken place between himself and his wife.

Tuesday 31 December   Saw the old year out, in Dunn's company, at Cheyne Walk—the most painful year I have ever passed, owing to the ill-health of Christina, and more especially of Gabriel. Were I to limit myself to what concerns myself personally, there would have been nothing to complain of. However, the year is much less black at its close than at some stages of its course.

[1] It was a bronze medal reproducing the likeness of Gabriele done by D. G. R. on the obverse and, on the reverse, bearing the inscription: A Gabriele Rossetti, degl'invidiosi veri che da Dante fino al Muratori si gridarono propugnatore magnanimo la Italia riconoscente. A. MDCCCXXXXVII.

1873

Wednesday 1 January An uncommonly mild and bright New Year's Day (but rainy again in the evening). It might very well have been a day in April, or even in May.

Thursday 2 January Met Stephens in the street. He enquires whether Gabriel would like him now to publish in the *Athenaeum* a long article (which he sketched out some while ago) on the large picture of *The Death of Beatrice*. I will ask Gabriel about this when next I write.

Friday 3 January Howell called, to speak about the plaguy Botticelli affair. The packages which Pinti was expecting from Italy have now arrived, but none of them contains the Botticelli. Pinti therefore, in uncertainty as to the date when the picture may actually return, and to close the case, has drawn a cheque for £80, payable to Gabriel. Cheque now in Howell's hands.—£80 is the minimum sum which I named some months ago to Howell (without direct consultation of Gabriel) as the amount which might be accepted for the picture: but I fear that Gabriel would not now like it, as it is only very lately that he offered the picture to Graham for £200. Howell consulted me as to what he had best do under these rather vexatious circumstances.—I advised him not needlessly to volunteer any statement of the exact details to Gabriel: but, if Gabriel should press him with queries about the Botticelli (which seems just now not unlikely) to explain the facts, and forward him the cheque—subject to repayment of the money to Pinti, and repossession of the picture by Gabriel in case the work should eventually turn up, which indeed may, I suppose, still be regarded as the most probable upshot at some indeterminate time. Yet perhaps after all the better course would have been to take the present opportunity, when at least the £80 cheque is in hand, of explaining the whole affair to Gabriel.— Howell tells me that Gabriel is buying through him a number of articles of household decoration—velvet for curtains etc. etc. with very little seeming regard for economy. Howell entered into various explanations about his own affairs of two or three years ago—especially the charges made against him of mis-dealings with Ruskin's money as connected with Jones. I am rather disposed to believe in the substantial correctness of Howell's account.[1] Nolly Brown brought round the printed address which his Father has issued, with a view to the Slade Professorship at Cambridge.[2] There is a good deal of sound matter in it, and well put too in a certain sense; but I rather fear the executive mould of the whole thing is not such as would tend to advance his cause with University dignitaries, and the other persons on whom the election depends.

Saturday 4 January   Ordered a copy of my Selection of Humorous Poems to be sent to G. Hake at Kelmscott.

Sunday 5 January   Finished the new catalogue of my books— which has indeed been rather a tough job. I mean now to resume the buying and binding of books, which I had wholly discontinued since the troubles at beginning of last summer.

Monday 6 January   Mamma is now a good deal troubled with tenderness in the soles of the feet. She consulted Dr. Holland Fox about it a little while ago: he recommended tonics, but no local application. She now thinks of speaking to Mr. Stewart about the matter, and receiving something like regular attendance from him regarding it.

Tuesday 7 January   At Cheyne Walk. An agreeable young painter named Britten[3] (who it seems was lately very near winning the gold medal of the R.A.) called on Dunn. Murray[4] also called,

[1] This entry refers to the dismissal of Howell by Ruskin as his secretary and factotum on the charge of dishonesty. For more details, see H. Rossetti Angeli, *Pre-Raphaelite Twilight*, pp. 138–9. See also p. 16 n. 1.

[2] The *Address to the Very Reverend the Vice-Chancellor of the University of Cambridge* was privately printed in London on 20 December 1872 for Ford Madox Brown.

[3] William Edward Frank Britten, decorative painter. Exhibited at the R.A. after 1884.

[4] Charles Fairfax Murray (1849–1919) was one of the artists employed by Ruskin to copy pictures. It was through Ruskin and Howell that he became known to the Rossettis. Later he became an art collector, as shown by the catalogue of the Birmingham Art Gallery—between 1903 and 1910 he presented the Gallery with five Pre-Raphaelite pictures—and by the catalogue of the Fogg Museum of Art, Harvard University.

along with young Hughes:[1] Murray is about shortly to go to Italy, for a somewhat lengthened stay in Rome and elsewhere, at Ruskin's expense. He is to make copies from the Botticelli frescoes in the Sistine Chapel: also thinks of examining the Old Master drawings in the various galleries, and drawing up a catalogue of them correcting errors of attribution, tracing connexion between drawings and pictures, etc. etc. He is under the impression that nothing (or next to nothing) of the kind has yet been done, in relation to such collections in *any* Italian Gallery.

Wednesday 8 January Called at the lodgings of Joaquin Miller, 11 Museum Street, who asks me to dine with him next Saturday. He proposes asking Morris, Brown, and a Mr. Williams, who is a Diplomatic Agent (American by birth) for the Japanese Government. Miller saw Whitman various times in America, and says he spoke a good deal about me. Miss Wynn Jones called on Maria in the evening. She tells me that Miss Traherne (whom I knew years ago as a conspicuous beauty entering into London society), now Mrs. Weldon, wife of the Rouge Dragon,[2] lives at Tavistock House, and has had Gounod[3] domesticated there for some while past. Gounod is without his wife, and causes some little scandal: but Miss Jones does not seem to attach any particular importance to it. He is of simple and genial habits—and is allowed for instance to smoke a pipe after dinner in company. Mrs. Weldon has for years been wholly devoted to musical enthusiasms and projects: she has sung in public, but, it would seem, with rather adverse result.

Thursday 9 January Called at Woolner's, to see after a cast of Hähnel's[4] *Asiatic Lion*, which he has sent over for my acceptance. Woolner is now engaged on a colossal statue of Sir H. Lawrence,[5] statue (now finished, I think) of Whewell,[6] and other matters, and seems to have his hands full of work. He renewed the offer (which

---

[1] Edward Robert Hughes (1851–1914), painter; a nephew of Arthur Hughes and a pupil of Holman Hunt.

[2] One of the Pursuivants of the Royal College of Heralds.

[3] Charles Gounod (1818–93). He remained in London from 1870 to 1875.

[4] Ernst Hähnel (1811–91), German sculptor.

[5] Sir Henry Montgomery Lawrence (1806–57) had a military and administrative career in India, was promoted Brigadier-General in 1857 and killed during the siege of Lucknow. See Edwardes and Merivale, *Life of Sir Henry Lawrence*, 2 vols., 1872.

[6] William Whewell (1794–1866), Master of Trinity College, Cambridge, scientist and philosopher who defended 'intuitionism' against John Stuart Mill. The marble statue is now in the antechapel of Trinity College, Cambridge.

he made to me a year or so ago) of a painting by Blake (or rather,
I have understood, by Linnell[1] after Blake)—the 'spiritual heads'
of *Wallace* and *Edward I* on a large scale:[2] I see the work now for
the first time, and it is a very important acquisition for my Blake
collection. As Woolner urged me to take it, and refused re-
imbursement of the sum (some trifle) that he paid for it, I was fain
to accept with thanks.—Brown called on me at night. He is lately
back from Cambridge, and seems to think his chances of success
in competing for the Slade Professorship there by no means bad,
though also still unassured. He hears that Colvin's chance is next
to none: but he informs me that Robinson[3] also is now a competitor, and to me it seems more than probable that Robinson will
succeed. He hears likewise that Woolner is in the field. I have no
knowledge otherwise as to this matter, and incline to doubt it.—
This is the day of Louis Napoleon's death—I had to pass through
the Soho district, 2 or 3 hours after the news was known in London,
and rather expected to see some symptoms of stir among that
French and refugee population: but there was nothing discernible.

Friday 10 January   Woolner sent me round the Blake picture: he
had bought it at the sale of Pierce the picture-dealer. In consequence of my conversation yesterday with Brown, I looked
through his Cambridge Address, making all verbal alterations
which seem to me desirable; and shall post the pamphlet to him.
This however is shutting the stable-door after the horse has been
stolen, as there seems no prospect of Brown's ordering any new
issue of his address. Got to-day a copy of my Selection of American Poems—the first time I see it as a published volume.

Saturday 11 January   Dined at J. Miller's: his American-
Japanese friend was ill, and could not come, and my only

[1] John Linnell (1792–1882), engraver, miniature portraitist, and landscape
painter. Blake was introduced to him towards 1818 and after that date Linnell
constantly helped and encouraged Blake. He commissioned the *Job* and the *Dante*
series. 'Linnell's "Spiritual Heads" after Blake have not been traced since the 19th
century though they appear to have been fairly well documented then. They probably
were by Linnell.' (Information given to me by Mr. M. Butlin, Keeper of the British
Collection, Tate Gallery.)

[2] Blake had found in John Varley, another painter of the Linnell circle, a kindred
spirit and in the evenings they would call up some well-known figure of the past,
which Blake would draw 'with the utmost alacrity': Wallace and Edward I were
among these visitors from the other world. See Alexander Gilchrist, *Life of Blake*,
London, 1863, pp. 271–2.

[3] See p. 141 n. 3.

fellow guest was Knight.[1] The latter says he suffers much from sleeplessness: does not venture to counteract this by Chloral, as the systematic use of that drug produces paralysis of the lower intestines. I hope this assertion is subject to some qualification, considering the free use that Gabriel makes of chloral. Miller gave us American oyster soup and American salmon: the former with a strange gamey taste—no doubt highly agreeable to many palates and not obnoxious to mine; the latter uncommonly fine and delicate. Miller says that 17,000 copies of his poems have sold in America: there is also money to his credit at Longmans' for the English edition. He is now writing a poem in the Spenserian stanza—being a kind of *Childe Harold* treatment of American wild scenery etc. The general structure and tone of the verse are superior to what I should have expected from Miller in so regular and stately a metre. I noticed however one Alexandrine in the middle of a stanza, and three or more lines of four (instead of five) feet. I informed Miller of this: but, until I told him exactly what was amiss, and what would amend it, he could not undertake to set it right. This is proof positive that poets having a genuine vocation and a strong metrical sense are capable of falling into the grossest blunders of rhythm—blunders which I and all of our family would have been at once struck by even in early childhood. I have sometimes seen this fact called into question: Keightley, for instance, in his *Shakespeare Expositor*,[2] lays it down that a poet never makes such blunders, and therefore, when they occur in print, one may be sure they are errors of the press.

Sunday 12 January   Wrote to Proudfoot to fetch some books for binding. It must be, I think, considerably more than a year ago that I sent him the last lot. The heads of Wallace and Edward I that Woolner has given me appear (on the authority of Gilchrist's book)[3] to be executed not by Blake himself, but by Linnell after the pencil-drawings of Blake.[4]

[1] Joseph Knight (1829–1907), editor of the *Sunday Times* and of *Notes and Queries*, and a contributor to the *Literary Gazette* and the *Athenaeum*. He was a friend of J. W. Marston and of D. G. R. whose biography he wrote in the 'Great Writers' series, published in 1887.

[2] *The Shakespeare Expositor: an aid to the perfect understanding of Shakespeare's Plays*, London, 1867.

[3] *Life of Blake with Selections from his Poems and Writings*, London, 1863, by Alexander Gilchrist (1828–61), biographer. He was a friend of D. G. R. who, with W. M. R., contributed to his book on Blake published posthumously by his widow, Mrs. Anne Gilchrist.   [4] See p. 226 n. 1, 226 n. 1.

Monday 13 January   Lyster lately proposed to present me with such books as I might select from Mr. Keightley's library, prior to the sale of remainder, or more especially of the foreign books. I replied however that I would rather purchase (and should be glad to do so) any which I might wish to own. To-day I went down to the house, and looked through the foreign books, and selected a moderate number of volumes (*Roman de la Rose* etc.) to the value of £3.12.—Poor old Miss Keightley has a grave and saddened aspect and manner; but on the whole bears herself vigorously, after such a breaking-up of her life-long ties as the death of her sister in a moment, and of her brother a few weeks afterwards. The large old black cat, Tip, is still flourishing. It used always to sleep with the deceased Frances Keightley: has hitherto, since her death two or three months ago, invariably avoided entering her bedroom, but a day or two back resumed this habit.

Tuesday 14 January   Looked out at Chelsea some books that will be serviceable to Gabriel in setting about a translation which he now proposed to execute of M. Angelo's poems.[1]

Wednesday 15 January   I am much concerned to-day to hear of the death of my old friend Hannay[2] at Barcelona: Dwelly, who is brother-in-law to Sutherland Edwards,[3] informs me that very recently Hannay was found dead in his chair. The details are not known, but apoplexy or heart-disease is surmised as the cause— He was nearly 46 years of age. This is painful news in itself, but more especially when one reflects on the condition in which his family must be left. He had, I think, five (or perhaps six) children, and, as far as I know they are still all alive. He took them all over to Spain when he settled there; but I rather believe the eldest child, a son now nearly 19, returned to England some while ago

[1] D. G. R. never made the planned translation of Michelangelo's poems.

[2] James Hannay (1827–73), novelist and journalist, edited several periodicals, became acquainted with the Rossettis as early as 1849. W. M. R. had the highest opinion of his talents. His first wife (d. 1865), a woman of exceptional beauty, sat as Beatrice in the water-colour of D. G. R.'s *Dante's Dream*. Hannay, who had five children by his first wife, married a distant cousin in 1868 who died two years later. When he himself died, he was British Consul in Barcelona. See *Memoir, passim*, and for more details, G. J. Worth, *James Hannay, His Life and Works*, University of Kansas Press, 1964.

[3] Henry Sutherland Edwards (1828–1906), musical expert and critic, also journalist, was correspondent of *The Times* during the Franco-Prussian War of 1870–1.

to complete his education. The youngest may, I suppose, be as young as 7 or 8. There is not even a stepmother to look after them, as the second Mrs. Hannay[1] died a year or two ago. The mother belonged to a poor struggling family; most of them, I rather think, now in Australia; Hannay, I believe, had no near relative living (he may perhaps have a stepmother living); and I can't suppose he has left behind him anything but debts and complication in money-matters. The present Police-Magistrate Hannay is, I believe, the James Lennox Hannay,[2] whom I used to meet years ago—cousin to James Hannay: he, I believe, is well off, but whether he cared enough about Hannay to attend zealously to the interests of his orphans I rather doubt.—In writing to Gabriel in the evening I mentioned this afflicting matter to him.

Thursday 16 January   Called at John Marshall's[3] to see about some more chloral for Gabriel. He was not in; but I saw for the first time his son, now aged (I suppose) twelve or thirteen, who from a very early age indeed has distinguished himself by executing very clever landscapes. He told me that he used to wish to be a painter, but does not now particularly; he was engaged in some geometrical work when I entered.

Friday 17 January   Settled this job of the chloral—the object being to continue a reduction of one-half of the proportion of chloral to water, as taken by Gabriel which reduction was made by Hake without Gabriel's knowledge some while ago, but is now less easy of continuance, seeing that Gabriel has lately taken to pouring out the chloral for himself. The arrangement which has now been made will, I hope, meet the difficulty. Marshall does not seem to think that Gabriel can yet awhile wholly leave off chloral, and he regards the present doses as strictly moderate: he knows nothing of 'paralysis of the lower intestine' (see 11 Jan.) as a consequence of chloral.—This winter has been as yet singularly

[1] David Hannay, the eldest boy, was born in 1853. The youngest child by the second wife was born in 1869.

[2] James Lennox Hannay, a London police magistrate, cousin of James Hannay. When a young man, he sat for the head of Valentine in Holman Hunt's picture, *Two Gentlemen of Verona* (1850). See *Reminiscences*, p. 169.

[3] Dr. John Marshall (1818–91), anatomist and surgeon. His fame rests upon the ability with which he taught anatomy in its relation to art. In May 1873 he was appointed Professor of Anatomy to the Royal Academy.

mild: shrubs are fast coming out into bud now, and have been so these few days past—I see in the newspaper the death of Mr. Waugh, father-in-law of Hunt and of Woolner.[1]

Saturday 18 January   Went up Great James Street trying to find the house in which Dr. Hake now has chambers, along with his sons; but, not knowing the number, I failed.

Sunday 19 January   Going on with the Memoir of Pope, for Moxon's volume.

Monday 20 January   Having heard from Brown that he has been laid up these few days with gout and neuralgia, I called to see him; he can now just set his foot to the ground, but is still confined to his bedroom. He urges me to resume writing about fine art, and especially to undertake a Life of Titian[2]—not so much involving an account of his individual pictures as exhibiting his position and surroundings as a man. Assuming (of which I am not entirely sure) that this work has not been already done in some efficient way, it would no doubt be a fine thing to achieve: also a laborious one, and I cannot but view my own qualifications for the task with some mistrust. However, as the work for Moxon is now near its close, I shall no doubt soon have to take up with some other settled literary employment. There are more things than one in connexion with Shelley that I should like to do; also my old project (or rather Palgrave's[3] as to suggestion) of a collection of 'dicta on art' by English artists,[4] for which transcripts of some considerable bulk were made years ago; also the *Christianity of Christ*, which I began in 1868 and have done nothing with these three years or more.[5] That is a work which interests me, but no doubt there is some presumption in so unscholarly a person as myself attacking it. One consideration as to the whole question of literary work for my handling is its chance of sale, or at any rate of ready publication. Another thing I *might* take up is the

[1] See p. 273 n. 3.

[2] Although W. M. R. never wrote a life of Titian he nevertheless contributed an article on Titian together with I. A. Richter to the *Encyclopaedia Britannica*.

[3] Francis Turner Palgrave (1824–97), the literary critic and anthologist.

[4] W. M. R. collected information and notes for this compilation which was never completed.

[5] This work remains extant in MS.

translation of *Dante*, in which I had got beyond the middle of the *Purgatorio*.[1]

Tuesday 21 January   In going to Cheyne Walk, I passed a little Oriental shop in Ebury Street—Inman's—which I have often noticed these three or four years past, but never made close acquaintance with. Found here a good stock of Japanese, Indian, etc., articles, and bought some—principally Japanese crape-pictures.—Dunn has now about finished his cartoon-work at South Kensington—the section of the 'Charge to Peter' that contains the figure of Christ—and the time within which the competitors were to complete their performances is just expiring. Some of them however have solicited an extra week, which has been granted: and Dunn will avail himself of this to add some finishing touches. He apprehends that the only competitor who will be regarded by the umpires as fairly contesting with himself in successful result will be the one who is occupied on the other section of the 'Charge to Peter'.

Wednesday 22 January   Since Monday night the weather has greatly changed. Yesterday was a sharp frosty cold; to-day about equally cold, but to some extent damp again. Perhaps we are now at last in for a considerable spell of real winter.

Thursday 23 January   Christina thinks of looking up a number of her old poems, that were considered hardly good enough to be printed in her two volumes and offering these for publication in some magazine (*Argosy* or other)[2] under a pseudonym. She would adopt a pseudonym partly because the works are not of her best quality, but more especially because, being written many years ago, they derive from a tone of feeling necessarily not very congruous with her present age. This, I think, is a good reason for not publishing the poems in magazines with her real name; but I am not much in favour of a pseudonym in this or any instance. Besides, the chief reason for publishing—which in this case would be money in hand—would be greatly thwarted by a pseudonym.

[1] W. M. R.'s translation of the *Inferno* was published in 1865; see p. 125 n. 1. The *Purgatorio* remained unpublished.

[2] C. G .R. did publish two sonnets 'Venus's Looking-glass' and 'Love lies bleed-ing' in the *Argosy* for 1 Jan. 1873, but under her real name; so was a third poem, 'Amor Mundi' composed on 21 February 1865 and reprinted in the same maga-zine on 1 May 1873.

The poems, not being in themselves first-rate specimens, would perhaps hardly be welcomed by the editor at all if, instead of coming out with Christina's name, they were to be published with a newly invented pseudonym.—Called at Dr. Hake's house, 15 Great James Street, but find that he is now staying at Bath.

Friday 24 January   Mrs. Brown and Nolly called, asking Maria and me to meet two of the Hakes tomorrow at Dinner.—I have lately been noting down at Somerset House such remarkable names (whether euphonious or odd) as come before my eyes in official correspondence : There is something in the real *de facto* combinations of this sort superior, I think, to almost any effort of combination that a novelist could make, and my object in drawing up the list has been mainly to supply Nolly with the names, for any use he might turn them to in writing his novels. I therefore gave him to-day a first instalment, with which he seemed pleased. Smith & Elder, he tells me, have now agreed to publish as a book his novel of sea-life : subject however to important modifications in the conduct of the story, such as will almost make it a new tale. Anyhow this is very encouraging.—I looked through, at Joaquin Miller's request, the first printed sheet of his Spenserian poem, *By the Sundown Seas*, noting slips of metre etc, and shall return him this sheet, and go on afterwards with the residue. There are several blemishes to note, but on the whole the poem has excellent quality.

Saturday 25 January   Dined with the Browns. Dr. Hake expects to be in Italy at no distant date : as Scott and I are not unlikely to be there as well some time this year, we might perhaps all meet. Nolly expects his novel to be published towards Easter.

Sunday 26 January   Finished making notes and suggestions on J. Miller's proofs.—One of the most annoying outward symptoms of Christina's illness, the enormous protrusion of the eyes, is now very sensibly diminished : this diminution has been going on for some while past, but I am more particularly struck with the stage it has reached just now. The swelling at the throat is also so far subdued as to excite no particular attention when Christina is dressed.

Monday 27 January Dined with Stillman. His son is still very weak and ailing but has progressed to some noticeable extent, being able to go out of doors on crutches a goodish deal. The infant Euphrosyne (just about a year old) recognised the other day as 'Papa' and 'Mamma' the crayon portraits[1] which Gabriel did three years or so ago of the parents: this must, I think, be an act of considerable precocity. Mrs. Stillman has painted a very good portrait of her. The other guests were chiefly photographers: Stillman being now mixed up in a row going on in the Photographic Society. A letter complaining of the hanging of the Society's last Exhibition, particularly of unfairness to the contributions of Colonel Stuart-Wortley[2] was lately received by the Editor of the *Photography Journal*, purporting to come from, and enclosing the card of Mr. Bouverie-Pusey,[3] and this letter was followed by others in like strain, in different handwritings: but Mr. Bouverie-Pusey, on being asked, wholly denies having had any sort of connexion with the matter. Col. Stuart-Wortley also denies it explicitly: but strong suspicions against him exist. There are at least two disguised hand-writings, and very cleverly disguised they are, as compared with Col. Stuart-Wortley's ordinary writing: still, the experts, Chabot and Netherclift, on being consulted, positively affirm that the same person was really the writer of all the letters. I (who know my own eye to be a very sharp one) am distinctly, though hardly so positively, of the same opinion. What ulterior steps will or can be taken is a little uncertain. Stillmand has some grounds of personal resentment against Stuart-Wortley —Chabot was present at the dinner: on the evidence of handwriting (besides other matters) he is most entirely convinced that the Tichborne claimant is an impostor, and is Orton.[4] He is of French descent, but of a family a long way back settled in England, (Revocation of Edict of Nantes). He says that experts in handwriting very seldom differ in the conclusions they arrive at— seldomer than any other experts he knows of. Does not believe in

[1] Mrs. Stillman's red chalk portrait was made in 1869. It is reproduced in Marillier's *Dante Gabriel Rossetti*, 1899, facing p. 152, and is the property of R. M. Ritchie, the sitter's grandson. William Stillman's portrait, dated 1870, now in the Museum of Fine Arts, Boston, appears more as a red chalk than as a pastel. See Surtees, nos. 519 and 518, p. 197.

[2] Colonel H. Stuart-Wortley (1832–90), a grandson of the first Baron Wharncliffe.

[3] S. E. Bouverie Pusey, son of Philip Pusey, M.P. (1799–1855), and nephew of Dr. Pusey, one of the leaders of the Oxford Movement.

[4] See p. 146 n. 1.

the decipherment of character by hand writing. I myself do decidedly believe in it to some extent—as for instance that you could hardly get a very firm handwriting, or a very elegant one, from a person who was not in some definite way or degree firm or elegant-minded. Chabot thinks that even this does not hold good to any marked extent.

Tuesday 28 January   Dwelly showed me a letter addressed by David Hannay (the eldest son) to Sutherland Edwards: it shows that the family though in very narrow circumstances, are not plunged into quite such a quagmire of difficulties as I had feared. David has been taken on as Clerk, at a small salary, by the acting Consul at Barcelona (it would appear I was mistaken in supposing David to have been just of late in England), and has some hopes that the next Consul will retain him. His eldest sister has succeeded in getting at Barcelona some families wherein she teaches English; and I gather that a second sister will remain seeking similar employment. Another, Robina,[1] is to come to England—to be taken care of, I suppose, by some relative: two boys remain, for whom David hopes his father's influential friends may succeed in obtaining schooling on some foundation. A Miss Cole[2] (who I believe had for years past been governess to the family, and of great service to all) is still with them.—David says there was only about £6 in the house when his father died: some one (who remains anonymous) produced some money for immediate necessities, otherwise they would have been floored altogether: now he hopes that, among them all, something like £200 a year may be got together. Hannay was found dead with a very placid look, and seemingly without any pain: but on this subject David does not enter into details.

Wednesday 29 January   Wrote at Stephens' suggestion, and sent to him, a letter to Reid[3] of the British Museum representing the claims of Stephens to an increase of pay for the work which he does at the Museum regarding satirical prints.[4] Also sent

[1] Robina was the daughter of the second marriage; she was then 4 years old.

[2] Charlotte Cole was an old family friend of the Hannays who took care of the children after their mother's death.

[3] George William Reid (1819–87), Keeper of the Department of Prints and Drawings in the British Museum.

[4] F. G. Stephens had undertaken to draw up a Catalogue of Prints and Drawings (Satire) in the British Museum. It was published in 4 vols. from 1870 to 1883.

Keningale Cook[1] a testimonial for which he asks, with a view to a class of English literature at Queen's College, Harley Street.[2]

Thursday 30 January Allingham called. The first time I have seen him for several months. He referred to Mrs. Bodichon's offer of letting to Gabriel her house at Robertsbridge: but, as I informed Allingham there would not appear to be in this plan any particular advantage to Gabriel, who, as long as he remains at a considerable distance from town, is at least as well suited at Kelmscott as he well could be elsewhere. I see in the *Daily News* that Brown has not succeeded in obtaining the Slade Professorship at Cambridge. Colvin is elected. For Brown's sake I regret this result much.

Friday 31 January Going on with the Prefatory Notice of Pope.

Saturday 1 February Took a second short spell at the British Museum, for the purpose of looking up a few dates etc. still wanted before I send to the printers the materials for the Miscellaneous Selection of Poetry—*Via Lactea*,[3] as I christened it some while ago.

Sunday 2 February A rather considerable fall of snow to-day: the cold continues steady since 21 January. Wrote Moxons, asking for payment in respect of the American Selection.

Monday 3 February Christina more unwell than she has commonly been of late, with a gathering in the nose, hysterical attack, etc.: she has been in bed all to-day, and the earlier part of yesterday. Dr. Jenner had been expected to call to-day, but did not appear.

Tuesday 4 February Went to Cheyne Walk, and had the satisfaction of seeing there the Botticelli picture, lately returned after its prolonged wanderings. Howell called. He was going round to the

---

[1] Keningale Cook (d. *c.* 1886), editor of the *Dublin University Magazine*. He was the writer of poems and of a book named *The Fathers of Jesus*, referring to the moralists who taught the moral truths of the Gospel before the advent of Christ. See *Reminiscences*, p. 506.

[2] Founded by F. D. Maurice (1805–72), the Christian socialist, in 1848 for the advancement of women's education.

[3] This selection of poetry was never published.

chambers of Watts[1] the solicitor, to state what he knows about the arrangement which was made years ago between Swinburne and Hotten with regard to publication of Swinburne's books,— Watts being now engaged in negotiating for a final close of all connexion with Hotten, and transfer to some other publisher, perhaps Chapman and Hall. Howell tells me that Swinburne (who is at present at Holmwood)[2] has at last found the notes I took on the occasion of the conclusive interview between Swinburne and Hotten, when the business arrangements were first made; which notes I returned some years ago to Swinburne at his request, and which he forthwith proceeded to mislay. With them, I believe the rights and wrongs of the whole affair will become much more apparent. Howell is shortly to visit Gabriel at Kelmscott.

Wednesday 5 February   Christina still in bed: Dr. Wilson Fox, however, saw her yesterday, and has ordered remedies which seem to be producing a good effect. Maria plagued with toothache.

Thursday 6 February   Obtained at Howell's request, and sent to him, the papers as to election etc. at the Astronomical Society and the Geological Society: he wanted also the Society of Antiquaries, but those papers are not so readily procurable. It seems he has lately been elected into the Royal Society which astonishes me not a little: but he says that his pretensions as a Civil Engineer were the *raison d'être* of the election, and that in fact he was Engineer-in-chief for one of the Portuguese Railways—the first constructed in the country, I rather think he says.

Friday 7 February   Spent the evening by invitation at Wallis's, at Red Lion Square, meeting there Dilberoglue, Webb, etc.

[1] Theodore Watts (1832–1914) (Watts-Dunton after 1896) had been educated as a naturalist; then he qualified as a solicitor. He was introduced to D. G. R. by Dr. Hake and for many years he acted as D. G. R.'s, Morris's, and Swinburne's legal adviser. His first visit to D. G. R. at Kelmscott in 1872 was the starting-point of his literary career. He became a regular contributor to the *Athenaeum* after 1876. He decided to rescue Swinburne from a disorderly life and harboured him in his own house at Putney after 1879. He then became the owner, after Swinburne's death in 1909, of the latter's valuable MSS. and works of art. His novel, *Aylwin* (1898), describes the literary circles into which he had introduced himself: D. G. R. appears as 'D'Arcy' while the semi-Portuguese Howell is christened 'De Castro'; the little Gipsy is Watts-Dunton himself.

[2] Holmwood, near Shiplake and Henley-on-Thames (Oxfordshire), the seat of Swinburne's parents.

Conversation more social-political than artistic, about the colliers' strike, the Commune, etc.: Webb is strong in upholding the action of the colliers in carrying out their strike to the extreme uttermost, as being practically a state of 'war', which having undertaken they are right in enforcing. He speaks with utter disgust of the restoration of St. Alban's Abbey, now going on under Gilbert Scott's[1] direction. Wallis has a very fine show of Spanish-moresque lustreware: also Burgkmair's[2] *Petrarch*, one of the most admirable illustrated books extant. I hardly think any cinquecento book of the same class quite equals it.

Saturday 8 February   A curious man named Stronsberg, a foreign contractor, has called on me sometimes at Somerset House on matters of business. He called again to-day, and talked at large on all sorts of subjects. He has a plan for the extinction of drunkenness, which I suppose would be too paternal and despotic ever to be tried in this country, but if tried might have some considerable effect. He would require every person who wishes to be served with drink in a public-house or drinking-shop of any kind to take out an annual shilling license. Whenever such a person was convicted of drunkenness, the license should be endorsed—or forfeited (I forget which, but at any rate no drunkard, however desperate, should ever be precluded from taking out a new license). Any liquor-seller who sold liquor to a person not duly provided with a producing license should be liable to very severe punishment—say 6 months' imprisonment, without option of fine. The gain to the Revenue would be large, for millions of people would take out a drinking-license, however little practical use they might make of it.

Sunday 9 February   Finished the Prefatory Notice of Pope. Except some finishing-up jobs (such as looking out a suitable edition of Pope, attending to proofs of *Via Lactea*, etc.) this is the last thing I have to do on Moxon's series: the publishers *may* however be

[1] Sir George Gilbert Scott (1811–78), architect, President of the Royal Institute of British Architects, restored many cathedrals in England.

[2] Hans Burgkmair (*c.* 1473–1531), German painter, miniaturist, and wood-engraver, pupil of Albrecht Dürer and father-in-law of the elder Holbein. The *Petrarch* mentioned here is a German translation of Petrarch's prose treatise on Fortune, *Glücksbuch beydes des Guten und Bösen*, with 260 designs that modern scholars attribute not to Burgkmair but to Hans Weiditz (*c.* 1492–1537). See. D. G. R., *Letters*, iii. 1137.

adding other volumes to the series from time to time.—On awaking from my Sunday night's sleep I was rather impressed with two peculiarities in the quality of my dream: 1) the extreme distinctness of visual faculty, just the same as if I had been exercising my physical eyesight: I had dreamed of picking up various very brilliant and beautiful pieces of oxydized glass and other iridescent objects, and I saw and appreciated the various qualities and tints of colour—pink, blueish, etc, the difference in quality of surface-tint between an oxydized piece of wood and the oxydized glass, the comparative failure of colour when the objects were afterwards (in my dream) produced by lamplight, etc. 2) I dreamed that there was a man whose real name was Murphy, but some one was in the habit of latinizing his name into Murphius. Forthwith it passed through my mind that the ingenious way of doing the thing would be to call him M. Ulpius (pronouncing Marcus Ulpius), because 'l' is linguistically interchangeable with 'r', and because of the punning reminiscence from the name of the Emperor Trajan. All these rather far-fetched tricks of mind came to me just as readily in sleep as they could have done in waking. Nothing in my occupations of the preceding day had tended in a like direction: nor can I fix upon anything nearer than reading casually, two or three days ago, some details connected with Trajan. I have more than once, on waking, noticed that similar ingeniosities, of a verbal or other such like kind, had been passing through my mind while asleep: but of course the instances are few comparatively.

Monday 10 February Resumed the reading up of books about Shelley (Essays and Letters at present) with a view to collecting together all the materials which he left of an autobiographical character. I should much like to see this job done, but can't say whether there is any substantial likelihood of finding a publisher.

Tuesday 11 February Called on Scott: he has recently been engaged on a dozen or so of woodblocks for Keble's *Christian Year*:[1] had indeed had the offer of doing the entire series (60) of illustrations needed for the book—which is rather ludicrous,

---

[1] John Keble (1792–1866), one of the leaders of the Oxford Movement with Newman and Pusey. *The Christian Year: thoughts in verse for the Sundays and Holydays throughout the year*, 2 vols., Oxford, 1827. It was published anonymously.

considering his religious views—but this he declined.—He showed me a copy of a letter of Burns[1] (sent to him by Mr. Scott-Douglas), narrating his interview with Jean Armour when he re-visited her after the first separation between them, consequent on her pregnancy: this letter is written in terms of the broadest indecent outspokenness, and of riotous delight in the incident which probably had laid the foundation of Jean's second pair of twins.—Scott and I came to a provisional understanding that we may be going to Italy together towards 1 May.

Wednesday 12 February　Christina has been somewhat better these few days. Today again hardly so well.—Spanish Republic determined on,[2] but I suppose the decree must be regarded as for the present merely provisional, pending a plébiscite or some such move. I fear Spain is too disturbed a country to allow of a very good chance for long to a Republic: at the same time, the existence of the neighbouring Republic in France, supposing that to endure, may materially improve the chances in Spain. Were both to endure and flourish, it would be a glorious result, fruitful probably of much in no very remote future.

Thursday 12 February　Went to see the Exhibition of Old Masters at Burlington House. Examined two or three rooms, and looked casually through the others. There is a stupendous Botticelli (heaven and earth picture of beatification of the Virgin):[3] Blake's

[1] In 1785 Robert Burns had given Jean Armour, who was pregnant, a written declaration of marriage to which both put their signatures, but her parents requested a public and regular marriage in legal form. In April 1788 their old contract of marriage was recorded in front of the justice of the peace. Burns commented: 'I am so enamoured of a certain girl's prolific, twin-bearing merit that I have given her a legal title.' See Catherine Carswell, *The Life of Robert Burns*, London, 1930, p. 335.

[2] Queen Isabella II of Spain, after having been overthrown by a military rebellion, had taken refuge in France and Switzerland in 1868; nevertheless the Cortes of 1869 had voted for the continuance of the monarchy and Prince Amadeo of Savoy was chosen, but was regarded by most of the Spaniards as an intruder; he had to abdicate in February 1873; a republic was proclaimed which lasted till 1875.

[3] *The Assumption of Our Lady* was painted for the church of San Pietro, Florence, as a commission of Palmieri. When the church was demolished in 1783, the picture went into the Casa Palmieri and was sold by one of the descendants to the Duke of Hamilton, from whom the National Gallery, London, bought it in 1882. The authenticity of the picture was questioned by Bode in 1886; it was reattributed to Botticelli in 1933 and, in 1951, Mr. Martin Davies declared it to be the work of Francesco Botticini (1446–97) who worked in Botticelli's studio. See R. Salvini, *Tutta la pittura del Botticelli*, Milano, 1958, i. 173.

picture of *Gray's Bard*[1] is a wonderful piece of colour, gilt being freely used in it.

Friday 14 February   Wrote to Gabriel explaining how the question of going to Italy stands between Scott and me, as Gabriel shows some disposition to come as well. I don't at all count on him.

Saturday 15 February   Brown called. He does not know any details about the election to the Slade Professorship at Cambridge—only that Colvin obtained the appointment. Lucy, I am sorry to hear, is suffering from cough etc, and told by Marshall that she must not venture out of doors for the present: she is not ordinarily subject to coughs, and Brown does not seem to understand that there is anything really serious in the case.

Sunday 16 February   Wrote to Moxons, sending the notice of Pope, and asking whether they, or Ward and Co. would be disposed to publish the Selection I made some years ago of the Dicta of British Artists on Subjects of Art.[2]

Monday 17 February   Gabriel writes that both Dunn and Howell are now about to visit him.

Tuesday 18 February   Called at Brown's, principally to enquire after Lucy, who still confines herself to the house, but is going on fairly. Brown is preparing to paint on a large scale his design of Byron's *Sardanapalus*[3]—also that of the *Two Foscari*:[4] he would like also to paint a subject, of which he showed me an interesting and attrative design, 'Apelles painting Phryne as Venus Anadyomene'.[5] He has now seen (I have not) Hunt's picture of the *Shadow*

---

[1] *The Bard from Gray* was painted by Blake in 1809. (Tate Gallery.)

[2] This compilation was never published and is still extant in MS.

[3] In 1870 Madox Brown had prepared several designs to illustrate Moxon's *Byron*. Subsequently he executed some of them as pictures. The *Dream of Sardanapalus* mentioned here is a large oil version of the subject. See F. M. Hueffer, *Ford Madox Brown*, p. 281.

[4] *The Two Foscari* (1821) is the name given by Byron to his tragedy, whereas Madox Brown's picture is generally referred to as *Jacopo Foscari*.

[5] This picture was commissioned by Frederick W. Craven of Manchester, one of Rossetti's and Madox Brown's patrons, but the nude being considered as a necessary element of the design by the painter, 'Mr. Craven boggled at the idea.' So the picture was finally abandoned. See F. M. H., *Ford Madox Brown*, p. 263.

of the Cross,[1] and in several respects admires it heartily. Agnews[2] are going on with some sort of negociation [*sic*] regarding this picture, and Hunt therefore has to discourage visits to inspect it.

Wednesday 19 February Went round to Cheyne Walk, and find that Dunn left for Kelmscott on Monday.

Thursday 20 February We heard some little while ago that all the pictures in Bath House (Lord Ashburton's) had been burned: Gabriel used to know them well in the time of the now Dowager Lady Ashburton and he speaks of the catastrophe as a serious loss to art. To-day, he has received a letter from my Aunt Charlotte, saying that all the pictures in the drawing-room were destroyed, except a Titian and a Rubens (subjects not mentioned), and a *Christ, John and Lamb*, which must be the so-called Leonardo which Gabriel regards as peculiarly precious. These three are only slightly damaged. How far the pictures in the drawing-room may go, as representing the entire collection of pictures, I do not know.

Friday 21 February At Cheyne Walk. F. came, and spent most of the evening with me: she professes herself resolved not to marry again.[3]

Saturday 22 February Went again to the Old Masters at Burlington House. One of the excellent things here is a grisaille picture by Dürer of *Christ carrying his cross*—a number of small figures. It does not appear to be mentioned in Scott's book.

---

[1] *The Shadow of the Cross* also known as *The Shadow of Death*. There are three versions of the picture: one is a study in oil for a large picture now in Manchester Art Gallery. They were painted concurrently at Bethlehem and Jerusalem in 1869–72 and completed in London. They were sold to Thomas Agnew and Sons for £5,500. Hunt made a quarter-size replica in 1873 for the engraver Frederick Poole. The study is in Leeds City Art Galleries and the replica belongs to the Trustees of the Middlemore Estate. See M. Bennett, *Catalogue of the Holman Hunt Exhibition in Liverpool and London, May–June 1969*, pp. 48–51.

[2] Thomas Agnew and Sons, the art-dealers. William Agnew (1825–1910) founded the National Liberal Club. The firm is now established in Bond Street, London.

[3] Fanny's first husband was a Mr. Hughes, a mechanic, who died in 1872. He had sat for the figure of David in the Llandaff triptych. In 1879 she married a Mr. Schott, a widower who had been her lodger for two years. After D. G. R.'s death, Schott organized an exhibition of the drawings and pictures Fanny received from D. G. R. See P. F. Baum's introduction to *D. G. R.'s Letters to Fanny Cornforth*, Baltimore, 1940.

Sunday 23 February   Wrote to Gabriel, offering to give him for Kelmscott, if serviceable, an old oak carved panel that I bought the other day in Cleveland St. for 7 shillings representing the *Creation of Eve*, and the *Temptation*: not a bad piece of work.

Monday 24 February   Christina, besides the more serious aspects of her loss of health, is hardly rid of one minor cause of discomfort and disquietude than another comes on. It is now a gathering in one ear: Sir W. Jenner called to-day, and gave directions about it, not apparently attaching any particular importance to the matter.

Tuesday 25 February   Rapid thaw after a considerable fall of snow yesterday. It has now been unpleasantly cold ever since 20 January but I should not be surprised if the change to-day were the forerunner of Spring weather. Streets excessively dirty.

Wednesday 26 February   Christina pretty well again, so far as the gathering in the ear is concerned.

Thursday 27 February   Went to Brown's, where were Joaquin Miller, O'Shaughnessy and a few others. Miller means to print in his forthcoming volume of poems a tart paragraph written by Bayard Taylor[1] against his previous volume, saying that I and other English critics of it had been taken in by its pretence at *couleur locale* which is however altogether delusive. Along with this, Miller will print a statement made by some distinguished geologist, to the effect that Miller's scenery is so true as to serve the purpose of a guide-book—also a statement which (according to Miller) Humboldt[2] once made, that Taylor has been further and seen less than any man he knew. I recommended Miller to drop any such litigious appendages to a volume of poetry, but did not persuade him. As his description of Walker[3] has been

[1] James Bayard Taylor (1825–78), American printer, journalist, dramatist, and poet. W. M. R. says that he was better known in the United States as a traveller than as a poet. In 1854 he published *Poems of the Orient*, and later, books about his travels: *Journey to Central Africa* and *Northern Travel*. He was also one of the editors of the *New York Tribune*. See the *Academy*, 19 December 1874.

[2] Alexander Von Humboldt (1769–1859), German naturalist and traveller.

[3] William Walker (1824–60), an American filibuster who, according to Miller, shared his wild exploits in Nicaragua. See F. M. Hueffer, *Ford Madox Brown*, p. 289.

impugned—one paper saying that Walker was an undersized man, of Methodist-parson aspect—I asked Miller about this point. He admits that Walker may probably have been a very quiet-looking man when seen in every-day life; but maintains that he made a considerable personal display when engaged in military expeditions. His height was about the same as Miller's own; if this is accurate, he was certainly the reverse of undersized—getting on towards being tall. Brown has now sketched out on canvas, for a well-sized picture, his design of *Byron and Miss Chaworth*:[1] thinks also of painting on a somewhat similar scale his old design of *Cromwell at St. Ives*.[2]

Friday 28 February   At Cheyne Walk. I am now (during Dunn's absence at Kelmscott) going there every Friday as well as Tuesday.

Saturday 1 March   Looked, at Joaquin Miller's request, through some more of his poems—*Isles of the Amazons* etc. This stands in considerable need of condensation.

Sunday 2 March   Having to reply to a letter from Mr. Campbell, my Shelleyan correspondent in the Mauritius, I informed him of the compilation of Shelley's letters, etc. on which I am now engaged; adding that failing other arrangements I may perhaps have a few copies of the collection printed off for private circulation.

Monday 3 March   Brown writes informing me of the death of J. Marshall's second son, aged about thirteen.[3] I trust (and incline to think) this is not the son who showed several years ago such astonishing gifts for landscape-painting, and whom I for the first time saw about a couple of months ago.

---

[1] In 1873 Ford Madox Brown prepared a cartoon of the *Byron and Mary Chaworth* subject, then a water-colour; in 1875 he completed the oil picture, and the design of it formed the 'Little-Vignette' for the Moxon's *Byron* edited by W. M. R. See F. M. Hueffer, *Ford Madox Brown*, pp. 281, 292, 298.

[2] *Cromwell at St. Ives*, later known as *Cromwell on his Farm* (Lady Lever Art Gallery, Port Sunlight), begun in 1852, was not completed until 1874; it is a large oil-painting and water-colour versions were made of the subject. See Mary Bennett, *Catalogue of Ford Madox Brown's Exhibition*, Liverpool, 1964.

[3] There is an unpublished letter (at Fitzwilliam Museum, Cambridge) from D. G. R. to Marshall on the death of his son.

Tuesday 4 March   Met Dr. Heimann in the morning. He expects his son Charles back from Japan next month to stay till the close of the year, and then return. Horace in New Zealand is now Book-Keeper to a German shoemaker: not perhaps a very satisfactory employment for a youth who threw up city-life here on account of its drudgery, but it seems he is content, and eventually Dr. Heimann expects to place him along with Charles. Finished at last looking through the Burlington House Exhibition of Old Masters. Met Howell there, who says that he used in his childhood to know, in the hands of some Portuguese owner at Lisbon, the remarkable grisaille by Dürer of *Christ bearing the cross*, which connaisseurs here (it seems) deny to be a Dürer: I can see no rational reason for the denial. Dunn returned in the evening to Cheyne Walk. Scott looked in there. He has received an appointment as Joint-Examiner, with Hart[1] and another, of the drawings sent up in competition by the schools of Art: this will occupy him (£3.3 per day) from about 15 April to 15 May: I therefore proposed to postpone till 25 May our projected starting for an Italian trip. Some one at Dukinfield is now in correspondence with Scott about certain Blake drawings in his possession. He has sent Scott a photograph of a battle-subject, one of these drawings: it is a spirited piece of work, and not a common one, but neither Scott nor I perceive in it any true sign of Blake's handiwork.

Wednesday 5 March   Going on with the Shelley compilation.

Thursday 6 March   Allan McClounie, the husband of Gabriel's servant Emma, died this morning in the Cheyne Walk house, of consumption, which had been wearing him out these two years or more.—Hüffer and Brown called on me in the evening—first time I have seen Hüffer since his marriage to Cathie Brown in September.—He says that the Tauchnitz edition of Gabriel's poems, with an introduction written by Hüffer will be shortly published. He had made some reference to Buchanan in this introduction, and asked me whether I think it would annoy Gabriel: my impression is that Gabriel will not now much care whether it is in or out, but that certainly of the two it would be better to omit it. Joaquin Miller also called: looks much worn, and professes to be very tired

[1] Solomon Alexander Hart (1806–81), painter; Professor of Painting at the R.A. from 1854 to 1863.

of all work connected with his forthcoming volume of poems, and anxious to get it off his hands, and himself away, as soon as may be. He thinks of returning to California by the Indo-Australian route. His indifference to plain matter-of-fact in his descriptions is remarkable, and certainly far from approvable, and I can easily think now that his Walker (see 27 Feb.) is rather a fancy-picture. In his Spenserian poem he has spoken of Byron in early youth as black-haired: I have assured him that Byron was neither black-haired, but dark auburn-haired in mature manhood, and pretty sure therefore to have been light-haired in adolescence, and that the passage as it stands becomes by this mis-statement hardly intelligible (no direct mention of Byron's name occurring in it), not to speak of untruthful: yet he leaves the passage as it stands, simply because he doesn't quite see what epithet to substitute, and because Mary Chaworth (who is referred to in the same passage) being fair, he thinks Byron ought as a matter of contrast to present himself to the imagination as dark. I am not sure whether I did at last persuade him to make the needed alteration, but rather think I did.

Friday 7 March Scott called on me at Somerset House, having been invited by Routledge to undertake the editing and illustrating of a series of English poets, not unlike that which I am doing for Moxon. Routledge, he says, was called in as arbitrator or the like in Moxon's affairs, and probably saw reason for thinking Moxon's speculation a good one. I gave Scott all the information I could as to the nature of the work, terms, etc., and he thinks the like terms (apart from the question of illustrations) would content him.

Saturday 8 March Louisa Parke called. There seems some (not perhaps much) chance of her having to relinquish her situation as governess to Leyland's girls, on the ground that she is confessedly not good at arithmetic, in which on the contrary her pupils have very good capacity, inviting proportionate cultivation.

Sunday 9 March I see in the *Athenaeum* that Howell has become a member of the Anthropological Institute:[1] he seems resolved to take a position as a 'solid' man.

[1] The Anthropological Institute was founded in 1871 as a result of its amalgama-

Monday 10 March   Going on with the Shelley compilation. I have now looked through all the more substantial books needing to be extracted from, and have nearly completed the chronological compendium of materials. I counted up those I have already set in order, and they amount to 368 items—no inconsiderable number. This is the great majority of what will be needed, but several other items have still nevertheless to be added.

Tuesday 11 March   Dined at Howell's, Northend Grove: the first time I have ever been in that house, though Howell has resided there since 1868. Burton,[1] Sandys, etc., there. The beautiful getting-up of the house is equal to the many praises I have heard of it: and several of the precious and tasteful objects have been acquired at fabulously small prices. Kate Howell[2] exceedingly gracious to me. Before dinner we got talking about religious opinions, à propos of Cathie Brown's marriage at the Registrar's only. Mrs. Howell expressed a considerable degree of free-thinking, and asked what my opinions amount to. I explained to her that they amount to absolute disbelief of many matters of religion, and total uncertainty, without express disbelief, as to the remainder. I hardly know why, but this precise point of view seemed to very convincing to her, and she at once avowed herself a convert to it, with regard to any questions as to which she had heretofore differed. Burton very indignant against Gladstone's Irish University Bill,[3] as spoiling a number of things that are at mation (!) with the Ethnological Institute which had been founded in 1843. It still exists today.

   [1] Sir Frederick William Burton (1816–1900), water-colourist, director of the National Portrait Gallery, and later of the National Gallery. He was associated with Sandys and Howell in 1866. See Swinburne, *Letters*, i. 215 n. 1.
   [2] Charles Howell married his cousin Frances Catherine Howell in 1867. 'She was in her own way as popular as Charles.' D. G. R. made two portraits of her, one before she was married in 1865, the second in 1869. She died in 1888. See Helen Rossetti Angeli, *Pre-Raphaelite Twilight*, p. 212, and for the portraits, Surtees, nos. 338 and 339, p. 169.
   [3] William Ewart Gladstone (1809–98), Prime Minister when he introduced the Irish University Bill proposing the establishment of a new university in Dublin which Roman Catholics would be able to attend on equal terms with the Protestants. The latter claimed that there was already a University college in Dublin—Trinity College—founded under Queen Elizabeth in 1570, but until the Catholic Emancipation Act of 1829, the Catholics were not allowed to attend Trinity College and after 1829 they refused to join because it was an Anglican institution. The Irish University Bill was defeated at the second reading. To understand Gladstone's position it should be remembered that, brought up as a strict Evangelical, Gladstone during

present right, and for no object save to accommodate the more ignorant and priest-ridden classes of Catholics and even this without conciliating the priests. I am not quite sure what his own opinions are: infer that he is a Protestant, or as likely a sceptic, fond of enlightenment, and conservative in the main. Howell has been flattering some of his colleagues on the School Board[1] a little, and apparently gaining ground with the more liberal members. I saw the Japanese black-and-white lapdog: a seemingly obtuse, slightly snappish, and very ugly animal, with immense unmeaning eyes, and flat puggish face: has even some resemblance in visage to the Japanese stoneware toad that I keep in our sitting-room.

Wednesday 12 March   Going on with the Shelley compilation.

Thursday 13 March   D°—Have now finished (save as regards certain outlying publications etc. not for the while in my possession) the noting down and indexing of the materials for this compilation, and have begun the actual work of compiling—beginning this evening with the cutting up of a copy of the poems (my two-volume edition) and of the Essays and Letters.

Friday 14 March   Ordered various Shelley books needing to be cut up for the compilation. Received the first proof of the forthcoming reprint of Gabriel's *Early Italian Poets*:[2] I have agreed to do the main work of proof-correcting.

Saturday 15 March   Dined by invitation at Hüffer's, and was glad to

his time at Oxford became a staunch High Churchman and even considered taking Holy Orders. A few years later, he met the future Cardinal Manning, then still an Anglican, who became godfather to Gladstone's eldest son. Gladstone's views were never pro-Catholic, but all through his life he remained a sincere and devout Christian dedicating himself to the task of giving effect in politics to the Christian religion. See Philip Magnus, *Gladstone*, London, 1954.

[1] In a letter to his mother, dated 7 March 1873, D. G. R. wrote: 'You will be astonished to hear that Howell has been elected as Catholic representative to the School Board, and seems to have made some remarkable débuts at the meeting in the way of speechifying . . . He seems to think he has found his true vocation, and that a few years will see him in Parliament.' See *Family Letters*, p. 285.

[2] In 1861 D. G. R. had published *The Early Italian Poets* (Smith and Elder). The book, in D. G. R.'s words, was 're-arranged to make more evident its important relation to Dante', and appeared with a new title, *Dante and his Circle*, in 1874 (Ellis and White).

find him and Cathie presenting an appearance of happiness, mutual affection, and comfort. He tells me that Joaquin Miller intends to dedicate his forthcoming volume of poems 'to the Rossettis', or some such phrase. I have a vague idea that Joaquin Miller told me something about a proposed dedication in which *I* was to be concerned, when I dined with him: but I certainly never did nor could commit others to the acceptance of the dedication, and am not at all sure they would wish for it, and I must make Miller understand as much. Brown was the only person who dined along with me at the Hüffers. In returning home by rail, changing suddenly at Wimbledon from a smoking to a non-smoking-carriage, he had a narrow escape from a terrible or even fatal accident; as the train jerked forward just as he was mounting, and he might have been expected to lose hold and footing—which happily however was avoided. The railway people wanted to get his name, with a view to prosecuting him: but old Brown resolutely declined to give it, and seems to have remained master of the situation.

Sunday 16 March Wrote in reply to a letter from Kirkup, informing him of the death of Keightley, and of the Dantean MS. writings of my father which I found about a year ago.

Monday 17 March Bought a pair of Japanese swords with some capital metalwork, £1.10; also a pair of carven shells with religious subjects—I suppose Italian (perhaps Neapolitan) work, 15 shillings; all at a curiosity-dealer's, 13 Bloomsbury Street.—I consider the swords a very good bargain, and don't remember having ever seen a true *pair* for sale before. They must be fifty to eighty years old at least, I should fancy.

Tuesday 18 March Passed the evening at Cheyne Walk. Dunn has now received notice from South Kensington that neither his own copy from Raphael's cartoon, nor any of the other copies, is approved by the judges as up to the mark: this naturally annoys him. He suspects—and to me also it seems not improbable—that the reason assigned for not giving the work to *someone* to do (and, as far as I can gather, Dunn was decidedly the best man in the competition) is not wholly a candid one: the real reason being that, in consequence of the retirement of Cole[1] from South Kensington matters there are altogether in an unsettled and provisional state, and the project practically abandoned.

Wednesday 19 March   Joaquin Miller looked me up at Somerset House, and left with me the remaining proofs of his forthcoming volume. He showed me the dedication 'To the Rossettis': I strongly recommended him to write direct to Gabriel as to this matter, before anything further is done. I mentioned the dedication to Christina: she feels some hesitation in sanctioning it, not knowing what the book may contain: if she makes up her mind to object, she is to write to Miller. I looked through the proofs, and noted down some remarks on them. They include a series of poems about Christ, named *Olive Leaves*, implying a sort of religious or at least personal enthusiasm, mixed up with a good deal that has more relation to a sense of the picturesque than of the devotional. These poems, though far from worthless from their own point of view, are very defective, and would I think be highly obnoxious to many readers and reviewers: I have suggested to Miller the expediency of omitting them altogether. Christina, I find, has already read these particular poems, and to some considerable extent likes them—which is so far in their favour, as affecting religious readers.

Thursday 20 March   Lucy Brown called, wishing to look at the print of old London hung up in our passage—to see how London Bridge used to look, with a view to her picture of *Margaret Roper and head of Sir T. More*. I did not know that this picture was still in hand.

Friday 21 March   Received and passed the proof of the notice of Thomson, for that volume in Moxon's series.

Saturday 22 March   Mamma not well—troubled with cold and cough.

Sunday 23 March   The cough better, but general condition low. Sir W. Jenner came and says it is an attack of influenza, easily to

[1] Sir Henry Cole (1808–82), secretary of the Science and Art Department of the South Kensington Museum from 1853 to 1873. He produced several water-colours and etchings and was also an illustrator.

be remedied. Mamma may have to remain in bed two or three days.

Monday 24 March   Mamma somewhat better.

Tuesday 25 March   Nettleship called, asking me to look at his new picture of lions for the R.A. His usual ill-luck attended a picture which he lately sent to the International Exhibition, and which was declined: this is however the less surprising seeing that his subject was the disagreeable one of two lions eating up a negro. He has a commission for *Jacob wrestling with the Angel*; and on the whole I think, seems more settled and at ease with himself than he has sometimes been within these two or three years.

Wednesday 26 March   Bought eleven Japanese and Chinese books (£1.10) at Wilson's. They are not rich in designs, but have considerable interest of one kind or another. Mamma still in bed, and languid, but I hope on the mending hand.

Thursday 27 March   Am now very near the end of the actual putting-together of the materials for my Shelley work—cutting up books, copying extracts, etc. The only printed materials still outstanding (I think) are the letters published by Peacock in *Fraser's Magazine* in 1860, which I have as yet failed to procure. As to the unpublished materials, I wrote the other day to Locker, and he authorizes me to use any autographs etc. in his hands; but there is scarcely anything beyond what I have a copy of already. He will also introduce me to a Mr. Mitchell, who has something or other, and will, Locker thinks, make no difficulty in placing it at my disposal. The important question of the letters in Slack's hands, addressed to Miss Hitchener, still remains: I have not yet applied to Slack on the subject (partly thinking that I had better get my present materials into some shape first, so as to put the matter practically before him), and am doubtful of the result if I do apply: must however attend to this at no distant date.

Friday 28 March   Called on Rose by appointment, to discuss the Chancery proceedings pending in Mrs. Wieland's case. The immediate question is whether the property shall be partitioned between Mrs. Wieland and Captain Taylor, or the whole of it sold and the mortgages paid off. Mrs. Wieland is understood to be in favour of the partition, and so should I be if feasible: but it seems that the court is not likely to acquiesce in this view unless cogent reasons can be shown for it; that these would be traversed on Captain Taylor's part; and that some troublesome litigation would be likely to ensue, and after all the reasons not be ratified (probably) by the Court. Rose thinks therefore that a sale will probably be the practical and right solution of the difficulty: he has appointed a meeting at his office between the Wielands and myself for Monday next.—I finished the piecing together of my Shelley work, and began the needed annotation or connecting remarks—which no doubt will be of some considerable volume.

Saturday 29 and Sunday 30 March   Much engaged at Somerset House on Saturday.

Monday 31 March   Met the Wielands at Rose's. Mrs. Wieland was somewhat reluctant to the idea of selling the property: but, as it appears to Rose and myself—and also apparently to Wieland—that a sale will be decreed by the Court, whether opposed by us or not, she consented and Rose is to carry out the arrangement. Mrs. Wieland would like to invest the proceeds partly in some business for her husband and self (Wieland, as I now gather, having at present no sort of occupation): but Rose explained to me that this is decidedly inadmissible under the terms of the will and marriage-settlement. Rose tells me that Miss De la Ramée (Ouida)[1] is one of his clients: fast, and very extravagant, running up great accounts at hotels etc., and leaving them unpaid. He likes her, however, and thinks her very clever. Lent me her new novel to read: I have not yet read anything of hers, but fancy her reputation for genuine talent of a certain class is well deserved.

Tuesday 1 April   Called to see Chapman's pictures: two portraits, skilful and attractive, and likely, I think, to do him good if sent

---

[1] Ouida was the pen-name of Louise de la Ramée (1839–1908), one of the lesser novelists of the period, but extremely popular in her day. In the midst of Victorian conformity she held aloft the banner of rebellion. The new novel mentioned by W. M. R. was *Pascarel, only a story*, 3 vols., London, 1873.

to R.A., but he seems after all hardly likely to be sending them. Also called on Scott, who showed me a series of wood-blocks that he has designed for the edition of Keats he is about to edit for Routledge—very successful designs, taken collectively: he has similarly done Coleridge, and sent the blocks off to be engraved, and he tells me that is the better series of the two. He and I again talked about our projected excursion to Italy. The start had at his suggestion, been postponed till 25 May, and it now seems not unlikely that he may then be still unprepared to start, and moreover unwilling again to start at any later period of the hot season. On this assumption, my only course will be to go off by myself—or rather in the first instance to learn how Dr. Hake's Italian project stands, and, if feasible, fall in with it, which indeed I must see about even if Scott does come. As regards Scott there is a rather strong suggestion that, if he goes, his wife and Miss Boyd may come also—to which I would not think of raising any objection: and he tells me that Mrs. Linton[1] also wishes to come, and probably to be accompanied by a friend of her own. This would, in my view, make the whole affair utterly overgrown and unmanageable: so I plainly told Scott that if Mrs. Linton goes, I drop out of the scheme. Scott told me some startling news about S. Solomon[2]—of which indeed Nettleship had dropped some hint a few evenings ago. That there really has been a final catastrophe seems positive, though the precise facts are apparently not well known.

Wednesday 2 April Mamma came downstairs to-day, for the first time since her influenza began: she is not yet well, but pretty tolerable. Maria much out of sorts. Our housemaid Catharine, a cheerful mannered person who suits us very well, so shaky in general health that at last she has definitely decided to leave. I replied to Skelton[3] of Edinburgh (Shirley) who recently wrote

---

[1] Elizabeth Lynn Linton (1822–98), married W. J. Linton, the engraver, as his second wife in 1858; but in 1867 when he went to America she remained in England, and they never met again. In 1864 she had published a book, *The Lake Country*, with engravings by her husband. She was to be the first woman journalist: she contributed several hundred (250 in 1872) articles to various papers and magazines supporting liberal principles; she also published several books and essays. See G. S. Layard, *Mrs. Lynn Linton*, London, 1901.

[2] See p. 120 n. 1.

[3] John Skelton (1831–97), writer. He took the pseudonym of 'Shirley'; his

to Gabriel, saying that some Edinburgh paper announces that Gabriel is about to leave the Cheyne Walk house on account of his ill-health. Of course I informed Skelton that the statement and the assumed reason for it are now both untrue. Did not send on the letter to Gabriel, as it would be sure to annoy him.

Thursday 3 April   Mamma is still anything but well. She saw Dr. Fox again to-day and he recommends her to go to Hastings as soon as she is sufficiently recovered, though not quite yet. I called at Davis's, the Curiosity Dealer at the corner of Green Street, with the view of seeing whether I could procure anything (something in the nature of the setting of a locket) suitable for preserving the fragment of Shelley's skull which Trelawny gave me last year. Did not find anything this time: but shall probably return there within a few days, taking with me the object itself.

Friday 4 April   Called to see Trelawny, whose niece notified to me the other day that they are now in town for a short while. I see no diminution in his energy and vigour. Mrs. Hogg, he tells me, has picked up to some extent since last year in health and strength: her memory however is not good. He asked her lately to tell him deliberately whether she had ever known so admirable a character as Shelley, and she after reflection replied no. Trelawny has a very good opinion of MacCarthy's recent book, the *Early Life of Shelley*: of MacCarthy himself he knows nothing beyond what I was able to tell him. I informed him of my present work regarding Shelley and enquired whether he would allow me to insert in it such hitherto unpublished letters of Shelley as he possesses— chiefly those which Miss Clairmont has lately sent him. He replied 'I don't know what they contain.' It appears to me that if he can be brought really to consider the matter, he is likely enough to accede to my request, but that the 'if' is dubious. I abstained from pressing the matter; he has lately sat to Millais for a picture of an old Mariner amid his grandchildren,[1] narrating some of his adventures:

Essays of Shirley, 1882, and *Table Talk of Shirley*, 1895, are full of reminiscences of the Rossettis.

[1] *The North-West Passage* was completed in 1874. The 'grandchildren' were reduced to one granddaughter. Swinburne declared the Mariner to be 'an unmistakable likeness' of Trelawny. It is in the Tate Gallery.

speaks highly of the unsparing labour that Millais gives to his pictures. Says it is true that Byron went to Greece, partly to be away from la Guiccioli[1] to whom he was by that time sufficiently indifferent, and of whom he would speak somewhat slightingly among intimates : all his ardour was in pursuit, not in possession. His letters to la Guiccioli during the earlier stages of the courtship are, Trelawny believes, about the finest things ever done of their kind. They filled a good-sized box, and Mrs. Shelley read them, and told Trelawny about them. He supposes them to be still extant.[2] Shelley knew nothing of boxing, or other athletic work for the hands; his power was in the lower limbs. Rogers, Hobhouse,[3] and Moore,[4] were all decided infidels but hypocritically held aloof from Shelley : when dining in his company along with Byron, they would wholly ignore him (as I have before remarked, Trelawny's memory must be at fault regarding Moore, whom he certainly never saw in the company of Shelley or of Byron), to which Shelley paid no heed : every now and then Shelley's scholarship would be in requisition on some point or other. And then he outshone all the 'convives'. He had a certain respect and sympathy for Taafe[5] (at Pisa) on account of his undertaking the great

[1] Byron met Teresa Gamba, Contessa Guiccioli (1800–73) at Venice in 1819. They lived together in Ravenna, Pisa, Genoa, and Florence until he left Italy for Greece in 1823 where he died at Missolonghi (April 1824). After Count Guiccioli's death in 1840 she married the Marquis de Boissy and lived in Paris. She published in French *Lord Byron, juge par les témoins de sa vie*, 2 vols., Paris, 1868; it was translated into English with the title *My Recollections of Lord Byron*, London, 1869.

[2] These 139 letters written in Italian by Byron belong to the Gamba family; they were published by Iris Origo for the first time. See *The Last Attachment*, pp. 423–77.

[3] John Cam Hobhouse, Lord Broughton (1786–1869), statesman, travelled with Byron all over Europe, and wrote an account of their journey which illustrates *Childe Harold* (1818). As Byron's executor he advised the destruction of the poet's memoirs. Hobhouse published *Recollections of a Long Life* in 1865, but the 1909–11 edition contains a diary and notes which were not to be published before 1900.

[4] Thomas Moore (1779–1852), the Irish poet, met Byron in 1811. After Byron had left England it was through Moore that he kept in touch with English literary circles. Byron gave him his memoirs to have them published after his death, but they were destroyed in 1824, as advocated by Hobhouse. In 1830 Moore published *Life, Letters and Journals of Lord Byron*; in 1847 a one-volume edition of the *Life* appeared.

[5] Count John Taaffe (or Taafe) (*c.* 1788–1862), Irish poet and expatriate; after 1815 spent the remainder of his life in Italy. At Pisa he met the Shelleys and Byron in November 1820. He produced a translation of the *Divine Comedy* and a two-volume *Comment on the Divine Comedy of Dante Alighieri*, London, Murray, 1822. Byron said of Taaffe : 'He will die if he is *not* published, he will be damned if he *is*; but that, *he* don't mind.' See C. L. Cline, *Byron, Shelley and their Pisan Circle*, London, 1952, and H. R. Angeli *Shelley and his Friends in Italy*.

task of translating Dante : did not however want his company, and, if he had reason to think him coming, would say 'I smell a bore in the wind.' Trelawny insists that Sergeant major Masi,[1] with whom the row in Pisa occurred, was substantially in the right. The English party was straggling all about, and obstructing the road, and Masi, being on duty, had to pass as best he might—in his doing which, Taafe, a bad rider, took needless offence, and appealed to Byron. It was Byron's coachman who used the pitchfork on Masi —the coachman generally being a very inoffensive man. Trelawny is convinced Shelley would not have come to his death, had Trelawny been freed from the quarantine embarrassment, and at liberty to accompany him. Captain Roberts, who built the *Don Juan*, is just dead : was in straitened circumstances at the close— died in or near Leghorn. Leigh Hunt's incessant punning—the puns themselves being far from good—was a great infliction—I presented to Trelawny one of the two Japanese swords that I bought two or three weeks ago. He is not just now in correspondence with Miss Clairmont, nor has he taken any steps with regard to her correspondence of recent years : he thinks however of communicating with her again soon.

Saturday 5 April Mamma was better yesterday, and not amiss to-day. Towards night however her cough came on very troublesome, and she passed a bad night. Maria far from well.

Sunday 6 April Maria and I agree that it is noxious to Mamma to change from room to room in the course of the day; more especially for the purpose of retiring to bed. We therefore prevailed on her to stay entirely in her bedroom to-day and some advantage appears to have ensued from this course. I opened in the evening a newspaper which reached me some days ago from Whitman, and was much concerned to find in it that he had a

[1] Stefani Masi, Sergeant-major in the Tuscan Royal Light Horse. One afternoon, Byron, Shelley, Taaffe, and friends were riding near Pisa; when they came near the city gates, a mounted dragoon, Sergeant Masi, grew violent and behaved insolently towards Taaffe; Shelley was knocked off his horse, Byron sent for his servants, and one of them wounded the sergeant who was reported to be dying. Taaffe reported to the police in so boastful a manner that Jane Williams referred to him as 'False-Taaffe'. The story is told by all the biographers of Shelley and Byron, in different versions according to their sense of the picturesque. See N. I. White, *Shelley*, 1947, ii. 351–4, and C. L. Cline, op. cit.

paralytic stroke some little while back. It was a severe and disabling attack, but confidence is expressed as to his eventual recovery.

Monday 7 April   Mamma is likely to go to Hastings with Christina next Monday. It seems that my two aunts will also be going there about the same time: and there is some talk of Henrietta Polydore's joining them. Her illness seems to have reached almost its final stage now. If my aunts are there, the other three, all invalids, may manage to get on somehow: otherwise I think the plan an impracticable one.

Tuesday 8 April   Called at 15 Great James Street to see Dr. Hake: it appears that he is still not back in London *permanently* from Bath, nor his health very good. I asked him what he thinks of doing about going to Italy. His plan is to visit his daughter in Germany some time this year, and to go on to 'some nook on the Mediterranean': he wishes to avoid the very hot season, and would therefore not be postponing his start far beyond the present date. I rather doubt whether it will turn out practicable for him and me to combine, taking Scott into consideration more especially but (as I told Dr. Hake) I should have no personal dislike at all—rather the contrary—to the quiet and seclusion of the sort of trip he contemplates. Watts told me something about Swinburne's publishing affairs: Chapman and Hall are fully prepared to publish for Swinburne and to take over the stock on hand from Hotten; but just at present they are rather holding back, because they expect Hotten to become bankrupt at an early date, and a more advantageous bargain for themselves would thereby become feasible. Watts has made enquiries, and fully believes Elizabeth Rovedino to be out of England for some while past. At Chelsea I gave to Guérant (the French Officer who got mixed up in the affairs of the Commune) a few of Gabriel's books to bind. He rather fears a Bonapartist restoration, owing to feeling in the army, and apprehends an increase of anti-republican intrigues and influence from the election of Buffet[1] as President of the Assembly. Guérant was in Mexico: Bazaine behaved very badly there, and

---

[1] Louis-Joseph Buffet (1818–98), French politician, was one of the promoters of a liberal Empire. He was a violent opponent of Thiers and was elected President of the French Assembly in 1872 for three years.

in the Metz affair he regards him as distinctly a traitor. Very many Frenchmen deserted from the army in Mexico, and joined the Mexican Nationalists : Maximilian was an agreeable well-meaning man, but of no capacity. Guérant does not seem sanguine as to getting back to France at any early date : he is already obtaining some modicum of employment in book-binding. F.[1] tells me that Emma is greatly indisposed to remain as servant at Cheyne Walk, unless a second servant is employed. To which Gabriel, under present circumstances, naturally demurs. Mrs. Nicholson ('Red Lion Mary')[2] with her husband and daughter, has offered to come as Emma's successor : on many grounds I should regard this as a very desirable arrangement, but Gabriel has not as yet decided with respect to it—nor indeed has Emma actually given warning.

Wednesday 9 April Thomson (author of *Weddah and Om-el-Bonain*) sent me some very sensible notes to *Witch of Atlas* and *Epipsychidion* the other day—some of which I answered to-day. Before sending off my reply, I received from him another set of notices, applicable to *Adonais* and *Hellas*.

Thursday 10 April Received the proof of my Prefatory Notice to Mrs. Hemans.[3]

Friday 11 April A Mr. Thomas Cory wrote to me lately, asking me to read, and give my opinion on, certain poems he has written. Afterwards he sent me the MS. of a long poem (still in progress) about Theseus. He seems to be a man of meagre education, and there are very frequent solecisms in his poem, both in metre, diction, etc. : at the same time I don't think it wanting (as far as I read it) in a certain poetic sense and power of presentation. I wrote to him to-day to this effect, suggesting that he should not attempt so great an effort as the 'Theseus' until his executive training is more assured.

---

[1] See n. 1 p. 195.

[2] 'Red Lion Mary' was D. G. R.'s, William Morris's and E. Burne-Jones's servant when they resided in Red Lion Square in 1856. They were young men then and 'Red Lion Mary' helped them not only by housekeeping, but also in their professional work, making models' draperies, etc. See G. Burne-Jones, *Memorials of Edward Burne-Jones*, London, 1904, i. 169–72.

[3] *The Poetical Works of Mrs. Felicia Hemans*, ed., with a Critical Memoir, by William Michael Rossetti, London, 1873.

Saturday 12 April   Going on with the Shelley compilation. I am now writing the introductory observations and notes to the several items, and am getting on (chronologically) towards the close of 1811. There is a good deal to do in this line.

Sunday 13 April   In the morning George Hake and his brother Henry called—George being up from Kelmscott since Friday. In the afternoon we received a telegram to say that Gabriel also would be coming up; and he made his appearance late in the evening. Mrs. Morris, he informs me, is ill; otherwise she would now be going down to Kelmscott. He seems likely to remain here some few days. I wrote to Mr. Slack asking whether he would allow me, in my Shelley compilation, to make any and what sort of use of the Shelley letters in his possession; suggesting that, were he to do so, the publishing value of the book would be largely enhanced, and he could command (as far as I am concerned) his own terms as to share in any profits. Also wrote to Scott who informed me the other day that his wife and Miss Boyd will accompany him on the proposed Italian trip. I informed him that I have no sort of reluctance to be one of the party under this arrangement; but that at the same time the whole question deserved reconsideration by himself, according to the altered circumstances especially as regards Mrs. Linton (see 1 April). Gabriel tells me (what I am very glad to hear of) that Brown has been commissioned by a Mr. Brockbank to paint in oils for about £400 the *Cromwell*[1] subject of which he made a water-colour many years ago. He had been projecting this oil-picture for some little while past.

Monday 14 April   Called on Trelawny in the afternoon. He tells me he has given away the Japanese sword I lately presented him (Gabriel, by-the-bye, is much pleased with the companion sword, still in Euston Square); and he showed me another sword—far from identical, but bearing a considerable resemblance to the one I gave him, as to arrangement of metal work etc. This sword, Trelawny tells me, is one which he looted on a Chinese junk (the same case, I understand, that he describes in the *Younger Son*), and he considers it to be Chinese, and that mine was also the same— not Japanese. I still adhere to the opinion that mine at any rate is Japanese: as to Trelawny's, I feel no great confidence either way.

[1] *Cromwell on his Farm.* See p. 243 n. 2.

A Mr. Dillon being present most of the time, I got less Shelleyan conversation with Trelawny than usual. He says that Shelley was of a silent turn. During Shelley's lifetime (I think between the first period when Trelawny was in the way of seeing Shelley, and the second) Trelawny met Shelley's sisters, including Elizabeth, at an evening party: he says they were quite unlike Shelley in appearance, though this seems contrary to the evidence of others. On again seeing Shelley, he mentioned this fact to him: Shelley looked at him very earnestly, and then walked straight out of the room, his feelings being too strong for him. Trelawny thinks (but I fear not very resolutely) that he will produce a Shelley–Byron book this year; reissuing his previously printed matter, with some more added.[1] Mrs Williams, whose beauty in her youth he extols, possesses a good portrait of herself by Clint,[2] done when she was young. Shelley never spoke about himself.

Tuesday 15 April   Stayed away from Somerset House, and spent most of the day with Gabriel at Cheyne Walk: he expects to return to Kelmscott to-morrow afternoon. F., Dunn, George Hake, Scott, Brown and his wife, Howell, Boyce—all there at one time or another. Howell says that Brown has unfortunately lost the commission for his *Cromwell* picture, through having imprudently advanced suggestions as to payments in instalments during progress etc.: the proposing purchaser took offence or alarm, and called off. This is a thousand pities. Hunt, it seems, has sold his *Shadow of the Cross* to Agnews for £10,000—a colossal price indeed: I have not yet seen that picture. Howell is going to issue a circular winding up the whole affair of the Cruikshank subscription.[3] He read it to us in MS., and I discern in it something

[1] *The Recollections of the last Days of Shelley and Byron* by Trelawny were published in 1858. Twenty years later and not in 1873 as suggested here, they were republished in an enlarged form (a preface of thirteen pages instead of two and 459 pages of text instead of 304) and with a different title: *Records of Shelley, Byron, and the Author*, London, 2 vols., 1878. R. Garnett thought that 'every alteration in the text is a change for the worse'. Edward Dowden who reprinted the first version of 1858 in 1906 is not so categorical. See E. Dowden's introduction to the reprint of the first version.

[2] The portrait of Jane Williams by Clint is reproduced facing p. 95 in Trelawny, *Recollections*, a new reprint of the 1858 version, ed. J. E. Morpurgo, 1952.

[3] George Cruikshank (1792–1878) the caricaturist and illustrator. In his old age he had become poverty-stricken; C. A. Howell, acting as Ruskin's secretary, started a subscription for the old artist in 1866. Ruskin contributed £600 and many contemporary artists were very generous. See H. R. Angeli, *Pre-Raphaelite Twilight*.

of an aggressive character against various sorts of people other than Howell's intimates. It is well put however, and not in any very marked sense injudicious. Scott definitely settles for me to join in his Italian trip, along with his wife and Miss Boyd.

Wednesday 16 April   Since Monday, and more especially since yesterday, there has been a rapid advance in heat: to-day I dispensed with a fire altogether, and never felt the want of it. Began, in my Shelley work, verifying, from a little manual published by Fuller, all indications regarding days of the week, and supplementing this point in the letters wherever I can. The scrutinising of this detail throws a good deal of light on a point here and there, and the like should certainly never be omitted in any investigation which relies on dates and sequences.

Thursday 17 April   Mr. Slack replies to me that he does not feel bound to withhold any longer the Shelley letters in his possession, and would trust to my discretion as to the use to be made of them. He asks me to talk over the matter with him some time at his house in Sussex—has given up his London residence. Though his letter does not perhaps amount to an actual consent to publish the letters in my compilation, it is certainly not very far removed from this, and is therefore most highly gratifying. With this addition, even apart from the letters in Trelawny's hands, my book would contain a large amount of new matter, Shelley's own writing, and ought to command a publisher.

Friday 18 April   Went to the British Museum, to look up the proper edition of Pope to be printed in Moxon's series. It was however so near the closing hour that I could do nothing effectual.

Saturday 19 April   Went again to the Museum, and looked into editions of Pope as required. Also looked at the sort of tale—unfinished—named *Recollections of Childhood*, which Hogg published in the *Monthly Chronicle* many years ago,[1] thinking I might possibly find there some reference to Shelley, or some character

---

[1] 'I was asked to contribute to the *Monthly Chronicle*, . . . I gave portions of my unpublished novel. It commences with No. 30, and terminates with No. 40, for then the *Chronicle* ceased, under the title *Some Recollections of Childhood*.' See T. J. Hogg, *The Life of P. B. Shelley*, ed. Dowden, 1906, p. 546.

founded upon his. However, I can see nothing of the kind: the story (though Hogg calls it a novel in his *Life of Shelley*) seems vague and essay-like to the last degree. I also made at the Museum a little list of the various blunders in the Museum Catalogue concerning books written by our family (as for instance calling Christina's second name 'Gabriela' and converting 'Pietrocola' into a Christian name, 'Pietro Nicola'), and shall send this tomorrow to Ralston.

Sunday 20 April Wrote to Slack, proposing to visit him in Sussex on 3 or 4 May: I would combine with this (or try to do so) a visit to Mamma and Christina, who will then be in Hastings.—Looked through Godwin's *Political Justice*,[1] as needful to the full understanding of Shelley's letters, etc.

Monday 21 April Got the piece of Shelley's skull, which Trelawny gave me more than a year ago, enclosed in a locket, having glass on both sides.[2] I have found somewhat more difficulty than I expected in getting something adapted for this purpose. The locket selected is wholly plain, and hardly worthy of its contents: it is however at least inoffensive.—Wrote to James Thomson further about the very many serviceable notes on Shelley[3] that he has sent me, and asked him to give me a call some evening.

Tuesday 22 April Called on Trelawny. Showed him the piece of Shelley's skull in the locket; also (in a very summary way) the portion which I have as yet gone through of Shelley's correspondence, etc. Shelley's face, Trelawny says, was very mobile: the look of it, as centred in the eyes, very impressive at a distance.— Trelawny having often been fixed hereby when he happened to see Shelley at some considerable distance up the Lungarno of Pisa. Trelawny is much in the habit of saying 'Good God'. In relating to me this evening something that Shelley had said to him, he began by observing that Shelley said 'Good God, Trelawny', but he then corrected himself, explaining that Shelley did not in fact ever use that expression. Shelley when he was

---

[1] Published in 1793. [2] See the *Athenaeum*, 22 July 1882, p. 145.
[3] Published in *Shelley, A Poem, with other writings relating to Shelley*, by the late James Thomson (B.V.) Printed for private circulation, London, 1884.

alone or supposed himself so, would sometimes recite passages of his own poetry: would, especially, when out in the country, recite poems then in course of composition, so as to try on his own ear the effect of the metre and diction: was extremely fastidious as to diction, thinking that there would be always some best word or phrase of all discoverable for any particular passage, and that the fashioning of the verses ought not to be given up until this was attained. Trelawny again told me (what he had said more than once) that Shelley cared nothing about children; once, in Trelawny's presence, Shelley stepped over his own child Percy, near the threshhold of the house, without observing that it *was* Percy till the nurse told him. On that occasion Trelawny made a jocular remark about 'a wise man who knows his own children'; when Shelley rejoined, 'a *wise* man wouldn't have any'. Trelawny also reiterates a denial (so far as his observation and belief extend) of the statement (Medwin's, I think) that Shelley was short-sighted. He strongly believes that Shelley never had any sexual knowledge of any woman other than his two wives: any statement or suspicion of intrigue with Mrs. Williams is preposterously untrue to any one who, like Trelawny, knows how passionately attached Mrs. Williams was to her own husband—not to speak of Shelley's share in the question. Trelawny confesses to having a considerable sneaking kindness for Louis Napoleon, to which the Italian war of liberation powerfully conduces: he thinks however he wanted resolution. Knew something of him in England. Trelawny showed me a book of 'Reminiscences' by Villemessant[1] recently published. Here some mention is made of Trelawny, as he was known in Paris at one period of his life, and among other instances of Trelawny's extraordinary strength, it is stated that he would take three '*noisettes*', each between one several pair of fingers: would then close his fingers together, and shatter the nuts. Trelawny tells me this is true. He spoke of the fine form (which he has often mentioned) of Shelley's legs, and how 'finished' his hands and feet were. I asked whether a cast of the hand had ever been taken. No—no one ever

---

[1] Jean Hippolyte Auguste Cartier de Villemessant (1812–79), French Conservative journalist. In 1854 he became the editor of *Le Figaro*, a newspaper which till then had been rather unimportant. When Villemessant took it in hand it appeared twice a week; in 1866 it became a daily newspaper with a wide circulation. The book mentioned here is the first volume of J. H. A. de Villemessant, *Mémoires d'un journaliste*, 6 vols., Paris, 1872–8.

paid any attention of that sort to Shelley. Trelawny had tried hard to get Eastlake,[1] then in Italy, to paint Shelley's portrait, but couldn't rouse his interest in the matter. Eastlake had evidently no sort of idea that Shelley was a truly illustrious personage.

Wednesday 23 April Brown called: has completed a series of cartoons (15, I think) for painted glass. Has received from Gabriel a letter addressed to Gabriel by a Mrs. Davies (who writes in the *Quarterly* etc.)—intimating, in reply to queries from Gabriel that the recent statements about S. Solomon are true. What is his present exact position—whether he is detained in an asylum, after production of some sort of legal evidence of unsoundness of mind, or what else may be the fact—is not defined.—Morris back from a recent trip in Italy with Jones.—I wrote to Garnett, asking him some questions that arise in the course of my Shelley work, especially whether he knows anything about Horsham, so as to lead to a verification of the statement made by the 'Newspaper Editor' (*Fraser*, 1841) to the effect that many of Shelley's early verses were printed by a Horsham Printer named Phillips.[2] I find in Shelley's correspondence some confirmatory indications; and quite think the statement is true, and the verses thus printed would include the *Victor and Cazire* volume. One ought to try to ferret out the present successors or representatives of this Phillips (which seems to be the correct spelling), and see whether anything can be discovered.—Henry Hake called, will leave tomorrow for a course of study (some two years) at German Universities: that at Giessen will be the first.

Thursday 24 April Rae[3] of Birkenhead writes me that William

---

[1] Sir Charles Lock Eastlake (1793–1865), painter, Director of the National Gallery, President of the Royal Academy. D. G. R., aged 19, showed him one of his first oil paintings representing three medieval figures, one being the Devil. Eastlake 'did not encourage him to proceed with any such subject'. See *Memoir*, p. 100, and C. L. Eastlake, *Contributions to the Literature of the Fine Arts*, with a Memoir by Lady Eastlake, London, 1870.

[2] The 'Horsham printers' mentioned here were C. and W. Phillips of Worthing. They first printed for Shelley *Original Poetry by Victor and Cazire* in 1810, sold by J. J. Stockdale. In the following year they printed the *Necessity of Atheism*, but Stockdale refused to sell the pamphlet, being afraid of the consequences, and also thinking, as he wrote to Sir Timothy, that he should not encourage the young man in his subversive attitude. See *Stockdale's Budget*, 1826.

[3] George Rae, manager of the North and South Wales Bank, had been an important purchaser of D. G. R.'s pictures since 1862.

Davis[1] the landscape-painter is dead, which I am sorry to hear: he was not only a painter full of faculty and insight, but an example of modest single-minded worth, and genuine soundness and simplicity of character, amid all the troubles of narrowest fortunes and general want of appreciation and encouragement. I regret that I had not managed to see a little of him since he came, three or four years ago, to settle in London. Rae wants me to write something about Davis in the *Athenaeum* or other review: I am not quite clear what I can do, but I wrote to Stephens, committing the matter to his hands so far as the *Athenaeum* is concerned. No doubt poor Davis's large family must be left in deplorable straits. Rae seems handsomely disposed to do whatever he can, and I expressed to him my readiness to join in any subscription etc. I quite think that one day the ownership of Davis's works will be a handsome property: possibly (but I fear not probably) a vigorous effort now might tend towards this result, and enable the family to turn his remaining sketches, etc into money to some considerable amount.—Went to see Delacroix's *Sardanapalus*[2] at 168, Bond Street, and found it interesting and fine.—Not much like what I had expected. A large landscape in same Gallery, *Riverside Pastures*, by Dupré,[3] is a most astonishing piece of force—date 1835. Various other interesting things, including one or two incredible legerdemains by Whistler, as well as other leading works of his. Some uncommonly choice tasteful pottery by Chavin (now in London, I am told)—also some by a gentleman

[1] William Davis (1812–73), Irish landscape painter, was little known in London as he exhibited mostly in Liverpool. An obituary article appeared in the *Academy*, June 1873, p. 205, in which the main characteristics of his art were described.

[2] It was sent to London on the occasion of the sixth exhibition of the Society of French Artists. Delacroix painted two pictures on the same subject, probably inspired by Byron's drama (1821); the first was a sketch for the very large one which he exhibited at the Paris *Salon* in 1827. Its full title was *La Mort de Sardanapale*. It roused a storm of indignation and Delacroix wrote to a friend: 'J'ai eu à subir les tribulations assez nombreuses de MM. les très ânes membres du jury' (Letter to Soulier, 6 February 1828). Such was not the opinion of the London visitors: Miss Mary Margaret Heaton referred to Delacroix's picture in the *Academy* (1 May 1873) as 'an opium dream in its evil beauty and splendid horror'; she adds that it fetched 96,000 francs at a recent sale in Paris. Both versions mentioned above are in the Musée du Louvre.

[3] Jules Dupré (1811–89), French landscape-painter, a member of the so-called School of Barbizon. Spent some years of his youth in England, was influenced by Constable and when back in France, influenced in his turn Courbet, Cézanne, and others. He returned to England in 1870. See E. Bénézit, *Dictionnaire des peintres, sculpteurs, etc.*, Paris, 1948.

of fortune (French) very cleverly working up Japanese motives into a different and more sturdy quality of handling.

Friday 25 April　Received through Mrs. Townsend six copies of the bronze medallion of my Father struck in Italy in 1847, which is now being dispersed with a view to raising funds for the proposed monument to him in Vasto: it is a very respectable piece of art, and not wanting in truth of feature, though the general look of the face is hardly *like*. Spent the evening at Brown's, principally for the purpose of talking about Davis and his family—widow and *ten* children, or (if Rae is right) even twelve. Some immediate succour has, it seems, been forthcoming from Mr. Miller of Liverpool:[1] the two eldest sons (about 18 and 16) are studying as painters: arrangements will probably be made for an exhibition of Davis's works along with some others for the benefit of the family. The look-out seems of the gloomiest. Davis died of angina pectoris. He had been suffering from this disease on and off for a year or two: lately got a very bad attack, brought on in a moment from the shock of suddenly finding one of his fine pictures ignominiously hung on a staircase in the International Exhibition: rallied from this attack, and was well for some days: then had another attack, and succumbed on Tuesday. Stephens replies to my letter of yesterday, and asks *me* to write something about Davis for the *Athenaeum*: must see to this.[2] Brown showed me the large photograph taken from his picture of *Professor and Mrs. Fawcett*:[3] it does excellent justice to the work, and should impress those who see it with the signal merits of that. Brown tells me that Joaquin Miller is to marry Miss (daughter of Sir Duffus)[4] Hardy: she is greatly in love with him. Morris was here, looking uncommonly fresh and vigorous after returning from a brief trip (with Jones) to Florence: he has delighted greatly in Italy.

[1] Mr. John Miller of Liverpool is described by W. M. R. as 'the most open-handed of merchants, and the most lovable of Scotchmen and picture collectors'. He used to show great generosity to the artists he liked to gather in his house. See *Reminiscences*, p. 226.

[2] W. M. R.'s unsigned article on Davis appeared in the *Athenaeum* for 3 May 1873.

[3] The *Portrait of Professor and Mrs. Fawcett* was painted by Madox Brown for Sir Charles Dilke in 1872. See p. 156 n. 1.

[4] Sir Thomas Duffus Hardy (1804–78), archivist, Deputy Keeper of Record Office from 1861 to 1876; had been a friend of the Madox Brown family for many years. See *Reminiscences*, p. 491.

Saturday 26 April Mr. Rae having informed me that it is proposed to purchase the large picture by Davis now at the International Exhibition, for the benefit of the family, and having
asked when I could go round to look at it, I went for this purpose,
but failed to find it. The catalogue does not name this important
picture, but only the other far from important one on the staircase,
which, after looking all over the building, I at last found. I saw
for the first time the Royal Albert Music Hall,[1] the size and
space of which are really noble and vast.

Sunday 27 April Wrote a little article about Davis, as suggested
by Stephens; and sent it to him, for insertion in the *Athenaeum*,
or to be turned to account by himself in the same quarter, as he
may prefer. Wrote to Rae, offering to contribute to the fund
which he tells me is being got up for the Davis family: I offer
£20 if wanted, or (by preference for the present) £10. Also wrote
to Millais, appointing to call on him Wednesday week to see the
figure of Trelawny that he has lately painted in a subject-picture,[2]
and taking occasion at the same time to mention about the calami-
tous position of the Davis family. Millais is not only a leading
man on the Artist's Benevolent Fund, but I have more than once
been assured that he is himself extremely liberal in such matters.

Monday 28 April J. Thomson called on me. I find him to be
a man of about 33 or 34, of appearance and manners rather of the
commercial traveller type than the long-headed working man
type; in essentials agreeable and well-mannered, and with a good
deal of sound knowledge, and readiness in producing it. He
learned Italian for the purpose of reading Dante, and seems to
have a very competent knowledge of the language and literature.
Thinks Leopardi shows some Shelleyan influence, and might
possibly have met Shelley: this may be worth looking into.[3]
Though he doesn't profess to have devoted himself to the special
study of Shelley, I find him very familiar both with Shelley's
poems, and with what has been written about him by Hogg,
in my memoirs, etc. I offered to communicate (and had before

---

[1] Erected in 1867 to the memory of Prince Albert.   [2] *The North-West Passage*.
[3] In fact, Leopardi (1798–1837) never met Shelley. In 1890 W. M. R. delivered a
lecture on 'Shelley and Leopardi' to the Shelley Society, and repeated it at the
Taylorian Institute, Oxford, on 24 November 1891 (published in *Studies in European
Literature, 1889–99*, Oxford, 1900, p. 55).

made this offer in writing) the more important of his Shelley notes to *Notes and Queries*, and to express therein my high opinion of Thomson's own doings as a poet: in this he acquiesced. His opinions in religion and politics are of course of a very extreme kind, writing as he does in the *National Reformer*: but he does not seem to be much mixed up with the practical movements of the Republican etc. party. He knows and likes Bradlaugh: considers him a man of considerable oratorical gift, ambitious, and likely to achieve somewhat. Odger[1] he has rather a distaste for, and other popular leaders he does not seem to know very much about. Thomson passed some of his early youth in Ireland; but, to judge from his speech, he is quite an Englishman, and perhaps a Londoner. He got to know something of Whitman's poems through my selection, and has become a very ardent admirer of them.

Tuesday 29 April Called on Scott, to settle about the time for starting on the Italian trip with him, his wife and Miss Boyd: it will to all appearance be 26 May—the goal, Rome and Naples, and what else is manageable *en route*.—Called again on Trelawny. He wrote lately to Miss Clairmont, offering to give her £50 for any Shelley letters etc. in her possession, which Trelawny would then turn to such account as he might see fit. She however, is not willing to close with this offer, and speaks of some money-difficulties in which she is involved, and generally straitened circumstances, and ill-health. Trelawny thinks under the circumstances (and I concur) that it would be desirable to ascertain distinctly what are Shelley's documents in Miss Clairmont's possession; and, assuming their value to be at all commensurate, then to see about getting up a subscription for their purchase. Trelawny would still produce his £50; I said that I would contribute £20 or £25, and could probably get four or five other persons to join in the plan. Trelawny says that Shelley left Miss Clairmont by will no less a sum than £12,000. He had left £6,000 in the body of the will, and then (whether by inadvertence or otherwise) another £6,000 in a codicil. Miss Clairmont, however, did not manage the money prudently—one unfortunate speculation

---

[1] George Odger (1820–77), a shoemaker, Radical Working Men's candidate in several by-elections; though supported by Dilke and Fawcett, he failed and became President of the International Association of Working Men after 1870.

being the purchase of a box or boxes in Lumley's Italian Opera-house,[1] now burned down. She is now (as stated in her late reply to Trelawny) reduced to £120 a year, and her niece goes out teaching. She is still in Florence, Via Valfonda. I asked Trelawny whether he thought I might call on her if I am in Florence this year, but he considers she would not be pleased at my doing so. He and I continued talking about Shelley's will, which he says was regarded as a remarkable document in a legal sense; and we agreed that I ought certainly to endeavour to procure a copy of it, and insert this in my compilation. Miss Taylor now tells me that she believes her uncle to be seventy-four years of age. I am strongly of opinion that this is below the mark, and about seventy-nine the true age. He never wears a great coat, nor any under-clothing. He has lately renewed his acquaintance with Leigh Hunt's book *Lord Byron and some of his Contemporaries*; and though his dislike of Hunt is strong, he says it gives a very good idea of Byron and Shelley, especially the former: any deficiency in this regard being solely due to the unfavourable conditions of intercourse sub-sisting between Byron and Hunt, showing to Hunt only a partial and unpleasant side of Byron's character. Shelley used to say that the best thing Hunt had done was a paper about a drunken char-woman in the *Indicator*.[2] I will endeavour to look this up some day.

Wednesday 30 April Going on with the Shelley compilation. I have now reached, in order of time, the arrival of Shelley at Lyn-mouth,[3] July 1812.

Thursday 1 May Went again to the International Exhibition, having now some definite information as to where Davis's more important picture is to be found. Traced it out; but regret to find it, so far as my judgment goes, far from being among his best works, and not attractive to any ordinary eyes. There is a pic-ture by a man whose name is new to me—Marsh[4]—remarkably

[1] Benjamin Lumley (1811–75), manager of Her Majesty's Theatre from 1842 to 1858.

[2] See the *Indicator* for 22 November and 27 December 1820; for 3 and 26 January 1821.

[3] W. M. R. actually spelt it 'Lymouth' and had it printed in that form in his various books and articles on Shelley.

[4] Arthur H. Marsh (d. 1909), painter. See the *Art Journal*, 1909, pp. 85–7.

sober, pathetic, and efficient: *Looking Out for the Missing Boat*. It would be scarcely possible to paint a better picture, in essentials, of the subject. Looked at several of Phillip's[1] pictures here: the general impression of his force and ability is certainly not diminished by seeing the collection of his works as a whole, though I have never been among his more pronounced admirers. Looked also, for the first time, at the Albert Monument in Hyde Park—confining myself very principally to the podium, with its pantheon of great artists etc. I quite agree with Brown in entertaining a high opinion of Armstead's[2] portion of this work: it shows a vigorous comprehension and nervous apprehension of the subject, and has plenty of matter and arrangement. Philip's[3] section is also more than creditable, though it has less *cachet* than Armstead's.

Friday 2 May Met Garnett in the street, and asked him whether he considers the authorities of the British Museum would be the proper persons (for national purposes) to whom to leave, at my death, the fragment of Shelley's skull.[4] He says he knows of no institution more appropriate and decidedly thinks the Museum would accept and preserve the relic: but is not very sure they would set store by it, and make it accessible to enquirers. He says the Museum have down in their records several relics or curiosities of a like kind, of old date; and he has never been able to find where these are, nor indeed whether they still exist.—Colonel Hinton[5] (U.S. Army) called on me in the evening with a letter from Whitman, who expresses cordial approval of what I have done affecting him in my Selections of American and Humorous Poetry. Whitman is now fairly recovered from his paralytic seizure, which at first numbed the whole left side: he is still in

---

[1] John Phillip, R.A. (1817–67), a painter who specialized in scenes of Spanish life.   [2] Henry Hugh Armstead (1828–1905), sculptor.

[3] John Birnie Philip (1824–75), sculptor and architect. They were both engaged on the decoration of the Royal Albert Memorial Monument. 'Round the podium was a processional frieze showing the great painters, poets, musicians, sculptors, and architects of the world, carved by Armstead and Philip.' See T. S. R. Boase, *English Art, 1800–70*, Oxford, 1959.

[4] It seems that the authorities of the British Museum were not interested. The relic remained in the possession of the Rossetti family until Mrs. Rossetti Angeli presented it to an American scholar.

[5] Colonel Richard J. Hinton had written an article entitled 'The Poet Walt Whitman—His Fame and Fortunes in Europe and America: His Present Position', which appeared in the *Rochester* (*N.Y.*) *Evening Express*, 17 March 1868, and was reproduced in the *Kansas Magazine* on 8 December 1872. Hinton showed that

the Office of the Solicitor General.[1] Mrs. O'Connor[2] nursed him with great affection during his illness. Burroughs has left Washington, having received some other government post. Hinton is about to traverse Europe as Inspector of Foreign Consulates: this position however, he tells me, is more nominal than real, the essential object being of a commercial character. He was immensely busy on Grant's side during the late Election. Went through the War of Secession (of course on the Northern side), and had before that been one of the raiders with John Brown,[3] though not (as I understood him) actually present at Harper's Ferry. He was in serious danger for some while afterwards. He considers that, if the Secession and War had not occurred, there would before now have been a slave Revolution. The American Nation is, since the War, all the more abhorrent of war for any purpose other than absolute necessity: it would be very difficult to make them re-engage in any war. Hinton is a native of England, but practically an American, by profession a journalist: age 41, but looks younger. His culture does not seem to amount to much, but I dare say he has ability, and personally he is prepossessing. He says that Whitman has lately issued some scattered poems, as the beginning of a series which is to have more especially a national character— the *Leaves of Grass* being regarded, in this comparison as personal rather than national. Hinton is surprised to hear that some specimen of this undertaking has not yet reached me.—I sent to Rae for the Davis' subscription, a cheque for £7, and wrote him my opinion about the Cornfield picture in the International Exhibition: my article on Davis, sent to the *Athenaeum*, is published to-day, with but little variation.

Saturday 3 May   Received a large packet of the proofs of Gabriel's

Whitman was very much more appreciated in Europe, particularly in England, than in his own country. W. M. R. greeted him as 'the sum and expression of the great democracy of the West'.

[1] Whitman was suddenly stricken by paralysis in January 1873; he gradually improved and returned to his office, but in June had to ask for leave of absence. See 'Walt Whitman as Civil Servant', *PMLA*, pp. 1094–1109, January 1943.

[2] The wife of W. D. O'Connor, Walt Whitman's friend. See p. 10 n. 3.

[3] John Brown (1800–59), American slave-trade abolitionist who believed that he had a divine commission to destroy slavery by violent means. He led an attack on an arsenal at Harper's Ferry, but he and his forces were overpowered by a body of American marines.

Early Italian Poets. This work is now, I think, not far from completion.

Sunday 4 May Went down to Mr. Slack's, Ashdown Cottage, Forest Row, Sussex; a house high up in a fine country, and commanding several very agreeable views. To my great joy, he handed over to me the entire packet of Shelley letters along with such letters or drafts of Miss Hitchener's,[1] by way of answer, as pertain to the series. He authorizes me to publish the letters as they stand; taking due care to avoid any such reflections on individuals as might possibly lead to legal complications, and also not to bring him prominently into the question, so as to raise needless questions of proprietory right, right of prohibition, etc., on the part of the remote and dormant connexions of the Hitchener family. I again raised (as I had previously done in writing) the point that he ought to stipulate for and receive a substantial share in any profits which may possibly be forthcoming from publication: but he did not pause over this suggestion—saying (what is indeed true) that, were the letters to be regarded as negociable [*sic*] property, his power of dealing with them would become all the more limited and precarious, in view of the un-mooted claims of the Hitchener family—now represented by a German lady, Mrs. Buxton.—Heard the cuckoo for the first time this year. In the evening began copying out the Shelley letters: this will be a serious job, and I think I must call in a transcriber, not however allowing the letters ever to leave my own house. The numbered series of letters mounts up to 49: a few are wanting, but only some seven or eight, I think. Indeed it appears to me the

---

[1] When Miss Hitchener left England after her short-lived marriage, she deposited the Shelley letters with her solicitor, Mr. John Slack, together with transcripts of some of her own letters, and never reclaimed them. John Slack's widow, Mrs. Charlotte Mary Slack of Croydon, bequeathed the letters to the Revd. Charles Hargrove in March 1907 with a request that he would bequeath them to the British Museum; but the legatee presented them to the B.M. immediately (Add. MSS. 37496). The correspondence includes forty-six letters from Shelley to Miss Hitchener, one from Harriet Shelley, and twelve letters from Miss Hitchener (9 to Shelley and 3 to Harriet). At the beginning is a long MS. note by W. M. R. on the history of the correspondence, dated 2 August 1874. A transcript of the letters made by W. M. R. was used by E. Dowden for his *Life of Shelley* (1886). They were published by Bertram Dobell in 1908 (*Letters from P. B. Shelley to Elizabeth Hitchener, now first published*). They are reproduced in Shelley, *Letters*, i, interspersed with other letters between nos. 81 and 195.

gaps are less considerable now than when I read the letters in 1869, but Mr. Slack says there is no difference.

Tuesday 6 May   Called again on Trelawny, and showed him one of the letters from the Hitchener correspondence. Trelawny is a decided depreciator of women, both as regards intellect and character; and he says that Shelley, in his later years, found that his ideal notions about women were not correct. I however reminded Trelawny of the great regard Shelley had entertained for Mrs. Williams in his last year or two, and he admitted that this told against his statement, but was accounted for by the fact that Mrs. Williams was really a very superior woman. My own impression is that Trelawny overstated the matter generally. He spoke again about the excellence of Owen Jones[1] as a designer, saying that one day he will rank next to Flaxman.[2] He designs for various leading silversmiths etc., makes some £1500 a year, and cares nothing for large money-gains. Trelawny has (as I found some while back) a great dislike to Woolner, on the ground partly of his self-assertion. Byron never read his own writings, after once they were published: Trelawny himself has not read *The Younger Son* these forty years. At Cheyne Walk I find there is now a second female servant, engaged under Gabriel's instructions.

Wednesday 7 May   Hunt called in the evening; he is now living at Wilton Place (or some such name), Campden Hill: has a studio elsewhere, but the Agnews keep it dark, like all else connected with his bargain for the sale of the picture of Christ.[3] He substantially, though not explicitly, admitted the accuracy of the report that he has sold this work for £10,000; also that the Queen wants to have a replica of a portion of it, but the upshot of this, owing to Agnew's copyright claims, is a little uncertain. He expects to be off to Jerusalem, with his son, in less than three or four months. Is now on very indifferent terms with Woolner, arising principally from the fact that Fairbairn[4] had bought of

[1] Owen Jones (1809–74), architect and ornamental designer. He had decorated Trelawny's house, 7 Pelham Crescent. 'I did not think it more than moderately successful' (W. M. R.'s unpublished note).

[2] John Flaxman (1755–1826), designer and sculptor.

[3] *The Shadow of the Cross.* See p. 241 n. 1.

[4] Thomas Fairbairn was a friend and patron of Woolner who, in 1857, modelled the two Fairbairn children's heads. They were both deaf and dumb. On seeing the

Woolner for £500, three pictures (said to be a Vincent[1] and two early Stanfields),[2] and that Hunt, under a sort of compulsion, expressed to Fairbairn a strong opinion against the genuineness of the Stanfields, and thereby thwarted some further negociations [*sic*] that were going on between Fairbairn and Woolner. Mr. Waugh[3] left his property divided (after Mrs. W.'s death) between his various children; and Hunt's son[4] will come in for the share which had thus been assigned to his mother. Hunt told me a good deal about Monk (the prophet): he has been and probably is, decidedly insane—meeting Jesus-Christ in the Regent's Park etc. etc.—and has been persuaded to make his way back to Canada. He is to take ship shortly: but I should doubt whether his departing is so certain as the convenience, to all his acquaintances in London, of his so doing.

Thursday 8 May Called to see Millais's portrait of Trelawny in the picture of the Arctic veteran: (in *The North-West Passage*). It is truly excellent in character and likeness, though perhaps Trelawny is right in thinking the body rather too huddled with age, and not showing sufficient physique. Saw Millais's three youngest children, and Mrs. Millais, and spent an hour with him in very frank and cordial chat. He urges prompt action on the part of Mrs. Davis with the Artists' Benevolent Fund, and anticipates a ready and handsome response. Spent the evening again with Trelawny. He thinks he may reprint, for private circulation, his book about Shelley, etc. adding various anecdotes and details; also urges strongly that Byron's letters ought to be republished (extracting from the narrative those especially in Moore's *Book of Byron*),[5] and that I would do well to attend to this job. I should have no objection to do it, yet no extreme inclination either.

marble group, Browning was so struck by its pathos that he wrote a stanza: 'Deaf and dumb.' See Amy Woolner, *Woolner* (cited p. 20, n. 3).

[1] George Vincent (1796–*c*. 1836), landscape painter; one of the later members of the 'Norwich School'.

[2] Clarkson Stanfield, R.A. (1793–1867), marine and landscape painter. Ruskin spoke highly of him.

[3] Dr. George Waugh, who had died in January 1873, had been a chemist in Regent Street. He had three daughters: Fanny who married Holman Hunt and died in 1866, Alice who married Woolner and died in 1864, and Edith who married Holman Hunt as his second wife and died in 1876. See p. 214 n. 2.

[4] Cyril Hunt.

[5] *The Poetical Works, with His Letters and Journals, and His Life, of Lord Byron*, ed. Thomas Moore, 17 vols., 1832–3, London.

Friday 9 and Saturday 10 May   Busy at Somerset House. Called on
Mr. William Mitchell, 16 Grosvenor Street, who possesses the
original *Epipsychidion*: the only copy I have seen or heard of.[1]
Both his Shelley letters have been published.

Sunday 11 May   Wrote to Mr. J. Russell, whom Dunn mentioned
to me last Tuesday, asking whether he would come to transcribe
some of the Shelley–Hitchener correspondence. I am making
myself good progress with this heavy transcribing job: am also
looking through the Globe Edition of Pope (to be used for
Moxon's edition), to take care that no copyright matter, in notes
etc., is encroached upon.

Monday 12 May   Had to attend before a Committee of the House
of Lords (Lord Rosebery's[2] Committee on Horses) to give evidence
as to the incidence of the horse and horse-dealing license-duties.
Acquitted myself, I hope, pretty well; though I was led into a little
pit-fall by some figures Lord Halifax[3] handed me, and asked me
to speak to—after doing which Lord Rosebery queried regarding
an addition to them which ought properly to have been made,
and which I had frankly to admit. Lord Rosebery is a very prepossessing handsome specimen of the young aristocrat. Am to
receive a copy of this evidence to revise, and only hope no thwart-
ing of my projected Italian trip, as to day for starting, etc., will
ensue hence. In the evening Brown called on me, saying he would
like Lucy to accompany the Scotts and me abroad. This will be
most entirely to my liking: it is proposed partly in the interest of
her health, which continues to cause some anxiety. Mrs. Scott had
replied to Brown alleging in opposition the objection I had raised
to Mrs. Linton as an addition to the travelling party: I however
do and must look on Lucy as very different from Mrs. Linton
and I wrote to Mrs. Scott urging this point of view in emphatic

[1] An original draft of part of the poem is at the Bodleian.
[2] Archibald Philip Primrose, 5th Earl of Rosebery (1847–1929), was at Christ
Church, Oxford, but went down in 1868 by request of the Dean rather than abandon
his small racing stud. He later acquired a country house at Epsom, had a famous
stable and won the Derby three times. In 1894, after serving as Gladstone's Foreign
Secretary, he succeeded him as Prime Minister, but his government fell a year later.
He was also a man of letters and published *Napoleon: The Last Phase*, London, 1900.
Four other editions followed.
[3] Sir Charles Wood (1800–80), created Viscount Halifax in 1866, Lord Privy
Seal, 1870–4.

terms. Brown lately back from Liverpool where he has seen Rae, Miller, etc. and talked over the Davis affair. Nolly has received £50 from Smith & Elder for the copyright of his naval story, now in course of printing. Maria troubled with erysipelas in one of her feet.

Tuesday 13 May Called at Brown's and saw there young Davis, who is cleaning and completing various oil and water colour sketches left by his father: several of these are very talented works, and attractive too to some eyes, though they had been totally neglected for some while past. They ought to be saleable in the collection that is to be got up at Liverpool. Young Davis has a strong sturdy aspect, and does not look the sort of young fellow to mope when he might be doing: I find him rather older-looking (say 21 or 22) than I had expected. Talked to Lucy about the Italian project, and saw her picture of *Margaret Roper receiving the head of Sir T. More*—which, though a little wanting in qualities of surface etc., is really a good and interesting picture, and ought not to have been rejected from the R.A.—Charles Heimann[1] writes to let me know that he has returned to London from Japan.

Wednesday 14 May Garnett came to dinner, and to look at the Hitchener correspondence. He gave me a copy of a letter by Shelley[2] to the Olliers[3] regarding Taaffe's translation of Dante. The original exists in an edition in the British Museum of Moore's *Life of Byron*,[4] illustrated by numerous autographs, portraits, etc., etc. He showed me a pamphlet (belongs at present to Wilson the bookseller) published by Clarke[5] in 1821—same publisher and year as the pirated *Queen Mab*. It is to oppose the views of Shelley as expressed in that poem concerning marriage, and to debate the degree and kind of his atheism. There is no author's name: the pamphlet is not amiss, nor yet particularly good.

[1] Charles Heimann was the son of Dr. Adolf Heimann. See p. 118 n. 2. The whole Rossetti family, especially Christina, considered the Heimanns as great friends.

[2] See Shelley, *Letters*, ii. 303.

[3] Charles (1788–1859) and James Ollier, Shelley's publishers since 1817, were two enterprising young liberals whom Shelley had met in Leigh Hunt's circle.

[4] See p. 254 n. 4.

[5] William Clarke, radical London bookseller published a pirated edition of *Queen Mab* in 1821, was prosecuted by the Society for the Suppression of Vice and sentenced to four months' imprisonment. For further details, see p. 149 n. 3, and H. Buxton Forman's article in *The Shelley Society's Papers*, 1888, part I, pp. 19 ff.

Thursday 15 May   Called again on Trelawny, at his suggestion, to see a letter from Miss Clairmont that he has just received. She gives some details as to letters, etc., of Shelleyan interest in her possession; thinks she may own forty to fifty related to the subject.[1] One is a letter from Shelley complaining of Byron's misrepresentation of him. Trelawny considers however that all that Miss Clairmont says on this matter is coloured by vindictiveness: she suffers much now in health, and can't look up the papers for the present. Trelawny proposes to give me a letter which I can present to her on my approaching stay (probably a very short one) in Florence. He recommends me to ascertain what papers she possesses, but not to lend myself to any move for damaging the reputation of Byron—and certainly I would of my own accord steer clear of anything of that sort. Trelawny leaves London for Sompting to-morrow.—Maria confined to bed all day with the erysipelas in foot and more especially by a very violent attack in the throat. The latter was abating as night came on.

Friday 16 May   In consequence of Maria's illness, Mamma returned to-day from Hastings: Christina and my aunts will come back next Tuesday. Maria is however a good deal less unwell to-day. The Scotts acquiesce in the arrangement for Lucy Brown to join our Italian party.

Saturday 17 May   Called to see Dr. Hake, and am sorry to find him still far from vigorous in health. He says London is, as it always has been, unsuitable to him, and he seldom goes out of doors. He may be going pretty soon to see his son Henry and his daughter in Germany, and then on towards the autumn to Italy, where he would probably winter. He informs me that George lately wrote to him from Kelmscott, saying that Gabriel, after any moderate exertion such as taking a walk, shows symptoms of faintness sometimes, and George thinks the action of the heart may not be quite right. To this Dr. Hake does not at present attribute any special importance, but he has recommended a tonic.

[1] A few days after Shelley's death Trelawny wrote to Clare Clairmont suggesting they should become 'firm and staunch friends'. A long correspondence ensued which lasted till 1875, when the ageing Clare Clairmont wearied Trelawny with her constant suspicions and recriminations. Trelawny wrote to her on 17 June 1875: 'The past is past . . . We have both lingered beyond our time . . . so goodbye.' *Letters of Edward John Trelawny*, ed. H. Buxton Forman, 1910, p. 249.

Sunday 18 May Took round to Lucy Brown's the very handsome travelling-case which Mr. Spartali gave me about two and a half years ago; as I think it may be found very serviceable for the united purposes of the three ladies and Scott. For myself, I should not draw upon its stores. Wrote Miller (Liverpool) offering to take two shares (10/– each) in the Art-Union project for Mrs. Davis's benefit: also, if wanted, to give up to that collection the little picture by Davis (Mrs. Davis and infant) which Miller himself gave me in 1857.

Monday 19 May Went to the R.A. Looked adequately through two and a half rooms, and cursorily through others. There seems to be a great dearth of inventive or ideal pictures; but a good deal to look at, and, in landscape especially, considerable signs of life. About the most poetical picture in the place appears to me to be the *Pastoral in Wales*; a landscape by C. G. Lawson[1]—exceedingly graceful and delightful: I do not remember this artist's name before. Anthony[2] has a magnificent specimen—*Evensong*—a church by sunset: one of the fullest expressions his great powers have yet received. Brett very fine. Millais has nothing but portraits and fancy portraits (Mrs. Heugh etc.), masterly and consummate. Gilbert's *Naseby* is most spirited and splendid—a real *chef d'oeuvre*.

Tuesday 20 May Called on the Wielands, to discuss about Mrs. Wieland's money affairs; there does not appear to be anything very particular for me to do just at present. Thence to say goodbye to the Howells, by whom I was so much pressed to stay to dinner that at last I consented—not without some ensuing repentance, as the thing was kept dragging on till 9.15 before any dinner appeared, and a message sent round to Dunn at Cheyne Walk more than half miscarried. An awkward affair has just occurred concerning certain subscriptions for the Cruikshank

---

[1] Cecil G. Lawson (1851–82), a landscape artist. He painted large subjects; his first picture exhibited at the R.A. was 'Cheyne Walk, Chelsea' in 1870; he was a regular exhibitor at the R.A. See *Cecil Lawson, A Memoir* by Edmund Gosse, London, 1883.

[2] Mark Anthony (1817–85), also a landscape painter who became known to the Rossettis and Ford Madox Brown as early as 1847. W. M. R. wrote 'He became anxious to graft something of Praeraphaelitism upon the style which came natural to him and in which he excelled.' *Reminiscences*, 141. *Evensong* was purchased by the Walker Art Gallery, Liverpool, in 1873 and is still there.

affair stated to have been handed in to Rose: this will have to unravel itself in some way or other—presumably not too pleasant a one for some one or other. Hence to Scott's, where we discussed some needful preliminaries to our start, and settled not to take tickets under the Cook's Tourist system—though I heard lately through Brown that, according to Lowes Dickinson, that system is most convenient and satisfactory, and Miss Boyd has lately heard from another quarter to the same effect. The Lawson who painted the picture I liked so much at the R.A. is, Scott informs me, an extremely young man, son of an old family acquaintance of his: he lives in Cheyne Walk.

Wednesday 21 May   Young Davis called, and I gave him such information as I could with a view to an application to the Artists' Benevolent Fund. Also Howell, who paid me £2 for the Chinese hawthorn-pot that I bought years ago in Paris: this being the arrangement which I finally proposed, although the price he first volunteered was £10, which I lowered to £7, and neither of these sums seemed prompt at forthcoming. Also Dr. Hake, who may perhaps still be in town by the time I return from Italy, and thinks he and I might be in the way of meeting in Italy some time next year. He sold his house at Roehampton to his neighbour there, Mr. Levy. Has been writing a poem (rather fine drawn in respect of its treatment of miracle, as he explains it to me) on the blind man cured by Christ: he offered this to the *Fortnightly*, but they thought it hardly in their line, and he now thinks of *Good Words*.[1] Hake considers this his most successful work of art.—Asked Garnett (Somerset House) a few particulars about the Medwins, and the Pilfold family into which he married. His wife is the granddaughter of a Captain Pilfold, who was in the army: and this Captain Pilford must, I apprehend, have been a son of that other Captain Pilfold of the Navy, who was Shelley's maternal uncle.

Thursday 22 May   Changed my money in preparation for the Italian trip. I turned £31 into Italian paper-money, and realized an extra 73 francs on it. Went in the evening by invitation to Mrs.

---

[1] A magazine edited by the Very Revd. Donald Macleod and published by Isbister & Co. It lasted from 1860 to 1906.

Gilchrist,[1] and there re-encountered Mr. Haines,[2] who has grown much broader, and I think better-looking than he ever had been. Herbert Gilchrist[1] has just painted his first oil-picture, a portrait (life-sized head, or nearly so) of his mother. As far as I could judge by lamplight, it shows considerable aptitude in expression, look of life, handling of flesh etc., but is painted on a dangerously offhand principle, with a view to obtaining general effects and impressions, instead of strict realization. He is still studying at Cary's[3]—not having as yet succeeded as Probationer at R.A.

Wednesday 6 August Many things have passed in this interim, which I am not minded at present to record, nor yet to resume the regular keeping of my diary. As a matter of business, I note that to-day Mr. Bell, of the publishing firm, called on me at Somerset House and agreed to the terms set forth under 8 May 1872 regarding an edition of Blake's *Poems*[4] in his Aldine Series. He would like the introductory notice to be only about 32 to 48 pages and the arrangement of the poems mainly chronological. the *Prophetic Books* would not be included: I think however an exception must be made in favour at any rate of the *Marriage of Heaven and Hell*, if only for the sake of making the volume of a moderately substantial thickness.[5]

[1] Widow and son, respectively, of Alexander Gilchrist. See p. 10 n. 4.

[2] William Haines, a friend of Alexander Gilchrist, compiled the list of Blake's engravings in Gilchrist's *Life of Blake*, pp. 483–90.

[3] Francis Stephen Cary (1808–80), artist and art teacher, studied at the R.A. and painted in the studio of Sir Thomas Lawrence; studied also in Paris, Italy, Munich, and after 1842 managed the Art School in Bloomsbury where Millais and D. G. R. received early art instruction. Cary retired in 1874. See the *Athenaeum*, 17 January 1880.

[4] *The Poetical Works of William Blake*, ed., with a Prefatory Memoir, by William Michael Rossetti, London, George Bell and Sons, 1874.

[5] In fact, the *Marriage of Heaven and Hell* does not appear in the Aldine edition of Blake, whereas there are a few excerpts from the *Prophetic Books*.

ACKNOWLEDGEMENTS

A WORK of this kind cannot be achieved without contracting many debts. I have been fortunate enough—thanks to W. M. R.—to meet many interesting men and women, some of them have become close friends. I shall first mention the departed. It was Professor Georges Lafourcade who introduced me to Thomas J. Wise—I wish to ignore what happened later—the fact remains that his generosity to students and scholars who wished to peruse the precious manuscripts and books in his library was boundless; moreover, I owe to him my introduction to Mrs. Rossetti Angeli and to Miss Mary Rossetti without whom this volume would never have seen the light.

Mr. Hopkins and Mr. Frederick Page of the Oxford University Press took an interest in the work as it was then planned. After the long interruption due to the war and the academic and family duties that were mine, the work was resumed with a somewhat different object in view. I was then given the most courteous, enlightening assistance by the authorities of the British Museum Library, Messrs. Ellis, Randall, Angus Wilson, Dr. Flower. More recently I met with a similar reception at the Bodleian Library. Mrs. Imogen Dennis, by allowing me to work in her own house on the documents in her possession, showed me the same generous hospitality as her mother, Mrs. Rossetti Angeli.

I am grateful to Miss Mary Bennett and Mrs. Virginia Surtees for kindly answering my queries about some of the pictures mentioned in W. M. R.'s Diary, and also to Professor Fredeman who was good enough to verify a few points in the text. Mr. D. McN. Lockie, Fellow of the Royal Historical Society, has kindly helped me to revise the proofs and read through my editorial notes which have greatly benefited from his suggestions and historical knowledge.

For assistance of various kinds I wish to thank Mlle Suzanne Lafourcade who patiently and competently copied out passages from manuscripts, the late Miss Cecily Hale-White, Mme de Savignac, Mme Henri Peyre, Mr. David Caslon, and all those whose names are not mentioned here, but not forgotten.

INDEX

Pictures, literary works are indexed under their headings except in the case of the Rossetti family and poets and artists most often mentioned in the diary, such as: Byron, Madox Brown, Shelley, Swinburne, Trelawny.